Apartheid's Reluctant Uncle

Apartheid's Reluctant Uncle

The United States
and Southern Africa
in the Early Cold War

THOMAS BORSTELMANN

New York Oxford
OXFORD UNIVERSITY PRESS
1993

Oxford University Press

Oxford   New York   Toronto
Delhi   Bombay   Calcutta   Madras   Karachi
Kuala Lumpur   Singapore   Hong Kong   Tokyo
Nairobi   Dar es Salaam   Cape Town
Melbourne   Auckland   Madrid

and associated companies in
Berlin   Ibadan

Copyright © 1993 by Thomas Borstelmann

Published by Oxford University Press, Inc.,
200 Madison Avenue, New York, New York 10016

Oxford is a registered trademark of Oxford University Press

Library of Congress Cataloging-in-Publication Data
Borstelmann, Thomas.
Apartheid's reluctant uncle: the United States and Southern Africa in the
early cold war/Thomas Borstelmann.
p. cm.   Includes bibliographical references and index.
ISBN 0-19-507942-6
1. United States—Foreign relations—South Africa.
2. South Africa—Foreign relations—United States.
3. Apartheid—South Africa. 4. Cold War.
5. South Africa—Race relations. 6. United States—Race relations.
7. United States—Foreign relations—1945–1953. I. Title.
E183.8.S6B67   1993
327.73068'09'044—dc20   92-29686

9 8 7 6 5 4 3 2 1

Printed in the United States of America
on acid-free paper

For Lloyd and Lynn,
and in memory of Jane

Preface

Twenty-five years of Cold War historiography have made it clear that certain costs accompanied the choice of the administration of President Harry S Truman to interpret the Soviet Union and the forces of left-wing reform and revolution around the world after World War II as the most evil and powerful conspiracy against human freedom in history. Foremost among these costs was the embarrassingly oppressive behavior of the anticommunist but distinctly nondemocratic allies the United States often found itself supporting as part of the supposed "free world." The governments of Vietnam, Portugal, Argentina, China, Greece, South Korea, Nicaragua, and the Philippines come readily to mind as examples.

Among American allies in the early Cold War, by far the most striking exception to the "freedom" the United States government espoused was provided by the policies of the government of the Union of South Africa. The accession of the first apartheid regime in 1948 brought with it the only national government of the post–World War II period to proclaim openly and enthusiastically the virtues of racial discrimination and segregation. Ironically, the victory of apartheid coincided with Harry Truman's strong stand in the 1948 U.S. presidential campaign in favor of greater civil rights for all Americans. Nonetheless, the Truman administration, despite some misgivings, chose in these same years to build an unprecedentedly close relationship with the government in Pretoria. While other important factors influenced this decision, the key for Washington, it turned out, was uranium. Similarly, the United States government gave strong support to the white European rulers of the neighboring colonies of southern Africa, the most important of which was the Belgian Congo— due also to uranium.

As I began to investigate the significance of this story, my curiosity was stimulated by the responses of others to my work. Archivists were invariably friendly and helpful, but also surprised; they had rarely, if ever, thought of American relations with southern Africa. One distinguished historian listened to my description of the topic and responded simply, "Well, that's a bit offbeat." Another, while more sympathetic to the subject, warned me to avoid any "special pleading" for the importance of southern Africa to the United States during the Truman era. The latter advice I have taken to heart, and the evidence I have found stands on its own without needing artificial emphasis.

With rare exceptions, historians and others remain surprisingly uninformed today about the relationship between apartheid and the Cold War in the formative years of each, despite considerable recent interest in the current volatile situation in South Africa. The centrality of southern African uranium to American national security policy in the Truman years seems comparably unrecognized.[1] The crucial relationship between domestic race relations in the United States and American policy toward the Third World and its nonwhite residents—including southern Africa—during the early Cold War awaits comprehensive treatment. And the connections between racism and anticommunism, two of the most powerful and troubling themes in American history, have yet to receive much attention.

One of the fruits of the easing of Cold War tensions in the 1990s will surely be a new openness to looking more comprehensively, and with less partisan defensiveness, at the consequences of American anticommunism in the post–World War II period. United States government decisions made in the interests of "national security" have had an enormous impact on almost every aspect of American life, not to mention on other parts of the world, like Vietnam. Such important stories as the momentous environmental impact of American nuclear policy, for example, or the effects of a highly militarized global foreign policy on gender relations at home and abroad deserve extended consideration. So, too, do the racial consequences of the Cold War, and this is the part of our unexamined recent history that I offer a small piece of here.[2]

Generous financial assistance from the Department of History of Duke University and the Harry S Truman Library Institute in Independence, Missouri, has been critical to the completion of this project. The staff of Perkins Library at Duke, especially the Inter-Library Loan office, provided superlative professional services at every stage of the research for this study. The entire staff of the Harry S Truman Library has been an extraordinary model of professional expertise and personal hospitality. I had no idea that I would feel so at home, or learn so much, on my visits to Independence. The helpful staff of Oxford University Press contributed the title and the fine editorial skills of Gail Cooper.

This book has benefitted enormously from the kind assistance of many people, whose ideas helped stimulate whatever is of merit here but who bear no responsibility for the interpretations and conclusions I make. Carlos E. Pascual and Lawrence Goodwyn offered insightful suggestions in the initial stages of this project. John L. Platt provided critical doses of literary expertise, brotherly encouragement, and sustaining enthusiasm during the early chapters. Richard S. Kirkendall gave freely of his time and considerable historical knowledge in commenting on drafts of all chapters, while demonstrating unusual hospitality to a fellow scholar exiled to his city for a period. William H. Chafe and Calvin D. Davis generously offered important encouragement and suggestions on the entire manuscript, as did William Minter. Bruce R. Kuniholm contributed critical insights in the final stages of the project, and Gary Y. Okihiro provided help at the end. I am deeply grateful to them all.

Peter H. Wood has long provided guidance and wise counsel at so many levels that it would surely embarrass him if I enumerated them all. Suffice it to say that without him this project would probably never have been started and would certainly not have been finished in a form like the present. I have yet to meet his peer in either scholarship or teaching, and I am profoundly grateful for his friendship.

My wife, Lynn Denise Borstelmann, bears more responsibility than anyone for ensuring the completion of this project. Her encouragement, sympathy, editorial skill, and computer expertise have been crucial. Her presence has deepened and broadened all of my life, and I celebrate our journey together with often unspeakable joy. It is to her and to my parents, Jane Millis Borstelmann and Lloyd Joseph Borstelmann, who first introduced me to the beauty and importance of history, that this book is dedicated.

Ithaca   T. B.
January 1993

Contents

Note on the Text

The terminology employed to identify people of different races in South Africa can be confusing. I follow standard current usage: "white" refers to people of predominantly Afrikaner or English descent; "black" includes all people of color (that is, all nonwhites); "African" describes people with dark skin whose ancestors were indigenous to sub-Saharan Africa; "Indian" means people whose ancestors came from the Indian subcontinent; and "Colored" identifies those people, mostly resident in the Cape province, whose ancestry is a mix of white, African, and Malay.

The city of Cape Town was still referred to as "Capetown" in the 1940s, and for the sake of consistency in the text and notes I use the older spelling. Similarly, I refer to the states, colonies, and territories of southern Africa by the names that were common in the years under discussion: South West Africa (Namibia), Bechuanaland (Botswana), Southern Rhodesia (Zimbabwe), Northern Rhodesia (Zambia), Nyasaland (Malawi), and the Belgian Congo (Zaire).

Occasional use of "Washington," "Pretoria," and "London" is made for the purpose of literary felicity in referring to the governments of the respective countries. I have done this only when the issues involved were largely matters of consensus within the particular government in question.

One of the compromises involved in the South African Act of Union in 1909 designated Pretoria, a largely Afrikaner community, as the country's administrative capital, and Cape Town, a more English city, as the seat of the legislature. The U.S. Minister (after 1948, the U.S. Ambassador) and at least some of his staff therefore spent about half of the year in each city, depending on when Parliament was in session. This double residence will become apparent in the notes.

Southern Africa in 1945

Apartheid's Reluctant Uncle

South Africans tend to hold up a mirror to America so that Americans are struck, however ambivalently, by a weird family resemblance.

—Joseph Lelyveld, *Move Your Shadow*

But alas, I did not ride away: for a while I stopped my ears to the noises coming from the hut by the granary where the tools are kept, then in the night I took a lantern and went to see for myself.

—J. M. Coetzee, *Waiting for the Barbarians*

Introduction

The Cold War produced some remarkable bedfellows. Under the leadership of President Harry S Truman, the United States government from 1945 to 1952 built alliances around the world against what it viewed as a pervasive threat by the Soviet Union to human freedom. The most important new commitment came in war-torn Europe, for the Truman administration had no doubt that Western Europe was the key to containing the spread of Soviet influence; its long history of industrial and military power made it the cornerstone of American policy. The enormous colonial territories controlled by England, France, Belgium, Portugal, and the Netherlands in Asia and Africa heightened the significance of these countries. The United States also developed formal alliances in these years in its own hemisphere and moved toward stronger ties with the countries of the Middle East, East Asia, and Southeast Asia. One of the most troubling and problematic relationships to emerge for the United States in this period, however, was with a nation far removed from the Soviet Union and Europe: the Union of South Africa.[1]

Still a self-governing Dominion of the British Commonwealth until 1961, South Africa evolved during the Truman years from minor member of the victorious Allies of World War II to a status approaching that of international pariah. The cause, simply put, was its race relations. Elsewhere, successful prosecution of the war against Nazi Germany and the revelations of the Third Reich's efforts at racial genocide had discredited racial discrimination in international politics as never before. The long-established tradition of exploiting nonwhite peoples overseas would die hard in nations like England and Portugal, but in practical terms the war had devastated the European colonial powers, victors and vanquished alike. Moreover, the two most powerful nations to emerge victorious from the war shared an anticolonial tradition and reputation that seemed to offer a basis for greater racial equality. The Soviet Union had outlawed racial discrimination, and in the United States the movement to end segregation was growing steadily stronger. But the white minority in South Africa during these same years set its face resolutely against this tide of world history, moving forcefully to strengthen its position in what would become the world's last redoubt of white supremacy.[2]

Nevertheless, strategic and economic interests were simultaneously drawing the United States into closer alliance with South Africa. The apartheid regime that had come to power in 1948 in a surprising victory over the United Party of internationally renowned statesman Jan C. Smuts solidified and expanded previous South African segregation, further impoverishing and debilitating the vast majority of people in the Union. The Nationalist Party government of Dr. Daniel F. Malan made no apologies for this policy to the world abroad or to critics at home, and ignored all threats and pleas to change course. But South Africa's ties with Great Britain remained close, and American trade and investment in the Union expanded rapidly during the late 1940s and early 1950s. The white government's fervent anticommunism and steady support for the United States during the various crises of the early Cold War brought it much credit in Washington. Most important of all, South Africa's agreement in 1950 to produce and sell large quantities of uranium ore exclusively to the United States and England made the Union central to American national security policy. Thus an apartheid regime came to rest prominently among the nations of President Truman's self-proclaimed "free world." By the end of the Truman administration in January 1953, South Africa had become the greatest political embarrassment to the United States in the now vociferous Cold War.

An examination of American support for the white minority government of South Africa and for the colonial rulers of the rest of southern Africa offers a window on the complicated interplay of two major themes of twentieth-century American history: racism and anticommunism.[3] The direct relationship between race relations in the international sphere and racial behavior in the United States will also become clear, for it was no coincidence that the Cold War and the civil rights movement in America happened simultaneously. American relations with South and southern Africa both reflected and, in turn, influenced the manner in which the decolonization of most of Asia and Africa proceeded in the context of the Cold War. An exploration of these themes properly begins with a survey of American relations with Africa before 1945 and the impact of World War II on southern Africa, especially the Union of South Africa.

PART ONE

COMMON INTERESTS

CHAPTER 1

The United States: American Race Relations and Ties with Africa Before Truman

Momolu Massaquoi came to Nashville during the Reconstruction years to attend Central Tennessee College. A son of the royal family of Sierra Leone, Massaquoi had gone to a mission school at home and had become a baptized Christian. In 1872, early in his undergraduate career in the American South, he happened upon a revealing but not uncommon scene of American life that would trouble him for decades thereafter. A large crowd of white people were taking a black man out of the city jail and parading him in a public square. They then tied a rope around his neck, secured it to a nearby bridge, and threw him over the side. What horrified Massaquoi even more than the brutality of the murder was the happy, festive atmosphere of the crowd. Hundreds of white men and women were laughing and joking at what they apparently thought of as sport. Describing this event years later to an audience of distinguished clergy in Boston, Massaquoi noted that despite white Americans' views of Africa as a "savage continent," he had never seen anything there to compare with the savagery he had witnessed in Nashville.[1]

The racial contours of American society that shocked Momolu Massaquoi in the nineteenth century were quite familiar to men who grew up in those same years in the South and the border states, like Harry Truman of Missouri and his first appointed Secretary of State, James Byrnes of South Carolina. The long, dark history of race slavery and its aftermath in the United States had left a legacy of racial segregation, discrimination, and violence that still prevailed on the home front during World War II. The struggle of black Americans for equality in their own country gained momentum during the war, laying the foundation for important symbolic changes during the years of the Truman administration and for the massive civil rights movement of the 1950s and 1960s. But in 1945, despite four years of war against the most destructive racists of the twentieth century, the United States was not well prepared as a society to deal with the rising power of the people of color who made up the vast majority of the world's population. African Americans remained almost exclusively at the bottom of the American socioeconomic ladder. Parts of the Third World had become familiar to some American soldiers during the war, but white Americans as a whole continued to have as little knowledge of the nonwhite world abroad as they had of black communities in the United States. If most white Americans could barely notice black Americans, they could scarcely imagine black Africans.[2]

Governments tend to share the perspectives and limitations of the societies from which they emerge. The members of the Truman administration were products of a racially hierarchical culture whose values they shared and celebrated. The competitive ideological atmosphere of the Cold War would help move them eventually to adopt certain policies more sensitive to the desires of people of color at home and abroad, but their own experiences before coming to power trained them to identify with Europeans rather than with other peoples in international affairs. Truman and his advisers saw a vital and friendly Western Europe as the cornerstone of American foreign policy. They knew little of southern Africa, and when they considered it at all, they viewed the region through European rather than African eyes. They showed much more interest in events in Asia, where the end of the war revealed highly unstable conditions in China and almost all the colonial areas. Left-leaning revolutionaries threatened European control with far greater immediacy there than did any of the more preliminary discontents in sub-Saharan Africa. Relatively safe and little noticed by the public, American interests in southern Africa—especially in the Belgian Congo and the Union of South Africa—were already substantial by the eve of the Cold War. In the crisis-filled years of the Truman administration, the United States government would continue to define its interests in the region in a manner that would tie it closely to colonial and white minority rule.

I

American images of Africa before World War II emphasized topography and wildlife rather than people or cultural achievements. Few Americans had traveled to the continent, and most who had were either tourists or big-game hunters; while there, they usually shared in the comfortable and even luxurious life of European whites in a still-colonial world. The little information about Africa that reached the United States tended to be welded into a single, simplified image utterly at odds with the marked diversity of African environments and cultures. In this stereotype of the mysterious "Dark Continent," endless jungles teemed with savage and exotic beasts: lions, crocodiles, and huge snakes. The occasional person with dark skin who appeared in this story fell into one of two categories, depending on the degree of his independence from whites: he was either an obedient, childlike servant accompanying white hunters or explorers, or a practically naked savage bent on cannibalism. Africa and North America represented polar opposites in economic development, and people from the richest continent rarely bridged the cultural gap to understand those from the poorest one. Even an American journalist genuinely sympathetic to the lives of African people could still refer casually in 1948 to "the vast, sad wilderness of Africa."[3]

Two sources of information in the United States proved particularly important in creating and sustaining the image of Africa as exotically beautiful and culturally primitive. The first was the print media. From its inaugural issue in 1889 onwards, *National Geographic* magazine portrayed Africa as the essence of all that was not Western and therefore not civilized in the world. Other magazines followed its lead in the early decades of the twentieth century by showing stunning African landscapes peopled by women with bare breasts and men with bare buttocks. American schoolbooks and children's literature spoke similarly of primitive savagery, and even most black-owned newspapers and magazines viewed Africa in largely negative terms.[4]

The second prominent medium to work the same ground was the American film industry, which built on these established stereotypes and ventured deeper into realms of fantasy and thus farther from African realities. Africa in the movies before World War II appeared as a kind of manifestation of the unrestrained id: savage to the point of cannibalism and thoroughly sensual. Black magic and voodoo abounded, while notably simian African men not under white control provided a steady subtext of sexual menace to white women. Africans were portrayed in uniformly derogatory fashion as American filmmakers constructed a fantasy Africa out of their own projections of supposed white superiority and convoluted fears of black sexuality. Decency and morality were almost exclusively associated with the presence of white people. In Richard Wright's powerful 1940 novel, *Native Son,* the impoverished black protagonist Bigger Thomas and his friend Jack go to the movies in Chicago:

> Two features were advertised: one, *The Gay Woman,* was pictured on the posters in images of white men and white women lolling on beaches, swimming, and dancing in night clubs; the other, *Trader Horn,* was shown on the posters in terms of black men and black women dancing against a wild background of barbaric jungle. . . .
>
> [Bigger] looked at *Trader Horn* unfold and saw pictures of naked black men and women whirling in wild dances and heard drums beating and then gradually the African scene changed and was replaced by images in his own mind of white men and women dressed in black and white clothes, laughing, talking, drinking and dancing. Those were smart people; they knew how to get hold of money, millions of it. Maybe if he were working for them something would happen and he would get some of it. . . .

The most famous of these films were the Tarzan series and the King Kong movies, which reached the height of their popularity in the years right before World War II.[5]

Americans of a more entrepreneurial bent and their allies in the United States government regarded Africa as an undeveloped treasure house of natural wealth. In contrast to the tremendous commercial exploitation of natural resources in the United States, African wealth remained largely untapped. Accustomed to viewing black Americans as lazy and carefree, most white Americans assumed that a similar passivity in Africans hindered them from making capital of their vast resources. This apparent failure to contribute to their own economic development troubled commercially minded Yankees. Africa appeared to them to be almost another American West, an inert land of enormous potential just waiting for whites, with their modern knowledge and motivation, to come and develop it. Most Americans associated progress in Africa with white settlement, just as they had in the United States decades earlier. Continuing European colonial control of almost the entire continent seemed to confirm African helplessness. Africans, like African Americans, might make obedient laborers in the development of their own continent, it seemed, but only under the direction and discipline of whites.[6]

Few white Americans had encountered people of color as peers or equals, knowing them instead almost exclusively in positions of inferiority. Blacks, especially, seemed always the poorest, least educated, least healthy, and most submissive and vulnerable of Americans. By the late nineteenth century, as attitudes towards the poor in general became less sympathetic, supposedly scientific theories of Social Darwinism further bolstered long-standing assumptions in the United States and Europe of white superiority. White dominion around the globe seemed evidence of the "survival of the fittest." American and British scientists defined human intellectual development in explicitly racial terms, theorizing that different races had differing natural capacities; black people were always put at the bottom of any list. As the United States seized its own colonial empire in the Spanish-American War at the turn of the century, "Anglo-Saxonist" thinking prevailed as white Americans identified increasingly with the English and disdained newer immigrants from southern and eastern Europe. Racial attitudes changed little in the United States in the early decades of the twentieth century, and with Africa firmly under European control and African Americans still in the lowest echelons of the American working class, most white Americans were not prepared in 1945 to respond to Africans as they did to people from Europe or of European descent.[7]

Among the few Americans who took any serious interest in the 150 million people of Africa, missionaries made up the largest group. Years of living on the "Dark Continent," however, rarely overcame the cultural and racial assumptions they had been deeply imbued with, and Africans seemed always like children to them. American missionaries up to World War II regarded technologically unsophisticated Africans not only as in need of religious redemption, but also as lacking a meaningful history or culture of their own. These apparently passive creatures were seen instead as needing to be molded and outfitted for life in a modern world dominated by Western economic and political, as well as religious, realities. In their efforts to legitimate and fund their own work, missionaries tended to emphasize to their churches and organizations at home what they understood as the moral and sexual depravity of Africans, including nudity, polygamy, and what evidence they could find of cannibalism.[8]

The American scientific and academic communities seemed rarely even to notice that there were people in Africa before World War II, showing instead considerably more interest in the continent's animal life. In 1936 the American Museum of Natural History in New York was prepared to unveil its long-awaited Akeley African Hall when it received from a patron one last gift for display: a bronze figure of an African drummer. The museum director, F. Trubee Davison, expressed pleasure at this final addition to the collection, noting that it would "add a human touch to the African Hall."[9]

The first modern anthropological survey of an African country, demonstrating the indigenous origins of remarkable cultural achievements in the West African state of Dahomey (now Benin), was not published until 1938. Even after this landmark study by Melville J. Herskovits, evidence of ancient African political empires and artistic legacies went largely unnoticed outside the anthropological profession or was explained away as the result of outside influences. Working from the same assumption, that social and political success depended on the degree of white influence, American writers and even some anthropologists portrayed independent African rulers in Ethiopia and Liberia as virtually incompetent and often comical. Isaiah Bowman, president of Johns Hopkins University, one of the foremost American geographers, and an important adviser to President Roosevelt on "dependent areas" issues, summarized these feelings in his preface to a 1941 book of aerial photographs of Africa: "In the air Africa can be seen and enjoyed without perpetual reminders of the desperate human problems on the ground."[10]

The most obvious solution to the maze of social problems Americans believed inherent in African societies south of the Sahara was an infusion of large numbers of white settlers. In contrast to western and central Africa, the milder, drier climates of eastern and southern Africa had long attracted substantial numbers of European immigrants. South Africa had the largest white population on the continent, whose technological modernity and European culture made the country, in the eyes of Americans, a beacon of Western progress on the "Dark Continent." White Americans who paid any attention to Africa usually felt considerable identity with the descendants of tough, self-reliant European settlers of a new continent who had tamed the "wilderness" and made a plentiful life for themselves. Unlike the non-Western, "undeveloped" land use associated with the rest of the continent, the very landscape of the European areas of southern Africa impressed American visitors with its familiarity: roads, automobiles, telegraph poles, barbed-wire fences, farmhouses, and

neatly cultivated European-style farms. The presence of genuine European cities in South Africa, complete with familiar architecture and land-
scaping and the efficiency of skyscrapers, electric street cars, and telephones, contrasted dramatically with rural African life and reassured
Americans of the superior ingenuity of white people. The juxtaposition
of Europeans with Africans also created dangers to be guarded against,
as suggested by one white visitor in 1948 who described the quarter
million Colored people of Capetown as "a pathetic and frightening display of centuries of dock-side inter-breeding." But with its balls, theater,
formal evening wear, yachting, and other trappings of Western high society, white Capetown seemed the very pinnacle of culture in Africa.[11]

II

On the eve of World War II, world politics and wealth were, to a remarkable degree, still largely controlled by a handful of small white nations in Western Europe. While the growing power of the United States,
Japan, and the Soviet Union already threatened that hegemony, most of
the world's nonwhite peoples still lived in territories officially ruled from
London, Paris, Brussels, Lisbon, and The Hague. The primary lines of
power ran between these metropolitan centers of the North and colonial
"dependencies" in the South.[12] The connections between Western Europe and the Southern Hemisphere would be irretrievably weakened,
however, by the global warfare of 1939 to 1945. The decade and a half
after 1945 would see 800 million people in forty new countries free
themselves from colonial bondage, followed by the creation of another
twenty-five new nations, mostly in Africa, in the first half of the 1960s.
At its founding in 1945, the United Nations consisted of fifty-one nations, of which only three were African, three Asian, and seven from the
Middle East; by 1965, membership had more than doubled and white
Western nations were in a distinct minority in the international organization. The speed and extent of decolonization following World War II
represented a revolt against the West and a clear sign of a new era in
world politics. "Never before in the whole of human history had so revolutionary a reversal occurred with such rapidity," concluded one prominent world historian.[13]

   Such changes resulted, to a considerable extent, from the nature of
the Second World War. Responding to the overtly racial theories of the
Axis powers, the Allies mapped out an ideological high road for the war.
While Adolf Hitler fashioned a Nazi ideology rooted in supposed "Ar-
yan" superiority, and the Japanese appealed to other Asians to throw off
their white colonial overlords and claim Asia for the Asians, the United
States and England declared their war aims to be freedom, democracy,
and human rights. In his annual message to Congress on 6 January 1941,
before the United States had officially become a belligerent nation, President Franklin D. Roosevelt laid out his vision of a world founded on

"four essential human freedoms": freedom of expression, freedom of religion, freedom from economic privation, and freedom from fear of aggression. He repeatedly emphasized that these were to be effected "everywhere in the world."[14] When Roosevelt met with British Prime Minister Winston Churchill later that year aboard ship off the Newfoundland coast, the two leaders issued a joint declaration of war aims that became known as the Atlantic Charter. While noting their desire for global free trade and unhindered access to raw materials, they emphasized their opposition to all forms of aggression and expansion by one nation against another. Most important for the colonial peoples of the world was the third of the eight points in the statement: that the two countries would "respect the right of all peoples to choose the form of government under which they will live."[15]

Anticolonial nationalists throughout the British Empire and the rest of what would soon be called the Third World[16] took substantial encouragement from such rallying cries to a democratic future. While not naïvely expecting colonialism and white rule to disappear without considerable struggle, these men and women appreciated the ideological and political weapon provided by such declarations by the powerful United States and acceded to by a stout defender of empire like Churchill. In South Africa the African National Congress (ANC) responded in December 1943 with a detailed sixteen-page pamphlet applying the Atlantic Charter principles to its country. Prime Minister Smuts did not appreciate Africans' taking his allies Roosevelt and Churchill so seriously. Having earlier made it clear that such lofty principles of the Charter as the right to self-government could only be put into effect in South Africa in the distant future, due supposedly to the complexity of the country's multiracial society with its different "levels" of civilization, Smuts labeled the ANC pamphlet "propagandist" and "wildly impracticable."[17]

Churchill himself backed away from the explicit message of the Charter within weeks of its issuance. He reassured the House of Commons on 9 September 1941 that he and Roosevelt had intended the third principle of the declaration "primarily" for the European states under Nazi occupation and that the progressive evolution of "dependent" peoples in the British Empire was a separate issue. Over the next six months, Roosevelt waffled on Churchill's interpretation. He refused to contradict his ally explicitly, but he simultaneously reaffirmed a global application of the Charter as he tried to shore up Allied support among Southeast Asian colonial peoples facing imminent Japanese attack. Both the President and the State Department fully anticipated the propaganda potential of the Charter among Asian and African people not yet living under governments of their own choice.[18]

Opposition to colonialism was deeply rooted in the American psyche. The founding of the United States two centuries earlier had marked the first successful revolution of a colonial people against their European rulers in the modern era, and the American Revolution had continued to inspire anti-imperial nationalists throughout the world. Their belief in the principle of self-government formed the foundation of Americans' understanding of themselves as a distinctive people. Initially, exclusion of the majority of Americans by race, gender, and wealth from the application of this principle had severely limited the practice of democracy in the United States. But the elimination of property qualifications, the abolition of slavery, the achievement of women's suffrage, and the beginnings of the shift away from official federal support for racial segregation during World War II indicated the enormous power of the ideology of self-government to encourage dramatic social and political change.

By the end of the nineteenth century, however, an expanded and industrialized United States increasingly resembled the European nations it had originally set out to be different from, especially with the acquisition of its own overseas colonies in 1899. Americans fought alongside the French and British, the most important imperial powers, in World War I. But most Americans were never comfortable in the role of official colonialists, and by the mid-1930s the United States had promised to grant independence in ten years to its largest colony, the Philippines. Strong American business interest in expanding trade throughout the world meant opposing the closed trading blocs of the European colonial systems. This desire for an "Open Door" for American trade and overseas investment bolstered traditional American opposition to formal colonialism.[19]

Entering the war in 1941 with the declared aim of promoting self-government in every corner of the world, while also joining forces in a uniquely close alliance with the greatest colonial power, Great Britain, the United States was squarely confronted with its own ambivalent position. The result was an often-sharp difference between American words and actions in the early years of the war. While working hand in hand with the British military staff and refusing to press Churchill on granting independence to India and other colonies, the Roosevelt administration continued to tout the promises of the Atlantic Charter, and the State Department promoted the idea that the European powers should announce specific future dates when colonial peoples would achieve full independence. This belief in timetables for decolonization reflected both the satisfaction of American policymakers with their own schedule for the Philippines and their need to produce more support for the Allied cause among Britain's unhappy colonial peoples in Asia. Former Republican presidential candidate and prominent internationalist Wendell Willkie returned in September 1942 from a seven-week world tour, which included a visit to British West Africa, to call unequivocally for an end to European colonial rule abroad. The long-standing admiration of the American public for such features of English domestic life as parliamentary democracy, the rule of law, civility of manners, and policemen without handguns did not extend to British imperial rule overseas. This was made clearest by the unusually blunt "Open Letter to the People of England" published by *Life* magazine on 12 October 1942, which declared that Americans "may have some disagreement among ourselves as to what we are fighting for, but one thing we are sure we are *not* fighting for is to hold the British Empire together."[20]

Roosevelt's own anticolonial feelings were apparently genuine. He seemed to have been shocked by the squalor and technological backwardness of the British colony of Gambia in West Africa on his stopovers there in January 1943 en route to and from the Casablanca conference with Churchill and the combined British and American chiefs of staff. His anticolonial pronouncements appeared to take on more of an edge thereafter, and he referred frequently—both publicly and privately, and with some indignation—to the poverty of Gambia as vivid evidence of the failings of colonial rule.[21] Throughout 1943 and at least until the summer of 1944, Roosevelt indicated considerable enthusiasm for the State Department's plans for some form of postwar international trusteeships to preside over the decolonization of the European empires. As late as a month before his death in April 1945, the President spoke of his concern "about the brown people in the East." He regretted that Churchill did not understand their resentment of white rule and emphasized how important it was that these billion Asians not come to see the United States as an enemy for failing to support their independence.[22]

Supervising the enormous expansion of the United States economy driven by wartime demand, Roosevelt was also fully aware of the advantages to American business of gaining access to traditionally closed colonial markets. Postwar international trusteeship of colonial areas would allow for the President's and Secretary of State Cordell Hull's cherished "free trade," known grimly by British officials sensitive to American manufacturing superiority as "freedom of American trade." Resenting such pressures, the British nonetheless moved from 1943 on to appease their increasingly powerful ally as well as the growing opposition to British rule in India and elsewhere by gradually liberalizing their colonial arrangements.[23]

Despite its sympathy for independence movements in the colonial world and its interest in expanding postwar trade with those areas, the United States government's clear priority in the war years was the defeat of the Axis powers. If strongly anticommunist Americans could ally themselves with the Soviet Union in order to stop the Nazis, they could certainly accept close working relations with Western, Christian, democratic, capitalist peoples like the British and the Free French. Roosevelt may have subjected Churchill to monologues about India and hoped that the French could be prevented from returning to Southeast Asia after the war, but he never considered endangering his wartime alliances by raising a serious challenge over such peripheral concerns. And if this was true for Asia, it was all the more true for Africa, where the United States had little contact or experience and where nationalist movements for independence were not yet generally as organized and vocal as in Asia and the Middle East.[24]

The wartime willingness of the United States to acquiesce in its allies' continued colonial control of most of the nonwhite world was powerfully solidified during the final year of the war by the growing sense in Washington that the Soviet Union would soon replace the Axis powers as the strongest threat to American national security. As victory over Germany and Japan became certain in 1944 and early 1945, with Soviet troops pouring into Eastern Europe and American soldiers fighting their way across the Pacific island chains toward Japan, the first glimmers of the Cold War could be seen. The anticolonial rhetoric of the Roosevelt administration gradually declined as American military planners demanded that several Pacific islands be retained for postwar forward air bases. The rebuilding of a noncommunist Western Europe closely allied with the United States rose to the top of the American agenda, precluding any weakening of the European states through the precipitate loss of their colonial assets.

The growing popularity of left-wing guerrillas in China, Indonesia, and Indochina combined with the Soviet occupation of Eastern Europe to create fears in Washington of a communist threat to a postwar liberal capitalist world order even greater than that posed by colonialism. Roosevelt even seemed to acquiesce in the return of the French to Indochina, which he had strongly opposed earlier. The President and the State Department eased their mild pressure on the British about colonial matters, carefully limiting their postwar trusteeship formula to the mandated territories from World War I and parts of the Italian empire by the start of the United Nations conference in April 1945. By the time Harry Truman took office that same month, security concerns regarding the Soviet Union and left-wing forces in Asia were rapidly replacing a flagging anticolonialism within the United States government. In the coming Cold War, the United States would ally itself not only with colonial empires but also with forces much farther right on the political spectrum, including the government of South Africa.[25]

III

General surveys of the history of American foreign relations rarely mention Africa before the late 1950s. Like the State Department at the time, diplomatic historians since have largely viewed pre-independence Africa as a colonial concern of the Europeans' with little strategic significance for the United States. One of the few exceptions to this trend, Thomas J. Noer, has suggested that an essay on American relations with Africa could well be entitled "the invisible chapter" of any book on American diplomacy, a description aptly matching the near-invisibility of African people and even African Americans to most white Americans in the 1940s.[26]

This historical blind spot follows closely the attitude of the United States government at the time. The State Department before World War II dealt with Africa almost exclusively through the European colonial powers, creating its first African desk only in 1938. The officer assigned to the position, Henry S. Villard, had no specific training for it, although the familial tie to his famous abolitionist great-grandfather, William Lloyd Garrison, could perhaps have been considered some form of credential. Of the Africa desk's placement within the Department's Division of Near Eastern Affairs, Villard noted that "Africa didn't really belong in the near East, but nobody knew where else to put it." Villard then became the head of the new Division of African Affairs created in 1944, but as late as 1958 the State Department maintained more diplomats in the single country of West Germany than in all of Africa. In continuing to deal with Africa and its peoples through their colonial overlords in Europe, the United States necessarily risked identification with the imperial tradition of Western Europe in the eyes of many Africans.[27]

Certain American traditions and interests raised African hopes that the United States might, with the approach of World War II, avoid a complete alignment with the Western European powers. Politicized Africans in South Africa and British West Africa deeply admired the anti-colonial history and democratic traditions of the United States, while many Americans emphasized that this would not be a war to protect European imperial interests. The expanding interest of American business in unfettered international trade suggested a more concrete conflict of interest with the European powers and their systems of exclusive or preferential trade with their colonies. Antagonism toward the British system of Imperial Preference within the far-flung empire seemed especially likely.

But the necessities of war in the face of Axis victories up to 1942 bound the United States tightly to the survival of the British Empire, and official American support for an Open Door trading system in Africa was muted by the realization in Washington that America's European allies could not afford to be further weakened by the loss of their African colonies. The need for close Allied cooperation and full mobilization of the resources of colonial Africa for the war effort moderated American interest in colonial independence. Established American trading routes ran mostly elsewhere, and while United States trade and investment in Africa did rise sharply during the war, they remained a small fraction of total American commerce and capital abroad. No short-term commercial advantage seemed worth the risk of antagonizing Washington's closest allies in the midst of a war.[28]

The invasion of Ethiopia by the fascist forces of Benito Mussolini in 1935 offered a preview of how the United States government would respond during and after World War II to conflicts involving Europeans and Africans. Since the Ethiopians' defeat of an earlier generation of Italian invaders four decades before at the battle of Adowa, this poor but proud country in northeastern Africa had stood as a symbol of black independence and self-respect. As the largest community of people of African descent outside of the continent, African Americans were particularly alarmed by Mussolini's conquest and displayed thereafter a sharpened interest in international affairs. While the Roosevelt administration registered protests with the Italian government, refusing to recognize Italian authority in Ethiopia and briefly limiting American commerce with Italy, United States policy continued officially as neutrality. Within a year, American trade with Italy, including arms sales, resumed.[29]

The course of World War II did little to increase official American interest in the people of Africa, but it dramatically altered American assumptions about the strategic importance of the continent. The location and considerable mineral wealth of Africa, especially southern Africa, brought it prominence in the emerging doctrine of American national security. The United States military learned from experience that Africa in wartime afforded a staging ground for any future invasion of Europe, a land bridge to the Middle East, and protection for shipping routes in the Atlantic. Axis control of Europe and the Mediterranean, especially after the fall of France and Italy's entry into the war in 1940, drove these points home. African foodstuffs and strategic minerals also proved crucial for the Allied war effort, especially industrial diamonds, cobalt, and uranium from the Belgian Congo, graphite from Madagascar, copper from Northern Rhodesia, chrome and manganese from Southern Rhodesia, and gold and manganese from South Africa. Colonel William Donovan, the head of American wartime intelligence services, valued African resources highly enough to show considerable concern for the potential for German sabotage of the material production of the African colonies. He placed agents from the Office of Strategic Services (OSS) throughout southern and central Africa to monitor any German action there until the threat retreated with the Allied invasion of North Africa in 1942.[30]

Even as the exigencies of war highlighted their continent's strategic importance as never before, the people of Africa remained largely mysterious and insignificant to American policymakers. American diplomatic representatives in the African colonies lived like other whites in the colonial world, with considerable comfort and privilege and ready attention from ubiquitous, inexpensive black servants. As emissaries from a racially stratified culture whose ideas and values they shared, American consuls sanctioned colonial authority by living amiably within it. They experienced Africans solely as servants and paid little attention to signs of nascent nationalism during the war. Having known African Americans only as denizens of the lowest social strata at home, American diplomats and policymakers assumed that first-class citizenship for colonial Africans, as for black Americans, stood far off in the future. Under-Secretary of State Sumner Welles, a point man for Washington on colonial issues, expressed the dominant view of his colleagues in the Roosevelt administration that Africans simply were "in the lowest rank of human beings." While Asians at least manifested an obvious yearning for independence with imminent revolutions in several colonial territories, American policymakers interpreted the less visible African nationalist movements as a sign that Africans apparently did not even desire freedom from colonial rule.[31]

For white Americans to have admitted that black Africans could and should rule themselves would have inevitably entailed acknowledging the same for black Americans. Such a racially democratic approach would have challenged the entire social structure of the United States, a task that would be braved, not by professional white diplomats in the 1940s, but by poor black civil rights workers in the American South a decade later. Several hundred years of racial neglect and misinformation had poorly prepared the new President, Harry Truman, and his administration for dealing with and understanding the peoples of Africa. Extensive racial discrimination in the United States helped prevent American officials from even considering significant support for African independence during or soon after World War II.[32]

IV

When novelist Ralph Ellison wrote in the late 1940s of the African American as "the invisible man" to white Americans, he gave poignant expression to the underlying racial tragedy of American history.[33] Americans of European descent had so long degraded Americans of African ancestry through the mechanisms of slavery and segregation that few whites could see blacks as the human beings they were. African Americans appeared in white popular culture almost exclusively as inferior, childlike creatures, often warm and funny but never responsible and mature. In prominent radio shows like "Amos 'n Andy" and in Hollywood's biggest movies like *Gone with the Wind,* blacks were consistently portrayed as lazy, comical, simpleminded, and rarely reliable. The Second World War initiated changes in American society that would lead eventually to the civil rights and Black Power movements and the evisceration of such racial stereotypes, but blacks were still only dimly visible to white America in 1945.[34]

Playfully derogatory images of "Sambo" shielded from the view of most white Americans the extraordinary, pervasive brutality and oppression faced daily by black Americans before and during the years of the early Cold War. Historians have rarely evoked the almost totalitarian control by whites of every aspect of the material lives of African Americans, especially in the South.[35] Public lynching, private murder, arbitrary capital punishment, rape, and mutilation constituted merely the gory veneer of a racial hierarchy in which blacks were usually kept "in their place" by the more mundane tools of poverty, miseducation, negligible health care, economic coercion, police intimidation, and the countless petty harassments and reminders of a Jim Crow society.

During World War II, racial violence in the United States escalated sharply in both the civilian and the military spheres. Among the victims of the six recorded lynchings in 1942, for example, was cotton-mill worker Cleo Wright of Sikeston, Missouri. Alleged to have attacked a white woman, Wright was seized from jail by a mob of hundreds of white people and dragged to death through the black section of Sikeston by a rope attached to a speeding automobile. The crowd then burned his body. In 1943, 242 racial battles occurred in forty-seven cities across the country, frequently with police provoking or assisting white aggressors. Most spectacular were the full-scale race riots that summer in New York and Detroit, the latter exploding with enough viciousness to kill thirty-four people (mostly black) and force President Roosevelt to proclaim a state of emergency and send in six thousand soldiers to restore order.[36]

Racial fights and incidents broke out almost daily on public transportation in the United States during the war, usually involving the treatment of African American soldiers. Accustomed to blacks' occupying the lowest end of the social scale, many white Americans suffered distress upon seeing so many of them with the authority implied by their United States military uniforms. This proved especially true in the South, where uniformed black men with guns represented to most white people a virtual nightmare of racial insubordination. The segregated U.S. Army helped alleviate such concerns by refusing to protect black soldiers away from their bases and by using white military police to control and intimidate them. Black soldiers experienced frequent beatings and even death at the hands of local police and private individuals when they ventured from their military posts. Harrowing treatment by white fellow soldiers and military tribunals led to racial violence and riots at nearly every Army base in the South, and many in the North and West and even abroad, at some point in the war. Roosevelt's entrusting of racial matters in the armed forces during the war to two Southern aides, one of them the avowedly racist director of the war mobilization effort, James Byrnes, exemplified the scale of the problems facing black servicemen who hoped for democracy at home as well as abroad.[37]

Abiding white hostility to African Americans reached remarkable extremes during the war. More revealing in some ways than the most brutal murders was the positive treatment accorded German and Italian prisoners of war incarcerated in the United States. Captured soldiers of the Nazi Wehrmacht were able to eat and even enjoy some hospitality in public establishments in the United States that refused to serve uniformed officers of the United States Army who had dark skin. Many white Americans felt more kinship with their country's sworn enemies, who were killing American soldiers by the thousands in the service of one of history's most ruthless dictators, than with fellow Americans who were sacrificing their lives to defend the United States and the freedoms for which it was supposed to stand.[38]

While ironic on a superficial plane, this telling comparison suggested stark tragedy at a deeper level. Racism could transcend even the most fiercely felt patriotism and allegiance to democratic ideals. Black Americans fighting to preserve the very existence of the United States appeared to be more of a threat to the structure of American society than the soldiers of Adolph Hitler. The subversive possibilities of African Americans, feared for centuries by slaveholders and their descendants, concerned the United States government as well, as the Federal Bureau of Investigation (FBI) and intelligence operatives of the War Department infiltrated and monitored black political organizations and watched at least one of the two black U.S. Congressmen during the war.[39]

Refusing to be intimidated by these considerable obstacles, many black Americans seized the opportunities created by the war to press their demands for equality and justice at home. A. Philip Randolph's threat to lead a massive march on Washington in 1941 helped persuade Roosevelt to create the President's Committee on Fair Employment Practices (FEPC). Service in the military, despite its numerous problems, offered social and economic mobility to many African Americans, especially those from the South, as did employment in the rapidly expanding wartime manufacturing plants. The black-owned *Pittsburgh Courier* declared a "Double-V" campaign for victory both abroad and at home for democracy and freedom. Bolstered by the experience of thousands of newly assertive and confident black veterans, African Americans realized the unique opportunity for advancing their cause while their goals were so clearly in line with those of the country as a whole in its struggle against worldwide oppression. Strong black opposition to Byrnes contributed to Roosevelt's decision not to choose him as his vice-presidential running mate in 1944, and thereby indirectly helped Truman in his swift ascent to the presidency. In *An American Dilemma,* his massive and influential study of American race relations published in 1944, sociologist Gunnar Myrdal concluded that "not since Reconstruction has there been more reason to anticipate fundamental changes in American race relations, changes which will involve a development toward the American ideals."[40] Even if such expected improvements in the status of African Americans were to follow the war, however, it remained to be seen whether they would affect American relations with Africa.

CHAPTER 2

Southern Africa:
The Impact of World War II

On the day of the atomic bombing of Nagasaki, less than a week before the Japanese surrender, the Non-European Unity Committee of Cape-town issued a "Declaration to the Nations of the World," which high-lighted the ironic situation of black South Africans involved in World War II. Non-Europeans in the Union of South Africa, announced the declaration, lived under "a tyranny very little different from Nazidom," despite the Union's presentation of itself to the world as a parliamentary democracy. Like the Nazis in Germany, continued the Committee, white South Africans were a people obsessed with their supposed racial supe-riority and divine mission to rule people of other races in perpetuity. Even "liberal" Prime Minister Jan Smuts publicly branded whites who refused to adopt this *Herrenvolk* ideology as "mad, quite mad." Noting the comprehensive restrictions on every aspect of black lives in the Union, the declaration reminded its readers that "the life of a Non-European is very cheap in South Africa. As cheap as the life of a Jew in Nazi Ger-many." The Committee concluded that the defeat of Hitler and the im-minent surrender of the Japanese did not constitute the final chapter in the struggle against tyranny. In passing along this document to the State Department, the American consul general in Capetown admitted to his superiors that these claims about the treatment of the vast majority of residents of an Allied nation were not exaggerated.[1]

While it did not bring the immediate demise of white dominion in Africa, the Second World War did create an international environment that helped raise African political expectations throughout the continent and especially in South Africa. Italy's invasion and occupation of inde-pendent Ethiopia in 1935 had aroused considerable black interest in in-ternational affairs, and Africans in South Africa were thrilled about the fighting role of Africans from West and Central Africa in the Allied ar-mies that drove the Italians and Germans off the continent. The experi-ence of hundreds of thousands of black South Africans as noncombatant support troops in the war exposed most of them for the first time to an outside world different from South Africa in many ways, especially in

regard to the Union's traditional racial hierarchy. South Africa's participation in the Allied cause of freedom, democracy, and human decency
indeed had much richer implications for black South Africans than for
their white countrymen.[2]

I

In 1939, the European colonial powers seemed as firmly entrenched in
Africa as they ever would be. Metropolitan capital was successfully and
intensively exploiting colonial resources, and the Europeans were even
legitimated in the eyes of many African elites, who tended to identify
their political and social ambitions with European culture. A significant
amount of African criticism of the colonial structure focused on its character rather than its mere existence. The four independent states on the
continent on the eve of the Second World War offered little encouragement for black self-government: South Africa was controlled by whites;
Ethiopia had been overrun and occupied by Italian forces; Liberia was
considered largely an unimportant protectorate of the United States; and
Egypt viewed itself as part of the Middle East. Missionaries and big game
hunters provided the majority of the minimal American interest in the
"Dark Continent," while the United States government had no significant interests there. The Soviet Union had even less concern for Africa.
Few people anywhere, either white or black, imagined how rapidly African society and politics would change in the next two and a half decades.[3]

In important ways, the war transformed Africa and Africans' perceptions of their relationships with Europeans. North and northeast Africa
formed an important theater of battle, and Africans from every part of
the continent volunteered for or were conscripted into European armies.
The essential myth of imperial invincibility was fatally weakened by the
capitulation of France and Belgium to the Germans, and even more so
by the Japanese defeats of the vaunted British in the Southeast Asian
theater. This deeply symbolic victory of a nonwhite nation over the greatest
of the imperial countries echoed the Ethiopian defeat of the Italians at
Adowa in 1896, redeemed the Italian occupation of Ethiopia of 1935,
and served notice that European power abroad was in its ebb tide. Of all
the colonial powers in sub-Saharan Africa, only neutral Portugal emerged
from the war largely unscathed, a development critical for enabling it to
remain in Africa a decade longer than the other imperial states. The lords
of most of Africa—Britain, France, and Belgium—could claim victory in
1945 only because of the intervention of the Soviet Union and the United
States. These real victors fought under an anticolonial banner, while the
Europeans had been financially and emotionally drained by the war effort.[4]

The increasing technological complexity of the weapons used in the
Second World War, from machine guns to atomic bombs, also con-

tributed to a dramatic shift in Africa's relationship with the outside world. Access to the vast natural resources of the continent took on enormous strategic significance for the Allies. The unprecedented production of raw materials demanded by "total war" rendered the global conflict in one sense a struggle for the control and exploitation of the world's strategic minerals. In the early years of the war in particular, German control of continental Europe and the Japanese occupation of Southeast Asia denied the Allies access to many of their traditional sources of strategic materials, thereby increasing the importance of Africa. Throughout the war, the United States itself remained the foremost mineral-producing nation in the world, but heavy wartime demands necessitated the use of other sources. In its production of four specific minerals, Africa helped determine the outcome of the conflict: industrial diamonds, cobalt, gold, and uranium. The first two, of which over 90 percent of world production during the war occurred in Africa, were essential for iron and steel manufacturing, while African gold helped keep the British Empire financially afloat, and uranium from the Belgian Congo, when enclosed in atomic bombs, brought the war in the Pacific to an abrupt close. Important quantities of chrome, manganese, vanadium, platinum, and copper from southern Africa pushed the continent's wartime significance further beyond its previously limited political and economic role in international affairs. Long-standing colonial and Commonwealth connections greatly facilitated Allied access, usually at bargain prices, to the wealth of Africa.[5]

Most important for the future of the continent, World War II served as a powerful stimulus for the development of African nationalism. After being cloistered within the narrow confines of the colonial state, over a million Africans from throughout the continent propelled themselves outward by enlisting and serving in the Allied armies and in support industries. American intelligence officials noted that African soldiers figured prominently in driving the Italian and German forces out of Africa and saw action on battlefronts throughout the world in the British, French, and Belgian armies. Gaining skills, education, and experience previously inaccessible to them, Africans witnessed the power of fellow colonial subjects in India peacefully persuading their colonial overlords to promise them independence. They took note of fiercely nationalistic yellow soldiers defeating white ones in the China-Burma-India theater. And they were moved and encouraged by the Allies' anti-Nazi and antiracist propaganda and apparent promises of postwar freedom embodied in the Atlantic Charter.[6]

Having been told that they were fighting abroad for freedom, African soldiers returned victorious from the war with stronger ideas about liberty at home as well. They joined another stream flowing back into Africa at the end of the war: African students, especially from British West Africa, who had sojourned in American colleges and universities and who were similarly convinced that democracy should now come to their own countries. The U.S. Office of Strategic Services reported on this rising tide of African nationalism in the last months of the war and the concomitant European colonial plans for a rapid, extensive demobilization of African soldiers in order to disperse them swiftly and minimize the social and political effects of their return. Belgian administrators in the Congo, for example, apparently feared the return of the African Force Publique from the Middle East due to reports of how its troops were being treated as equals by white Allied soldiers. The Belgian authorities were concerned that such worldly experience might have diminished the Africans' willingness automatically to respect and obey whites; that respect could be mutual between Europeans and Africans remained largely a future idea for Belgians in the Congo. African troops in the Portuguese Army in Mozambique were known to be unhappy with their restriction to menial tasks from which they could learn no new skills. The OSS understood that the potential impact of large numbers of returning black soldiers on the existing political and social structures of Africa, while feared by Europeans, was anticipated eagerly by the "more sophisticated and politically alert natives," particularly in South Africa and British West Africa. "The African nationalist," concluded the OSS, "sees in military service for the native a wedge with which the fight for equality and native development can be broadened."[7]

While greatly encouraged by the results of the war, African nationalists were not naïve about the difficulty of the tasks that confronted them at home. The Europeans showed no signs of liberating their African colonies out of gratitude for African contributions to the war effort. Though weakened by the effects of six years of global war, the economic and political structures of colonialism remained in place. A returning West African soldier suggested the seriousness of the obstacles still confronting his people's quest for freedom in a version of the Twenty-third Psalm, which he sent to the *African Morning Post* of Accra in 1944:

> The European Merchant is my shepherd,
> And I am in want;
> He maketh me to lie down in cocoa farms;
> He leadeth me beside the waters of great need. . . .[8]

But as the first postwar years swept European colonial rule out of most of Asia, it became clear to those who sought an end to white rule in Africa and to observers abroad that independence would come to most of Africa in a matter of years rather than generations.[9]

II

As the only rapidly industrializing state in Africa and the one with by far the largest number of white settlers, the Union of South Africa was perhaps more affected by the World War II years than any other territory south of the Sahara. In order to understand this important and distinctive impact, certain features of the development of southern Africa since the first Dutch settlement at Table Bay in 1652 need to kept in mind. One is the character of the northwestern Europeans who populated the Cape of Good Hope and came to call themselves Afrikaners. From their earliest days, the Afrikaner people have felt themselves threatened to an extent few other peoples or nations have experienced, both from within their borders and from without. The story of Afrikaner nationalism carries at its core an almost paranoid sense of danger.[10]

Dutch emigrants of the seventeenth century took with them two profound fears stemming from the national experience of Holland. The most basic was of the sea. The constant danger of enormous floods from storms on the North Sea, which had killed thousands of people and drowned dozens of villages in the past, induced in the people of the Netherlands a fear of inundation comparable to the terror of the Black Death in other parts of Europe. Their national survival depended on the communal building and maintenance of defenses against the sea, and they constructed dikes, dams, and windmills to reclaim from the ocean tens of thousands of acres of fertile low-lying land. The dread of drowning could even be seen in a device created by the strongly Calvinist Dutch to discipline recalcitrant young delinquents who refused to work: the youth would be placed in an enclosed chamber with only a pump; the valves then opened to let water in, and the only way to survive was for the youth to work the pump with supreme vigor.[11] On the arid expanses of southern Africa, the small group of Dutch and other northwestern European settlers would come to believe that while the ocean no longer threatened them, the large indigenous population did. In this new land the Afrikaners feared that their cultural and racial identity might be submerged forever in an inland sea of black Africans.[12]

Related to this preoccupation with inundation by water was another deep concern deriving from the national history of the Netherlands: the threat of invasion by foreign imperial powers. The Dutch who emigrated to southern Africa in the seventeenth century left a Protestant country still ardent in its desire to defend its relatively recent independence from the Roman Catholic Spanish Empire. The Calvinist Dutch believed that their independence from the sea and from external authority represented divine approval of their national endeavor. By the nineteenth century, the Afrikaners had come to see themselves as a new incarnation of the chosen people of God, analogous to the ancient Israelites, with a special and exclusive covenant with God and a fresh mandate to "smite the heathen" in order to occupy the new Canaan.[13] When the British gained political control of the Cape Colony in the early nineteenth century and sought to moderate some of the more brutal aspects of the extremely authoritarian relations between Afrikaners and Africans, the ghost of external imperial intervention seemed alive again to these fiercely independent descendants of settlers from the Dutch republic. Their determination to be free of the restraints of British liberal imperialism led to the Great Trek inland of 1836 to 1838 and the founding of the Boer republics, which became known eventually as the Orange Free State and the Transvaal (north of the Vaal River). The discovery of diamonds in the 1870s and gold in the 1880s drew the British inland, however, and the British defeat of the Afrikaners in the Boer War of 1899 to 1902 resulted in the unification of the Cape and Natal colonies with the two Boer states in 1910 as a self-governing Dominion of the British Commonwealth.

South Africa's failure after World War II to evolve with the rest of the world in the direction of racial egalitarianism can be traced to the peculiar development of its social structure and political history. In all African territories with substantial European populations, such as Kenya, Algeria, Mozambique, and Southern Rhodesia, white settlers exerted disproportionate influence on the administrative policies of their metropolitan governments and opposed granting significant political power to Africans. But the longer colonial rule continued, the greater the possibility became of transferring eventual control to an increasingly politicized African majority. The largest and most established white settler community was in South Africa, and only there and in neighboring Southern Rhodesia did self-government come early enough to create powerful white settler regimes. Historian Leonard Thompson has referred to the transfer of power to European settler communities who remain dominant over indigenous peoples as "secondary colonialism." This phenomenon differs from the "primary colonialism" of the European power because in secondary colonialism the stakes for the ruling whites are much higher: all members of the ruling oligarchy live in the colony and view the maintenance of the colonial system, with their clear economic and political interests in it, as crucial for their own survival. In Southern Rhodesia, limited white self-government began in 1923, but the minority regime did not declare its complete independence from Britain until 1965, a time when vastly different racial assumptions in world opinion brought almost universal condemnation of an action plainly designed to prolong white minority rule. In South Africa, by contrast, the transition to independent rule by the local white population was completed in 1910, when racial discrimination was still endorsed and practiced by the European nations and the United States. The founding of the modern South African state was therefore unquestionably legitimate in the eyes of the existing international community.[14]

The white rulers of the new Union of South Africa built their hopes for permanent minority rule on an avowed foundation of racial segregation. The government of Louis Botha and the young Jan Smuts, both generals and Afrikaner heroes of the Boer War, set out to guarantee perpetual white supremacy in every aspect of South African life. The Mines and Works Act of 1911 and subsequent legislation firmed up the industrial color bar by reserving most categories of skilled labor for white workers only. The Native Affairs Act of 1920 reinforced administrative segregation by giving limited self-government to Africans within the "native reserves," a policy leading eventually to the establishment of the nominally independent African "homelands" within South Africa. The Natives (Urban Areas) Act of 1923 confirmed urban areas as exclusively the domain of whites, in which nonwhites were allowed only as long as they served white needs; cities could now create "native locations" nearby as ready labor pools and regulate the movement of Africans with pass systems, thereby preventing them from competing for jobs with poorer whites. Most important of all was the territorial segregation established by the Native Land Act of 1913, which designated 87 percent of South Africa's land—including the most fertile for farming and ranching—for the 20 percent of the population who were white. Most white South Africans disliked Africans as independent peasant producers, preferring to keep them available instead as extraordinarily cheap migrant workers for white farmers and urban dwellers. The Native Land Act had a devastating impact on previously self-sufficient African farmers, who were forced off their land in large numbers. They joined the gathering tide of rural Africans who sought to survive by finding employment in the cities or as migratory laborers, with consequently devastating social effects on traditional family lives. This was the manner in which most Africans were incorporated into the racial capitalism characterizing South Africa's modern economy. Yale sociologist James Leyburn concluded in 1944 that "discrimination against the blacks in the Union of South Africa is more far-reaching, more cynical, than in any other self-governing country in the modern world."[15]

The economy black South Africans found themselves increasingly drawn into in the years before and during World War II had been built on gold. Since the original discoveries in 1886, the gold-mining industry had provided the driving force in South Africa's economic expansion. The geological formation known as the *Witswatersrand* ("reef of white waters," or simply, "the Rand") on which the city of Johannesburg had been built produced far more gold bullion than any other single source in the world. In addition to attracting capital and skills from abroad and stimulating a host of secondary industrial development, gold mining had functioned as a stabilizing force in the South African economy and had kept the Union free from the serious balance-of-payments problems endemic to so many other countries. The economical production of gold in the South African mines depended, as all South African mining and governmental leaders acknowledged, on the extremely low wages paid to migrant African laborers, who worked under difficult and dangerous conditions. White South Africa's remarkable wealth and consequent international importance were the fruits of black labor. The maintenance of a steady supply of Africans needy enough to be willing to work for so little remuneration remained, therefore, a central concern of the South African government.[16]

A newer stage of industrial capitalism had already begun to replace this older, extractive capitalism when World War II intervened to accelerate the transformation. Demands by the Union government for man-ufactured war materials and the disruption of international trade stimu-lated an enormous boom in industrial production, more than doubling the value of South African manufactures between 1939 and 1945. In-dustrial expansion created new jobs, which drew rural South Africans of all colors to the cities in even greater numbers than before the war. Fleeing drought and starvation in the native reserves and squatter evictions in the white farming areas, impoverished Africans came to Johannesburg and other urban areas during the war in such numbers as to constitute a demographic reordering of South African society. Industrialization brought the races into increasing contact as Africans even worked side by side with whites in some of the newer factories, despite regulations against doing so. White unease with the growing black population in urban areas and consequent slippages in segregation would propel the Nationalist Party with its apartheid platform to power soon after the war. In purely economic terms, the manufacturing boom of the war years created in South Africa a more diversified and self-sufficient modern economy, which was attracting considerable capital and thousands of immigrants from abroad by 1945.[17]

White ambivalence toward black workers deepened as wartime labor needs dramatically illustrated the South African economy's nearly total dependence on them. Chronic labor shortages had hindered South Afri-can development since the nineteenth century, a problem that whites had tried to solve by such means as recruiting workers for the Rand mines from neighboring colonies like Mozambique and requiring "hut" taxes of rural Africans in the Union, which forced them to seek work in towns in order to earn currency.[18] As Africans flooded into the cities during the war and took work in factories as well as mines, white authorities were pleased but also determined that they should remain passive and willing workers. As actual and potential American investors in the Union were reassured a few years later by the United States Department of Commerce, black workers in South Africa were not allowed to organize, strike, or bargain collectively. The South African government wanted to forestall any doubts of its commitment to keeping cheap and docile the black work force it depended on.[19] An American businessman working for the Nash Motor Company in South Africa during the war pointed out to the OSS the tendency of white South Africans to associate a lack of dignity with manual labor and the consequent fact that whites con-tributed "so little actual work" to South African industry. "Native labor in South Africa is the worst treated labor in the world," continued Fred-erick Spencer. "In South Africa only natives work. Every white artisan and even the white apprentices must have native helpers who actually do the work."[20]

South Africans of Indian descent[21] received treatment similar to that accorded South Africans of African descent by South Africans of Euro-pean descent. The vast majority of Indian South Africans lived in Natal

Province on the Indian Ocean, where they numbered fewer than the African residents but roughly the same as the mostly English (rather than Afrikaner) white population. Fearing the much higher birthrate of the Indians and resenting the commercial success of many middle-class Indians, whites talked openly about deporting them "back" to India, despite the fact that most of them had been born and had lived only in South Africa. The American consul in Durban, Natal's leading city, reported during the war that "the usual 'Jim Crow' discriminations against negroes in our Southern States exist here against the Indians," with the explicit approval of Prime Minister Smuts.[22] Just as white Americans, with the aid of local, state, and federal governments, prevented black Americans from moving into their segregated neighborhoods, the South African government enacted the Pegging Act of 1943 to stop affluent Indians from buying real estate in European areas of Durban for either residential occupation or investment.[23]

While suffering the same lack of political representation in their own country, South Africans of Indian descent had a crucial advantage over their African countrymen: external support. An assertively nationalistic India had already journeyed far down the road to self-government and Dominion status alongside South Africa within the British Commonwealth. India was led in its struggle against colonialism by Mohandas K. Gandhi, whose early years of residence in the Union and political work against racial discrimination there gave him particular empathy for the situation of South African Indians. Indian nationalists eagerly took the side of Indian South Africans protesting the restrictions of the Pegging Act, thereby elevating the issue from the realm of domestic South African politics to that of international relations within the British Empire. In this preview of postwar Indian–South African relations can be seen the power of foreign-policy concerns in persuading the internationalist Smuts to alter his course. The Pegging Act so antagonized Indian elites in Natal and public opinion in India that Smuts removed some of its most irritating clauses before joining the conference of fellow British Empire prime ministers in London in April 1944. The influence of India, the rising "Crown Jewel" of the Empire, on London and therefore on Pretoria was apparent.[24]

Tensions between Europeans and Indians in Natal continued to grow during the last two years of the war, attracting the worried attention of American diplomatic observers. Anxious about their declining relative numerical status in the province and dismayed at Indian economic success and movement into some formerly all-white areas, white Natalians called for a return to complete segregation. White children in the neighboring Orange Free State even refused to eat bananas supplied in school lunches due to rumors that Indians had injected them with infantile paralysis germs in retaliation for anti-Indian legislation in Natal.[25] U.S. officials in South Africa hoped that the more liberal and humane proposals of Jan Hofmeyr, the United Party deputy leader and Smuts' heir-apparent, might prevail in decisions regarding what they called the "Indian problem," but they also recognized the power of the forces working against liberal white South Africans like Hofmeyr. While hoping to placate growing Indian demands for decent treatment and political representation, Smuts was even more determined to maintain the support of white voters in the traditional United Party stronghold of Natal in the face of segregationist Nationalist Party efforts to make headway in the province by manipulating the Indian issue. Nationalist Party newspapers attacked Smuts for supposedly failing either to support segregation or to repress racially egalitarian communists strongly enough because of his desire not to offend India or the Soviet Union. Overwhelming white hostility to Indians moved the Prime Minister to propose new legislation by the end of the war to establish complete segregation in Natal.[26]

III

In addition to the economic changes that brought Africans and Indians into greater contact with Europeans and increased white determination to maintain segregation, the war years stimulated a transformation of black politics in South Africa. Swelling numbers of impoverished Africans arrived in urban areas determined to create a better life than that of rural poverty they had left behind. Their persistent struggle against the crippling racial discrimination they encountered in the cities inspired a rising movement of African nationalism among younger members of the African National Congress, which reinvigorated the organization and lifted it into national and international prominence. The Communist Party remained the only political party in South Africa to oppose racial discrimination and accept blacks as members, and the ANC developed important ties with white radicals in the late 1940s. Anticommunists in the United States and South Africa would later spend considerable time and energy trying to determine the degree to which the ANC was influenced or "controlled" by communists and "the international communist movement." A half-century of Cold War thinking since the Second World War has made it necessary to recall some of the origins and development of the Congress in order to understand the importance of the 1940s for black politics in South Africa.[27]

By 1945 it was not communism, but Christianity, nationalism, and Western liberalism that had made the strongest marks of any foreign influences on black South Africans, as State Department intelligence reports admitted a few years later. The vast majority of politicized Africans in the Union opposed colonialism and racial discrimination on the basis of liberal ideals of democratic self-government and Biblical claims of the dignity and equality of all persons, not on the grounds of Marxist analysis. Sojourns in the United States and experiences with Americans, both black and white, had profoundly influenced African religious and political leaders in South Africa since the nineteenth century. The founding president of the ANC (then called the South African Native National Congress) had attended Oberlin College in Ohio. John L. Dube and the men who succeeded him in the leadership of the Congress came from the small group of African bourgeoisie and sought to maintain their own elevated status among Africans while also working to restrain the advancing subjugation of all blacks in South Africa. Booker T. Washington, not Vladimir Lenin, was a heroic model to them. But their mildly reformist goals and tactics brought little success in the face of growing white dominance, and the ANC reached the nadir of its influence in the late 1930s with the final disenfranchisement of all Africans in the Union.[28]

In the decade following the outbreak of the Second World War, social and ecological crises in South Africa's rural African areas joined with the demands of the wartime economy to speed the creation of a huge new urban black political constituency. Urbanization laid the basis for greater intertribal African unity than had ever existed before in the Union, and the vast expansion of the black proletariat led to a revival of trade unionism and growing class consciousness. The political awareness and determination of urban black South Africans in the 1930s had impressed a black American visitor, Eslanda Robeson, the wife of renowned American singer and activist Paul Robeson: "I am surprised and delighted to find these Africans far more politically aware than my fellow Negroes in America. They understand their situation and the causes for the terrible conditions under which they live, and are continually seeking—and are firmly resolved to find—a way to improve their lot."[29] Newly arrived urban workers did not passively accept the overwhelming poverty that confronted them in the black townships and squatter camps of Johannesburg and other cities, but moved, often spontaneously, to resolve their immediate problems. Using a tactic made famous more than a decade later by the American civil rights movement, they boycotted buses to resist fare increases and organized squatters' movements in Johannesburg to deal with severe housing shortages. The successes of such popular resistance movements and of wartime strikes by illegally organized African factory workers encouraged the development in urban black communities of a fresh, assertive nationalism. The established leadership of the ANC, with its traditional middle-class unease with unplanned populist organizing, lost credibility in the black neighborhoods and was forced to move toward greater militancy in order to keep up with its potential constituency.[30]

The force that emerged within the ANC during the war years to push the organization to a more radical and activist political stand was the Congress Youth League. ANC president Alfred Xuma had been successfully recruiting politically committed younger Africans into the Congress for some time in an effort to reinvigorate it, and a group of them formally established the Youth League in 1944 with Xuma's approval. These younger men sought to infuse the national liberation movement with the spirit of African nationalism and to be a pressure group that would spur the ANC out of its long-standing elitism and into greater militancy on behalf of Africans of all classes. Under the leadership of Anton Lembede, their ideology was strongly "Africanist": they sought to overcome African feelings of inferiority—resulting from their degrading treatment by whites—by asserting pride in their racial and cultural history and in the very blackness of their skin.

Like the "Black Consciousness" movement associated with Steve Biko in the 1970s, this Africanist approach was sensitive to the importance of healing the deep psychological and spiritual wounds of centuries of racial discrimination. Lembede and other Youth Leaguers like Oliver Tambo, Walter Sisulu, and Nelson Mandela had been inspired by the popular resistance and labor movements in wartime Johannesburg, and worked to project their Africanist appeal to African workers in order to promote the unity of all Africans in the struggle for national freedom. They were extremely wary of the political left and especially the Communist Party, as they believed Africans suffered oppression as a racial group rather than as part of an economic class. Youth League members suspected Marxist radicals, both white and black, of seeking to use Africans for their own ulterior purposes, much as hostile whites always had. The Youth League endorsed such tactics of mass action as boycotts, strikes, civil disobedience, and noncooperation with the white authorities. The movement of white politics in South Africa to the right after the war and the eventual victory of the Nationalist Party in 1948 on a platform of apartheid would confirm the Youth Leaguers' belief that the traditional lobbying tactics of the ANC were no longer relevant to the current situation in the African struggle for liberation.[31]

IV

South Africa's entry into World War II created ominous rumblings along the political fault line that divided the white population of the Union. The coalition United Party of Smuts and J. B. M. Hertzog had ruled South Africa since 1933, but the former Boer War generals split over whether to join the rest of the British Commonwealth in the Allied cause when war broke out in Europe in 1939. Smuts won a close Parliamentary vote, moving Hertzog to support Daniel Malan's anti-British Purified Nationalist Party[32] in opposition to the government. Unlike the English and the moderate Afrikaners who backed Smuts, Malan and his followers still nursed the wounds inflicted by the British imperial armies in the Boer War four decades earlier. They resented the economic and cultural dominance of South Africans of English descent, represented by South Africa's continued membership in the British Commonwealth. Centered in the strongly Calvinist Dutch Reformed Church, of which Malan was an ordained minister, these Afrikaners eschewed the liberal capitalism they associated with England and leaned instead toward the authoritarian national socialism represented by Nazi Germany and Portugal. They admired Hitler's emphasis on the racial purity of the *volk,* on a disciplined, authoritarian party involved in every aspect of its members' lives, and on national unity and pride. Malan and his followers considered themselves the true descendants of the earliest Afrikaners and the bearers of the same Zionist covenant to rule the heathen races around them. They sought to preserve Afrikaner culture by uniting into one party the long divided Afrikaners, who made up over half of the Union's white population, and ultimately reestablishing an independent Boer republic like those of the late nineteenth century.[33]

The weight of internal strife and even subversion lay heavily on South Africa throughout the war. Many ardent opponents of the government were jailed for what amounted to treason, while Malan and other "responsible" leaders of the Nationalist Opposition openly hoped for a Nazi victory in the early years of the conflict when Hitler's armies were overrunning continental Europe. Malan declared publicly that a victorious Germany "will want a government sympathetic to itself," a role that only "the National[ist] Party can fill."[34] Many Nationalists believed that a defeat of the hated British would provide an opportunity to secede from the Commonwealth and establish a republic. Although one out of three Afrikaners of military age responded to Smuts' call to enlist in the South African armed forces, an equal number joined the anti-British, paramilitary *Ossewa Brandwag* ("Ox Wagon Sentinels"), which served as one rallying point for antiwar sentiment. Frequent brawls and riots between antiwar protestors and soldiers, including a massive two-day running battle in the streets of Johannesburg in January 1941, forced South African soldiers in uniform to walk in groups in order to avoid assault. Afrikaner policemen were frequently implicated in the antiwar activities.[35] On a level above the street frays, the powerful *Broederbond* ("Band of Brothers"), a secret society of elite Afrikaners founded in 1918 and by this time intertwined with the Nationalist Party, continued its efforts to gain control of the country and free it from British economic domination. The United States Minister in South Africa, former Marine Corps commandant General Thomas Holcomb, reported to Washington at the end of the war that the shadowy Broederbond seemed still fixated on a trauma almost a half-century old: "The favorite Afrikaans phantom of the Anglo-Boer struggle—the internment and death of the Afrikaans women and children during that period."[36]

Like the fascists and national socialists in Europe, the Nationalists in South Africa may have disdained Western liberalism, but they loathed communism. Just as the Soviet Union had outlawed racial discrimination, the Communist Party of South Africa remained the only political party in the Union to oppose white supremacy. Malan declared during the war that white South Africa was threatened, not by the Axis powers, but by "the doctrine of equality [that] is preached by the Communists." He blasted the Smuts government for embracing the Soviet Union as an ally.[37] Nationalist Members of Parliament ridiculed the reports of horrifying Nazi atrocities that were emerging from Europe in the final months of the war, calling instead for investigations of Soviet concentration camps in Siberia as well as memorials to the tens of thousands of noncombatant Afrikaners who died while in British detention during the Boer War.[38] From the Nationalist perspective, South Africa and the rest of the Western world should have been fighting *with* Germany *against* the Soviet Union. With Bolshevism the real enemy, the Nationalists viewed the entire Second World War as a costly mistake. American diplomats in South Africa, noting the tiny electoral support for the Communist Party, reported that Malan's emphasis on the danger of communism "looks like [a] red herring to distract attention from his pro-Nazi record."[39] This was a tactic that would prove quite effective in the Cold War to come.

V

The wiry, erect figure of Jan Smuts dominated South African politics throughout World War II. The experiences of this commanding native Afrikaner and British field marshal included a record-setting performance at Cambridge University as a student, leadership in the Afrikaner military forces against the British armies in the Boer War, subsequent close collaboration with the British government in World War I, prominence in the establishment with Woodrow Wilson of the League of Nations and its mandate system for colonial territories, and four decades of symbolic leadership of the South Africans who supported the Union's membership in the British Commonwealth. His political enemies referred to the Prime Minister as "slim Jannie" ("clever little Jan") in bitter acknowledgement of his considerable skills at political manipulation. Smuts believed as much as any white South African in the necessity of maintaining white supremacy in the Union through segregation and legal discrimination. His sensitivity to international politics and his desire to maintain an important personal role on the changing world stage led him, however, to disguise some of the substance of his racial beliefs and policies with a stylistic flexibility at odds with the unadorned racism of his narrowly nationalistic opponents like Malan. ANC leader and Nobel Peace laureate Albert Lutuli noted that Smuts succeeded in being seen as "a world statesman beyond the Union's borders" while remaining "a subtle and relentless white supremacist at home."[40]

Smuts' unusually broad exposure to the world outside South Africa convinced him that white minority rule was on the way out in Asia by the end of the war. He believed that white dominance in Africa could be maintained much longer by tact and clever strategy than by "precipitancy" in dealing with black dissent.[41] He showed some of that wiliness when the Japanese advance into Southeast Asia and their capture of Singapore from the British in 1942 elicited visible black sympathy in the Union for the nonwhite conquerors of the Europeans. In order to shore up black support for the Allied cause, the Prime Minister declared publicly that segregation in South Africa had "fallen on evil days" and raised black hopes that the Union government might move away from racial discrimination with the rest of the world after the war. He dropped this ruse as soon as the Japanese offensive was halted.[42]

Smuts continued to urge white South Africans to exercise subtlety and care in the administration of racial discrimination, including preserving the constitutional franchise of light-skinned Coloreds in the Cape Province who provided important political support for the United Party. But U.S. Minister Holcomb reported to the State Department that Smuts did agree with the Nationalists about the need for intensified residential segregation of Coloreds and Indians, as well as Africans, from whites. Smuts acknowledged that more African labor was needed in the industrializing cities, but he reminded Parliament that whites could not allow this migration to proceed randomly: "When the native comes to the (urban centers) . . . we want him to go to a definite place, to a definite organization, to be dealt with there, *to be under control* so that if there is no work for him or if he cannot get employment, he can be sent back." In language that precisely foreshadowed the later Nationalist Party policy of apartheid, Holcomb paraphrased Smuts' belief that "the natives," with the exception of temporary urban sojourns, "were to develop along their own lines in their own territories, in a manner suited to their traditions and their past."[43]

In order to maintain white dominion in southern Africa, Smuts argued that the Union needed to retain the friendship of the outside world, even at the cost of some criticism of South African racial policies. He reminded white South Africans that they constituted "one of the most vulnerable points of European civilization in the world today" due to their small numbers, and therefore could not afford to provoke needlessly either the black majority at home or allies abroad.[44] By the end of the war Smuts and the United Party increasingly shared Nationalist fears that communist agitators might be organizing black South Africans to overthrow white rule.[45] To the Nationalists, this called for cracking down on the Communist Party in the Union, but Smuts' internationalism and his preference for co-option over conflict led him instead to support improving South Africa's relations with the Soviet Union in order to deal with the problem at what he saw as its root.[46]

Smuts' interest in diplomatic solutions did not preclude an aggressive and expansive view of South Africa's postwar destiny. He promoted the idea of a more integrated southern African region under Union hegemony, with wider markets for South African manufactured goods and a bigger labor pool for its industries, farms, and mines. Smuts envisioned the annexation of South West Africa and the three British territories of Bechuanaland, Swaziland, and Basutoland, as well as South African dominance over Mozambique, Angola, Southern and Northern Rhodesia, and Nyasaland. He foresaw South African regional leadership boosting European settlement in colonies as far north as the equator and bolstering

South Africa's racial policies at home. Citing what he called the need for a *"modus vivendi"* of black labor and white entrepreneurial and political leadership in southern Africa, Smuts declared in a speech at Lourenco Marques, Mozambique, in July 1945 his conviction that "white civilization in this region has been justified and can bear the scrutiny of history."[47]

To the United States government as much as to Great Britain, Smuts represented enlightened South African opinion. He was a renowned international figure and ally who had worked closely with the United States in the two great global conflicts of the twentieth century. Against considerable domestic opposition, he staunchly supported the most important American ally, Great Britain. The Prime Minister respected American industrial and military might and seemed comfortable with the likely dominance of the postwar world by the United States.[48]

Like the British and American governments, the Union government under Smuts seemed to operate from an unspoken assumption of white superiority with some sense of obligation to members of supposedly inferior races. American diplomats in South Africa assured the new Truman administration in 1945 that Smuts' United Party would continue as a moderately liberal one, eschewing even the nominal socialism of the British Labour Party, while moving gradually toward a more liberal racial policy under the leadership of the elderly Smuts' first lieutenant, Jan Hofmeyr. This contrasted sharply, they said, with the explicit racial prejudice, anti-Semitism, and Anglophobia of the Nationalist Party, characteristics disturbingly familiar to people who had just fought a war against Nazi Germany. In spite of Malan's growing popularity among many white South Africans at the end of the war, U.S. Minister Holcomb believed that most South African whites were fairly liberal and would continue supporting the United Party in the next election. He reported optimistically to Washington in April 1945 that progressive forces "are in the ascendancy in South Africa, despite surface appearances to the contrary." Three years later, in the much more troubling context of the full-fledged Cold War, Holcomb's prediction would be proven dramatically wrong.[49]

CHAPTER 3

The Truman Administration and Southern Africa: 1945

The rise of Harry Truman to the office of President in April 1945 had uncertain implications at the time for people of color in the United States and abroad. The former border-state legislator had grown up and come to political prominence in the Jim Crow world of rural and small-town Missouri, and his early life reflected the pervasive racism of that society. One of the foremost scholarly authorities on the President, Alonzo Hamby—himself a product of rural Missouri and a strong admirer of Truman overall—has described the young Truman as "a typical rural bigot."[1] As late as 1946, as the occupant of the nation's highest office, he was still known to speak privately of blacks as "nigs" and "niggers." His prejudices had extended to most foreigners as well, except perhaps the British, as indicated by ready references to Mexico as "Greaserdom," Slavs as "bohunks," Italians as "Dagos," and New York City as "kike town."[2]

On the other hand, as Hamby notes, Truman seemed to grow out of much of his provincialism and racism as his political career expanded his contacts with the broader world. He recognized the growing power of black voters in Kansas City and St. Louis and established a relatively progressive record on civil rights as a senator. He supported the FEPC, the abolition of poll taxes, and federal anti-lynching legislation. These stands and his sympathy for organized labor helped persuade Roosevelt to run for re-election in 1944 with Truman rather than Byrnes, whom Roosevelt knew better and had worked closely with during the war. In the months following Roosevelt's death, the new President seemed determined to carry on the liberal tradition of the New Deal. Within three years Truman would in fact establish himself as the strongest proponent of civil rights to occupy the White House up to that time.[3]

I

The State Department generally agreed with Truman's reading of the domestic and international political situations, which encouraged him to move as President toward stronger support of racial equality at home. Diplomats saw this as a way to limit damage from racial discrimination in the United States to the American image abroad. But the foreign policy establishment in Washington that Truman inherited from his predecessor showed little interest in any fundamental alterations in the international racial status quo in 1945.

The white men who managed the State and War Departments and the intelligence services had achieved their considerable personal successes in a segregated society and had known black people almost exclusively as social and economic inferiors.[4] Many white people of their grandparents' generation—including both sets of Truman's grandparents—had owned black people as slaves.[5] Western European perspectives dominated their view of the world abroad, due to historical ties of culture and language, assumptions of white racial superiority, long-standing European dominance of international politics, and the close alliance of World War II. In the face of what American policymakers saw as the emerging postwar threat of expansion by the Soviet Union, their concern for the defense and reconstruction of the battered nations of Western Europe quickly overshadowed all other interests. The primacy of Western Europe in American foreign policy during the Truman years disposed the administration to accede to continued European control of the natural wealth of the colonies of southern Africa. The men who were emerging at the end of the war as America's Cold Warriors took little interest in the fifty million black people of that region.[6]

The fervent anticommunism of Truman's foreign policy advisers focused on freedom from Soviet and leftist influences but often masked vigorous racial prejudice. Truman's choice of prominent segregationist James Byrnes as his Secretary of State made plain the lack of concern at the highest level of United States policymaking with the welfare and opinions of people of color. Byrnes' public castigation of the Soviet Union and its Eastern European allies for not allowing free multiparty elections inspired considerable outrage among liberal and progressive Americans, who doubted the propriety of such statements from a man whose home state of South Carolina did not allow a third of its own population to vote.[7] But the institutional powers of the United States government had no such objections to Byrnes. FBI director J. Edgar Hoover, for example, sought to help Byrnes by sending him at least one intelligence report giving advance notice of planned acts of opposition to his nomination by specific black organizations.[8] Truman's later and more famous Secretary of State, Dean Acheson, did not share Byrnes' overt racism, but he manifested a Eurocentric and Anglophilic world view rooted in his own background as the son of an Episcopalian bishop and an enormously successful product of the wealthy all-white world of Groton, Yale, Harvard Law School, and corporate Washington and New York. He was no more inclined to support racial democracy in southern Africa than his Southern predecessors, Byrnes and George Marshall, had been.[9]

As the original articulator of the containment doctrine and the most intellectual and reflective of the top policymakers in the Truman administration, George Kennan perhaps best exemplified the limitations implicit in the Eurocentrism and racial assumptions of the early Cold War. A self-described geopolitical realist and a specialist in Soviet-American relations, Kennan had little interest in the potent ideals of national liberation rumbling through the Third World at the end of World War II. Despite his specific assignment to take the long view of future American interests as head of the State Department's Policy Planning Staff, Kennan's attitudes on colonial and racial issues were strictly traditional. He consistently supported the European imperial powers in their relations with their colonies. He viewed Africa as marginal to the global balance of power and paid it less attention than any other region of the world.[10]

Kennan felt personal revulsion toward most Third World peoples— Asians, Arabs, Latinos, and Africans—whom he tended to lump together as impulsive, fanatical, ignorant, lazy, unhappy, and prone to mental disorders and other biological deficiencies.[11] He showed particular distress at their mistrust of the West as the Cold War intensified, branding it "almost hysterical," "violent," and "a sort of orgy of rejection and defiance." He interpreted any unwillingness to ally wholeheartedly with the West against the Soviet bloc as evidence that nonwhite peoples were childlike and perhaps even canine, needing to be seized "by the scruff of the neck" and forced to defend their independence from the supposedly ubiquitous Soviet threat.[12] Not surprisingly, Kennan indicated comparable disdain for those he regarded as inferiors in the United States, including blacks, women, and recent immigrants from southern Europe, whose influence he considered detrimental to the country. On the eve of World War II, Kennan apparently believed that all three of these groups should be disenfranchised and that the United States would in fact be better served by a "benevolent despotism" of elite white males rather than a democratic government.[13]

Both Acheson and Kennan continued to support white minority rule in southern Africa long after the rest of the continent had been decolonized and most Westerners had backed away from overt approval of the white governments there. Acheson defended the legitimacy of Rhodesia's white minority government and its actions when it declared its independence from Great Britain in 1965 to a chorus of worldwide criticism.[14] In the mid-1960s, Kennan not only opposed putting external pressure on South Africa to change its racial policies, but even felt some personal attraction to apartheid. He apparently believed that a modified version of the South African system of "separate development" might work well in the American South, as he disliked the idea of whites anywhere being pressured into racial desegregation. Prevented by the success of decolonization elsewhere on the continent from arguing any longer that Africans in general lacked the capability for self-government, Kennan narrowed his scope by 1967 to suggesting that blacks in southern Africa might be

intellectually more limited than other Africans and thus unable to participate responsibly in modern society.[15] With the foremost diplomats of
the Truman administration so openly supportive of white minority rule
in the region even decades later, there was little likelihood of the United
States government's supporting color-blind democracy in southern Africa
in the early Cold War.[16]

II

American governmental obtuseness about the rising significance of race
in world affairs and the Truman administration's inclination to see white
imperial governments as its closest allies did not prepare the United States
well in the 1940s for the domestic and international racial issues that
would soon confront it. With greater prescience, the noted black American sociologist Dr. W. E. B. Du Bois had declared forty years earlier
that "the problem of the Twentieth Century is the problem of the color-
line."[17] The fighting in World War II had demonstrated, often brutally,
the enduring intensity of racial loyalties and hostilities, especially in the
Pacific theater, where a nonwhite nation had effectively challenged
the global dominion of the white West.[18] Japan had steadily ridiculed
the Western Allies' belief in white superiority, manifest in European colonialism and American segregation, and had made considerable psychological capital in the colonial world by advertising the living conditions
of black Americans. The psychological-warfare offices of the Axis powers
had beamed the news of every lynching in the United States throughout
the nonwhite world.[19] Within forty-eight hours of his torture and execution in the streets of Sikeston, Missouri, in 1942, Cleo Wright's name
and story had been relayed in sordid detail to the Dutch East Indies and
India in order to help break down resistance morale in the face of the
advancing Japanese armies by showing how the democracies treated people of color.[20] German propaganda leaflets dropped over Libya had re-
produced a graphic picture from the *Detroit Free Press,* showing an elderly African American man being struck full in the face by a member of
a white mob during the Detroit race riots of 1943, while his arms were
pinioned by two uniformed police officers. Written in Arabic, the leaflets
had appealed to Arabs to fight the Allies who treated nonwhite people
this way.[21] Despite the prominent American role in eventually defeating
the racist Nazis, the war had previewed the vulnerability of the United
States in a postwar international order of increasing color equality.[22]

The founding conference of the United Nations, held from April to
June of 1945 in San Francisco, revealed the depth of American ambivalence about racial equality in world affairs. The fate of the colonial world
loomed large as the delegates committed their countries to avoiding future wars by promoting "fundamental human rights," "justice," "social
progress," and "the equal rights" of all people around the globe.[23] Soviet
representatives argued for complete national independence and self-

determination in all colonial areas, raising hopes among non-Europeans that the United States, with its own equally anticolonial history, might take a similar stand and thereby pressure the weakened imperial powers to move swiftly toward decolonization.[24]

Sharply differing opinions within the Truman administration reflected conflicting American interests. The State Department and more racially liberal elements generally supported a strong trusteeship system for all colonial areas in order to encourage democratic development and free trade. The War Department and more conservative anticommunists, on the other hand, wanted to maintain American military bases in the western Pacific indefinitely and strengthen the imperial nations of Europe for the emerging conflict with the Soviet Union. Similar differences marked the American delegation at San Francisco. When the final test came on the disposition of colonies, the United States cast its lot with the colonial powers by using its decisive influence to weaken its own original proposals for an extensive system of international trusteeship. The term "independence," deemed "provocative" by U.S. delegates Harold Stassen and John Foster Dulles, was omitted entirely as an explicit goal for the "dependent" areas of the world.[25]

The Truman administration's decision at San Francisco to oppose the aspirations of colonial peoples for complete independence from their European overlords resulted in considerable disappointment in the Third World and among blacks and liberals in the United States. General Carlos P. Romulo, representing the Philippines at the conference, spoke for billions of people of color when he denounced "self-government" as a meaningless and deceptive goal for U.N. trusteeship when the European imperial powers were so clearly excluding the ultimate prize of independence.[26] Americans—including a large number of newly politicized blacks—who had hoped that the forum of the United Nations would bring out the most progressive elements of United States policy were troubled by American accommodation of European imperial desires, although they were pleased by the strong statement of ideals embodied in the U.N. Charter.[27] The American delegation at San Francisco, however, viewed even the principles of the Charter with suspicion. Foster Dulles, only eight years from becoming Secretary of State and already a leading Republican spokesman on foreign policy, and most of the other American representatives opposed the human-rights clause because, as Dulles put it, "the Negro question in this country might become the subject of investigation or other action" by the United Nations.[28] From its earliest months, the Truman administration recognized this American vulnerability in a postwar world for which the genocidal atrocities of Adolf Hitler had greatly discredited racial discrimination.[29]

The Union of South Africa was probably the most comforted of any nation at San Francisco by American support for the colonial powers and rejection of any international intrusion into its domestic racial situation. As the senior statesman of the British Commonwealth, Jan Smuts chaired one of the four major commissions at the U.N. conference. With no apparent sense of irony, the leader of the most racially discriminatory society in the world wrote the first draft of the preamble to the U.N. Charter, including its noble claims of "fundamental faith in human rights" and respect for "the dignity and worth of the human person."[30] Most Americans knew of Smuts only as a strong supporter of the British Empire and "Western civilization" in Africa and a firm ally in the war. They understood little about the conditions black South Africans lived under, and they were scarcely concerned with the racial limitations of British imperial liberalism. The American delegates at San Francisco treated Smuts with profound respect, considering him "a great man" and even "a glamorous figure . . . still slender and straight in spite of his age."[31] Although white South Africans looked forward to the fruits of victory after the war and in general had no idea of the persistent and increasing hostility their country would soon face in the international arena, Smuts himself indicated some awareness that the United Nations would probably become a forum for a color-blind ideology of equal rights.[32] At the birth of a new era in international relations, marked by an increasing number of nations governed by people of color and a sharply declining tolerance for traditional racial hierarchies, the South African Prime Minister could find some reassurance in the policies and inclinations of the newly dominant United States.

III

The foremost American interest in southern Africa in 1945 was in the Belgian Congo. World War II had demonstrated the significance of the vast treasure house of strategic minerals buried in the rich soil of "the hostile wilderness" of its southernmost province, Katanga.[33] In the quantity and diversity of its forest and mineral products, this sole colony of Belgium—which was seventy-six times larger than its tiny European possessor—contributed far more than any other African territory to the Allied supply of strategic raw materials. Despite the German occupation of Belgium itself, prior planning by the Congo governor-general and the colony's leading mining enterprise, Union Minière du Haut Katanga, kept control of the Congo in hands friendly to the Allies. Most of the colony's traditional trade with Belgium was diverted during the war to the United States, and economic ties with the Americans became close enough to spark rumors in the Congo that it might become an American dependency after the war.[34]

In addition to the colony's increased wartime production of copper, tin, and rubber, the Allies benefitted particularly from the Congo's control of two-thirds of the world's industrial diamonds, essential components in precision cutting instruments for the production of all military weapons. The OSS indicated even greater concern about the security of the colony's enormous supply of cobalt, as American and Canadian steel producers had recently converted their equipment to operate with the particular quality of cobalt ores found in the Congo. The American intelligence service concluded that a German conquest of the area "would constitute a major Axis victory."[35] Postwar planners in the Truman administration also recognized the vital importance of the Congo's wealth, including its sizable gold production, to the reconstruction of the Belgian economy.[36]

The continued exploitation of agricultural and mineral resources required a steady supply of labor, and in this regard the situation in the Belgian Congo created considerable uncertainty in Washington. The combined efforts of the Belgian colonial bureaucracy, the Roman Catholic Church, and European capital over more than half a century had established a colonial system in the Congo unparalleled in the depth of its penetration of African societies and the breadth of its control over all human activities. Belgian authorities in the colony faced little of the criticism at home that influenced their British and French counterparts in Africa, as almost all Belgians shared a marked sense of superiority about their formula for colonial administration.[37] Hampered by a lack of colony-wide organization, African resistance to such Belgian practices as forced agricultural labor, nominally disguised as "education," tended to be sporadic and unsuccessful.[38] Poor housing conditions, wartime demands for increased productivity, the use of coercion, the example of striking European miners in the region, and wage rates that were low even by colonial African standards did, however, lead to a major strike by African miners in the Katanga Province in December 1941. As riots broke out, white officers used privately hired African soldiers to fire on the strikers and their families, killing as many as eighty people. The massacre ended the immediate work stoppage, but only at the cost of increasing local hostility toward Union Minière and the Congo government. The OSS worried that the restless labor situation in the colony might interfere with the important mining activities there.[39]

By the end of the war, one previously insignificant mineral from the Congo had impressed itself on the Truman administration as the single most important resource for American national security after the war. Uranium powered the atomic bombs that brought the war in Asia to a sudden end, and its presence in the largest single deposit in the world in Katanga's Shinkolobwe mine dramatically increased American interest in the stability of the Congo's colonial regime and of the southern African region as a whole.[40] Before World War II, uranium's only commercial use had been as a coloring agent in the ceramics industry, with some supplies coming from the Colorado plateau and Canada, but most from the Congo. Scientific experiments in Germany and the United States on the eve of the war had indicated, however, that uranium was fissionable and could be used as the fuel for a limited nuclear chain reaction, and physicists in the United States expressed concern that the Congo ores be kept out of German hands. With the Nazis occupying Belgium in June 1940, Roosevelt's Advisory Committee on Uranium encouraged Union Minière to move its aboveground supplies to the United States for safe-keeping. The company's managing director, Edgar Sengier, had learned a year earlier from British scientific contacts of uranium's extraordinary potential significance, and he had already arranged for stockpiled ore in the Congo to be shipped to New York. In October 1940, the African Metals Corporation, Union Minière's American affiliate, received twelve hundred tons of hand-sorted uranium ore of high quality and stored it in a warehouse on Staten Island.[41]

The secrecy of the Manhattan Project prevented officers of the State and War Departments and even the OSS from initially realizing the significance of uranium.[42] For two years they remained cool to offers by Sengier, who had come to New York from Brussels for the duration of the war, to sell it to the United States government. The appointment of Brigadier General Leslie R. Groves to oversee the project of developing an atomic weapon brought a swift end to that delay. Within one day on the job, Groves and his assistant, Lieutenant Colonel K. D. Nichols, had found Sengier and reached an agreement with him to buy all the ore on Staten Island and to have first option on the one thousand tons stockpiled aboveground in the Congo, which would be shipped immediately to the United States. In contrast to North American ores of .2 percent uranium concentration, the hand-sorted initial batch from Shinkolobwe averaged an extraordinary 65 percent uranium. Later shipments from the Congo declined somewhat in quality but remained still many times richer than American and Canadian ores.[43] Roosevelt himself recognized the dramatic potential importance of Groves' African purchases, asking a briefing officer in 1944 to point out on the map the location of the uranium deposits in the Congo.[44] In September 1944, the British and American governments finished negotiations with Sengier and the Belgian government in exile in London and signed the Tripartite Agreement, under which Union Minière agreed to ship all of its production of uranium ore until 1956 to the United States and England.[45]

Although Truman may have known of the existence of the Manhattan Project as early as August 1944,[46] he discovered the importance of the Belgian Congo only after being sworn in as President in April 1945. Groves informed him at their first meeting that a uranium bomb of unprecedented power (the so-called Little Boy) would be ready without requiring a test by about August 1, and that the construction of a plutonium bomb (known as "Fat Man") was also nearing completion.[47] News of the successful detonation of a plutonium device in the New Mexican desert reached Truman in late July at the Potsdam Conference in Germany. When minerals from the southern border of the Belgian Congo exploded in the air above Japan, abruptly ending the war and ushering in the atomic age, few people in the world had any idea where the ingredients for this extraordinary power came from. The men of the Truman administration, however, knew that they had found the key to unprecedented power in the mines of southern Africa.

IV

By 1945, the United States government had acquired another interest in southern Africa by promising to respect Portuguese imperial authority in Angola and Mozambique in exchange for the use of a strategically critical air base in the Portuguese Azores. Domestic economic weakness kept Portugal essentially a dependency of other European empires, especially the British, and Portuguese overseas expansion had always involved capital from other, wealthier nations. Western Europeans, North Americans, and South Africans had invested prominently in the rail and port facilities of Mozambique and Angola. The British-owned Benguela Railway in Angola provided the major outlet for transporting the strategic minerals of the Katanga Province and the Northern Rhodesian copper belt to the Atlantic Ocean at Lobito. The landlocked Rhodesias and the South African province of Transvaal also depended on Mozambican ports for much of their exporting, a trade that bolstered the Mozambican economy, while inexpensive migrant labor from the Portuguese colony enabled the mines of the South African Rand to operate at enormous profits.[48]

Considerable national pride combined with close links to the stronger powers of the region made the Portuguese deeply sensitive about their African colonies, especially given the important role of Mozambican and Angolan natural resources in the Portuguese economy.[49] During the 1940s, the Portuguese government sought to strengthen its imperial claims by promoting the theory of "luso-tropicalism," which posited that a historically unique absence of racism among the Portuguese people had allowed Portuguese colonization in tropical areas to develop without the racial discrimination so evident in the colonies of other European powers. By the early 1950s, the Portuguese government was mobilizing this mythic idea to claim that Angola and Mozambique were in fact not colonies but "overseas provinces" integral to "Greater Portugal," as Portugal sought to avoid United Nations investigations into reports of oppressive conditions there. The evidence for "luso-tropicalism" was supposed to be that all "civilized" people in the colonies, regardless of race, were to be equal citizens of Portugal. By 1950, however, fewer than 1 percent of Africans in Mozambique and Angola were considered "assimilados," while the rest were allowed no political or civil rights.[50] More than 99 percent had never attended a school, and American missionaries, U.S. consuls, and the OSS all reported home that forced labor, starvation wages, and extraordinary brutality characterized Portuguese rule in southern Africa in the 1940s.[51]

The man ultimately responsible for the welfare of the several million people in Angola and Mozambique was Antonio Salazar, the President of Portugal and a self-proclaimed "nineteenth-century man" convinced of the cultural superiority of his country over the materialistic rest of the Western world. Repelled by what he saw as the dehumanizing aspects of modern technology, Salazar refused to allow his secretaries to have telephones or typewriters in the presidential office and enjoyed reading in his candlelit study. His government openly espoused national socialism and Italian-style fascism and effectively repressed all political dissent. He kept Portugal assiduously neutral during World War II.[52]

At first glance, Salazar would not have seemed a likely candidate for close relations with the United States and Great Britain, but the exigencies of war soon moved the Roosevelt administration to sign an agreement of considerable strategic significance with Portugal. The Azores offered an important forward base for Allied operations against a Nazi-occupied Europe. The British government used its centuries-old ties with Lisbon to help convince the Salazar regime, which feared the Germans despite certain ideological affinities with the Third Reich, that they should let British forces land there in October 1943. American forces soon followed, and Washington began negotiating for a long-term arrangement to use the Lagens airfield on Terceira Island. As the counselor in the American Embassy in Lisbon during 1942 and 1943, George Kennan had emphasized in his cables to the State Department the importance to the United States of "the stability of the Portuguese Empire in general." After some hesitancy about departing openly from the American anticolonial tradition, Roosevelt personally instructed Kennan to offer Salazar the *quid pro quo* of a United States "assurance to respect the sovereignty of Portugal and its entire colonial empire" in return for access to the Azores. The Portuguese dictator agreed, and with the Santa Maria Agreement of November 1944, the United States acquired the use of a crucial military base in the North Atlantic at the cost of tacitly supporting the continued colonial domination of Africans in Angola and Mozambique by the Portuguese.[53] The strategic importance of the Azores and Salazar's passionate anticommunism would continue to link the United States to Portuguese colonial stability in southern Africa throughout the Cold War years of the Truman administration.

V

While not as immediately important in 1945 as Congolese uranium or access to the Azores airfields, American interests in the Union of South Africa had grown during World War II and would expand dramatically in the postwar decade. Americans had long noticed the parallel histories of the United States and South Africa, dating back to the Protestant European settlers who sailed to each country from Dutch ports in the seventeenth century. Theodore Roosevelt and others saw the Great Trek of 1836 as an American-style odyssey, in which a small group of brave and determined white pioneers sought freedom from British imperial rule while overcoming nonwhite residents who blocked the path to the economic development of a continent. One American in 1900 articulated a common assumption that South Africa was the heart of "the New England of Africa, whose enterprising sons are doggedly conquering the wilderness step by step, carrying with them Christianity and constitutional government."[54] The religious and political luggage of these pioneers also included a fierce determination to preserve white supremacy, and they paid close attention to reports of racial unrest in the United States, which they tended to blame on inadequate segregation and allowing blacks too much hope for advancement.[55]

The United States and South Africa have shared certain patterns of racial domination throughout the twentieth century, despite their almost reversed population ratio of blacks to whites. No other fully self-governing societies have been founded so clearly on legislated white supremacy. In the early years of this century, the two nations' systems of racial hierarchy seemed especially comparable. The decades after World War II would reveal a sharp contrast in the directions they were moving in, however, as the United States by the 1960s eliminated the last legal barriers of segregation, while South Africa quit the now multiracial Commonwealth and added more bricks to its domestic edifice of apartheid.[56] Inklings of these divergent paths appeared occasionally even in the war years,[57] but the dominant impression Americans held of white South Africans in 1945 was of English-speaking, Christian, capitalist, anticommunist Western allies who had carved out a corner of European civilization on the "Dark Continent." The sense of international emergency that pervaded the early Cold War years would help hide the substantial differences between the two countries behind a solid, if not iron, curtain of anticommunism.

As a steadfast loyalist of the British Commonwealth, Prime Minister Jan Smuts symbolized South Africa to most of the outside world. For Americans in particular, including Harry Truman, Smuts seemed to represent values and a history very similar to their own. He had fought the British as an anticolonial war hero, but he built his long political career on an attachment to English values and a commitment to maintaining close ties with Great Britain.[58] Smuts believed strongly in the importance of the Commonwealth, whose white-ruled member nations collectively proved throughout the war to be the closest allies of the United States. Despite the dissent of more Anglophobic Afrikaners, South Africa's gold production played an important role in Allied wartime economic strategy, and South African troops contributed significantly to Allied campaigns against Axis forces in North Africa.[59] Officials in the Roosevelt administration valued South Africa's role as one of the Allies and worked to provide lend-lease materials to the Union in order to bolster the prowar Smuts government against its antiwar domestic opponents.[60]

In addition to their historical parallels as English-speaking multiracial societies and their experiences as allies in both world wars, the United

States and South Africa by 1945 were also increasingly linked by economic connections of trade and investment.[61] While most of the world's economies limped through the depression of the 1930s, the rising price of gold fueled rapid, steady industrialization and growing consumer demand in South Africa after 1933. Great Britain continued to hold the largest share of the South African import market, but American manufacturers gained steadily during the 1920s and 1930s by providing machinery, vehicles, and other capital goods crucial for the Union's industrial growth. The value of South African imports from the United States increased more than eightfold between 1933 and 1941 as the Union became a leading non-European market for American goods. By 1936, the American magazine *Business Week* was referring to South Africa as "one of the most spectacular markets in the world."[62] The domestic demands of World War II caused British exports to the Union to drop sharply, allowing the United States to become in 1941 the largest supplier of goods to South Africa while the Union emerged in turn as the fourth-biggest foreign market for American goods.[63] American exports to South Africa continued to grow throughout the war, strengthening an already favorable balance of trade with the Union.[64] American businessmen and the State Department appreciated the South African government's sympathetic handling of American business concerns and its minimal import restrictions during the war, which were then almost entirely removed in September 1945.[65]

The need of the United States at the end of the war to invest abroad in order to maintain American economic prosperity matched up well with what Truman's Commerce Department called "the pivotal importance" to South Africa "of uninterrupted capital inflow from abroad."[66] British capital remained foremost for the Union, but American investments climbed in a manner similar to that of American trade during the 1930s and 1940s. South African tariff policies encouraged American industries to set up local manufacturing subsidiaries in the Union. Considerable American capital was invested in petroleum production, and by 1943 the value of American-owned assets in South Africa had grown to $87 million, a figure that would quadruple during the Truman years.[67]

By 1945, it was clear to the State Department that American investment in and trade with South Africa would continue to expand rapidly after the war. The Truman administration also realized that the group in the Union most pleased about American commercial penetration was the Nationalist Party. Noting that Malan believed that "Americans would try to break down the walls of Empire preference from the outside while the Afrikaners would seek to do so from the inside," the State Department concluded that "the Nationalist ideal of a South Africa independent, economically and politically, is obviously in accord with the American hopes of freer world trade without discrimination."[68] This coincidence of interests would take on greater significance when the Nationalists came to power three years later.

Strategic links supplemented economic ones between the two countries. The war had demonstrated the importance of South Africa's location abutting the East–West shipping lanes around the Cape of Good
Hope, especially with the Mediterranean in hostile hands during the early
years of the conflict.[69] The war had also depleted many of the accessible
reserves of key minerals in the United States, ending traditional American self-sufficiency in raw materials and increasing the need for imports
and for friendly governments in mineral-rich areas like southern Africa.[70]
By 1945, the United States had established itself as the major purchaser
of such important South African materials as manganese, industrial diamonds, platinum, and vanadium.[71] But the mineral that would bind most
closely together the futures of South Africa and the United States
throughout the tenure of the Truman administration was the same one
as in the Belgian Congo: uranium. The radioactive ore had long been
known to appear alongside gold in the mines of the Rand. Surveys con-
ducted by geologists working for the Manhattan Project and its subcon-
tractor, Union Carbide, revealed in 1944 and 1945 that South Africa
had the world's largest undeveloped reserves of uranium ore capable of
early commercial development. This news brought considerable comfort
to the national security planners of the Truman administration and dramatically raised the value of South Africa to the United States on the eve
of the Cold War.[72]

VI

"It may be, and I believe is, the manifest destiny of this country to grow,
as a white man's country, into a powerful industrialized modern state,"
wrote the United States Minister in South Africa, Lincoln MacVeagh, to
his old friend Franklin Roosevelt in 1942. MacVeagh's language revealed
the feeling of many Americans that South Africa had much in common
with the United States. Given racial tensions in the segregated United
States, Roosevelt would have had no difficulty understanding Mac-
Veagh's sympathy for "the difficult matter of handling the natives" in
South Africa, the issue that "must be faced" for the Union to build a
hopeful future. MacVeagh argued that the industrial color bar restricted
economic progress by limiting African productivity and consumption, a
problem whose solution "along cooperative, liberal, and progressive lines"
was prevented by the Afrikaners' stubborn devotion to a religiously based
doctrine of white supremacy. He informed the President that while Smuts
would probably defeat Malan in the 1943 election, the Nationalist Party
leader's "potent dream . . . of the good old days . . . of patriarchal
white supremacy, Kaffir servitude, and Boer Republican isolation" was
"perhaps better fitted to the average [white] mentality in this country
than that of his opponent." After Smuts' victory that year, MacVeagh
warned presciently that Malan "is yet a figure whose eventual comeback

is so possible as to be dreaded still. He is the Satan of the Dutch Paradise Lost."[73]

Two years later, President Truman reassured Americans in a major speech that "the foreign policy of the United States is based firmly on fundamental principles of righteousness and justice." In implementing those ideals, he declared, "we shall not give our approval to any compromise with evil."[74] Truman was referring to forces of darkness on the left end of the political spectrum, especially the Soviet Union, rather than those on the right as described by MacVeagh in South Africa. For almost all white Americans who had grown up in a racially discriminatory and deeply segregated society, the very idea of actual color-blind democracy—rule by the majority of people—in southern Africa in the 1940s, if even imagined, could only have seemed absurdly premature.[75]

Americans and their government had very little contact with the fifty million Africans of southern Africa, and they saw the region almost exclusively through the eyes of whites. MacVeagh himself, while critical of Malan's extremism, openly equated blacks there with "savagery" and whites with "civilized life"; he informed Roosevelt that continued white supremacy was "the only possible road of progress" in the Union.[76] His successor as U.S. Minister, Thomas Holcomb, had spent his entire career in the all-white United States Marine Corps and, as commandant after 1936, had steadfastly opposed allowing African Americans to enlist in the Corps. "If it were a question of having a Marine Corps of 5,000 whites or 250,000 Negroes," he told the Navy General Board when it was considering an expansion of the service in 1941, "I would rather have the whites." After Franklin Roosevelt decided to admit blacks to the American naval services in 1942, Holcomb ensured that all black recruits were kept in a rigidly segregated and self-sufficient battalion, which was trained in isolation from white Marines and assigned to a remote station rather than included as part of the Corps' amphibious units.[77] Having not yet been confronted by its own massive civil rights movement and unable even to outlaw the terrifying public spectacle of lynching, the United States in 1945 had not positioned itself well as a people or a government to oppose racial totalitarianism as well as totalitarianism of the left.

Throughout the years of the Truman administration and even long afterwards, the international role of South Africa would remain much more important to the United States government than the Union's domestic politics and race relations. Outlining commerce as the primary American interest in Africa, the official United States policy toward South Africa that Truman inherited from Roosevelt emphasized the need for "establishing closer relations of all types between the two countries."[78] Despite the widespread poverty and even famine among rural Africans in the Union and the rising power of apartheid-minded, pro-Nazi Afrikaners, ties of uranium, economics, military strategy, and culture bound the United States closely to the white minority regimes of southern Africa at the beginning of Truman's presidency.[79] As American concerns about Soviet aggression and communist expansion grew rapidly after the end of the war, the anticommunism of the Pretoria government and the British, Belgian, and Portuguese colonial administrations made them increasingly precious in the eyes of American policymakers.[80]

PART TWO

DRAWING
CLOSER

CHAPTER 4

Containing Communism and Black Unrest: 1946–1947

H. Stuart Hughes became the director of the State Department's Division of Research for Europe in early 1946, just when Winston Churchill was announcing to Americans and the world that an "iron curtain" had fallen across Europe. While Hughes found the ideological atmosphere in Washington more tense and suspicious of the Soviet Union than it had been a year earlier, he did not, as he recalled later, "think that the future had been foreclosed. The range of choice might be narrowing, but alternative paths still lay open." But the next two years would reveal escalating conflict between the expanded definitions of national security wielded by Moscow and Washington. By the end of 1947, the former allies had, in Hughes' words, "together reached the point of no return."[1]

The transformation of superpower suspicions into open antagonism had some momentous, if unintended, consequences for American policy toward the colonial world, for the domestic politics of the United States, and for American relations with South Africa. As the Truman administration defined American security in increasingly anti-Soviet terms, the United States government sought to bolster its ties with the noncommunist governments of the Western European nations. Two years after the end of the war, almost all of Western Europe continued to face grievous economic hardships, and moderate and right-wing forces in France and Italy confronted domestic communist parties of increasing popularity. Reconstructing the economies of its European allies along capitalist lines and strengthening noncommunist political forces there emerged as Washington's chief priorities. Residual anticolonialism in the Truman administration was shelved, for European recovery depended on colonial raw materials as well as American capital. The administration's shift during 1946 and 1947 to a Cold War framework for understanding international affairs coincided with the rising tide of nationalist revolution in the Third World, leaving the United States squarely in the camp of the imperial powers.[2]

Waging the worldwide anticommunist struggle declared by President Truman in his dramatic "Truman Doctrine" address of 12 March

1947 required substantial domestic support in the United States. The experience of World War II had sated most Americans' desire for global ideological conflict. Nonetheless, the Truman administration and their Republican opponents evoked long-standing American fears of subversion as they competed for popular support, in part by promoting an exaggerated estimate of expanding Soviet influence throughout the world. The popular anticommunism Senator Joseph McCarthy would begin to harvest so effectively three years later, while deeply rooted in American culture, was growing quickly in the atmosphere surrounding the Truman Doctrine.[3] The deepening of the Cold War combined with Truman's public support for greater civil rights in these same years to swing most African Americans and their leaders into acquiescence in the politics of anticommunism. As blacks sought greater access to the benefits of American life, they found that they had to moderate their criticisms of American support for continued European rule in the colonial world. The advancement of African Americans toward fuller citizenship in the United States thus came at the cost of muting their belief in the international character of white racial dominion in the early Cold War.[4]

In addition to eviscerating American anticolonialism and narrowing the scope of dissent and reform within the United States, growing American-Soviet confrontations in 1946 and 1947 increased the importance of South Africa to the Truman administration. Ironically, this happened in the same period when white repression of blacks in the Union escalated sharply and resurgent Afrikaner nationalism moved to the threshold of power. Rejecting the trend of the rest of the world away from explicit racial hierarchies, South Africa slid in the opposite direction as the Cold War unfolded. The fierce anticommunism and racial hatred of the increasingly popular Nationalist Party pressed Smuts and the United Party to prove their own toughness on communism and black unrest. The Truman administration worried some about the Union's growing racial tensions but valued far more the alignment of South Africa in the emerging Cold War.[5]

I

The escalation of tensions between the United States and the Soviet Union in the immediate postwar years seemed almost a cruel joke to many residents of the colonial world. They had hoped that the victorious alliance of the two great anticolonial powers would combine with the economic vulnerability of the European nations and the declining imperial sentiments of the metropolitan publics to usher in a new era of national self-determination. In particular, the dominant position of the United States at the end of the war implicitly legitimated the principle of self-government as a right of all peoples.[6] The editors of a nationalist newspaper in Madagascar did note in early 1946 that "we know very well that the colonialism and racism which some persons claim to reject is still alive within them." But "such people must understand," concluded *La Nation Mal-gache,* "that the era of colonialist conquest and domination is ended. We are now in a new era, to whose existence . . . the Atlantic Charter and the United Nations are the historic witnesses."[7] The emergence of the Cold War dismayed nationalists in Asia, Africa, and the Arab world, who shared little of the West's concern for containing communism and wanted badly not to have a new conflict between East and West blur what they saw as the older and more important struggle of the colonies of the South against the European imperialists of the North.[8]

Tensions between the United States and the Soviet Union compli-cated the relations of the United States with the colonial world but did not stop the rising chorus of demands for national independence after World War II. The crucial precedent came in India. Great Britain re-mained the most powerful and far-flung of the European imperial pow-ers, and if it had been able to retain its empire in Asia, the demise of the other Western empires would have been slowed. Like its European neighbors, Britain after the war sought to minimize changes in the exist-ing relationship between itself and its colonies. But the organization and moral courage of Indian nationalists emerging from the war confronted London with an intractable problem, which it proved unwilling to try to resolve by force of arms. For the new British Labour government, the practical and intellectual difficulties of maintaining the restless Asian col-onies in the postwar world were overwhelming, and London committed itself in 1945 to rapid decolonization there.[9] The other imperial powers proved less willing to grant independence voluntarily to their colonies, but their often brutal efforts at repressing nationalist uprisings had the clear markings, in the wake of the British precedent, of desperate mea-sures to forestall what had become inevitable.

From the perspective of the Truman administration in 1947, colonial issues paled in comparison to what it understood as Soviet-inspired com-munist aggression in Europe, Asia, and the Middle East. Truman used a framework developed by George Kennan in enunciating in March an American policy of "containing" communism throughout the world, which became known as the Truman Doctrine. The President asked Congress for $400 million in aid to Greece and Turkey to bolster anticommunist regimes the British could no longer afford to support. More important, he declared that there were now only "two alternative ways of life" in the world, one "free" and the other based on "terror and oppression."[10]

Such a division of the world had little appeal or correlation with reality for anticolonialists in the Third World, who knew which camp their imperial overlords supposedly belonged to. In equating anticom-munism with freedom, the United States was joining forces, not only with European imperialists and military-dominated governments in Greece and Turkey, but also with right-wing regimes in such independent na-tions of the developing world as the Philippines, Argentina, and China.[11] As *The Christian Century* observed in an editorial published on the same day that Truman delivered his address to Congress, the United States was coming to be "regarded elsewhere as the great champion of conservatism, and on occasion even of reaction, in international affairs."[12]

The containment of communist and other leftist influence in the postwar world required not only vigilance against external aggression but also the rebuilding of shattered political economies along capitalist, democratic lines. The Truman administration believed that global economic recovery and American prosperity depended on the successful reconstruction of the industrial democracies of Western Europe, the leading trading partners of the United States.[13] The U.S. Joint Chiefs of Staff (JCS) warned in May 1947 that "the conquest or communization of no other country or area would be so detrimental [to the security of the United States] as that of France and/or Great Britain," while control of the uranium ore of the Congo made the stability of Belgium critical to the United States. The JCS argued that a revival of German economic and military power would be crucial for France's economic recovery and for British and American security against the Soviet threat; in words strikingly similar to those of Nationalist leader Daniel Malan in South Africa, the Joint Chiefs emphasized that "the German people are the natural enemies of the USSR and of communism."[14] Their devastating experience in the recent war meant, however, that the French needed considerable assurances in order to overcome their fears of a revitalized Germany.[15] Widespread poverty helped burgeoning communist parties in France, Italy, and Belgium create the possibility of a peaceful, democratic shift to communist rule in Western Europe, an ominous and even traumatic prospect to policymakers in Washington.[16] The Truman Doctrine clearly would not suffice by itself, and Secretary of State George Marshall announced in June 1947 that the United States would provide extensive economic aid for the long-term reconstruction of Europe.[17]

American assistance under the European Recovery Program, commonly known as the Marshall Plan, could not be used explicitly for economic development or military counterinsurgency in the colonies. But massive economic support for the metropolitan governments necessarily strengthened their hands in dealing with colonial rebellions. Marshall Plan aid freed other French, Dutch, and British funds for the often bloody work of sustaining their empires against the gathering forces of nationalist liberation. Determined to strengthen the noncommunist government in Paris, the Truman administration could not afford to oppose France's plans to restore its sovereignty abroad. While publicly dissociating the United States from counterrevolutionary activities, American officials acknowledged privately that Marshall Plan aid was enabling the French to fight what became large-scale wars of "pacification" in Indochina, Madagascar, and Algeria. French portrayal of the guerrillas in Indochina and Madagascar as pro-Soviet communists helped assuage American concerns about supporting imperial repression, while French forces slaughtered forty thousand residents of Madagascar in 1947 alone.[18]

Marshall Plan aid to the Netherlands began to flow in the spring of 1948 and, in the words of the foremost historian of American-Dutch relations in this period, "hopelessly compromised" all American pretensions to neutrality in the intensifying conflict between Dutch colonialists and indigenous nationalists in Indonesia.[19] The concern of the Truman administration for the establishment of stable, anticommunist governments everywhere outside the Soviet bloc did not always wed it blindly to the imperial powers, as evidenced by the later role of the United States in pressuring the Dutch to grant independence to the largely noncommunist liberation movement in Indonesia. But much more often than not, Truman's priorities of reconstructing Western Europe and containing communism led the United States to act as a guarantor of Europe's remaining colonies.[20]

From the perspective of the Truman administration, the best solution to the vestigial problem of colonialism in the new era of the Cold War was for the Europeans voluntarily to liberalize their relations with nonwhite peoples and progress steadily toward the ultimate goal of decolonization. Such a path might have avoided debilitating wars in peripheral areas and assured that new nations in the developing world would remain within the noncommunist "free" world along with their former colonial overlords. The weaker imperial powers—France, Belgium, the Netherlands, and Portugal—tended to believe that they could not afford the loss of formal political control over the vast natural resources of their colonies. But the British, with their stronger links to Washington and their greater confidence about maintaining close post-imperial economic ties with their colonies, proved more willing to move in this direction. Britain's announcements in the winter of 1946–1947 that it would swiftly grant independence to Burma and India delighted American officials. The final independence of India and Pakistan in August 1947 and Burma and Sri Lanka in early 1948 won great credit for the British government in the United States, convincing the American government and public of the wisdom and goodwill of British colonial rule in creating a newly multiracial Commonwealth as a basis for political stability and economic development in the noncommunist world.[21] This progressive British policy encouraged the Truman administration to ease its demands for the abolition of the Imperial Preference trading system within the British Empire in the negotiations for the General Agreement on Tariffs and Trade of 1947.[22]

The growing preoccupation of American policymakers in 1946 and 1947 with the Soviet Union precluded paying any substantial official attention to the question of self-government in Africa. The years immediately following World War II witnessed the reaffirmation of colonial power on most of the African continent, a process underwritten by the United States through the Marshall Plan and the developing alliance soon to emerge as the North Atlantic Treaty Organization (NATO). In comparison to the vocal and insistent demands for independence in the Asian colonies, African nationalism seemed still somnolent after the war and did not appear to require immediate attention. This pleased the Truman administration, which recognized the importance of the agricultural and mineral wealth of the African colonies for Western European economic recovery, especially in light of Western Europe's loss of its traditional Eastern European sources of raw materials.[23] To an American government increasingly concerned with preserving stability around the world, the absence of revolution in some of its allies' colonies provided a measure of comfort. Britain's apparently enlightened colonial policies in Asia masked the Labour government's determination to maintain its empire in Africa, and to most Americans the British were proving their credibility as trustees of progress in the developing world.[24]

As the Cold War and decolonization in Asia proceeded apace in 1947, the Truman administration worked both sides of the colonial street in its efforts to strengthen its European allies while also keeping the new nations of the Far and Middle East within the noncommunist fold. While increasingly concerned about the "dangers of premature independence," which it feared might lead to Soviet subversion of weak new states, the United States government tried to avoid the appearance of total accommodation of the imperial powers. This strategy focused on the United Nations, where Soviet bloc support for Arab and Asian calls for rapid decolonization of all imperial holdings helped dramatize colonial and racial conflicts. The American delegation sought to play a mediating role between the imperial and anti-imperial camps. The effort to promote a "middle way" of the gradual evolution of "dependent" peoples toward self-government required that the United States delegation "avoid associating itself with either the more conservative colonial powers or those intent upon the immediate liquidation of colonial empires."[25] Under-Secretary of State Dean Acheson later recalled that the Truman administration saw its role as helping resolve "the colonial-nationalist conflict in a way that would satisfy nationalist aims and minimize the strain on our Western European allies."[26]

The difficulty of such a task was clear from the start. At the 1946 and 1947 United Nations sessions, the United States delegation voted regularly with the colonial powers on African and other colonial questions, to the dismay of representatives from the nonwhite nations. Iraqi delegate Awni Khalidy warned the Americans of "the feeling among many of the smaller states that the United States, instead of taking a position of independent leadership, was acting merely as one of the colonial powers opposing progress and blocking the promotion of the welfare of independent peoples."[27] Even a representative of the government of the Philippines, which remained deeply dependent on American support, deplored the "weakening" of American "moral leadership on the questions related to dependent peoples and the colored independent peoples," which was undermining American influence in the developing world. General Carlos P. Romulo resented what he called the arrogance of most American Foreign Service officers, who apparently expected delegates of smaller countries to change their views to support those of the United States. Romulo reminded American delegate Harley Notter, as Notter recorded the conversation, "that since World War II, the colonial peoples were determined to get self-rule at once, and we had better do our best in that direction in order to have the friendship and support of their millions" of people.[28]

Many Americans as well as people of color around the world had believed at the end of the war that American influence would, in Paul Robeson's words, "be upon the side of progress, not reaction . . . [,] upon the side of the freedom-loving peoples and the forces of true liberation everywhere."[29] By the end of 1947, however, the escalating tensions of the Cold War had considerably dimmed such hopes. The Truman administration had temporarily shelved its plans for a free-market capitalist order in the noncommunist world in the belief that containing the threat of Soviet expansion required American support for the continued colonialism of its European allies.[30] American policymakers feared the opportunities for communist influence amidst the "chaos" that they assumed revolution and rapid decolonization would bring in many areas of the colonial world.[31]

Truman had no tolerance for Third World neutralism—what one Indian nationalist called the "unwillingness of Asia and Africa to accept exclusive intimacy with their European masters of yesterday"—in what he had come to understand as a global struggle for the very soul and future of the human race.[32] In the Portuguese and British colonies of southern Africa, the United States government would soon be ignoring unauthorized use of American aid for colonial development when it increased the production of strategic minerals for the West.[33] In December 1947, the administration's military strategists lauded the loyalty of the British Commonwealth and, to a lesser extent, of the other Western nations to the American cause of containing communism; American defense planners concluded with satisfaction that "Western democratic economic and military measures should assure short-term stability" in colonial Africa.[34] The increasing antagonism in East–West relations was drawing the United States closer to the colonial and white minority regimes of southern Africa.

II

Truman's declaration of full-scale ideological conflict between the Soviet bloc and the "free" world helped shape the course of politics and race relations within the United States as well as in the international sphere. The announcement of the Truman Doctrine was intended, in the words of Senator Arthur Vandenberg, to "scare hell" out of the American people in order to call up massive public support for a bold and expensive foreign policy venture. Painting so grim a picture of the extent and insidiousness of the communist threat to the peoples of the "free" world could hardly avoid encouraging fears in the American public of subversive activities within the United States. Since its creation in 1938, the House Committee on Un-American Activities (subsequently known as HUAC) had been emphasizing such a threat, and the Republican congressional victories of 1946 were aided by frequent accusations that the Democratic administration was harboring subversives in the federal government through its laxity about employee loyalty. In order to head off investigations of various executive departments and agencies threatened by the new Republican-controlled Congress, Truman created a Temporary Commission on Employee Loyalty in November 1946. Then, nine days after his Truman Doctrine speech in March 1947, he issued an executive order establishing the comprehensive Federal Employee Loyalty Program. The President thereby officially sanctioned the idea that the security of the United States government and thus the stability of the American social order were seriously threatened from within.[35]

For many white Americans, especially in the South, racial segregation and white domination constituted the essential foundation of their understanding of American culture and society. Age-old fears of black assertiveness, renewed after the war by the presence of thousands of returning African American veterans, fed on official reports of anti-American subversion and conspiracy.[36] White Southerners were determined to reinforce the comprehensive web of white supremacy—the "tripartite" system of economic, political, and personal domination sociologist Aldon D. Morris has described—against any challenges to their racial authority.[37] Never absent during the war, white violence against blacks escalated in 1946 with the lynching of at least six African Americans and the last-minute escape of twenty-two others from a similar fate. A blue-ribbon panel appointed by Truman to investigate the state of civil rights in the country noted that "lynching is the ultimate threat by which his inferior status is driven home to the Negro. As a terrorist device, it reinforces all the other disabilities placed upon him." The police chief of a small South Carolina town demonstrated some of the other levels of violence used to ensure racial subordination with his gory torture and blinding of black veteran Isaac Woodward in the summer of 1946. "Legal" murders by police forces included the 1947 shotgun slaughter of eight black convicts by their guards at a prison camp outside Brunswick, Georgia, after the prisoners refused to work without boots in a snake-infested swamp.[38]

The extent of racial violence and terrorism in the South after the war remains difficult to measure because of the absence of comprehensive reporting. Many victims of racial killings simply "disappeared" and cannot be included in statistics, a phenomenon familiar in more recent decades in several Latin American countries. It appears that at least sixty African Americans died violently at the hands of whites in areas strongly influenced by the Ku Klux Klan during 1945 and 1946; Southern police officers, an important element in Klan organization, were directly implicated in two-thirds of those cases. An unknown number of imprisoned blacks died in police custody and were recorded officially as "trying to escape."[39] Customary police treatment of black prisoners, male or female, in the South was suggested a few years later by the immediate response of Rosa Parks' mother to the news of her well-dressed, middle-aged daughter's arrest on a city bus. When Rosa called from the Montgomery jail, the elder Mrs. Parks' first words were: "Did they beat you?"[40]

Perhaps the most telling demonstration of the readiness of Southern authorities to reinforce racial subordination through the use of what can only be accurately described as large-scale terrorism against black communities came in Columbia, Tennessee, in February 1946. The incident began with a dispute between Gladys Stephenson, the soft-spoken black cook for one of Columbia's leading white families, and William Fleming, a white radio repairman at the Costner-Knight Appliance Store. Looking to avoid trouble, Stephenson paid the bill for repairs on her portable radio even though it amounted to more than double the estimate she had been given. When she discovered that the radio still did not work, however, she began to upbraid Fleming, who responded by slapping and kicking her. Recently discharged Navy veteran James Stephenson came to his mother's aid, punching Fleming and knocking him through a plate glass window. The police then arrived and arrested the Stephensons, beating James in the process.

A lynch mob formed in front of the city jail that night but was frustrated in its design by the sheriff's prior transfer of the prisoners out of town for their safety. Black residents responded to the presence of the armed mob by barricading themselves in Mink Slide, the African American section of town, and preparing to defend themselves. When four policemen entered the darkened neighborhood without identifying themselves, black defenders fired on them, injuring all four, in the apparent belief that they represented the advance guard of the lynch mob. The sheriff called for state assistance, and five hundred heavily armed state patrolmen and National Guardsmen soon ringed Mink Slide. At dawn they struck, firing machine guns randomly into unopened doors, wrecking several black businesses, arresting over one hundred residents of the neighborhood, and leaving "KKK" written on the property of at least one business. Weapons were confiscated from blacks while white citizens brandishing rifles and sidearms roamed the streets freely. Two of the people arrested were shot and killed in prison by the police two days later, and thirty-one blacks were indicted on a variety of charges including attempted murder. Despite black and liberal protests in the North, business in Tennessee continued as usual with Governor James McCord commending the behavior of the authorities in Columbia.[41]

Just eight days before the outbreak of violence in Columbia, the *New York Times* had commented in an editorial that "this is a particularly good year to campaign against the evils of bigotry, prejudice, and race hatred because we have witnessed the defeat of enemies who tried to found a mastery of the world upon such cruel and fallacious policy."[42] While most white Tennesseeans may not have agreed, many other white Americans joined their black countrymen in cheering for Jackie Robinson as he demonstrated new possibilities for greater racial equality in the postwar United States by breaking the color line in major league baseball. Following the earlier lead of Joe Louis in boxing and Jesse Owens in track, the talented and disciplined Robinson became the first African American to play in the minor leagues in 1946 and in the major leagues the following year. His superior play won him rookie-of-the-year honors from *Sporting News* in 1947 and a complimentary cover story in *Time* magazine that September. Robinson's courage and perseverance in the face of considerable hostility from some players, coaches, and fans captured the attention and respect of millions of other Americans who had previously ignored the racial dilemmas of their country.[43]

In a sports-oriented culture like that of the United States, the achievements of Jackie Robinson in the "national pastime" of baseball symbolized the ebbing social acceptability of flagrant racial discrimination among a large number of Americans. Other less visible changes coming through the judicial system in the mid-1940s helped lay the groundwork for Truman's eventual move to a stronger civil rights stand and for the modern civil rights movement, which would undermine the efforts of white Southerners to restore the prewar racial status quo. In a 1944 case involving the state of Texas, the Supreme Court had ruled that the exclusively white primary violated the Fifteenth Amendment and was therefore unconstitutional. This decision helped pave the way, despite much intimidation, for a quadrupling of registered black voters in the country in the following ten years, including 750,000 in the South by the time of the 1948 elections. Similarly, the Court ruled in 1946 in a case involving a Virginia statute that segregation by race on interstate buses was unconstitutional. A "Journey of Reconciliation" by an integrated Fellowship of Reconciliation group the next year in order to test this decision on the buses of the upper South proceeded with only one minor incident involving violence. While large-scale movement towards desegregation remained over a decade in the future, public opinion in the United States was beginning to shift in symbolic and substantive ways towards an acceptance of greater racial equality during 1946 and 1947.[44]

The plummeting legitimacy of white supremacy in international affairs after World War II gave an important boost to the struggle in the United States for greater racial equality. If the effort to contain communism could ally the United States with forces of reaction abroad, it could also pressure Americans to abide more fully by their own ideology of freedom and equality. Amidst the rapid decolonization of the early Cold War, the racial facts of American life became vital to the ability of the United States to gain the trust of the new nonwhite nations. The unwillingness of the Soviet Union to subscribe to the traditional Western color line and the Soviets' ready use of racial horror stories from the

United States in propaganda aimed at the Third World forced the Truman administration to acknowledge the skyrocketing cost of explicit racial discrimination.[45] Under-Secretary of State Acheson admitted in May 1946 that "the existence of discrimination against minority groups in this country has an adverse effect upon our relations with other countries." Frequently, he continued in a public letter to the Fair Employment Practices Committee, "we find it next to impossible to formulate a satisfactory answer to our critics in other countries" as "the gap between the things we stand for in principle and the facts of a particular situation may be too wide to be bridged." Acheson concluded that the State Department therefore "has good reason to hope for the continued and increased effectiveness of public and private efforts to do away with these discriminations."[46] Truman himself acknowledged the problem in typically terse fashion: "The top dog in a world which is over half-colored ought to clean his own house."[47] But the difficulties of doing so for an ambivalent American government and public were suggested by the deeply segregationist views of the nation's popularly acclaimed chief spokesman on foreign affairs, Acheson's boss, Secretary of State James Byrnes, who was named "Man of the Year" for 1946 by *Time* magazine.[48]

The United Nations from its inception became a forum for international interest in American race relations as well as in colonial racial issues. The United States government was regularly embarrassed in its role as host of the United Nations by formal complaints of discrimination encountered by the shocked delegates and staffs of non-European member nations.[49] Black Americans assumed that the rights outlined in the U.N. Charter should apply to them as well as to the rest of the world, and appealed to the United Nations for an investigation of their treatment that would lead to an end to racial discrimination in the United States. The left-leaning National Negro Congress and the more moderate National Association for the Advancement of Colored People (NAACP) filed petitions in 1946 and 1947 with the United Nations, and the scholarly NAACP document, edited by W. E. B. Du Bois and outlining the systematic denial of elemental human rights to African Americans, received considerable media attention around the world.[50] While public opinion polls in 1947 indicated that only a minority of Americans believed that the treatment of blacks in the United States affected the attitudes of peoples of other countries towards the United States, newspaper readers on every continent digested the details of white American violence against blacks.[51] The Soviet Union, of course, promoted the dispersal of such information, but even the closest allies of the United States registered dismay at the brutality of the racial exception to American democracy.[52]

Hampered by international criticism of American domestic life just as it sought to take the offensive in a global campaign against communism, the Truman administration looked for ways to brighten the image of the United States abroad. In February 1947, the State Department began a series of radio broadcasts to the Soviet Union to inform its people of the better way of life available in the democratic United States. Unfortunately, one of the events the Voice of America felt compelled to comment on in its very first broadcast was the vicious lynching of Willie Earle, a black South Carolinian accused of murdering a white taxi driver. The later acquittal of all twenty-eight men who had confessed to participating in the murder did little to improve the international image of the United States.[53]

A more successful effort to strengthen the reputation of the United States regarding civil rights came in June 1947, when Truman became the first American President to address an NAACP conference. The ten thousand people present at the Lincoln Memorial in Washington and a worldwide radio audience heard him acknowledge that "many of our people still suffer the indignity of insult, the harrowing fear of intimidation, and, I regret to say, the threat of physical injury and mob violence." Truman called for the federal government to become "a friendly, vigilant defender of the rights and equalities of all Americans" as "our case for democracy should be as strong as we can make it." Confirming that the nation could no longer afford the high cost of explicit racial discrimination in the new world of the Cold War and decolonization, the President concluded that "never before has the need been so urgent for skillful and vigorous action to bring us closer to our ideal."[54] Six weeks later, the administration prepared to meet further international criticism of American racial practices with some counterattacks of its own, as the State Department asked its overseas missions to report home any cases of notable discrimination in their host countries.[55]

The use of flagrantly extralegal intimidation throughout the South to prevent blacks from voting in the 1946 elections, promoted openly by the Democratic Senator from Mississippi, Theodore G. Bilbo, and the international attention that those efforts received embarrassed Truman both as chief executive of the federal government and as head of the Democratic Party. Rising public protests against this repression and against other violence against blacks led to a meeting of top civil rights leaders with the President in September 1946, in which he appeared genuinely astonished to learn of the extent of black oppression in the South. After the Democratic Party's losses in the November elections and amid signs that black voters might be drifting back to the Republicans, Truman appointed an elite President's Committee on Civil Rights under the leadership of Charles E. Wilson, the president of General Electric, to make a comprehensive investigation of the state of discrimination in the United States.[56]

Truman released the Committee's report, *To Secure These Rights*, on 29 October 1947, just six days after Du Bois had presented the NAACP petition to the United Nations and thus adroitly timed to forestall criticism of the administration as unconcerned with racial problems. The Committee's report noted progress made by African Americans but painted a grim picture of the trials they still faced daily in the United States. In order to eliminate racial discrimination, *To Secure These Rights* recommended a vastly expanded role for the federal government in preventing violations of civil rights, including an extensive array of legislative remedies such as federal statutes to outlaw lynching, police brutality, and poll taxes.[57]

Truman had known the liberal philosophical bent of most of those he appointed to the Committee and was not surprised by their report. He hoped to retain the support of both his party's progressive forces and the more conservative white South for the upcoming presidential campaign, but his closest political aide, Clark Clifford, persuaded him by December to focus his electoral strategy on urban black, labor, and liberal constituencies. Clifford believed that the white South was less important in terms of votes and less likely to revolt against Truman, as it seemed to have nowhere else to go. By the end of 1947, Truman had not yet done much to improve tangibly the lives of black Americans. One of his aides even summarized the President's civil rights strategy as starting with a bold statement and then temporizing "to pick up the right-wing forces. Simply stated, backtrack after the bang." But in the symbolic terms so important in presidential politics and cultural change, Truman was helping to make white racism much less respectable in the United States.[58]

An important consequence of the Truman administration's simultaneous moves in 1947 to contain communism and to discourage domestic racial discrimination was the effective separation of the issue of civil rights in the United States from racial and colonial problems abroad. Despite ambivalent feelings among African Americans about their kinship with Africa, the New York–based Council on African Affairs (CAA) had managed throughout World War II to provide a notable voice in support of decolonization in general and African independence in particular. The small but well-organized CAA reached the height of its influence in late 1945 and 1946, the narrow window between the end of World War II and the full flowering of the Cold War. The socialist-oriented Council built close ties with African nationalist organizations, especially in South Africa and British West Africa, and gained enough prominence through political rallies, lobbying at the United Nations, and distributing information about conditions in colonial Africa to have its journal, *New Africa,* banned in South Africa and other African territories.[59]

The rigidification of the Cold War in 1947 led to a split in the Council's leadership over the issue of anticommunism and the beginnings of serious harassment and intimidation by the FBI and the Department of Justice, which swiftly undermined the CAA's effectiveness. As the hunt for radicals and subversives gained credibility and the federal government made it increasingly clear that it now viewed the world in strictly bipolar terms, the NAACP and most other civil rights organizations chose to stay close to the Truman administration by taking anticommunist stands. Truman's support for stronger protection of civil rights at home and the rising cost for blacks of taking any position supported by leftists thus helped destroy whatever progressive criticism of the administration's policies toward South Africa and its colonial neighbors still existed in 1947.[60]

III

While black Americans in the early postwar years faced renewed violence but also found cause for hope that the days of flagrant racial oppression might be waning in their country, black South Africans confronted a grimmer situation. Despite promises by the Union government during the war that their living conditions would be improved, the years after 1945 brought little substantive progress, as Americans living in the Union recognized.[61] The four residential options for Africans—the rural native reserves, the urban slums, the mining compounds, and the white farming compounds—each offered some combination of severe poverty, ill health, inadequate housing, dramatic overcrowding, and brutal treatment by whites. The serious threat of starvation in the drought-stricken reserves continued to drive people into the black townships and squatter camps around the country's urban areas, where employment was more available but living conditions were in many ways even worse.[62] Visiting American journalist Martin Flavin wrote that "the real wealth of the country is cheap labor" rather than gold, but black miners, as events soon proved, enjoyed none of the political rights or protections that might have been expected in a country considered by many as part of "Western civilization."[63] Investigations in 1947 of the treatment of African farm workers on white farms near the town of Bethal revealed near-slavery conditions of abuse, assault, and forced labor, as American diplomats reported to the State Department.[64] Flavin wrote in *Harper's* magazine that what black South Africans resented was not hard labor or even low pay so much as "the vicious, devastating, and degrading color line."[65]

The South African government's minimal response to the deteriorating situation of blacks in the Union revealed limitations on racial reform that were similar to but much sharper than those in the United States. Like the Democratic Party in the United States, South Africa's ruling United Party included both liberals and racial reactionaries. Jan Hofmeyr, the deputy leader of the party and the man widely expected to succeed Smuts, held moderate racial attitudes that placed him well to the left of the Prime Minister and the majority of the party. As white racial fears increased in the Union after the war, however, Hofmeyr's political fortunes declined, even before his early death at the end of 1948. U.S. Minister Thomas Holcomb suggested to the State Department that Hofmeyr's "difficulties are those of a liberal in a country where liberalism is not expedient."[66] The conservative rural wing of the United Party, especially in Natal, was vulnerable to wooing by the Nationalist Party.

While opposition from extreme segregationists in his own party hampered Harry Truman, white Southerners never seriously threatened to take control of their national government as the Nationalist Party did in South Africa in the immediate postwar years. White politics in the Union shifted to the right after World War II, and Smuts moved with it, to the dismay of black South Africans. The Prime Minister clearly demonstrated the meaning of "moderation" in South Africa in his responses to the two major nonwhite protests of those years, the Indian passive resistance movement and the African mine workers' strike.[67]

The United Party government put the Asiatic Land Tenure and Indian Representation Bill into effect on 3 June 1946 in response to the increasing number of South Africans of Indian descent who were buying property in previously all-white neighborhoods in and around the city of Durban. The law provided for the resegregation of Natal and reassured the fiercely anti-Indian whites of the province, who were largely English-speaking supporters of the United Party. In the preceding months, however, Natalian Indians had been led by the wily Smuts to believe that he was concerned with their interests. They were shocked by what they quickly dubbed the "Ghetto Act" and unimpressed with its dubious compromise of allowing them token political representation for the first time. They refused to make use of the franchise and began, under the leadership of the Natal Indian Organization, a two-year campaign of peaceful civil disobedience to protest the legislation and the general discrimination against Indians in South Africa.[68]

The historic kinship connections between South Africans of Indian descent and a now fervently nationalist India brought swift international attention to the passive resistance campaign in Natal. Indian leader Mohandas K. Gandhi, who had lived in South Africa for two decades as an organizer of opposition to racial discrimination under an earlier government of Jan Smuts and whose son Manilal still lived in Natal, encouraged Indians in the Union in their use of the power of *satyagraha* ("passive resistance") to resist this latest act of segregation. Supported by an outraged and united public at home, the Indian government protested the legislation by withdrawing its High Commissioner from the Union, boycotting all trade with South Africa, barring white South Africans from hotels in India, and raising the issue of South African racial policies at the United Nations.[69] The State Department monitored criticism of the South African government's action around the world, typified by that of the Mombasa Indian Association in Kenya, which cited parallels, in a comparison that was proving tenacious, between the attitudes and policies of the Union government and those of the Nazis in Germany.[70] International support for the passive resisters became widespread and included many prominent Americans, ranging from Paul Robeson to Eleanor Roosevelt.[71]

The passive resistance movement also garnered important backing within South Africa. Amidst the rising tide of white racism and the increasingly precarious situation of all blacks in the Union, African and Indian political leaders after the war started to move toward overcoming the mistrust that had long divided them and their constituencies. African National Congress president Alfred Xuma confirmed the beginnings of this momentous transformation in a speech to the Transvaal Indian Congress in which he declared the support of South Africa's eight million Africans for the passive resistance campaign. Xuma noted that Africans in the Union had also known the experience of having the government take away their land and rights, in the Native Land Act of 1913 and the Hertzog "native bills" of 1936, and he concluded that "freedom is indivisible."[72]

The Rev. Michael Scott, an Anglican priest living and working in the African ghettos of Johannesburg, and other whites formed a committee of support for the passive resisters within days of the initiation of the campaign. The next month, Scott, who also played a significant role in prompting the investigations of the execrable conditions of African farm labor in the Union, became the first white person to be imprisoned for participating in the Indian protests. More typical of the white response to the passive resistance effort, however, were the angry cries of "We need a Ku Klux Klan!" These formed a striking contrast to the appeals of Indian schoolchildren who marched in the streets of Natal chanting "We want freedom" and "We want democracy."[73] The image the United States projected abroad was proving, as Truman and Acheson feared, profoundly ambiguous.

The Smuts government's utter lack of sympathy for the passive resisters in Natal, demonstrated by steady harassment and arrests, seemed almost friendly in comparison with its bloody repression of the more momentous African mine workers' strike in August 1946. U.S. Minister Holcomb warned Washington months earlier that "grievances among Native workers on the mines have been steadily accumulating"; food shortages were increasing while wages remained the same as fifty years earlier, a level that a South African government commission had declared in 1944 to be thoroughly inadequate for providing even a subsistence existence for an African family. Holcomb blamed the Smuts government for its continued refusal to acknowledge the legitimacy of the burgeoning African trade unions in mining and industry and "the crucial need" for their legal recognition. The unwillingness of the government to address the causes of rising discontent among African workers meant that unrest would continue to grow, Holcomb believed, and the most probable result would be "a widespread strike of Natives in the gold mines." The labor attaché in the U.S. Mission in South Africa, John F. Correll, noted that "any dispute among gold miners subjects the entire country to a state of apprehension and social nervousness." Holcomb concluded that the South African government would attempt to settle any strikes by black workers, "not through negotiation and conciliation, but by repressive methods, since there is at present no Government machinery capable of dealing with the situation without force."[74]

The Transvaal Chamber of Mines, an umbrella organization of the largely English-speaking owners of South Africa's gold mines, provided crucial financial backing for the United Party and therefore the Smuts government. The Chamber's only responses to the regular requests by John B. Marks and other leaders of the unofficial African Mine Workers Union (AMWU) for talks about the miners' grievances had been to ignore them and to continue its traditional harassment and intimidation of all labor organizers. The government's War Measure 1425 remained in effect, prohibiting any gathering of more than twenty persons on government-proclaimed mining ground. Reluctantly, the AMWU concluded on August 4 that only a strike could gain the attention it sought and, with Marks emphatically warning against the use of any violence, called publicly for the support of all African gold miners. Fully prepared ahead of time, a special detachment of sixteen hundred heavily armed policemen responded swiftly to the outbreak of the strike on August 12, firing on strikers and charging them with batons and bayonets, killing at least twelve and wounding over twelve hundred. Miners who struck by sitting down underground were driven up "stope by stope, level by level" to the surface where they could be more easily contained in the compounds. One anxious mine manager called the violence a "minor civil war." By August 17 the sixty thousand strikers in nineteen of the Rand's forty-five mines had been beaten into submission and were back at work.[75]

The brutally effective response to the miners' strike orchestrated by Prime Minister Smuts illuminated the direction of South African politics after the war. Smuts announced that he was not particularly concerned about the strike, because it had been caused by "agitators" rather than by miners with legitimate grievances. "The natives," he added, needed to be protected from these conspirators who were seeking to bring them and the country to ruin. Most whites applauded the government's actions, and Smuts ignored the outraged response of the members of Parliament representing the Union's African population, who called his statement "shocking." The Prime Minister used the obvious strategy for reassuring his American allies, telling the U.S. Minister that the strike was "definitely Communist inspired." Holcomb had his doubts, however, noting that the pressure for the strike "quite clear[ly]" came from the AMWU's rank and file rather than from Marks, a Communist Party member, or from the Communist Party itself. Holcomb suspected that Smuts, sensitive to his international image, did not want to leave on his scheduled trip to the Paris Peace Conference with a massive strike by African workers still under way at home. The government and the Chamber of Mines had had ample notice of the strike and plenty of time to "erect machinery to handle grievances without resorting to brute force," Holcomb reported to Washington, but Smuts was instead determined to crush the strike and use it as a pretext for moving against the Communist Party in the Union in order to fend off Nationalist charges that the United Party was too lenient with communists.[76]

The "danger" of the Communist Party in the Union was its espousal of racial equality, a doctrine whose implications terrified most white South Africans. Malan and other Nationalist politicians, unwilling to imagine Africans as capable of serious creativity and organization, had long accused white radicals of being responsible for African demands for equality. Since the war, the Nationalist Party had been enlarging its political base at the expense of the United Party by accusing Smuts and his followers of insufficient vigilance against subversives and nonwhites.[77] Hustling to keep up with changes in white opinion, the United Party, reported Holcomb on 26 July 1946, "has been moving to the right since the war. At the present writing there is little difference between the United Party and the Nationalist [Party] on most issues, and there is no difference on color issues."[78] Smuts and his party accelerated this rightward shift in the wake of the mine workers' strike by putting the leading figures of the Communist Party on trial in Johannesburg for their alleged role in the strike and by declaring a "political war" on the four Communist members of the Capetown City Council. Holcomb told the State Department on 3 September 1946 that the United Party seemed to be initiating a "general, nation-wide anti-Communist campaign."[79] This could hardly have been a strange or unreasonable idea to the Truman administration, which also faced a vociferously anticommunist opposition party and was constructing a very similar political strategy in response. In South Africa, however, anticommunism went hand in hand with "the old ideology of segregation and white supremacy" that the Smuts government was now busily reaffirming.[80]

Americans understood that the strike by the African Mine Workers' Union and the response of the South African government portended a troubled future for the nation of South Africa. U.S. Labor Attaché Correll warned the State Department that the strike, which was the largest by African workers in the history of the Union, "cannot be over-emphasized in importance." Africans were close to the end of their endurance of the abysmal conditions in which they were forced to live and work, he concluded, while the Smuts government "is moving more and more in the direction of oppression and repression of non-Europeans."[81] The American business community had been thrilled by the reports of a new gold discovery in the Orange Free State in April, but it was clearly concerned now about the future of investments in the Union. *Fortune* magazine ran an article in October 1946 that extolled South Africa as "one of this latter-day world's outstanding amphitheatres of ante-Delanian [pre-Roosevelt] rugged individuals," which had, it added enthusiastically if ungrammatically, "opportunity and to spare for venture capital." *Fortune* noted, however, that the Union's color bar kept its urbanized African work force unnecessarily unskilled and so poorly paid that they had to live "in such abysmal, crime-breeding squalor as might inspire concern even in a Bilbo or a Talmadge." *Fortune* was especially troubled by the "pyramid of hate" into which white attitudes and policies seemed to be transforming South African society, as the miners' strike and its repression demonstrated all too clearly.[82] The American consul in Durban agreed, warning even before the strike that it seemed inevitable that "there will be a terrible day of reckoning" for white South Africans someday.[83]

The repressive policies of the Smuts government and the rising tide of Afrikaner nationalism in 1946 and 1947 helped transform the black struggle for equality and democratic rule in South Africa. The Asiatic Land Tenure and Indian Representation Bill and the violent response of the authorities to the mine workers' strike made plain the futility of the dignified, constitutional means of protest traditionally used by the ANC and other black organizations. Even the conservative, elite Native Representative Council acknowledged in the wake of the government's response to the strike that Smuts would not listen to their mild petitions of concern, and its members unanimously voted to suspend the Council's sittings in protest. The government's actions strengthened the hand of the more militant Youth Leaguers within the African National Congress. At the same time, the prosecution of Communist Party leaders resulting from the strike softened the Youth League's suspicion of left-wing radicals and helped pave the way for an increasingly close alliance of the ANC with South African communists of all colors. The movement toward unity among non-European spokesmen gained formal status with the "Joint Declaration of Cooperation" of 9 March 1947 by Xuma and two leaders of the South African Indian Congress, Dr. G. M. Naicker and Dr. Yusuf M. Dadoo. The electoral victory of the Nationalist Party in 1948 would further accelerate the radicalization and unification of the black nationalist movement, which was rapidly replacing the older politics of patience and acquiescence with mass political action and nonviolent resistance.[84]

By 1947, rising racial tensions at home and ample criticism from abroad had encouraged white South Africans in what U.S. Minister Holcomb called their "mood for extremism." Malan and the Nationalists inflamed the political atmosphere in the Union by campaigning steadily on the theme of threatened white supremacy in preparation for the next year's election. American observers assumed that the internationally famous Smuts could not really lose at home to a party of extremist Afrikaners, but they did acknowledge the impressive organizational and strategic advantages the Nationalists seemed to hold. Certainly the United Party depended almost entirely for its unity and success on the elderly Prime Minister. Despite his desire to placate the growing international criticism of South Africa's racial policies, Smuts had little room to maneuver on the domestic front between his own record and the bitter attacks of the Nationalist opposition. At the end of the year, the American legation in South Africa was relieved to be able to report that Smuts still seemed likely to win in the upcoming general election. By his actions toward his black countrymen, the Prime Minister had shown the limitations of "moderation" in white South Africa, but he at least eschewed the Anglophobia and evangelical racism of his former Sunday school student Daniel Malan.[85]

IV

The relations of the United States with South Africa in the first two years after World War II were heavily influenced by the person of Jan Smuts. As international criticism of South Africa's racial policies under his government increased sharply in 1946 and 1947, many abroad came to doubt the Prime Minister's lofty reputation. The editors of the respected *Economist,* for example, noted after the first regular session of the United Nations in 1946 that "to every non-European delegate, his outward appearance of progressive international statesmanship conceals the inward convictions of a prejudiced reactionary."[86] But most white Americans, especially those in high political, diplomatic, and economic circles who had had any personal interaction with Smuts, continued to be impressed and even awed by his intelligence and international prominence.[87] Under-Secretary of State Dean Acheson, who admired British ways almost as much as the South African leader did, suggested the esteem in which Smuts was still held in a note he sent to Truman to help prepare him for the Prime Minister's visit to the White House in November 1946. Smuts was "respected as the originator, with President Wilson, of the League of Nations and it was he who gave the name 'British Commonwealth of Nations' to the system of Government uniting, under the British crown, the various self-governing dominions," Acheson wrote, reminding Truman that Smuts was "the respected elder statesman" of America's closest ally, the British Empire.[88]

Smuts himself acknowledged in early 1947 the contradictory image he projected as an internationalist representing a racially polarized country in an increasingly egalitarian world. "I can be quoted on both sides," he admitted. "The Preamble [to the U.N. Charter] is my own work, and I also mean to protect the European position in a world which is tending the other way."[89] Smuts was one of the last of a generation of statesmen whose world had been dominated by white nations that ruled over peoples of color and did not question each other's right to do so; the Eurocentrism of his internationalist outlook put him painfully at odds with the multiracial world order emerging from World War II. He lamented Britain's decisions to liquidate its empire in Asia and to allow nonwhite nations equal status with South Africa in the Commonwealth, writing to a friend in 1947, "Ceylon a Dominion this year? Am I mad or is the world mad?"[90] The world view of this aging imperialist was indeed proving to make little sense to the peoples of the decolonizing Third World. Smuts found some reassurance in American policies for rebuilding and supporting the Western European nations, but the Truman administration was learning in the new public forum of the United Nations how embarrassing it could now be to have South Africa as an ally.[91]

From the start of the first of the annual fall sessions of the United Nations on 23 October 1946, South Africa spent weeks in the spotlight of international attention. Attacks on the Union's racial policies, especially regarding its residents of Indian descent and the territory of South West Africa, marked a new stage of international involvement in the Union's race relations. Representatives from the Third World, led by India and supported by the Eastern bloc countries, kept Smuts and the other South African delegates at the U.N. meetings on the defensive by focusing debate on the chasm between the principles of the United Nations and the realities of life in this member nation. These representatives of the new wave of racial egalitarianism insisted that South Africa was part of the general colonial problem of unrepresented nonwhite peoples, an analysis bitterly resented by white South Africans who saw themselves as "natives" of the Union as much as any black person.[92] The Council on African Affairs, headquartered in New York, also lobbied U.N. officials and the American delegation on behalf of black South Africans, distributing information on their living conditions and supporting the efforts of the Indian delegation and other nonwhite representatives. The Council emphasized that unlike other nations that at least officially agreed with the U.N. Charter's ideal of racial equality, the South African government explicitly *required* racial discrimination, in defiance of the Charter, which it had signed.[93] If such pressure in the new public forum of the United Nations put Smuts, with his enormous personal prestige in international affairs, on the defensive in 1946 and 1947, it would serve only to harden the already defiant attitudes of his Nationalist successors after their electoral victory in May 1948.[94]

When Indian delegate Vijaya Lakshmi Pandit, the sister of Jawaharlal Nehru, raised the issue of South African treatment of people of Indian descent at the opening session of the General Assembly in 1946, the tension between two different principles of the U.N. Charter became quickly apparent. On one hand, members were enjoined from interfering in "matters which are essentially within the domestic jurisdiction" of one state; on the other, members were expected to promote the observance of "human rights and fundamental freedoms for all without distinction as to race." Smuts responded to Pandit's charges by emphasizing the domestic jurisdiction clause and suggesting that Indians in South Africa were better off than they would be in India, with its widespread poverty and traditional caste system.[95]

Other nations wishing to avoid having international attention drawn to their treatment of people of color, like the United States and the imperial powers of Western Europe, tended to support South Africa in the U.N. debates. The United States government preferred to view South Africa's racial problems as largely the Union's own business, but their international implications made this increasingly difficult. The Truman administration's concern for retaining the loyalty of the world's decolonizing areas and its desire to minimize public criticism of its South African ally led the American delegation to try to play a mediating role at the U.N. On the issue of the Union's treatment of South African nationals of Indian descent, the United States took the position that the matter should be referred to the International Court of Justice (the World Court) for an advisory opinion on whether it fell solely within the domestic jurisdiction of the Union. In place of the condemnatory resolution offered by India, the U.S. delegation succeeded in having a more moderate proposal passed by the General Assembly in December 1946: friendly relations between South Africa and India had been impaired, it said, and the two nations should meet to discuss and find a resolution to the problem. But the level of resentment felt toward the South African government by people who had known firsthand the costs of white racial dominance—and the eagerness of the Soviet bloc to support their sentiments—made it difficult for the United States not to appear supportive of South Africa, just as it seemed to be sympathetic to the European colonial powers.[96]

In addition to concerns about South Africa's treatment of Indians and other peoples of color, the other major issue involving the Union to emerge at the first United Nations annual session was the future of South West Africa. The former German colony had been turned over to South Africa in 1920 by the League of Nations as a "class C" League mandate. That status meant that the Union could essentially administer it as an integral part of South Africa, but the Union government was obligated to promote the well-being and progress of the inhabitants of the territory and to report annually to the League on its administration. The dissolution of the League of Nations led the Smuts government to inform the opening session of the United Nations in 1946 that South Africa now planned to annex the territory outright.[97]

Considerable dismay greeted the announcement of the proposed South African action. Most member nations believed that South West Africa should instead be placed under the new U.N. trusteeship system. This seemed especially important in light of intensifying racial discrimination in the Union, which suggested that South African rule of South West Africa could not be in the best interests of the 300,000 Africans who constituted over 90 percent of the territory's population. Black Americans and representatives of South Africa's Indian and African populations joined U.N. delegations like that of India in ridiculing Smuts' assertion that most Africans in South West Africa actually welcomed incorporation by the Union; they called instead for an evaluation of African opinion in the territory by a neutral party. Fearing a similar fate for themselves, Africans in the neighboring British High Commission territory of Bechuanaland pleaded with London to help block South African expansion. The Soviet Union also opposed Smuts' proposal for annexation and insisted that South Africa abide by the spirit of the U.N. Charter either by bringing South West Africa into the U.N. trusteeship system or by granting it independence.[98]

The disposition of South West Africa, like the treatment of South African nationals of Indian descent, seemed to the Truman administration a minor concern that should not be allowed to distract the United Nations from the great issue of Soviet and communist expansion. Like other colonial issues, the future of South West Africa provoked strong sentiment in non-Western delegates, whom American policymakers wanted instead to focus on helping to create a stable, capitalist world order. The United States government also wanted to minimize debate on South West Africa because of its potential implications for American policy toward the mandated islands of the western Pacific, which the American military remained unwilling to place under U.N. trusteeship.[99]

Eager to reduce antagonism between South Africa and its critics, the U.S. delegation worked to defeat resolutions condemning the Union while gently pressuring the Smuts government to consider a trusteeship arrangement for South West Africa as a way to maintain all its practical advantages there without provoking the anti-colonial delegates.[100] Smuts wanted to incorporate the territory as fervently as did his Nationalist opponents at home, but his desire for good international relations led him to postpone annexation and accept an American proposal that the United Nations defer action on the matter for a year while South Africa resumed making annual reports on its administration of the territory. The U.N. in turn limited itself to requesting, rather than requiring, that South Africa follow the example of the other mandatory powers by bringing South West Africa under a trusteeship agreement. American prestige and influence had helped restrain open conflict over the issue, but South Africa was proving itself a difficult friend to have in international affairs.[101]

The 1946 General Assembly session charted the course of future relations between South Africa and the rest of the world. Never before had a sovereign nation had its policies of racial discrimination so openly discussed and specifically condemned by a worldwide council of nations. The United States had partially protected its ally by helping moderate the tone of the final resolutions, but the United Nations had clearly indicated that South Africa's racial and colonial policies were out of line with those of the international community.[102] While many white South Africans rallied to Smuts' defense in the face of his embarrassment on the international stage, the Nationalist Party made further domestic political gains by condemning the Prime Minister's minor concessions and compromising tone at the United Nations.[103] Caught between conflicting pressures at home and abroad, Smuts tried to keep to a middle course, which was rapidly disappearing. He promised that South Africa would not annex South West Africa and would continue to administer it in the spirit of the original mandate. At the same time, however, the South African Parliament resolved not to place the territory under U.N. trusteeship, and Smuts moved toward greater political integration of South West Africa into the Union.[104]

International criticism of South Africa continued in 1947, further irking white South Africans while encouraging Indian passive resisters and African nationalists.[105] *Pravda* in Moscow lambasted the South African Parliament's decision to ignore the U.N.'s recommendation on trusteeship for South West Africa, and the Soviet media in general continued to stress discriminatory practices against blacks in the Union.[106] Despite efforts by the United States to shield South Africa by denying him an entry visa, Anglican clergyman Michael Scott finally arrived in New York in the fall as an adviser to the Indian delegation at the United Nations with a collection of dramatic statements and petitions from the Herero people of South West Africa. Scott distributed this information widely at the U.N., destroying in the process what little credibility the Smuts government had gained from its claims that Africans in the territory wanted to be annexed by the Union. Indentured and child labor, pass laws, and utterly inadequate educational and health services, it seemed, characterized South African administration of the territory. One missionary in South West Africa called the referendum on the annexation question that the South African government had held there "an absolute farce," while the Herero reported being intimidated, harassed, and deceived in order to vote the "proper" way. When their tribal representatives sought permission from the South African government to be allowed to travel to the United Nations to present their case, the request was dismissed on the grounds that Smuts already was their representative there. They then smuggled out their petitions with Scott instead.[107]

The American delegation at the United Nations in the fall of 1947 continued its efforts to moderate criticism of South Africa and keep the Union from becoming further isolated from world opinion. With the battle lines of the Cold War having been clearly drawn earlier in the year, all anticommunist Western allies were increasingly valuable to the United States government. Another resolution by the Indian government to convene an international round table conference to discuss the treatment of people of Indian descent in South Africa failed again by a handful of votes; instead, the General Assembly merely repeated the previous year's more moderate resolution calling on South Africa, India, and now Pakistan (which had just come into existence) to meet to resolve the issue. The U.S. delegation was also pleased that Smuts was continuing to provide annual reports on the South African administration of South West Africa and that the General Assembly merely repeated its request that the Union place the territory under U.N. trusteeship.[108] These efforts at damage control in the newly declared Cold War came, however, at the cost of the United States' being increasingly identified with the colonial and racial attitudes of white South Africa.[109] By the end of 1947, it had become clear to the Truman administration that shielding the Union and its antiquated racial policies at the United Nations was a considerable embarrassment to the United States in its struggle for the allegiance of the peoples and nations of the emerging Third World.

V

Outside of the United Nations, relations between the United States and South Africa continued to grow stronger and friendlier in the immediate postwar years as the Union's economic and strategic importance to Washington increased with the development of the Cold War. One exception to the general ease with which this relationship was developing surfaced in the protracted debate over settling lend-lease debts from the war. South Africa had contributed less to the war effort, in proportion to its national wealth and population, than any other Commonwealth country. In addition, the Union, unlike the rest of the Commonwealth, had refused to sign a reverse lend-lease agreement by which it would have supplied strategic materials as a contribution to the Allied war effort; instead, the United States had been forced to buy them from South Africa at the market price. At the same time, South Africa's financial and economic position had improved sharply during the war, putting it in a better position to pay off its debts than any other Allied nation. Secretary of the Treasury Fred Vinson reminded Byrnes in November 1945 of South Africa's relatively small material contribution to the war effort and seeming disregard for the spirit of lend-lease. Vinson encouraged the Secretary of State to keep this in mind during forthcoming negotiations regarding the repayment of lend-lease debts.[110]

American calls for a settlement of the lend-lease debt caused a stir in white South African politics at the beginning of 1946. During the war, Smuts and the pro-government press had misled the South African public about the nature of the debt to the United States, giving assurances that the Americans would expect no repayment. Opposition newspapers were now eager to embarrass the Prime Minister with the news of the American request.[111] U.S. Minister Holcomb was troubled by the attitude of the Smuts government, which he believed was making the United States appear duplicitous and unreasonably demanding. Holcomb advised his superiors in the State Department that "our Government should adopt a just but very firm attitude towards this Government which is obviously planning to evade its just debts" because "in the long run such an attitude will gain us increased respect."[112] Despite American evaluations of U.S. lend-lease provisions to the Union at $169 million in direct assistance plus $704 million in indirect military aid, the South African government initially offered a total of $40 million for settlement of the bill.[113]

Stubborn negotiating by South Africa during the summer and fall of 1946 frustrated American lend-lease administrators and State Department personnel, who believed they were already being amply generous with a country that seemed to have profited substantially from the war.

Holcomb continued to lobby Washington to take a tougher stance, arguing that the Smuts government would not receive a token settlement with any more grace than it would an agreement reflecting the Union's actual obligations and ability to pay.[114] Holcomb's assistant in Pretoria, Dale Maher, reported with some anger "the duplicity of the Smuts government, which, in order to escape from a political dilemma of its own making, did not hesitate to falsify the real position of the United States." Maher concluded that "once again General Smuts has demonstrated his ability to escape from an embarrassing political situation by a clever and not too ethical manoeuvre, this time at the expense of the United States."[115] While not pleased by "slim Jannie" 's demonstration of the meaning of his nickname, top policymakers in the Truman administration were impressed by Smuts' arguments about how a large debt would strengthen the hand of his extremist enemies at home and by the importance of maintaining good relations with a country so well endowed with strategic materials. Late in the year, the two sides agreed to a settlement of $100 million.[116]

Economic links and historical ties continued after the war to keep South Africa closely aligned with Great Britain and therefore with the United States. Like Truman, Smuts believed that rebuilding Europe should be the West's top priority. The Prime Minister saw the British Commonwealth as a natural counterweight in world affairs to the growing polarity between the United States and the Soviet Union. With his almost spiritual view of the bonds tying the Commonwealth together, Smuts was an exceedingly gracious (some said even fawning) host to the British royal family when they visited South Africa from February to April of 1947. In its several pages of pictorial coverage of this imperial occasion, *Life* magazine emphasized the loyalty to the British Crown of the King's "stalwart subjects" of all colors in the Union and their special affection for Queen Elizabeth. The Truman administration could only be pleased with such apparent devotion to the strongest ally of the United States.[117]

South Africa remained particularly important to Great Britain in economic and financial terms after the war. The Union was one of the few countries with which the British had a favorable balance of trade, and the enormous gold production of the Rand mines helped bolster the entire sterling area's currency reserves. In return, South African industrial development continued to depend on British capital, which flowed even faster to the Union after the election of the Labour government in 1945 led to rumors that British industries might soon be nationalized. With Britain's financial difficulties growing more serious late in 1947, the South African government provided a crucial gold loan of £80 million plus a gift of £1 million "from the South African people." London also looked to Pretoria for strategic minerals and for help in any future defense of British interests in the Middle East. Despite its distaste for South African racial policies, the government of Clement Attlee in Britain found itself closely entwined with South Africa for economic and strategic reasons.[118]

Direct American economic interests in South Africa expanded dramatically in 1946 and 1947. South Africa's relative wealth and its cancellation of wartime trade restrictions in late 1945 unleashed an extraordinary boom in demand for consumer goods, which American manufacturers were uniquely positioned to satisfy. Already three times greater in 1946 than in 1938, American exports to the Union almost doubled again in 1947 to a total value of $414 million. The South African government's financial policies encouraged American investment in South African industries as well, which grew quickly in such fields as automobiles, tires, petroleum, and textiles. General Motors, Goodyear, Firestone, and a dozen other major American corporations initiated or expanded their operations in the Union soon after the war. Appreciating what *Fortune* magazine called the "fantastically low operating costs" of companies that could buy African labor so cheaply, American capital also started to flow into traditionally British-funded mining interests in the Union and in South West Africa. One of the leading American groups that began investing in the production of the strategic minerals of southern Africa after the war was the Newmont Mining Company, whose president, Fred Searls, had worked closely with Secretary of State James Byrnes during the war and whose board of directors Byrnes would soon be sitting on.[119]

VI

Several patterns of enduring significance in international politics emerged in the first two years after World War II. Explicit racial domination had lost its legitimacy in the gas chambers of the German Holocaust. No longer bolstered by confidence about their "white man's burden," the greatly weakened European imperial powers, in their different ways, began at last to consider withdrawing from their colonial empires. Despite continuing white violence, the United States witnessed important symbolic and substantive victories for greater civil rights for its citizens of all colors. The United Nations emerged as a prominent public forum for those pressing for the end of colonialism and racial discrimination everywhere.

With the rest of the world thus moving toward greater racial equality, the Union of South Africa emerged as the great exception. The processes of industrialization and urbanization combined with resurgent Afrikaner nationalism to increase racial polarization and put the Union on a course for apartheid. With the Truman Doctrine and the Marshall Plan defining American strategy and priorities in the developing Cold War, the anticommunist South African state with its wealth of strategic minerals and long-standing ties to Great Britain became increasingly important to the United States. The Truman administration therefore found itself working hard by 1947 to moderate the chorus of international criticism of South Africa and, to a lesser extent, the other colonial powers.

While southern Africa did not receive the attention in Washington that Europe, the Middle East, or Asia did, the United States nonetheless developed important ties with South Africa during the last two years before the establishment of formal apartheid. Rapidly expanding trade with and investment in the Union gave it a status and reputation in the American business community unusual for a country of its size. The presence of the world's largest known undeveloped uranium ore deposits on the Rand, recognized since late in World War II, meant that South Africa's strategic importance to the West had become enormous. The willingness of the Smuts government to develop that ore, as indicated by its work on a pilot leaching plant in 1947, and its plans to sell the material solely to the British and the Americans greatly pleased the Truman administration.[120] Despite the absence of any substantial threat of leftist subversion in South Africa, the Smuts government seemed as determined as the Truman administration to prove its anticommunist credentials. Late in 1947 the South African Attorney General showed how closely his country's course could parallel that of the United States by requesting copies of the reports of the House Committee on Un-American Activities to help in his own work.[121] With the rising power of the even more fiercely anticommunist Nationalist Party, South Africa's stability as a Western ally in the Cold War seemed assured.

CHAPTER 5

The Coming of Apartheid: 1948

In the burdened trek of South African history, the all-white elections of 26 May 1948 marked a watershed. To the surprise of almost all observers, the Nationalist Party, in alliance with the small Afrikaner Party, won a slim majority in the Union Parliament, and Daniel Malan became Prime Minister in place of Jan Smuts, who lost his own seat to an obscure Nationalist candidate. Racial tension in South Africa had been increasing under the United Party government since World War II, but the rise to power of the Afrikaner nationalists and their determination to implement the more rigorous system of segregation known as apartheid accelerated the racial polarization of the country. Later elections would add to the Nationalist majority, and black South Africans in the second half of the twentieth century would suffer increasing economic debilitation and personal and political harassment at the hands of the South African government. The results of the 1948 elections put the Union on a different political path from the rest of the world and gravely damaged the hopes of the majority of South Africans for a more humane and democratic future.

South Africa's fateful choice of apartheid came in the midst of growing antagonism in the Cold War. In the spring and summer of 1948, the United States was seeking to stem the tide of left-wing politics in Europe and Asia. Anticolonial insurgencies persisted in Southeast Asia, with the French increasingly embattled in Indochina and the British facing leftist rebels in mineral-rich Malaya. Communist troops were sweeping towards victory in China. The Soviet Union strengthened its hold on the reins of power in the occupied nations of Eastern Europe, and popular communist parties in Italy and France continued to make American policymakers anxious about the possibility of a democratic turn to communism in Western Europe. In June, Soviet troops cut off Western ground access to West Berlin, dramatically raising tensions in Europe and provoking a massive year-long airlift of supplies to the isolated city.

At home, the Truman administration took a strong stance in favor of civil rights in 1948, partly for domestic political reasons and because of genuinely held principles, but also in order to help shore up support for its international struggle to maintain and expand Western-style capitalist democracy. As it sought to establish greater credibility with people of color at home and abroad, the administration did not welcome the prospect of apartheid in a nation of the British Commonwealth. But the fierce anticommunism of the Malan government, the growing economic interdependence of the two nations, and the promise of vast quantities of uranium ore from the Rand assuaged official American concern about the evidently troubled future of its South African ally.

I

South Africa nudged into the consciousness of educated Americans right at the beginning of 1948 with the publication in the United States of Alan Paton's *Cry, the Beloved Country*. This beautifully written novel by a white South African received immediate critical acclaim and a wide audience.[1] Paton's story warned of rising tensions in his "beloved country," due largely to the impersonal forces of industrialization and urbanization. He saw the mass migration of black South Africans into the cities in search of work as causing immense moral damage, forcing them to shed their traditional social patterns and be led astray by the immoral temptations of de-tribalized urban life. Paton's heroes, both white and black, were kind, generous, religious, and above all humble. This represented the quintessential white South African liberal perspective of the 1940s, in which extremists loomed on both sides of the color line, and the real issues were as much moral and spiritual as political. *Cry, the Beloved Country* held up moderation and forgiveness by South Africans of all colors as the only road to a peaceful solution of the escalating racial tensions in the Union. Paton's tone, however, was mournful and not optimistic.[2]

Attention to Africa in general was also growing among American national security managers in the early months of 1948. They were deeply concerned with rebuilding Western Europe into an economic, military, and political union strong enough to resist the influence and pressures of the Soviet bloc. The Policy Planning Staff of the State Department made it clear in late January that the Truman administration feared above all the "catastrophe" that would befall Europe if Congress did not adopt the European Recovery Plan proposed by Secretary of State George Marshall seven months earlier: "A Europe abandoned by ourselves at this stage of the game would be little different . . . than the Europe which would have resulted from a German victory in the recent war." The loss of its traditional access to Eastern Europe's raw materials stemming from the creation of the Soviet bloc meant that Western Europe would have to fulfill much of its resource needs from either the United States or Africa. The Policy Planning Staff believed the United States to be the more viable source of materials at this point but emphasized the tremendous potential for a joint Western European program of "economic development and exploitation of the colonial and dependent areas of the African Continent," including the resettlement of excess European population. Particularly encouraging in this regard was the fact that Africa thus far remained "relatively little exposed to communist pressures."[3]

Even if Congress did fund the Marshall Plan, however, American policymakers believed a still more dangerous threat menaced both the recovery of Western Europe and the stability of its African territories. The growing popularity of the Communist Party in France and in Italy portended possible communist victories in democratic elections, which would have eviscerated the nascent anticommunist Western union. The U.S. Embassy in Rome warned in March that the United States government needed to increase its clandestine funding of the moderate Italian political parties "in order to save Italy from the left."[4] The American Embassy in Moscow predicted that a communist electoral victory in either France or Italy would rapidly increase communist influence throughout Western Europe and open up avenues for the "extension of Communist activities in the colonial world from Dakar to Saigon." From Washington's perspective, legitimately elected communist governments in Western Europe not only would have extended Soviet control in Europe all the way to the Atlantic, but also would have offered Moscow a shortcut from a position of no influence in Africa to one of complete domination of the continent.[5]

A destabilized Western Europe with left-leaning governments would have had profound implications for American relations with European colonial areas and American access to natural resources there. By the end of World War II, American policymakers knew that they had seen the end of the period of the United States' self-sufficiency in strategic minerals and other raw materials; access to natural resources in the Third World would now be crucial to American economic and military security.[6] By 1948, the Truman administration's concern with stockpiling rare mineral resources led it to seek improved rail transportation and expanded port facilities in southern Africa in order to encourage the export of the region's strategic materials.[7] In a suggestive study completed on February 24, the Policy Planning Staff noted that the United States had "about 50% of the world's wealth but only 6.3% of its population" and that "in this situation, we cannot fail to be the object of envy and resentment. Our real task in the coming period is to devise a pattern of relationships which will permit us to maintain this position of disparity without positive detriment to our national security."[8] Being explicit about this goal of continued economic dominance would not have lessened such "envy and resentment." Secretary Marshall instead instructed American diplomatic officers a few months later to "use our information resources to convince the people of third [nonaligned] countries that [the] achievement of their own aspirations will be significantly advanced with the realization of U.S. [rather than Soviet] national objectives." Soviet domination of Europe and the wealth of natural resources in its colonial areas would have had alarming effects on this American "position of disparity."[9]

The day after the Policy Planning Staff had reminded Marshall of the need to maintain the current status of the United States in the world economy, the unfolding political drama in Czechoslovakia came to a head. The Czech Communist Party seized full control of the government. The Truman administration and the American public were shocked by what they understood as a bold new Soviet act of aggression against a nation that had sought to participate in the American plan for reconstructing Europe. Eight days later, General Lucius Clay, the American commander in West Berlin, cabled Washington that he detected a change in Soviet attitudes that might forebode an imminent outbreak of war. Later in March, State Department adviser John Foster Dulles expressed the fear of many Americans that "today there is hardly anyone in Europe or Asia who does not feel that if he asserts himself in a manner displeasing to the Soviet Communist Party, he will be, or shortly may be, liquidated." Dulles concluded that this Soviet "terror is having a tremendous effect upon the willingness of people to oppose Soviet penetration." The administration's worst fears about Europe and therefore European colonial areas seemed more realistic than ever.[10]

With anxieties increasing about European stability, Congress voted on March 31 to appropriate funds for the administration's European Recovery Program. France, England, and the Benelux countries signed the Brussels Treaty for mutual defense, with Under-Secretary of State Robert Lovett and Senator Arthur Vandenberg going right to work to lay the legislative groundwork for America's entry into what would become the North Atlantic Treaty Organization in 1949. And the Central Intelligence Agency provided large infusions of money and organizing skills to help defeat the Communist Party in the Italian elections in April. The most immediate threats to Western European security seemed to have been at least temporarily contained.[11]

II

In the context of intensifying American concern about Soviet and communist expansion in Europe and Asia, the surprising news reached Washington in late May that the Nationalists had defeated the United Party of Jan Smuts in the South African parliamentary elections. While the United Party won more popular votes than its opponents, the party of Daniel Malan, in alliance with the smaller Afrikaner Party, gained a majority of seats in the Union Parliament and would now form a new government. American observers in South Africa were startled. U.S. Minister Thomas Holcomb had predicted just six weeks earlier that growing fears among white South Africans about threats to world peace abroad were strengthening Smuts' hand, as he continued to symbolize international stability. The Nationalists, Holcomb had said in mid-April, were now accepting the "inevitability" of their defeat. Right up to the election, the American Legation remained certain that "General Smuts dominates the political life of the country." Given their assumption about "the general recognition [in South Africa] of General Smuts's pre-eminence as the last surviving architect of Union, a master politician and a world statesman," American diplomats in South Africa were shocked that the Prime Minister lost even his own seat in Parliament.[12]

Americans tended to identify with the generally affluent English-speaking and moderate Afrikaner South Africans represented by the United Party, and did not realize the extent to which the United Party had failed to champion a vision of South Africa's future that would have offered a robust alternative to that of the Nationalists. The Truman administration was surprised by the Nationalist Party's success in organizing enough of the Afrikaner majority of the white population—especially farmers, urban industrial workers, and Afrikaner cultural and economic institutions—to support its apartheid platform. Policymakers in Washington, like most foreign observers, generally failed to understand the extent of the domestic political damage suffered by Smuts as a result of his difficulties at the United Nations and the benefit to the more chauvinistic Nationalists of growing white resentment of international criticism of South African racial customs.[13]

The key to the Nationalist Party victory and the centerpiece of its campaign was the proposed policy of apartheid. The Nationalists successfully mobilized the racial fears and pride of South African whites who dreaded the growing African urban population and the resulting breaches in traditional South African segregation. Malan and his colleagues defined "apartheid"—a new Afrikaans word that had come into use only in the 1930s and that would be translated literally as "apart-ness"—as a separation of the races, a policy rooted in the experience of the established white population of South Africa and in "Christian principles of justice and reasonableness." Its aim was "the maintenance and protection of the European population of the country as a pure white race" and the preservation of "the indigenous racial groups as separate communities."[14]

The goal of apartheid contrasted sharply with the recommendations of the Smuts government's Native Laws Commission. Commonly known as the Fagan Commission, after its chairman, Justice Henry A. Fagan, this prestigious body spent two years studying the problems involved in African urbanization and produced a report made public by Smuts in March 1948. Among its many findings, the Fagan Commission's most important conclusion was that a permanent African urban population existed by this time in the Union and must be accepted; there was simply no way to relocate the huge number of settled Africans in urban areas, many of them resident there for several decades, to the woefully inadequate native reserves. The migration of Africans as well as poor whites to the cities over the previous two decades had been caused by the same industrial dislocation found in other developed countries and could not be reversed. Instead, the Fagan Commission reported, the South African government needed to take a more active role in mitigating the enormous social problems accompanying this demographic shift—problems that Alan Paton had touched on in his best-selling novel. The scholarly Commission report clearly indicated that the massive relocation of Africans to the native reserves implied in the theory of apartheid would be a wildly expensive and inhumane policy. In the fearful domain of white South African politics, however, the idea of racial re-segregation, carefully couched in appeals to Afrikaner pride, proved more powerful than the sober assessment of a commission appointed by the United Party government and more attractive than the moderate racial attitudes embodied in the United Party's second leading figure, Deputy Prime Minister Jan Hofmeyr.[15]

In addition to a commitment to return to the more clearly authoritarian race relations of an earlier era, the electoral victory of Malan and the Nationalists represented in some ways a final reversal of the outcome of the Boer War a half-century earlier. While downplaying its well-known desire for a South African republic independent of the British Commonwealth in order not to alienate English-speaking voters during the campaign, the Nationalist Party in 1948 clearly represented those in the Union who sought to diminish and ultimately to eliminate the special relationship of Britain and South Africa. In finally unifying a substantial majority of the long-divided Afrikaners with his calls for complete racial segregation, Malan also appealed to Afrikaner ethnic pride by seeking to halt the swift tide of English immigration into the Union since World War II. Resentful of the domination of South African economic and political life by their countrymen of English descent, Afrikaner nationalists feared the potentially liberal racial attitudes of English immigrants. Malan's new government soon moved to encourage immigration instead from the Netherlands and Germany. The anti-democratic tendencies of ascendant Afrikaner nationalism were clear in the loyalty owed by almost all of the Nationalist Party leaders to the powerful, Anglophobic Broederbond, the shadowy organization dedicated to creating an Afrikaner republic.[16]

In the decades since the establishment of the first Nationalist Party government, historians and other observers have not reached a consensus about the significance of the 1948 election in South Africa. Some have emphasized the continuities of basic content and direction in white racial policies between the preceding segregationist regimes and the subsequent apartheid governments. From this perspective, the foundations of apartheid were laid by earlier legislation and administration, while the Nationalist program after May 1948 had only to close loopholes in the system and tighten administrative control of more details of the lives of black South Africans. The essential goal remained, before and after 1948, the preservation of white minority rule by whatever means necessary.[17]

Other observers have focused attention on the innovations of the apartheid system, both the symbolic dismissal of the rhetoric of white "trusteeship" of supposedly inferior races and the substantive increase in actual oppression experienced by people of color in South Africa. Leo Kuper has described the implementation of apartheid as a carefully planned counter-revolution against the processes of urbanization and industrialization that were drawing South Africans of all races together into a common society. Leonard Thompson has argued that the 1948 election was the single most important political event accelerating the polarization between blacks and whites in South Africa and between South Africa and the rest of the world.[18] Regardless of differences in emphasis, however, there can be little doubt of the symbolic significance of Malan's victory in pointing South Africa toward a future different from the rest of the world's. After a visit to the Union a few years later, British journalist (and subsequently noted African historian) Basil Davidson concluded that "against the long slow crucifixion of the Africans in South Africa the battle of words and shaken fists between the 'English' and the Afrikaners of today can seem, to strangers, little better than a shoddy farce."[19]

While the extent to which the May 1948 election marked an epochal change in South African politics has remained uncertain, the contending white political parties clearly shared one piece of ideological ground that mattered greatly to the United States government: a strong antipathy for communism and the Soviet Union. The U.S. Legation in Pretoria had been assuring the State Department since the beginning of the year that any white government in South Africa would have to remain hostile to an ideology that explicitly challenged "the domination of a large colored population by a small European minority." The South African economy depended on a stable African labor force, reported U.S. Minister Holcomb, and no Union government would countenance efforts—by communists or anyone else—to organize black workers to gain more power. Holcomb registered his concern for "the admirable potentialities for agitation which South Africa's basically unhealthy race relations present," but policymakers in Washington were relieved by the assurances of South African loyalty to the cause of the West in the Cold War. American national security managers understood that South Africa's anticommunism would only be strengthened by a Nationalist Party electoral victory. Holcomb revealed the essence of official American attitudes when he noted in January 1948 that the solution needed for South Africa's racial problems was a course somewhere between "the two absurd extremes of complete segregation and complete equality." The victory of the proponents of apartheid in May, while representing the first of these apparently comparable "absurd extremes," at least did not threaten South Africa's international position in the Cold War.[20]

The news of the Nationalist victory nonetheless did cause some confusion and dismay within the educated American public and in Western Europe. Reports reached the State Department of concern in Norway and France, while the London Stock Exchange experienced an immediate near-panicked selling of South African industrial shares.[21] American newspapers and journals indicated the difficulty many Americans had in understanding how other "Westerners" who had so recently been allies of the United States in the war against Hitler could now freely elect pro-Nazi leaders. The *New York Times* mourned the defeat of Smuts, the "elder statesman of the world," and warned of the "totalitarian" inclinations of many of the new Nationalist Party leaders. *Time* saluted Smuts as "wise, venerable, [and] oak-solid," and regretted the "perverse, isolationist, acutely race-conscious road" now being taken by white South Africa in choosing a government to be led by the "myopic, paunchy" Malan. The general American preference for the relative racial moderateness of Smuts revealed a serious misunderstanding of the former Prime Minister's own record and his continuing commitment to unquestioned white supremacy in South Africa. But politically aware Americans were correct in believing that a South Africa ruled by explicitly racist Afrikaner nationalists could only weaken the prestige and credibility of the West in the international arena.[22]

The swiftness with which the Malan government released from prison those convicted of treasonous pro-Nazi activities during the war caused further consternation among American observers. In early July, *The New Republic* identified the serious danger posed by the Nationalists to the worldwide cause of democracy: the new South African rulers were openly interpreting the anticommunism of the Truman Doctrine as "justifying their own brand of extreme Nazi-type reaction."[23] Such an ally muddied the Manichaean view of the Cold War that the United States government was promoting. *The Nation* warned against the "sinister group of younger men" surrounding the elderly Malan who had proven during the war "how little they believe in democracy."[24] U.S. Minister Winship reported from Pretoria that while the Nationalist leaders would probably not act "impulsively or immediately" to attain their objectives of apartheid and independence from the Commonwealth, every act of the new government would nonetheless be "deliberately calculated to bring them closer" to fulfillment.[25]

In a July 1948 analysis of developments in South Africa, the State Department's Office of Intelligence Research brooded about the "Nazi-minded, anti-democratic elements whose influence will permeate the governmental structure." The report warned that "the traditions of the Afrikaans front are completely alien to Anglo-American democracy" and that "the dynamics of this Afrikaans brand of fascism" were already being felt in the administration of the country's affairs. Fortunately, concluded this generally grim intelligence analysis, South Africa's cooling military relationship with Britain would draw it closer to the United States, and the Union government's realization of South Africa's growing need for American capital and American trade goods "may be the most potent factor in tempering Nationalist extremism."[26]

III

The news of the Nationalist Party victory particularly worried the Truman administration's nuclear planners, who that spring faced an imminent shortage of their most crucial resource, uranium ore. Since the beginning of the Manhattan Project in 1942, the United States had received over 90 percent of its uranium from the Shinkolobwe mine in the Belgian Congo's Katanga Province. But U.S. Atomic Energy Commission chairman David Lilienthal and others feared dependence on Shinkolobwe, due to uncertainty about the extent of its supply. In a meeting just two days after the South African elections, the American members of the United States–United Kingdom Combined Policy Committee on the development of atomic energy agreed with their British counterparts that "by 1952 South Africa might be the principal source of uranium and negotiations should be undertaken now to procure the maximum amount" possible from the Union. Under-Secretary of State Robert Lovett concluded prophetically that the United States should "bear in mind the importance of South African uranium in all our future dealings with the Dominion."[27]

It would be difficult to overstate the importance of uranium to the United States in 1948. Concerned with America's leading role in the developing Western military alliance and faced with what it believed to be hostile Soviet aggression in the heart of Europe, the Truman administration found itself increasingly dependent on nuclear weapons for the defense of Western Europe and other American interests. The National Security Council (NSC) concluded in September that the security of Western Europe, "without which there can be no European economic recovery and little hope for a future peaceful and stable world," rested on exclusive American possession of atomic weapons, which provided "the present major counterbalance to the ever-present threat of . . . Soviet military power." Since the rapid demobilization of American troops at the end of World War II, political and military analysts in Washington had assumed that Western ground forces were vastly outnumbered by those of the Eastern bloc. The Soviets had not yet deployed an atomic weapon, however, and the developing American nuclear arsenal was expected to provide the crucial deterrent to communist expansion.[28]

Unfortunately for the Truman administration, supplies of uranium ore were believed in 1948 to be extremely limited. General Leslie Groves, the commander of the Manhattan Project, had warned Under-Secretary of State Dean Acheson about this two years earlier when he emphasized that there "are not sufficient foreseeable reserves of high grade raw material to satisfy . . . our own requirements for the next three or four years."[29] Acheson had relayed the message in May 1947 to the Joint Congressional Committee on Atomic Energy, explaining that it was "necessary to control as far as possible all the ore indispensable to the process [of building nuclear weapons] and also to insure a continued supply from abroad." Acheson had reminded the Committee of the almost complete dependence of the United States on uranium imported from southern Africa.[30] For the still small number of weapons in the American nuclear arsenal to grow, the supply of uranium had to increase.[31] Conversely, in order to hinder the anticipated Soviet effort to develop an atomic bomb and thereby maintain the American monopoly on nuclear deterrence, "the cardinal principle [of U.S. policy] . . . has been to increase our raw materials position and to deprive the Soviets of supplies from outside the USSR," the National Security Council reported to Truman.[32] The Atomic Energy Commission announced new financial incentives in the spring of 1948 for increased uranium ore production on the Colorado plateau, but domestic sources by the end of the year were still only providing five percent of the total supply of the United States government.[33]

Under-Secretary of State Lovett, Acheson's successor as Marshall's chief of staff, informed the Joint Congressional Committee on 21 January 1948 of a new diplomatic arrangement that would dramatically increase the American share of ore from the Belgian Congo. The earlier Tripartite Agreement of 1944 had assigned almost all of the ore produced in the Congo to the United States, which had been doing the bulk of atomic development work during the war. That arrangement had given way in May 1946 to a temporary formula apportioning equal shares to the British and the Americans. By the fall of 1947, American supplies of uranium had fallen low enough to restrict seriously the production of weapons, while Britain's much smaller need for the ore due to its less developed nuclear production capacity meant that much of its allotment was simply being stockpiled. Congressional leaders were dismayed to learn of this situation and added their voices to the demands of the administration's nuclear planners for renegotiation with the British. During the talks that took place in December 1947, American delegates managed to persuade their British counterparts to make substantial concessions, in part, apparently, because of the threat that Congress might not fund the European Recovery Plan otherwise. Accordingly, the new, more favorable "modus vivendi" Lovett was reporting in January 1948 allocated all Congolese ore to be mined in 1948 and 1949 again to the United States, and granted Washington access as well to any unused stockpiles of ore in the United Kingdom.[34]

The central role of Congolese uranium in American national security policy kept the Truman administration acutely interested in what it saw as the remote interior of the southern end of the African continent. From Washington's perspective, threats to the stability of the area abounded. First, African residents and workers of the Belgian Congo might seek greater self-government rather than continuing to accept white colonial rule. Poorly paid miners living in extremely unhealthy conditions in the Katanga Province were in fact attempting to organize themselves for collective bargaining, and had already gone out on strike in 1941 and 1946.

But white policymakers from a racially segregated society tended to discount initiatives by black workers, especially in the distant interior of Africa. In 1946, General Groves had assured Secretary of State Byrnes that such a development "indicated attempts by Communist-inspired elements to infiltrate" the area. Groves' insistence on using quotations for the term "organize" in reference to Congolese workers suggested his distaste for the very idea of an African union. Regardless of who was responsible for the growing economic and social unrest in the area, however, the general believed it could only imperil the "flow of strategic materials now needed for U.S. production and stockpiling purposes."[35]

More dangerous to the Shinkolobwe area than internal subversion was a second possible threat: a direct Soviet attack on the mine. As early as the September 1945 London Conference of Foreign Ministers, Byrnes expressed certainty that Soviet delegate Vyacheslav Molotov's interest in a Soviet trusteeship for the former Italian colonies of North Africa represented a desire for access not to the Mediterranean but rather to "the uranium of the Belgian Congo."[36] British Foreign Minister Ernest Bevin agreed with Byrnes. When Molotov chose to poke fun at this concern, joking that "if you won't give us one of the Italian colonies, we should be quite content to have the Belgian Congo," neither of the Western statesmen had been amused.[37]

With American fears of direct military conflict with the Soviet Union growing in early 1948, the State Department's atomic energy specialist warned that "it is obvious that the Congo is a prime objective of airborne operations in wartime, and that we are not necessarily in the most advantageous position in this respect."[38] As plans for the United States to join the Brussels Treaty nations in a mutual defense arrangement developed during the rest of 1948, the Truman administration avoided formally endorsing European colonialism by refusing to give a specific military guarantee to any African territory, to the disappointment of Belgian Prime Minister Paul-Henri Spaak.[39] But Lovett made it clear to the Belgian government in December that it was nonetheless "obvious and self-evident [that] our interest in [the] Congo makes its security of utmost importance in US strategic thinking."[40] In fact, as the head of the State Department's Division of Western European Affairs remarked after consulting with top U.S. military officials, "the great interest of the United States in the integrity of the Belgian Congo . . . [is] self-evident and . . . far more fundamental than any specific assurances."[41] Another senior official in the State Department later acknowledged that "the defense of the Congo was foremost in the mind of the U.S. military establishment."[42]

The people of Belgium constituted a third threat to continued American access to uranium from Shinkolobwe. Although specific arrangements of the 1944 Tripartite Agreement and the 1946 adjustment of it had not been made public, it was widely known in Belgium that the entire uranium production of the Congo was sold to the United States and the United Kingdom.[43] Demands were increasing in the Belgian press and the left wing of the Cabinet to know the details of the sale of such an extraordinarily valuable national resource, and the Spaak government wanted to relieve this political pressure.[44] But the Truman administration leaned heavily on Spaak not to reveal any specifics of the agreement. Marshall emphasized in March 1948 that such a disclosure "would at the least stimulate speculation as to amounts and tempo of individual ore shipments, our degree of dependence on the Congo, and the relation of the Congo to the over-all procurement program." The Soviets might get a clearer sense of American bomb production rates and use the information as propaganda intending to show that the United States was supporting European economic recovery in order to guarantee the delivery of uranium.[45] Even more problematic, as Acheson had pointed out earlier, was the likelihood of the Soviets' manipulating such information at the United Nations "to bolster a charge of bad faith and unilateral self-serving, at the same time that we are ostensibly trying to promote multilateral control of atomic energy."[46]

A final threat to the "very satisfactory relations" Washington had worked out with the private management of the Shinkolobwe mine lay in the possibility that publication of the terms of the Tripartite Agreement might create irresistible public pressure on Spaak in Belgium to nationalize the mines. According to Acheson, the Belgian government had in fact already been forced in 1947 to announce that it would do so, and had established a small atomic energy research program in Belgium. American nuclear planners believed that such an action could be disastrous for the American uranium procurement program as it would end the American monopoly on Congolese ore production.[47]

Faced with uncertainty about the productivity and security of its Congolese uranium source at the same time that rising Cold War tensions in Europe were highlighting American dependence on its limited nuclear arsenal, the Truman administration sought other sources of the crucial metal with intensifying concern in early 1948. Groves had known since 1945 that South Africa possessed sixty percent of the world's significant deposits of lower-grade uranium ore that could be profitably developed in the near future. Lovett was concerned that South Africa's economic stability gave the United States "very little leverage that we could apply . . . through credits or the Marshall Plan or other means" to guarantee American access to South African ore.[48] Similarly, Lilienthal and others worried about Britain's apparent desire to control unilaterally all uranium sources within the Commonwealth.[49] But preliminary discussions with South African representatives convinced Washington that the Union wished to sell its potential ore production to the Combined Development Trust (CDT) of both the United States and Great Britain, as it would be in South Africa's political and strategic interest to do so. Prime Minister Smuts had demonstrated his loyalty to the developing Western alliance by facilitating the establishment of a pilot leaching plant for uranium in the Union at the end of 1947. South Africa's primary concern seemed to be with the cost of developing its uranium production capability and therefore getting an Anglo-American guarantee to buy, over the long run, however much ore could be mined.[50]

Negotiations began in earnest in June 1948 between the Combined Development Agency (CDA, successor to the CDT) and representatives of the South African government and mining industry. Working from the assumption that further successful research into extractive techniques would allow actual production to begin by 1952, they agreed on a tentative formula for a contract: the Americans and the British would buy ten thousand tons of high grade uranium concentrate at a price guaranteeing a worthwhile profit for the South African mine owners. The Truman administration sought a purely commercial contract with the South Africans as suppliers, hoping to discourage any interest of the Union government in joining the CDA, taking part in atomic research, or stockpiling uranium itself. Lovett admitted, however, that the great need of the United States for what South Africa could offer meant that Washington might have to agree to some or even all of these possible conditions if South Africa insisted on them.[51]

Surprised by the election results of May 26, the State Department was at first uncertain what impact the new South African government might have on the concurrent CDA efforts to buy uranium from the Union. Lovett wrote Senator Bourke Hickenlooper, the chairman of the Joint Congressional Committee on Atomic Energy, on June 16 to suggest that Malan's coalition government did not have strong support in South Africa and that there was no reason for the new Prime Minister to differ from his predecessor on uranium policy. The Under-Secretary of State argued that Malan's nationalistic rhetoric about withdrawing South Africa from the British Commonwealth would in practice be neutralized by his even more violent anticommunism, leaving the Union solidly in the Western camp. There seemed little danger to American interests in the southern African region from the new government in Pretoria.[52]

In response to Lovett's request for a full appraisal of the new government, the new U.S. Minister in South Africa, North Winship—a career diplomat from segregated Macon, Georgia, who maintained a home and a membership in the all-white Idle Hour Country Club there—cabled the State Department two weeks after the election to report that the Union under a Nationalist government would most likely draw even closer to the United States. Winship did note certain trouble spots, such as probable restrictions on imports from the United States, a more rigid approach to the problem of South West Africa, and a less friendly attitude toward Commonwealth concerns. Similarly, traditional South African collaboration with Britain on such defense concerns as naval maneuvers and officer training might decrease in frequency and friendliness. But any loss for the British would probably be a gain for the United States, Winship observed, given the Nationalists' fierce hatred of communism and the Soviet Union. The new South African government ea-

gerly desired American capital as a balance to substantial British investment in the Union, and seemed likely to pursue closer military cooperation
with the United States as a substitute for close defense ties with Britain.
In sum, concluded Winship, South African relations with the United
States "may be expected to become even closer" because of the Nationalists' concerns about defense and economic development.[53]

IV

The Truman administration recognized that a Nationalist government in
the Union represented little threat to the substantial economic and strategic ties binding the United States and South Africa closely together by
1948. As a liberal South African weekly had noted at the end of the war,
the Nationalist Party had positioned itself as "the most capitalistic of all
the political movements in South Africa."[54] The Nationalists were eager
for American manufactured goods and capital to continue replacing those
of Great Britain, a process already well under way in the first two years
after World War II. In 1947, the United States had surpassed Britain as
the leading supplier of South African imports. The American share of
the Union market continued to expand in 1948, especially after the South
African government terminated the previous arrangement under which it
had sold a fixed quantity of its annual gold production to the Bank of
England. This move unleashed a huge South African appetite for imports
from the dollar area, and the total value of American goods entering the
Union soared to a postwar high of $492 million for 1948. This repre-
sented about four percent of all American exports, a remarkable share for
a country with only two and a half million (white) customers wealthy
enough to consider buying imported goods. This small but prosperous
minority now made South Africa the eighth-largest customer for exported American goods and provided a particularly attractive market because of the country's ability to pay for everything in the hardest of cur-
rencies: gold.[55]

   While U.S.–South African trade was expanding, American investments in the Union's booming industrial economy also continued to grow
throughout the postwar years. Within weeks of the Nationalist victory at
the polls, *Newsweek* surveyed the South African scene and declared that
Malan's government was unlikely to take any steps that might frighten
off foreign capital, especially from the United States or England. South
Africa, concluded the magazine's business editors admiringly, was "like
the America of half a century ago, when men with money to invest wed-
ded a virgin land to virile capital and produced a new empire of mines,
railroads, great factories, and booming cities."[56] Assuring potential
American investors a few years later that "capitalism and individualism
are basic economic tenets in South Africa," the U.S. Commerce Department emphasized the long record of South African governments' encouraging industrial and commercial development.[57] Despite its rhetorical na-

tionalism, the Malan regime quickly proved that it would not alter its predecessors' policy of freely permitting the repatriation of foreign capital as well as the unhindered transfer of dividends and interest.[58] The Central Intelligence Agency agreed with the Commerce Department that the profitability of the South African economy was "based on the exploitation of cheap non-European labor," guaranteed by the South African government's refusal to acknowledge nonwhite unions or to allow black workers to strike.[59] The high rate of return on investments in the Union was suggested by the doubling in value of direct private American investments between 1943 and 1949, and again between 1949 and 1952. American-owned assets in South Africa were worth well over $200 million by the end of the Truman administration.[60]

Growing American investments in the Union, substantial as they were by 1948, represented only a small portion—approximately 1 percent—of American capital invested abroad during the Truman years. But those investments were crucial for South African economic stability and growth as the country set forth on the path of apartheid. Noting the Union's sharply increasing capital requirements during the 1940s, the Commerce Department made it clear that "there is no lack of awareness on the part of the South African Government and private industry that the country must depend heavily on external sources on a continuing basis, if its development is to proceed according to current hopes and plans." The predominance of American economic power in the postwar years joined with the anti-British orientation of the Malan government to challenge South Africa's traditional dependence on British investment and encourage the penetration of American capital.[61]

Several strategic considerations also provided strands of the web of common interests between South Africa and the United States in 1948. World War II had depleted some of the most accessible reserves in the United States of certain minerals crucial for sophisticated military hardware, forcing the Truman administration to look abroad for additional supplies.[62] The State Department in June 1948 emphasized the importance of southern Africa for the American effort at stockpiling strategic materials, and urged that greater American attention be paid to the improvement of transportation facilities in the area in order to "produce the quickest results in terms of an immediate increase in the flow of materials."[63] The CIA warned in September that the movement of colonial areas toward freedom from their European overlords "deprives the US itself of an assured access to bases and raw materials in many of these areas." This was especially dangerous, noted the Agency, "in view of global US strategic needs and growing dependence on foreign mineral resources."[64] In addition to the all important uranium reserves it was poised to begin exploiting in 1948, South Africa was already exporting to the United States a substantial percentage of American requirements for such key minerals as chrome and manganese. Declining American stocks of manganese for steel production were causing particular consternation by the end of the year for Under-Secretary of State Lovett and other top officials in the administration, who began to make "strenuous efforts" to encourage greater production of the ore in South Africa for export to the United States.[65] In its November 1948 summary of U.S. policy toward the Union, the State Department emphasized the need to promote "the development of her natural resources, especially those which are important to our program for stockpiling strategic materials."[66]

Despite its overriding concern with the defense of Western Europe, the Truman administration also recognized the geopolitical importance of South Africa. The Western Hemisphere, the Middle East, and the Far East rated higher on Washington's priority list of areas to defend in 1948, but that ranking reflected the absence of significant Soviet or communist influence in Africa more than a lack of interest in the protection of the Union.[67] There was little doubt among American policymakers that the United Kingdom was "our staunchest and most valuable ally in all quarters of the world" and that the "Commonwealth taken together is our strongest and most dependable" partner.[68] South Africa's financial importance to Great Britain remained considerable. The deputy director of the Policy Planning Staff noted a few years later the strong attachment of the British Commonwealth countries, with the exception of India, to the Western alliance in the Cold War and the heavy reliance the United States would place on them in the event of a Soviet invasion of the Middle East or Western Europe. "Any division between us and the members of the British Commonwealth," he concluded, "would be a great disadvantage to us in deterring the Soviet Union or in combatting it."[69]

The electoral success of the Nationalist Party in May 1948 did fuel certain long-standing anxieties in England, however, and the Truman administration tended to share those concerns. The related problems of South African racial policies and the Union government's desire to expand its influence throughout southern Africa gained particular notice in London and Washington. The explicit racism of the Malan government clearly would not help the leaders of the "free world" in their political contest with the rhetorically antiracist Soviet Union for the allegiance of the peoples of the Third World. The State Department had been concerned since World War II about South Africa's policy of spreading its economic and political influence as far north as possible. The British government hoped to contain South African influence in the surrounding region because of Britain's responsibility for the High Commission territories and the central African colonies and its desire for the development of less confrontational race relations there. The apartheid plans of the newly elected Afrikaner nationalists seemed destined, especially if pushed aggressively northwards, to provoke an eventual race war on the African continent.[70]

But these long-range concerns about the direction of South African society and politics were outweighed by the strategic, military, and political importance of the Union for the United States and Great Britain.

American worries about possible South African import restrictions on goods from the United States were mitigated by the recognition that the Union government, in the interest of the country's economic stability, had to act in some way to correct its large imbalance of trade with the United States.[71] The continuing dependence of the South African Defense Forces on the British for equipment and technical training and Malan's interest in joining the developing North Atlantic military alliance assuaged most fears in Washington about Afrikaner hostility toward Britain. The Truman administration wanted above all to avoid a South Africa isolated by narrow nationalism. By the end of 1948, the clear policy of the United States government was to encourage the Union to remain active in Commonwealth defense efforts, to develop its strategic resources, to enlarge its economic ties with American companies, and to continue providing its political support to the Western bloc at the United Nations.[72]

V

The Truman administration had another important consideration in mind as it reaffirmed its policy of support for the existing governments of segregated South Africa and the neighboring colonial areas of southern Africa in 1948. Like the Belgians in the Congo and the British in the Rhodesias, Nyasaland, and the High Commission territories, the Portuguese maintained control of their imperial holdings in Angola and Mozambique. Unlike Great Britain and Belgium, however, Portugal had not had its economy decimated by World War II and was not as dependent on American aid through the European Recovery Program.[73] The key common concern of Lisbon and Washington was military defense against possible Soviet aggression, and more specifically the strategic Lagens airfield on the Atlantic island of Terceira in the Azores.

World War II had demonstrated the importance of American access to the Azores in the event of another war in Europe. A series of temporary extensions of the original November 1944 agreement with Portugal allowed American and British forces to continue using the air base long after the end of the war. As the Joint Chiefs of Staff contemplated a possible sparking of the Cold War into an armed clash in Europe in late 1947, they ranked the Azores as one of only seven military bases worldwide that were "required" for the national security of the United States. The National Security Council identified the islands as "the most vital single spot in the world" other than the war zone or the United States itself as a base for staging combat aircraft in any future conflict in Europe. The State Department negotiated with the Salazar government throughout the second half of 1947, finally reaching agreement on 2 February 1948 for a five-year continuation of American access to the Lagens Airport. Within fifteen months the Joint Chiefs were urgently demanding that American diplomats also get Portuguese approval for an expansion of American facilities at Lagens.[74]

There was, of course, a price for the United States government to renew this immensely valuable contract in 1948. A particular sticking point in the negotiations had been the Salazar government's sensitivity about having foreign troops on what it considered Portuguese soil. The Truman administration assuaged this concern by selling American supplies to Portugal at "an extremely favorable price," providing economic aid through the Marshall Plan, and continuing its tacit support for Lisbon's authority throughout the Portuguese Empire, meaning primarily Angola and Mozambique.[75] Truman had been notified upon his accession to the presidency of Roosevelt's "quid pro quo" agreement of 1944 with Salazar to respect Portuguese sovereignty in its overseas empire in return for American access to the Azores. In 1946, U.S. Ambassador Herman Baruch in Lisbon reminded Secretary of State Byrnes that although Washington could not explicitly support European colonialism by formally guaranteeing the integrity of the Portuguese Empire, the United States government should continue its traditional respect for Portuguese authority in all its overseas territories. A 1946 arrangement between Portugal and the United States for joint activities at Portuguese air bases in the Atlantic "further strengthens this policy and further cements the ties between the Portuguese and the Americans," the ambassador concluded. With the renewed agreement of February 1948, American assent to Portuguese colonialism guaranteed access to the Azores for the rest of the Truman administration's tenure in office.[76]

Like allying itself with the evangelically racist South African government and the traditionally imperialist British Crown, Washington's choice to tie itself even informally to the Portuguese government would prove a substantial liability in the Cold War struggle for the allegiance of non-Western peoples. This policy also dismayed reform forces within Portugal who hoped for Western pressure on the authoritarian Salazar regime to augment their own efforts to move their country away from its strong association with the ideologies of the defeated Axis powers.[77] The irony of the foremost nation of the "free world" allying itself with the unapologetic dictatorship and colonialism of the Portuguese government seemed not to trouble leading policymakers in the Truman administration. George Kennan admired the "deeply religious" Salazar as "one of the most able men in Europe and a man of high moral principle" and had assured him during the war that the United States did not consider him a fascist. By 1951, Kennan would speak of Salazar as "an old friend" whom he enjoyed seeing in a personal capacity.[78] Dean Acheson remembered Salazar's "delightful" company and feeling "drawn to him as rarely [to anyone] on first meeting." Acheson admitted that "political liberty, in the modern British and American sense, does not exist in Portugal and . . . would probably be incompatible with the economic stability and growth" he attributed to Salazar's leadership. Calling on one of the highest of traditional Western authorities, Acheson concluded that "a convinced libertarian—particularly a foreign one—could understandably disapprove of Salazar. But I doubt that Plato would have done so."[79]

American officials engaged in what they understood as mortal combat with the varied forces of worldwide communism valued above all the Salazar regime's profound antipathy to all politics of the left. The Soviet Union's veto of Portugal's application to join the United Nations, which the United States championed, represented to the Truman administration a seal of ideological soundness for the small Iberian country. The absence of a visible, organized African challenge to Portuguese rule in Mozambique and Angola allowed the United States government not to let the character of its ally in Lisbon affect Portuguese-American relations during the Truman years.[80] U.S. Ambassador Lincoln MacVeagh in Lisbon admitted in a cable to Marshall in November 1948, however, that the rule of "the commercial and banking classes . . . renders Portugal today essentially a fascist state, fearful of the advances of communism and trusting to the power of the United States for protection if necessary."[81] The Central Intelligence Agency confirmed this two months later, noting that "Portugal is under a closely controlled dictatorship" in which "all phases of the economy are closely controlled by the government."[82] The Truman administration harbored no illusions that this was a free-market, capitalist democracy that would promote progressive colonial development policies in southern Africa.[83]

VI

The political problems inherent in supporting the status quo powers in southern Africa in the postwar years continued to be highlighted at the annual fall sessions of the United Nations General Assembly. At one meeting of the American delegation in early October 1948, the discussion hinted at the troubling relationship between anticommunism and racism in the region. Delegates John Foster Dulles and Francis Sayre reported on a prior conference with representatives of the new South African government, in which the Nationalists had indicated their desire to "cut off all relations with the United Nations" because of the Soviet Union's "considerable influence" in that body as well as among the Indian and African populations of South Africa and South West Africa. Even such a devoted anticommunist as Dulles thought this would be going too far, although he was certainly not troubled by the intensity of the South Africans' hostility to the Soviets. On the other hand, fellow delegate Eleanor Roosevelt recalled another, earlier discussion in which the South African representative, referring to the proposed U.N. Declaration of Human Rights, "had made it clear that . . . [the Union government] believed a government had the right to discriminate in any way against any part of its population."[84] Because American opposition to communism and the Soviet Union was based on supposed support for democracy and freedom, explicit racial oppression by governments tied to the United States would suggest at least a contradiction, if not outright hypocrisy, on Washington's part.

The architects of apartheid in Pretoria were not about to help the Truman administration resolve this dilemma. Anticommunism and white supremacy were inseparable in the minds of the Nationalists. The State Department reported in November that the United States could depend on "a sympathetic reception in South Africa of our firm opposition to Soviet expansionism and Communist fifth-columns." But it was also clear that "South Africa has become increasingly aware of the dangers which Communist propaganda presents to the maintenance of its social structure[,] based as it is on the dominance of a large colored population by a small white minority."[85] Afrikaner nationalists were moving toward defining all who opposed absolute white supremacy in the Union as "communists."

That it was communist rather than capitalist or Western propaganda that threatened white power in the Union by supporting majority rule did not go unnoticed in the Third World. The Central Intelligence Agency emphasized in September the danger of the newly liberated and still "dependent" colonial areas' siding with the Soviet Union. This could happen, noted the Agency, in response to the American alliance with European imperial nations and the threat of American economic power keeping the new nations of the Southern Hemisphere economically dependent on the industrialized West. The Soviet commitment to an "assimilative racial policy," concluded the intelligence gatherers, contrasted starkly with the traditional Anglo-American color bar: American "treatment of its Negroes, powerfully played up by Soviet propaganda, embarrasses the US on this issue. Racial restrictions in areas like South Africa and Australia also arouse colonial resentment."[86] From the perspective of the nonwhite majority of the world's population, white racism seemed as much a part of the Western alliance as anticommunism.[87]

In anticipation of the November presidential election in the United States, Truman in 1948 was staking out a domestic political position increasingly, if haltingly, in favor of civil rights for black Americans, and at the same time escalating his opposition to communism.[88] His administration was therefore uncomfortable at home as well as abroad with having racial segregation in the United States be equated with South African racial policies. The State Department urged that American diplomats in the Union "avoid being drawn directly into discussion of South Africa's racial problems," as South Africans did not hesitate to point out their common ground with the United States on this matter. Whenever this happened, the U.S. Legation there should "rebut . . . the distortions and exaggerations which are often featured in foreign comment on this subject."[89] Washington thus found itself denying parallels between nascent South African apartheid and traditional American racial discrimination to its allies in the Union as well as to its critics in the colonial world, the Soviet bloc, and the United States.[90]

Writing to American diplomats in July 1948, Secretary of State George Marshall had underlined the importance of this struggle for the political identity of the United States in the eyes of the developing world. One of the "false or distorted stereotypes concerning the U.S. which are widely held among the people of third [unaligned] countries" and that the United States needed to correct, the Secretary emphasized, was the "belief that American democratic principles are loudly proclaimed as a cloak for undemocratic practices and for the purpose of concealing wide-spread racial and economic discriminations and extensive concentration of political and economic power in the hands of the few." Marshall admitted that the people of decolonizing areas were not much impressed with "pretensions of the righteousness of U.S. aims or the sincerity of U.S. motives" unless they had specific evidence of common interests with the United States.[91] But Marshall's address at the U.N. General Assembly two months later showed that "loud proclamation" of American principles would continue nonetheless, as he excoriated "governments which systematically disregard the rights of their own people."[92] Segregation in the United States and in the colonial world and apartheid in South Africa made such accusations against the Eastern bloc suspect in the minds of those less preoccupied with communism.

The election of a Nationalist government and its initial efforts at implementing apartheid heightened tensions between South Africa and the United Nations and placed the United States in an increasingly awkward position. On one hand, the Truman administration wished to moderate criticisms of the Union in order to encourage it to continue making annual reports on its administration of South West Africa and discourage it from simply annexing the territory. American policymakers were particularly concerned to prevent such a strongly anticommunist nation from withdrawing from the United Nations into international isolation. On the other hand, Washington needed to avoid appearing to be the defender of South Africa and its racial policies against the majority of the General Assembly, especially in light of continuing discrimination and violence against blacks and other people of color in the United States.[93] The strong views held by the great majority of United Nations members on "race discrimination and the exploitation of colonial areas," as the CIA phrased it, made this dilemma especially acute. The American delegation therefore took the position that South Africa was under "a moral but not a legal obligation" to submit a trusteeship agreement for South West Africa, and the U.S. representatives helped persuade other member nations merely to repeat in 1948 the resolutions of previous years asking South Africa to place the territory under U.N. trusteeship. American spokespersons continued working to restrain international criticism of the apartheid state.[94]

VII

In its effort to separate anticommunism from racism in the eyes of the world, the Truman administration did not welcome the rise of apartheid in a nation of the British Commonwealth. Maintaining a credible alliance of the "free world" in the Cold War depended to a large extent on the West's willingness to demonstrate that it was moving towards greater racial equality at home and self-government in its colonies.[95] Truman built his own campaign strategy in the 1948 presidential race on the twin principles of anticommunism and liberalism, which meant support for civil rights in addition to toughness against the Soviet Union. Responding in part to third-party candidate Henry Wallace's appeals to black and liberal voters, symbolized by his refusal to address segregated audiences in the South, Truman followed Clark Clifford's advice to move to the left rather than the right in the campaign. Truman became the first American President to advocate a full-scale civil rights program when he sent recommendations for legislation banning racial discrimination to Congress on February 2. The Democratic Party included a strong civil rights plank in its campaign platform a few months later, even at the cost of many of its Southern white members' revolting and supporting their own segregationist candidate, Strom Thurmond. Truman signed executive orders on July 26 that banned racial discrimination in federal employment and the armed services, and he became the first American President to campaign in Harlem. While in some ways more symbolic than substantive, Truman's actions nevertheless signified a marked shift in governmental support for the principle of racial equality.[96] His narrow electoral victory on November 2 resulted in part from strong black support, especially in the North and West where African Americans could generally vote.[97] The electoral results in the two countries in 1948 suggested that, at least in terms of racial attitudes and policies, the United States and South Africa were moving in opposite directions.[98]

The day before the American election, the State Department issued a policy statement on South Africa acknowledging that the apartheid state was, as the Central Intelligence Agency would delicately put it a few months later, "something of a propaganda liability to the US and the Western bloc." Noting that Africans made up eighty percent of the country's population but had no political representation, the Department emphasized that the "role of the native" was the key issue affecting essentially every aspect of life in the Union.[99] In its first several months in office, the Malan government had made it clear that "it would chip away at the [few] rights of the Natives and Colored[s] at every opportunity," reported U.S. Minister Winship from Pretoria; the Dutch Reformed Church (sometimes referred to by those outside it as "the Nationalist Party at prayer") meanwhile publicly blamed growing racial unrest in South Africa on miscegenation rather than segregation. The ruthlessness of the Malan government toward nonwhite South Africans made Winship worry that its readiness to silence dissent might eventually jump over the color line and "infringe on the rights of the 'unsympathetic' European."[100] In November, *The Christian Century* commented in dismay on the "racial witches' brew" the Malan government was heating up "to the boiling point" by its actions to further weaken the position of nonwhites in the Union: eliminating Africans from the national unemployment insurance act, disenfranchising Indian citizens, extending segregation regulations on the railroads in the traditionally more liberal Cape region, and preparing to eliminate even indirect African representation in the South African Parliament.[101] Whitney Shepardson returned from a visit to the Union and reported to the influential Council on Foreign Relations in New York on October 25 that with the absolute control of the country's wealth by whites and the desperate poverty of its much larger black population, "the political situation in the Union of South Africa is not good, and there is little prospect of its getting better in the near future."[102]

The Truman administration and other Americans worried that the Malan government's harsher enforcement of existing racial restrictions and creation of new ones might destabilize South Africa by radicalizing its black majority.[103] For the first time in the Union's history, a member of the Communist Party, Sam Kahn, was elected by a large majority to the South African Parliament in November as one of the three representatives for the country's Africans.[104] The Central Intelligence Agency acknowledged that "the genuineness of many of the native grievances provides an excellent opportunity for Communist agitation."[105] *The Christian Century* warned that the real danger of South Africa's new racial laws was their potential for transforming the entire African continent into "a happy hunting ground for Communist missionaries." The magazine suggested what was perhaps the worst nightmare for racially liberal, anticommunist Americans: "If the revolt of the blacks is stirred up by the Communists, then these South African white racialists will welcome the chance to make the preservation of white supremacy the great issue on which to appeal for a world anti-Communist crusade."[106] Such a conflation of racism and anticommunism might threaten the very foundation of the Western cause in the Cold War.

Other aspects of the Malan government's policies also troubled the Truman administration. The Nationalists' restrictions on immigration from England in order to maintain an Afrikaner majority in the white population might slow the country's economic development by excluding needed skilled workers. Increased economic repression of the African majority would restrict the growth of South Africa's domestic market and thereby hinder continued industrialization and limit the importation of American goods.[107] Rumors of possible import restrictions created fears in Washington about South Africa's commitment to liberal trading principles. Having freed itself in January from its previous arrangement for shipping gold to Great Britain, the Union sent 100 percent of its gold output in

1948 to the United States to pay for its skyrocketing imports of American goods. But South African industry and mining still depended heavily on British capital. Fearing that London might retaliate for the dramatic drop in its gold imports by restricting capital outflow to the Union, the Malan government moved in early November to re-establish a baseline of gold exports to England by limiting imports from the United States.[108]

The importance of South Africa as an ally in the increasingly volatile atmosphere of the Cold War nonetheless heavily outweighed these concerns. The Malan government could not properly be blamed for economic nationalism when all parties in the Union assumed that some kind of import restrictions were needed to stem the torrent of gold flowing to the United States and restore the country's hard currency reserves.[109] The Central Intelligence Agency admitted two years later that the trade restrictions not only helped remedy South Africa's international payments deficit, they "also tended to give the country a better balanced industrial complex which would make it more useful to the US and UK in time of war."[110] Late in 1948, the apartheid regime further ingratiated itself with American national security managers by confirming its close military cooperation with the Western powers. The Malan government decided to restore the traditional Union policies of sending South African officers to British war colleges and using British instructors in the South African Defense Forces. It allowed the South African Navy to continue participating in British fleet maneuvers in the South Atlantic. It repeatedly indicated to Washington its strong interest in joining the emerging North Atlantic Treaty Organization, an idea that the United States gently declined but appreciated. Finally, South Africa earned itself particular credit in Washington and London by sending sixty airmen to help with the massive airlift of supplies into beleaguered West Berlin. Whatever problems the Nationalists might have had with British influence in South Africa did not lessen the compatibility of their anticommunist foreign policy goals with those of the major Western powers.[111]

The Truman administration was encouraged by these signs that the new government in South Africa might not retreat into the isolation suggested by its nationalist and racial rhetoric. American policymakers remained wary of the Nationalists' sympathy for fascism, including their pardon on Christmas Eve in 1948 of the last prisoner in the Union convicted of treason for his work on behalf of the Nazis. Similarly, American officials in segregated Washington continued to indicate some concern about the detailed attention American segregation and racial incidents in the United States received in the South African press—in stories with titles like "Apartheid—American Style"—especially in light of the Universal Declaration of Human Rights passed by the U.N. General Assembly in December.[112] But the Truman administration noted carefully the Union's wealth of gold and strategic minerals, rapidly industrializing economy, expanding trade with the United States, strategic location on the sea lanes around the Cape of Good Hope, dominant position in the southern African region, historic ties to Great Britain and the Commonwealth, and zealous anticommunism. Impressed by what the State Department emphasized as the Union's "relatively large white population," American policymakers considered above all South Africa's expected status within a few years as the world's leading producer of uranium ore. On November 24, with his own election safely behind him, Truman approved the elevation of the South African and American legations to the status of embassies. In the international atmosphere of impending crisis in 1949 and 1950, the bonds between Washington and the new apartheid government in Pretoria would grow closer still.[113]

CHAPTER 6

Rising Tensions in South Africa and the Cold War: 1949

Writing in the January 1949 issue of the influential American journal *Foreign Affairs,* Max Beloff underlined the importance of progressive domestic reform in the United States as a means of counteracting the egalitarian ideological appeal of the Soviet Union in the colonial world. "If one agrees that in the long run events in Asia and Africa will be as decisive as those in Europe are proving in the short run," noted Beloff, "then to the preaching and practice of political democracy and social justice must be added that of racial equality." He argued that continuing racial discrimination was far too costly in the new world of the Cold War, even if immediate independence should perhaps not be granted to "dependent" areas that were still too weak to resist communist expansion on their own. Beloff concluded that for the West to succeed in the Cold War struggle for the loyalty of the world's nonwhite majority, "it must be admitted as a principle of action that no opportunities of social or political development shall be denied anywhere in the world on grounds of race alone."[1]

Truman's strategy and platform in the 1948 presidential campaign had demonstrated his belief that an improvement in civil rights protections in the United States fit with the nation's new status as the leading proponent of noncommunist freedom and democracy. Britain's willingness to grant independence to most of its Asian colonies without the pressure of large-scale military conflict suggested that white dominion over peoples of color abroad might also be on the way out as a defining characteristic of the emerging Western alliance. But the deepening of animosity between the Soviet Union and the United States in 1949 encouraged American policymakers to focus almost exclusively on the containment of Soviet and communist expansion, with the result that all other considerations—including the elimination of racial discrimination—received much less attention in Washington. The successful Soviet test of a nuclear weapon and the final victory of the insurgent forces of Mao Zedong in China profoundly exacerbated American anxieties about the growing strength of international communism. With the creation of the North Atlantic Treaty Organization and with Marshall Plan aid pouring into Western Europe, the United States drew even closer to the European imperial powers and thereby associated itself anew with the racial discrimination embedded in colonialism.

While East–West tensions preoccupied the Truman administration, significant racial polarization in southern Africa in 1949 portended a grim future for that corner of the world. White settlers in the British colonies sought to take control of the future of their territories in order to guarantee permanent white supremacy in the region. Racial violence flared in South Africa, and the Union government began to implement apartheid legislation. Aware that white voters were increasingly attracted to the Nationalists' racial program, the United Party opposition placed much of the blame for its defeat in the previous year's elections on Jan Hofmeyr's relatively liberal racial views and replaced him in the party leadership with the more conservative J. G. N. Strauss. Hofmeyr's subsequent early death on 3 December 1948 reinforced the acquiescence of the United Party in the politics of apartheid. Denouncing the Nuremberg trials of accused Nazi war criminals and openly supporting the dictatorial, right-wing regime of Francisco Franco in Spain, the Nationalists made it clear that their version of anticommunism had little in common with that espoused by the liberal democracies. South Africa's black nationalists responded to the reactionary policies of the Malan government by beginning to organize as a serious and increasingly radicalized opposition, centered in a revitalized African National Congress.[2]

By the end of 1949, the Nationalist government of South Africa had confirmed the Union as a political Achilles heel for the West in the Cold War. While neither a member of NATO nor a participant in the European Recovery Program, South Africa's ties to Britain and the United States and its fierce anticommunism put it squarely in the Western camp. The Union's strategic, political, and economic importance to the United States had been clearly established in the early postwar years, and would increase in direct proportion to American insecurity in the Cold War. But the Nationalists' explicit determination to reinforce white supremacy and racial segregation in southern Africa placed their country at odds with most of the international community, embarrassing the Truman administration by revealing a glaring exception to the democratic rhetoric and aspirations of the Western alliance.[3]

I

Having appealed for greater racial equality at home during the previous year's campaign, President Truman spent much of his inaugural address of 20 January 1949 calling for a new American program to aid nonwhite peoples in the world's colonial areas by providing technological knowledge to accelerate economic development. The President acknowledged that "more than half of the people of the world are living in conditions approaching misery" due to hunger and disease. He warned that "their poverty is a handicap and a threat both to them and to more prosperous areas" because of the opening it offered to leftist revolutionaries around the globe. Truman therefore proclaimed as "Point Four" of his speech that "we must embark on a bold new program for making the benefits of our scientific advances and industrial progress available for the improvement and growth of underdeveloped areas." The President took care to promise that "the old imperialism—exploitation for foreign profit—has no place in our plans. What we envisage is a program of development based on the concepts of democratic fair dealing." He concluded that as the United States and other "like-minded" nations sought to build a new international system of security and prosperity despite the direct opposition of a Soviet government "with contrary aims and a totally different concept of life," they would find allies in "the millions who hunger and thirst after righteousness."[4]

Truman could not have been more explicit in hailing the importance of the majority of the world's people who were not white and who were now emerging from colonialism into independence. The President and his political advisers saw Point Four as a way to balance the essentially negative concern of stopping communism with a positive outreach to the people of the colonial world, based on sharing superior American technical knowledge in order to help eliminate poverty. Benjamin Hardy, the administration official who had first suggested the idea for the inaugural address, believed that even the least technologically advanced people would be impressed by how far ahead of the Soviets the Americans were in this regard.[5] The traditionally European-oriented State Department, however, had opposed including Point Four in the President's speech on the grounds that, at this point, it was merely an idea rather than a fully developed program. Dean Acheson, newly appointed as Secretary of State, quickly reassured the American public that Point Four would not be another massive government aid program like the Marshall Plan, but would depend instead on private American investment in the "developing areas" of the world.[6] Truman himself, while eager to capture the imagination and loyalty of Third World peoples, envisioned a plan for sharing knowledge rather than lending government capital. He foresaw private capital from the United States helping to build dams on the Zambezi and Congo Rivers that would provide power, irrigation, and flood control, just as public funding had done earlier in the Tennessee River valley and on the Midwestern plains near his Missouri home. The President believed that Point Four would have "nothing in common with either the old imperialism of the last century or the new imperialism of the Communists."[7] Instead, it would be "our greatest contribution to world peace" and the best "hope for the prevention of World War III."[8]

Serious problems accompanied the Point Four concept from its beginning. Congress, like the State Department, showed considerably less enthusiasm than the President for the idea. More than a year and a half passed before any funds were actually appropriated for the program, and even then the relatively small amount involved meant that Point Four, in Acheson's words, "remained the Cinderella of the foreign aid family."[9] The program worked better with independent countries than with colonial possessions, and only in Latin America had Point Four been put into significant effect by the end of 1950.[10] As Under-Secretary of State James Webb acknowledged in a telegram to the U.S. Embassy in London, the successful development of technical assistance programs in colonial territories in Africa required the "complete understanding and coop[eration] of [the] metropolitan country" involved.[11] While enormous amounts of private capital were needed for real economic modernization in sub-Saharan Africa, the metropolitan powers generally resisted the penetration and influence of American capital in the African colonies. The net result of these difficulties of funding and jurisdiction was a minimal impact of Point Four on colonial areas, including southern Africa.[12]

A few months before Truman's inaugural address, the Central Intelligence Agency had issued a report on the process of decolonization, which also emphasized the importance of the colonial and newly independent areas to American national security. The Agency noted the "serious dilemma" for the United States of trying to forge close ties with the anticolonial new nations of the Near East and Asia while maintaining good relations with the European powers, especially given the importance of the remaining colonial territories to the economic stability of the metropolitan countries. The CIA argued that the unwaveringly anticolonial Soviet Union gained political support from the "deep-seated racial hostility of native populations toward their white overlords" caused by centuries of imperial exploitation. While the report called for steady progress toward the "inevitable goal of independence" for the remaining colonial areas and reducing racial discrimination in Western nations like the United States and South Africa, it assumed that economic nationalism in the Third World and resentment there of American economic power and free-trade objectives would continue to complicate American relations with the non-European world. The Agency concluded that the ongoing process of decolonization would reduce American access to military bases and raw materials in much of the Third World, at the very time that the United States was defining its security in increasingly global terms and becoming more beholden to foreign mineral resources. Being dependent on "dependent" areas complicated the efforts of the Truman administration to contain the growth of communism through an alliance with both colonizers and colonized.[13]

Tensions between the colonial powers and the anti-colonial countries at the United Nations continued to be sharp in 1949. While Secretary of State Acheson disliked what he described as the "heated debates in which many small delegations not directly interested in colonial matters are swept away by emotional arguments against colonial admin[istration] in general," other American representatives at the General Assembly noted that the supposedly more mature Western Europeans also demonstrated "considerable emotion" about colonial issues.[14] The Belgians, British, and French proved quite defensive about what they saw as hostile and ignorant assaults on their administration of colonial areas, particularly in Africa. The Europeans tended to resent even limited American efforts to act as a mediator between them and the anti-colonial nations, arguing that the United States was thereby undercutting its own highest priority of strengthening the Western alliance against communism.[15]

American policymakers worried about the opportunity for political advantage that strong differences over decolonization created for the Soviet Union. The massive European Recovery Program and the developing military alliance of the United States and Western Europe allowed the Soviets to argue with some credibility that the United States was encouraging and sustaining the oppression of colonial peoples. The Soviet Union, by contrast, maintained a consistently anticolonial line at the United Nations. Moscow gained favor with the newly independent nations by its efforts to extend the United Nations' considerable powers over trust territories to all colonial dependencies, an idea the United States opposed in order to protect its allies' sovereignty abroad. The British government warned the Truman administration not to try to "out-bid the Russians in 'liberalism' towards colonial questions," because the Soviets, lacking any colonial obligations, could always raise the stakes higher than either the United States or the Western European powers would be willing to go.[16]

The United States was not ready, however, to concede the entire anticolonial field to the Soviets. It hoped instead that continuing progress by the Europeans toward decolonization would keep the Third World allied with the West. The Truman administration was therefore sobered by the refusal of Indian Prime Minister Jawaharlal Nehru, on his first official visit to the United States in October 1949, to alter his policy of nonalignment in the Cold War and by his insistence that colonialism rather than communism posed the gravest danger to world peace. Even worse, from Washington's perspective, Nehru intended to offer official recognition to the newly declared People's Republic of China. George Kennan warned Acheson two weeks later about governments of "states with colored populations" that had no sense of responsibility for international stability. Inexperienced and "unsteadied by tradition," argued Kennan, representatives of such governments tended often to be "the neurotic products of exotic backgrounds and tentative western educational experiences, racially and socially embittered against the west." He concluded, in phrases echoed a month later by American delegates at the United Nations, that such people were "unreliable from the standpoint of cooperation in any serious and responsible task of international association."[17] American policymakers found their traditional European allies considerably more trustworthy than the governments of newly independent countries in the Middle East or Asia, much less the black nationalists of colonial Africa or segregated South Africa.

While rising in importance in 1949, colonial and Third World issues remained secondary for the Truman administration to the task of strengthening and unifying the industrial heartland of Western Europe. Secretary of Defense Louis Johnson reminded a national radio audience in August that the power of the Western European states, "added to ours, should make us invincible; but their facilities, once they fall into enemy hands, would make that enemy hard to beat."[18] The leftist orientation of the anticolonial rebellions underway in Malaya and Indochina encouraged the United States to stand by the British and French, especially after the communist victory in China. The State Department acknowledged that its "immediate interest in maintaining in power a friendly French government to assist in the furtherance" of American aims in Europe took precedence over any colonial plans; the Department also recognized that American economic and military aid to France was being steadily rerouted to the war in Indochina.[19] In response to constituents' concerns about giving Marshall Plan aid to countries like Britain with some socialist features, Senator Arthur Vandenberg reminded them that the Western European governments continued to "believe in God," remained part of "our very precious western civilization," and fought communism at closer range and with more physical courage than Americans had to.[20]

As part of the American effort to construct a rejuvenated, united Western Europe, Marshall Plan aid was helping to pay for the postwar reassertion of colonial power in Africa by 1949. The independence or open rebellion of most Asian colonies underscored the importance of African raw materials for European economic health. The legislation that had put the European Recovery Program into effect in 1948 specifically included the overseas territories of participating European countries. The Economic Cooperation Administration, which oversaw the implementation of the program, supported "taking full advantage of ECA funds for overseas territories development," especially in light of "the important interrelationship between economic development of the overseas territories and [American] military or political consideration[s] and objectives."[21] The National Security Council agreed with the ECA that within the southern African colonies controlled by Britain, Belgium, and Portugal lay "resources that are urgently needed for the rearmament and economic strengthening of the free world."[22] The ECA made it clear that, unlike the Point Four program, it was not designed to undertake "long-range programs related solely to the internal development of the overseas territories." The Marshall Plan aimed to benefit Europeans, even at the expense of Africans under their rule, and the continued course of imperial exploitation of African resources funded by the United States was determined by European and American, not African, requirements.[23]

The choice of the Truman administration to ally the United States closely with the colonial powers of Western Europe in the Cold War was emphatically confirmed by the creation of NATO in the spring of 1949. As one Canadian diplomat involved in the establishment of the anti-communist military pact later recalled, NATO was "an alliance of the white, wealthy, industrialized, western democratic world."[24] The United States did not formally agree to defend colonial rule in its allies' overseas territories, but the very fact of the alliance implied that African colonies were seen in Washington as most important for how they could contribute to the stability of the Western European nations.[25] Both the Nationalist government and its United Party opponents in South Africa welcomed NATO and hoped that it would soon be extended to include Africa.[26] The inclusion of Portugal, insisted on by the U.S. Joint Chiefs of Staff because of the strategic importance of the Azores, belied the claim of the alliance to represent democracy, as Salazar made clear from the beginning that his country's participation did not signify agreement with the liberal democratic principles outlined in the NATO charter.[27] The American military alliance with Western Europe against the Soviet bloc, in combination with the European Recovery Program, left no doubt that southern Africa would continue to be seen in Washington through essentially European eyes.

II

While American foreign policy decisions in 1949 kept the United States at odds with Africans seeking greater self-government, certain signs of improvement in the status of the fourteen million Americans of African descent suggested that the United States government was not completely insensitive to the declining legitimacy of racial discrimination in world affairs. Journalist Mary Heaton Vorse reported in *Harper's* magazine in July that progressive changes in race relations were steadily, if slowly, altering Southern life in the United States. Vorse emphasized the substantial gains in black voter registration in the South since 1940 and the highly symbolic appearance of black policemen in the region. She noted that black Southerners were less intimidated now than ever before in pressing for the full legal recognition of their rights as citizens, especially in light of Truman's open support for greater civil rights legislation. Like many other observers, Vorse believed that the sporadic violence of the Ku Klux Klan and the revolt of the Dixiecrats in the 1948 presidential campaign were not signs of the future but rather "the diehards' last stand against a changing Southern world."[28]

Truman's executive order banning segregation in the U.S. armed forces, issued during the 1948 campaign, became the official policy of the Defense Department in April 1949. Although the Army lagged behind in formulating specific plans for desegregation, the Navy and the Air Force moved quickly in announcing their new policies.[29] The shift in policy and the beginnings of integration in the American military in 1949 even made an impact in South Africa, where American racial politics were observed with considerable interest. The U.S.S. *Huntington* and the U.S.S. *Douglass H. Fox* had been warmly welcomed by white South Africans when they visited the ports of Durban and Capetown in October 1948; the friendliness of the American sailors and their interest in the Union favorably impressed thousands of South Africans, and the visit helped foster even better relations between the two countries.[30] By contrast, American sailors on port leave in Cape Elizabeth a year later were frustrating taxi drivers and hindering the introduction of apartheid into the city's taxi service by hailing cabs in integrated groups and insisting on riding together.[31]

Racial discrimination and assumptions of white superiority nonetheless proved tenacious in American society and within the United States government despite these progressive signs. White violence against blacks continued, especially in the South: black homes were bombed in Birmingham in June, and mob violence by whites against blacks broke out in Groveland, Florida, in July, following dubious accusations that three young black men had raped a white woman.[32] Segregation did not fully disappear from the American armed forces for several more years, and racial tensions remained common, despite the important symbolic change in direction at the top of the chain of command.[33] Dr. Ralph J. Bunche, the only prominent black American diplomat and soon to be a recipient of the Nobel Peace Prize for his work in the Arab-Israeli peace negotiations, turned down Truman's offer of the prestigious new post of Assistant Secretary of State for Near Eastern and African Affairs, choosing instead to remain at the United Nations. Bunche's decision apparently stemmed in part from the unattractiveness of moving from New York to the more racially discriminatory city of Washington, and in part from the new position's requirement of working closely with Congress when the two ranking Democratic members of the Senate Foreign Relations Committee, Tom Connally and Walter George, were white Southerners with segregationist records.[34] Truman then appointed George McGhee, a white oil executive from Texas who acknowledged later that his Southern roots inclined him to sympathy with white South Africans and "their extremely difficult racial problem."[35]

Late in the summer of 1949, two outbreaks of violence near the small Hudson River valley community of Peekskill just upstream from New York City provided grim evidence that the confluence of anticommunism and white racism now visibly in power in South Africa also flowed just below the surface in the United States. The confrontations stemmed from a scheduled concert performance by Paul Robeson, an African American political activist and one of the country's best-known singers and actors. Robeson chaired the anticolonial Council on African Affairs and had become a vocal critic of American Cold War foreign policy, an avocation that earned him considerable attention from the FBI.

He staunchly opposed racial discrimination in the United States and abroad, providing inspiration to a wide audience of nationalists in the Third World, while publicly admiring many aspects of life in the Soviet Union. He had particularly aroused the ire of anticommunists—including the NAACP, which had recently ousted founder W. E. B. Du Bois for his leftist beliefs—in April 1949 with a speech at an international peace conference in Paris in which he had declared that African Americans would never fight in a war against the Soviet Union.[36]

On 27 August 1949, at a picnic area outside Peekskill, several hundred vigilantes assaulted a much smaller group of mostly women and children who had arrived early for Robeson's concert. Unrestrained racial hatred and virulent anticommunist fervor prompted the mob, apparently including many war veterans, to prevent the black singer's appearance. Yelling "We're Hitler's boys!" "We'll finish his job!" "Lynch Robeson! Give us Robeson!" and anti-black and anti-Semitic expletives, the attackers used billy clubs, brass knuckles, and rocks to beat concertgoers, overturning fourteen cars and leaving more than a dozen people bloodied enough to require medical attention. They then burned a cross to underscore their message. The half-dozen sheriffs and FBI agents at the scene made no arrests and held no one for questioning.

After the concert was rescheduled for the following week, twenty thousand people showed up to hear Robeson sing. The performance proceeded without incident until those in attendance tried to leave afterwards in their cars. On the exit road they encountered a long gauntlet of vigilantes hurling rocks at them with the encouragement of a thousand local police officers and state troopers, many of whom pounded on the slow-moving cars with their nightsticks while cursing the occupants with racial epithets. Governor Thomas E. Dewey afterward blamed the incidents on what he called the deliberately provocative behavior of "these followers of Red totalitarianism," but to most of those present at the altercations, the violence represented the merging of two fierce American traditions: anti-radicalism and white racism.[37]

The Peekskill incidents suggested the enduring power and intensity of white racial animosity toward African Americans, especially when blacks could be linked to political subversion in the midst of the Cold War. This was a linkage that white South Africans understood and believed in very strongly; the events at Peekskill could only have encouraged those in power in Pretoria. Those seeking a more racially tolerant route to an anticommunist world, such as Truman and his advisers, were again stymied by the difficulty of cleanly separating anticommunism from white racism in the United States. In spite of his own racial prejudices, George Kennan articulated as well as anyone the scope and significance of this problem for the United States in a lecture at the National War College in December 1949: "I am afraid we have not yet found a satisfactory system of living together for people of different color in our own country which would make possible a fully satisfactory and fruitful and hopeful relationship between ourselves as a nation and the colored peoples in other parts of the globe." American domestic problems could not be kept remote from the Cold War, Kennan concluded, and only a stable and harmonious society at home would enable the United States to win real victories in the international realm.[38]

III

While racial issues continued to complicate American domestic life and United States foreign policy in 1949, the first full year of the Malan government in South Africa brought increasing racial polarization to the Union and the surrounding region. Living conditions continued to worsen in the desperately poor, overcrowded African ghettos on the edges of South Africa's major cities. Crime rates soared in these areas as gangs of armed youths, known as "tsotsis," controlled the streets after dark. White police paid little attention to "black on black" crime, focusing instead on enforcing new, stricter pass laws to control and monitor the movement of Africans in white areas. An Anglican priest working in one of the black neighborhoods described housing conditions there as "disgusting," while the lack of decent sanitation measures spawned extraordinary death rates from tuberculosis and other diseases. Educational facilities for Africans were utterly inadequate, forcing the few schools to turn away hundreds of students at the start of each year; the only response of the South African government was to cut funds for African education even further, supposedly in order to reduce African dependence on whites.[39]

The Malan government's absolute conviction about the rightness of racial segregation left no room for compromise and offered little incentive to appeal to the moral conscience of the Pretoria regime. Rather than ameliorate the oppressive conditions under which the vast majority of South Africans lived, the Nationalist government was determined, as U.S. Ambassador North Winship reported to Acheson, to place "greater restrictions and disabilities on the Natives by [both] administrative and legislative measures."[40] International attention and condemnation of the course of apartheid made no apparent impact on Pretoria, especially when such allegations as barbaric jail conditions and the torture of black prisoners often appeared in the Soviet press, which white South Africans—like Americans—assumed wrote only lies.[41] When confronted with the dramatic difference in the quality of life of nonwhites outside and inside the Union, South African government officials apparently felt little need to defend their system of officially sanctioned discrimination. The Minister of Labor, for example, explained early in 1949 that the government considered it "unfair to the non-European himself to allow him to go overseas, especially in a country where there is no color bar and no discrimination . . . and then have him come back to our conditions here." As long as the Nationalist Party remained in power, he concluded, "I don't think that will be permitted."[42]

American diplomats in South Africa kept the State Department informed of rising resentment among Africans toward such official attitudes and policies. Ambassador Winship reported that with Hofmeyr gone and the United Party determined to regain power by de-emphasizing any differences with the Nationalists' electorally popular apartheid policy, even the most conservative African nationalists in the Union could see that the direction of white politics was against them.[43] Acknowledging that "thus far, apartheid has meant only a taking away from the meager privileges held by these peoples," Winship feared that increasing numbers of blacks were coming to regard white South Africans as their enemies. Worst of all, argued the ambassador, the implementation of apartheid and the consequent radicalization of organizations like the ANC was providing "fertile ground for Communist adherents who are active in their midst" and who "might gain control with consequent disastrous results." When ANC president Alfred Xuma called for an end to racial discrimination and the establishment of basic African rights to the freedoms of movement, speech, assembly, the press, and employment, the South African government continued merely to scorn or ignore him. Therefore, Winship believed, race relations in the Union were likely to get much worse.[44]

Simmering African resentment exploded into violence in the streets of Durban on 13 January 1949, although it was directed against South Africans of Indian descent rather than whites. Years of white efforts at promoting racial hostility between Africans and Indians in the Natal province came to shocking fruition after an incident between an African youth and an Indian shop owner sparked three days of rioting, which left 142 people dead and almost two thousand injured. A large majority of the casualties were Africans, killed or wounded by white soldiers called in to quell the disturbance. Only five whites died, most accidentally, as African rioters carefully avoided harming most whites or their property. Well over a million dollars' worth of damage was inflicted on property belonging to Indian merchants, however, and forty thousand Indians were driven from their homes and sought refuge in temporary shelters. Another twenty thousand Indians and Africans saw their homes permanently destroyed. Tensions remained high for months thereafter, despite a large police presence, while random violence occurred again in late February and Africans boycotted buses and stores operated by Indians.[45]

The American consul in Durban, Robert McGregor, reported a few days later that "the people of Durban"—a category apparently excluding African residents of the city—"remain surprised and shocked over the speed with which the trouble spread, the viciousness of the attacks and the fact that un-armed Natives can cause so much trouble in so little time." Many white South Africans feared that such violence could easily break out again anywhere in the Union and that next time it might be aimed at them instead of at Indians. The Nationalist government could not help but feel justified at what it saw as evidence of the barbarism of nonwhite peoples and the need for whites to rule over them and keep them from each other's throats. North Winship reported from Pretoria, however, that he found it "difficult to believe that a maddened[,] uncontrolled mob still on the edge of barbarism would be so circumspect in their conduct towards European property."[46]

The significance of the violence in Durban stemmed from the signs it gave of the direction of South African social and political developments and the response of the black communities within the Union. Americans of differing political orientations agreed that the riots resulted directly from years of anti-Indian agitation by white political and business leaders of both major parties, which played on many Africans' experiences of exploitation at the hands of wealthier Indian merchants. The State Department pointed to specific efforts of the Malan government to incite Africans and Indians against each other. *The Nation* emphasized the legacy of white degradation of Africans in the Union, as well as the desire of whites to undercut Indian economic success and to gain a measure of revenge against Indians for having brought South African racial practices to the attention of the United Nations. Both *The Christian Century* and *The Crisis* noted evidence that white *agents provocateurs* had encouraged and abetted African violence and looting during the riots. In the face of this white racial animosity and devastatingly effective manipulation, shocked African and Indian leaders seized the opportunity in the aftermath of the violence to begin to work together toward a unified black and Indian opposition to their real enemy: the apartheid government and all forms of white domination. African-Indian animosity lingered long afterwards in Durban, but steady progress toward a mutual strategy of nonviolent noncooperation with the white authorities resulted within three years in the launching of the massive joint Defiance Campaign of 1952.[47]

In its first full year in office, the Malan government moved to check and eliminate what it saw as the twin subversive threats of racial integration and communism. Not surprisingly, the Nationalists targeted first the most intimate threat to their racial ideals: interracial sex. The Prohibition of Mixed Marriages Act extended the statutory ban on marriages between whites and Africans to those between whites and all nonwhites. This legislation, in combination with the Immorality Amendment Act of 1950, aimed to ensure that the substantial light-skinned Colored population would be permanently separated from the white community. Malan expressed the essence of Afrikaner racial fears in a speech to a Nationalist Party gathering in August 1949, in which he referred to the recent marriage of Seretse Khama, the young man in line to become chief of the largest tribe in neighboring Bechuanaland. "Are you surprised that Seretse Khama has a white wife from England and that that is largely approved by Liberals of this country?" asked the Prime Minister rhetorically. "Are you surprised that the subjects of Seretse Khama or any Natives here will say: 'If Seretse Khama can do it, why not me?' "[48]

Malan's warning that white liberals were abetting the subversion of white racial purity in South Africa suggested the close relationship Afrikaner nationalists saw between racial and political threats to their goal of apartheid. The Nationalists tended to view any disagreement with their policies as either "communist" or aiding the cause of communism; views as diverse as those of the United Party, the Labour Party, the African People's Organization, the Native Representative Council, and the non-European trade unions were increasingly lumped together under the label "communist." While not unique to South Africa in the Cold War, such red-baiting allowed all demands for democratic reforms in the Union to be dismissed by the government as emanating ultimately from Moscow. The tiny Communist Party of South Africa did, in fact, oppose racial discrimination and the severely skewed distribution of wealth in the Union, and thus provided an easy target for the Malan government as it accelerated its campaign to eliminate leftist influences from the country in 1949. Member of Parliament Sam Kahn and Indian leader Yusuf Dadoo, both members of the Communist Party, were banned from political gatherings and public speaking, and the government moved toward constant surveillance of left-wing organizations and legislation to outlaw the Communist Party.[49]

Stricter enforcement of long-standing segregation laws by the South African police and the Nationalist regime's frank commitment to further debilitating black South Africans eventually began to provoke hostile responses from the nation's urban poor. Rumors that the municipal administration planned to extend the degrading pass laws to African women as well as men led to a confrontation between Africans and white police in the black "location" of Munseiville outside Krugersdorp in early November. A crowd of several thousand people, at least a few of whom were carrying firearms, apparently refused to be intimidated by the police, leading to an exchange of gunfire that killed two Africans and wounded five others as well as five whites. Prearranged strategies for regrouping after the police assault, along with a comprehensive African work boycott in Krugersdorp that day and a recent tram boycott in the Johannesburg location of Sophiatown, indicated that the incident was neither isolated nor random. Winship reported to Acheson that "racial tension, heightened by the charged atmosphere of apartheid, is on the upward surge and the possibility of a more extended and prolonged outbreak cannot be excluded."[50]

Polarization along the color line in South Africa in 1949 inevitably affected neighboring territories in the southern African region, especially South West Africa. During the previous year, the U.N. Trusteeship Council had criticized the latest South African report on its administration of the South West African mandate, noting that the "indigenous inhabitants of the Territory have no franchise, no eligibility to office and no representation." Unlike its United Party predecessor, the Malan government was unwilling to seek a compromise with the international organization, which it believed had no supervisory rights over the area. Instead, the Nationalists moved a step closer to incorporating the territory into South Africa by passing legislation in April that gave white South West Africans six seats in the Union Parliament. This action soon strengthened the Nationalist Party's tenuous parliamentary majority, as the large number of voters of German descent in the territory helped elect six Nationalists to those seats a year later. On 11 July 1949 Malan sent a letter to the U.N. General Assembly announcing that South Africa would no longer submit reports to the United Nations on South West Africa. The Union thus became the only mandatory power from the League of Nations period that refused to accept the U.N. trusteeship system and its provision for the ultimate independence of mandated territories.[51]

The Malan government's actions towards South West Africa further alienated it from most of the international community. While Pretoria's declared policy of preventing individuals who might criticize the country's domestic policies from traveling abroad continued to hinder Africans in South West Africa from seeking help at the United Nations, anti-apartheid activist Michael Scott did manage to leave the country by first driving into Southern Rhodesia and then flying to Europe and on to New York. Truman and Acheson both declined requests by Scott to speak with them, but the Anglican priest was allowed to address the U.N. Trusteeship Committee on November 26 on behalf of the Herero and the other African peoples of South West Africa. He pleaded for United Nations protection for Africans in the territory and detailed their degrading treatment at the hands of white farmers and the South African government, including the bombing and strafing of one tribe in order to remove it from land that whites wanted to seize. A Haitian delegate remarked after Scott's speech that it was now clear why the South African government had fought so hard to prevent him from gaining a public forum outside the Union: South Africa's behavior in South West Africa had little to do with the "just treatment" of its inhabitants and "their protection against abuses" required in trusteeships by the U.N. Charter.[52]

South African recalcitrance about the colonial issue of South West Africa exacerbated the American problem of how to keep the Union a viable member of the international community and the Western anti-Soviet camp while not appearing to support colonialism and white supremacy. At the United Nations the U.S. delegation continued its difficult endeavor to moderate criticism of South African actions in the diminishing hope that, with more time, the Union government might still change the direction of its racial policies and its relationship with the international organization. The American delegation was again partially successful in this effort: it helped pass a resolution in December asking the International Court of Justice for an advisory opinion on South African obligations regarding South West Africa, while unsuccessfully opposing another resolution calling on the Union to resume its annual reporting and to submit a trusteeship agreement for the territory. Malan's actions and attitude did not facilitate the Truman administration's efforts at mediation, as the Prime Minister made it clear that, in the words of a report by the U.S. Embassy in Pretoria to Acheson, "apartheid and the mandate ideal just can't live together in Southern Africa."[53]

IV

By 1949, developments in the British colonies and protectorates of southern Africa also reflected the increasing racial polarization of the region. Mindful of the decolonizing precedents in Asia and Britain's weakened economic and military situation, colonial planners in London began after 1947 to put their African territories on the path to eventual self-government. This strategy reflected both African pressures for independence and the Labour government's goal of creating social democracy abroad as well as at home. American pressure on Britain to move gradually but steadily toward the creation of independent governments in all of its colonies in order to avoid leftist revolutions also influenced British policies. The Truman administration's threat to cut off its substantial economic and military aid to the Netherlands in the spring of 1949, unless the Dutch stopped escalating the war in Indonesia and came to a compromise with the noncommunist nationalists there, helped undermine the confidence of traditional imperialists in London and strengthened the position of liberal reformers.[54]

British imperial strategy regarding Africa was changing swiftly in the late 1940s. As pressures built for self-government in its African colonies, especially in Nigeria and the Gold Coast, the British government realized that its profitable economic connections with those areas could no longer be preserved through formal empire using traditional alliances with African kings and chiefs, but rather through accommodation with the more modern African intelligentsia and their desire for political independence. Having withdrawn from the more strategically important areas of India and Palestine, the British had little reason to risk the potential economic disaster of a colonial war in sub-Saharan Africa. An important warning signal had come in early 1948 in the Gold Coast capital of Accra, when police fired on an anticolonial demonstration by African ex-servicemen, sparking three days of rioting. From then on, London moved to avoid large-scale conflict through rapid political liberalization, leading to the colony's independence as the nation of Ghana within a decade.[55]

Britain's evident commitment to a relatively swift transition to African self-rule in West Africa brought a new urgency to talk of a central African confederation. White settlers in Northern Rhodesia and Nyasaland, governed directly by the British Colonial Office, had long been interested in creating a political union with Southern Rhodesia, with its larger white population and greater degree of independence from London, in order to preserve white settler rule throughout British central

Africa. The British government's formal commitment to protecting the interests of the African majority of Northern Rhodesia and Nyasaland had always required that it oppose such plans in the past. With the rise of Afrikaner nationalism to power in South Africa, however, London's attitude began to change. An economically viable federal union of the three territories might have the effect of quarantining Afrikaner racial attitudes and Anglophobia and preventing their influence from spreading northwards. A large conference of exclusively white delegates from the three territories met to discuss the idea in February 1949 at Victoria Falls, indicating to London the strength of white settler support for the project but also marking it from the beginning as an effort to preserve white supremacy in the region.[56]

Africans in the territories were dismayed by these developments and registered their opposition without delay. Led by the Nyasaland African Association and the Federation of African Societies of Northern Rhodesia, Africans in the two northern territories made it known that they wanted nothing to do with Southern Rhodesia and its segregationist policies, which they believed were little different in substance from those of South Africa. African workers in Southern Rhodesia had indicated similar discontent with their conditions in the self-governing colony by an array of strikes and other labor unrest throughout 1948. In the years before the threat of local white rule unrestrained by the more liberal British Colonial Office became so immediate, African nationalists in Northern Rhodesia and Nyasaland had been relatively submissive to British colonial authority. But after the Victoria Falls Conference, and all the way through the seven years of the ill-fated Central African Federation established in 1953, they mobilized to seek the color-blind independent governments that would eventually come into existence with the creation of Zambia and Malawi in the early 1960s.[57]

While developments in British central Africa received less attention in Washington in the late 1940s than did events in South Africa or the Belgian Congo, the Truman administration had one important interest in the region. Since the beginning of World War II, the United States had become a major buyer of the chrome, copper, and manganese produced in substantial quantities in the Rhodesias. Transportation facilities in the region consisted of limited rail capacity in the Rhodesias and inadequate port facilities in neighboring Mozambique. In order to effect its program of stockpiling these strategic minerals, Washington initiated discussions with London and Lisbon about improving shipping in the region. The State Department also dismissed reports in the American press in 1949 of abysmal living and working conditions for African miners in Southern Rhodesia, making instead the apparently laudatory claim that the situation of miners there was among the best anywhere in southern Africa. The need for the inexpensive production of strategic minerals continued to link official American interests with the colonial status quo in the region.[58]

One other piece of the story of racial polarization in southern Africa during the first full year of apartheid rule in South Africa emerged out of romantic rather than strategic concerns. The difficulty arose because love in this case crossed the color line. Seretse Khama was the young heir to the chieftainship of the Bamangwato people, the largest tribe in the British protectorate of Bechuanaland. After receiving his baccalaureate degree from Fort Hare College in South Africa, he had gone to Oxford in 1945 to pursue graduate studies in law. From there he moved to London, where he met Ruth Williams, a white Englishwoman, through mutual friends at a missionary society meeting. They had married on 29 September 1948, expecting to move to Bechuanaland for Seretse to take his place at the head of the tribe. But Seretse's powerful uncle, Tshekedi Khama, who had been the regent of the Bamangwato since the early death in 1925 of his brother, Seretse's father, opposed the marriage. Tshekedi wanted his nephew to marry a Bamangwato rather than a foreigner, and he opposed Seretse's ascension to the chieftainship as long as Ruth was his wife. The tribe split into two camps in the dispute, with a substantial majority supporting Seretse by June 1949 and welcoming his wife warmly upon her arrival in August.[59]

These events shocked whites in South Africa, where the Mixed Marriages Act had gone into effect in July. The arrival of a white woman as the wife of an African chief on the very border of the Union seemed a direct affront to the Nationalist regime and a threat to its domestic racial policies. Earlier South African governments had long sought the transfer of Bechuanaland and the other two British High Commission territories, Basutoland and Swaziland, from British control to South African sovereignty, a development foreseen and approved in principle by the South African Act of Union of 1910. With the growing split between South African racial policies and the British responsibility for protecting the welfare of Africans in the territories, British governments had been unwilling to effect such a transfer. But the issue was complicated by Bechuanaland's thorough economic dependence on South Africa, whose customs union, currency, and banking and postal systems it shared. Bechuanaland was even the world's only country without its own capital, being administered instead from Mafeking across the border in South Africa. So when the Malan government barred Seretse and his wife from entering the Union in October 1949, they could not even visit the territory's administrative office. Determined to fend off the threat of liberal racial policies on his country's borders, Malan renewed calls for Britain to transfer all three High Commission territories to South Africa.[60]

The British government faced an awkward dilemma in deciding, at Tshekedi's request, whether to approve Seretse as the tribal chief. It was unwilling to bow to pressure from Pretoria and turn over the territories' African populations to the architects of apartheid, but it wished to avoid conflict with South Africa, which remained an important member of the Commonwealth and the dominant power in the region. London was also concerned about re-establishing peace among the divided Bamangwato. After delaying for some months in vain hopes that Ruth Khama might find life in Bechuanaland unacceptable and return to England with or without her husband, and after failing to persuade Seretse to relinquish his claim to the chieftainship voluntarily, the British government finally decided in March 1950 to recognize neither Seretse nor Tshekedi as chief. Instead, the British High Commissioner would rule Bechuanaland directly, while Seretse would be banned from entering the territory for at least five years. In announcing its decision publicly, London took no position on interracial marriages and did not mention South Africa, explaining its policy almost entirely in terms of how best to re-establish domestic tranquillity within Bechuanaland.[61]

Jan Smuts, now the Opposition leader in the South African Parliament, apparently played a central role in the British decision. He convinced his numerous influential contacts in the British government that allowing Seretse and his white wife to become the rulers of the Bamangwato would encourage "native trouble" in the Union and play into the Nationalists' hands by arousing an intensely hostile reaction among white South Africans. In such an emotional atmosphere, Smuts argued, Malan might even decide to blockade or invade Bechuanaland in order to force the British to cede it to South Africa, a course the United Party would be politically unable to oppose.[62] White Southern Rhodesians also let the British government know their fears that an interracial ruling family in the region would have a negative impact on race relations in their country.[63] Domestic opinion across the political spectrum in England, on the other hand, registered dismay at the idea of sacrificing Seretse and Britain's long-standing commitment to African interests in the territory to South African racial prejudices.[64] But the British government decided that its interests in southern Africa—especially its significant economic, strategic, and political ties with the Union—would be best served by placating white power in the region, while London also was privately pleased to have a unique opportunity to eliminate the Khama ruling house, which had often proven inconveniently independent in the past.[65]

V

An expanding definition of American national security and deepening fears of revolutionary communist power in 1949 heightened the United States government's interest in preserving political stability throughout the noncommunist world, including southern Africa. The Policy Planning Staff of the State Department declared in March that the security and welfare of the United States could not be separated from "the peace and security of the world community"; aggression anywhere in the world, whether through armed force or by subtler acts of subversion, could "jeopardize the security" of the United States. The successful Soviet detonation of a nuclear test weapon, announced in September, ended the

brief American monopoly on atomic power and increased American anxieties about how to contain the expansion of communist influence. The
declaration of the communist People's Republic of China on October 31
unleashed a storm of partisan controversy in the United States over the
ill-phrased question of "Who lost China?" and stimulated American fears
of further leftist insurgencies in the Third World. In this atmosphere of
deep uncertainty about the direction of international politics, the firm
anticommunist position of the Union of South Africa, which Dean Acheson called one of "the more responsible" of the nations of the British
Commonwealth, and its considerable supplies of uranium ore provided a
measure of comfort to the Truman administration.[66]

In a report issued in January 1949, the Central Intelligence Agency
pointed out that South Africa's strategic location and minerals, its membership in the Commonwealth, and world sensitivity to the racial issues
dominating the domestic life of the Union gave an unusual international
significance to the partisan politics of South Africa's tiny white electorate.
The Agency noted that South Africa not only had considerable uranium
deposits but also produced twelve of the other twenty-three strategic
minerals listed by the U.S. National Security Resources Board as so critical that stockpiling was required. The Agency also underlined the importance of a strong British Commonwealth for American security. But
it worried about "Malan's repressive policy" of apartheid, which was contributing to the deterioration of race relations in South Africa and
throughout the rest of the continent. While Malan's handling of South
African racial issues both at home and at the United Nations was winning him greater support among white South Africans, the Agency warned
that international condemnation of apartheid would inevitably reflect some
on the United States "because of its close alignment with South Africa
in various other respects."[67]

South Africa's devaluation of its currency in 1949, in conjunction
with similar action by the other members of the sterling area, helped
restore the country's balance of payments by slowing imports from non-
sterling nations and by raising the price of gold. Concerned at first about
the restrictions that had been put on imports from the United States in
November 1948, the Truman administration was pleased to learn within
a few months that the Union government was making significant exceptions for American manufacturers with plants in South Africa. Pretoria
was also sending signals to Washington by February 1949 that discrimination against American shippers would soon be eased. South African
officials continued to emphasize in public speeches their country's need
for American investment capital and American technical skills. American
businessmen waxed optimistic about the potential for profits in the Union,
with one prominent New York merchant reminding the State Department in January that "in 1952 to 1953, the new gold fields of the Orange Free State will come into production, roughly doubling South Af-

rica's gold production and opening up a field of unlimited trade to the American trader."[68]

As part of its expanding program to contain communist influence around the globe, the Truman administration in 1949 developed the Military Assistance Program (MAP) to "strengthen the morale and material resistance of the free nations" of the world.[69] The distribution of this aid reflected American perceptions of where communism was most threatening, with the NATO countries receiving three quarters of the funds and equipment, and such less obviously "free" nations as Greece, Turkey, Iran, South Korea, and the Philippines getting most of the rest.[70] South African Defense Minister F. C. Erasmus visited Washington in August to talk with administration officials about acquiring military equipment from the United States, which he claimed the Union badly needed. Secretary of Defense Louis Johnson and Under-Secretary of State James Webb listened carefully but offered little help, citing the higher priority of other imperiled areas and the carefully circumscribed limitations of the MAP funding about to be approved by Congress. Erasmus' hints that the development of South African uranium ore and its export to the United States could perhaps become linked to American military assistance to the Union raised the potential stakes of the discussions considerably, and the Americans suggested that they would seek early amendments to the MAP legislation to give Truman the flexibility to make some provision of arms for the Union.[71] The South African government's security concerns in 1949 were plainly more domestic than external, and MAP had been designed in part to provide for "improvement[s] in the internal security situation" of recipient countries. Thus American weaponry moved a step closer to helping control dissent against apartheid.[72]

South Africa's declining gold reserves and the constant need for more foreign capital for its industrial development had led the Malan government in late 1948 to begin seeking a substantial loan from the United States.[73] Confident that its large gold mining industry, vital uranium ore deposits, and relative financial stability would guarantee it good credit with both the United States government and private American banks, Pretoria optimistically assumed that it could arrange a large loan at low interest and with no restrictions on the use of the funds. The governor of the Reserve Bank of South Africa, Dr. Michiel de Kock, and the South African Minister of Finance, H. C. Havenga, were therefore surprised and dismayed by the lack of encouragement they received in informal talks with American officials and bankers in Washington and New York in the fall of 1948. Credit was tighter than they had expected in the United States, and American bankers were put off by the South African government's arrogance in assuming that it could get whatever it wanted without restrictions on the use of the loans. Havenga and de Kock were able to arrange only a $10 million credit from New York banks, less than a fifth of what they had hoped for.[74] Pretoria demonstrated its temporary displeasure by delaying its response to American requests for increased production of manganese ore in early 1949 and by hinting that the lifting of its import restrictions on American goods could be linked to the loan issue.[75] State Department officials, especially Robert Lovett, were dismayed at these events, and argued that South Africa's strategic minerals were far too important for the United States government not to help arrange American credit for the Union. The Truman administration took South Africa's formal application in 1949 for a $100 million loan from the U.S. Export-Import Bank under careful consideration.[76]

No one in Washington doubted the commitment of white South Africans to the Western anticommunist cause in the Cold War. But the evangelical style of racial prejudice that characterized the Nationalists' policies kept the Truman administration faintly nervous about how the Union might also be detracting from the credibility of the "free world." The Malan government worked steadily at trying to convince Washington that in Africa black rule would mean a communist takeover, while continued white dominion remained the only guarantee of preventing such a scenario. Harry Andrews, the South African Ambassador in Washington, pressured Acheson to oppose the U.N. plan to cede the region of Eritrea to independent Ethiopia out of regard for the Italians living there, as Pretoria was determined to avoid any precedent of white people living under black rule, especially on the African continent. Andrews presented the problem to Acheson, however, in terms of the "danger of Communist penetration into Africa by way of Soviet representation in Ethiopia."[77]

The extent of the Nationalists' preoccupation with the supposed threat of dark-skinned peoples caught American observers by surprise at times in 1949. Noting that "we get along so well with you people that we don't have to beat around the bush," the Chief of Staff of the South African Defense Forces, General Len Beyers, told the Army attaché to the U.S. Embassy in Pretoria that South Africa's greatest help to the United States, besides uranium production, would be in the realm of containing Indian penetration of central Africa. The Truman administration hoped the Malan government would avoid being distracted from the larger issue of communist expansion by such peripheral or even spurious concerns.[78]

White Americans who had any knowledge of the Union nevertheless tended to see white South Africans as similar to themselves, which was a reassuring thought amidst fears that much of the world was slipping into anti-American darkness. The Central Intelligence Agency emphasized that "within the European community the usual forces and conventions of Western democracy operate." Robert McGregor, the American consul in Durban, even indicated considerable sympathy with what he admitted was the South African government's policy of "native repression." It was "quite possible, even likely," McGregor reported to Washington, "that we would act in the same manner if we endeavored to govern as a white race among a black population five times as numerous." Writing in *The Nation* in May 1949, Thomas Sancton observed numerous similarities between the two countries in their current racial practices and institutions, while noting differences in their apparent future directions. The Nationalist victory in South Africa, he believed, was as if the Dixiecrats—the breakaway Southern Democrats in 1948—had won in the United States; the political language and goals of the two groups had a great deal in common.[79]

Such comparisons pleased the Nationalists, whose press organs generally described the United States in terms of the Ku Klux Klan and the plans of Southern segregationists, such as Senator Richard Russell's suggestion for redistributing the black population of the South throughout the United States.[80] Acheson made efforts to portray the United States to white South Africans in terms of American progress toward racial equality and away from discrimination, hoping thereby to encourage them to shed their more extreme prejudices.[81] American policymakers were more comfortable on anticommunist rather than racial grounds with their South African counterparts. When the two issues could occasionally be brought together in ways that did not play into the Nationalists' racial phobias, the Truman administration was relieved. The two governments, for example, worked together on a case involving Max Yergan, a black former leftist and founder of the Council on African Affairs who had lived in South Africa years earlier and had recently split with Robeson and Du Bois at the CAA and become an avid anticommunist. Yergan requested permission in June 1949 to visit the Union again in order to warn black South Africans about the evils of communism. Acheson assured a cautious but delighted Pretoria that Yergan's new political commitment was apparently serious and not a fake, thereby paving the way for Yergan's South African visa.[82]

While substantial in their own right, all such military, economic, and political considerations in relations between the United States and South Africa in the Truman years paled in comparison to the ultimate question of uranium ore. Improving American intelligence capabilities in the late 1940s and early 1950s revealed the construction of new Soviet industrial plants with greater blast resistance east of the Ural Mountains. Air Force planners lengthened their lists of critical Soviet targets to hit in case of a full-scale war, sharply increasing American requirements for nuclear weapons. The Soviet Union's detonation of its own nuclear device in September 1949 added new urgency to this task. Soon thereafter Truman approved a sizable increase in the American production of fissionable materials. Certain that Soviet conventional forces in Europe greatly outnumbered those of the Western alliance, and formally committed now as a member of NATO to the defense of Western Europe, the United

States government privately acknowledged in late 1949 that its defense policies rested almost entirely on the nation's nuclear deterrent.[83]

"The cardinal principle" of all American actions regarding supplies of fissionable materials, the National Security Council reported to Truman in March 1949, "has been to increase our raw materials position and to deprive the Soviets of supplies from outside the USSR." The major world source of uranium ore thus far had been the Belgian Congo, from which the United States had received over ninety percent of its supplies; "the principal future source of uranium," the NSC reminded the President, "appears to be South Africa."[84] American and South African scientists were developing new chemical techniques that promised in the near future an economical method of extracting the enormous quantities of low-grade uranium ore present in the tailings of the gold mines of the Rand. American, British, and Canadian representatives of the Combined Development Agency traveled to the Union in the fall of 1949 for preliminary talks with the South African Atomic Energy Board about conditions for a commercial contract for the purchase of the Union's future ore production. On 30 November 1949, the American delegate cabled Acheson from Pretoria that they had reached a tentative agreement about the amount and price of ore to be produced.[85]

These "questions of utmost importance with South Africa," as Acheson called the uranium negotiations, colored all aspects of the Truman administration's relationship with the Union in 1949.[86] American observers of South Africa were frequently startled by the "tactlessness" and "penchant for creating ill-will" Ambassador Winship called "one of the principal attributes of the Nationalist Government."[87] After provincial elections in March revealed impressive gains by the Nationalists, the State Department worried that "we can expect the South African Government to be even less moderate than in the past" since the election results would strengthen the extremist elements of the ruling party.[88] Rising racial tensions in the Union persuaded the State Department to assign a new officer, Joseph Sweeney, to the U.S. Embassy in Pretoria for the purpose of studying and reporting on race relations there.[89] But the strategic significance of South Africa for the West seemed to require that the United States government maintain a policy of what a later American administration would call in the 1980s "constructive engagement," in which Washington would use its opportunity as a friendly power to apply what the CIA termed "indirect pressure" for liberalization in the Union.[90] Malan provided some encouragement for such an approach by declaring in mid-1949 that South Africa would not seek complete independence in the immediate future but would instead remain in the British Commonwealth, which he called an important vehicle for halting the spread of communism.[91] South African Defense Minister Erasmus summed up his government's satisfaction with its relations with the United States after a visit to Washington in August: "I leave the United States with a feeling of great encouragement that the strategic importance of South Africa as one of the far-flung bastions of democracy is well understood by our American friends."[92]

VI

By the end of 1949, the apartheid government's encouragement of racial polarization in South Africa had set the stage for greater racial conflict. The white electorate's rejection of the nominally moderate policies represented by Jan Smuts rendered any politics of compromise increasingly untenable. Fearful of losing further popularity with white voters, the United Party chose to distinguish itself from the Nationalists more by style than by substance in matters of race. Symbolic of the disappearing middle in South African politics, Michael Scott, the high-profile white Anglican clergyman who had devoted himself to working with South Africa's poorest blacks and against the rising tide of racial prejudice, lost his license to officiate as a priest in the Diocese of Johannesburg. Long burdened by extreme oppression but aware of the changing racial sensibilities of the world community outside South Africa's borders, Africans in the Union saw in the rise of apartheid the end of all reasonable hopes for progressive racial reform through the white political system. Growing numbers of blacks in the Union came to believe that the only path to improving their condition lay through their own unity and organization. Old animosities between different nonwhite groups began to disappear, with Africans in Natal—who less than a year earlier had been at war with their neighbors of Indian descent in the streets of Durban—showing open admiration for Indian Prime Minister Nehru and his unyielding stand in favor of nonalignment in the Cold War during his autumn visit to the United States.[93]

The direction of South African race relations and politics at the end of 1949 was vividly portrayed in the dramatic contrast of two events on December 16. One was the dedication of the Voortrekker Monument between Pretoria and Johannesburg in honor of the Afrikaner military forces who, on that date in 1838, had decisively defeated the army of the Zulu chief Dingaan at the battle of Blood River. That victory, in which some three thousand Zulus had reportedly been killed by superior firepower at the cost of only three white casualties, still had enormous emotional significance for many Afrikaners, who tended to see in it a sign of divine approval of their quest for freedom from British imperial control and for dominion over black people.[94]

One out of every ten whites in the entire country turned out for the massive celebration in 1949, which had been carefully orchestrated by the Nationalists as an emblematic capstone to their recent political triumph. Fears of Afrikaner-English tensions dissipated as speakers from both backgrounds, including Malan and Smuts, appealed for white unity in South Africa.[95] In his address, Malan railed against "godless Communism, which is the upsetting of everything the Voortrekkers regarded as sacred," including, most obviously, absolute white supremacy. While the government organizers of the festivities had contended ahead of time that it was designed as a celebration of "good faith" and not of triumph over blacks, South Africans of darker hues had their doubts. *The Sun,* a Colored newspaper, warned that if white South Africans did not "heed the writing on the wall[,] it may yet be that the hymn of hate which is being sung today may have a boomerang effect. The day may yet come when millions of blacks will still raise a mighty monument to Dingaan."[96]

Two hundred and fifty miles to the south of the Voortrekker Monument, in the city of Bloemfontein, another equally symbolic and portentous event was unfolding on the same day. At the annual convention of the African National Congress, a younger generation of African nationalists, organized as the Congress Youth League under the leadership of Nelson Mandela, Walter Sisulu, and Oliver Tambo, won the adoption of their "Programme of Action" by the Congress as a whole. The Programme rejected the traditional ANC strategy of polite lobbying through petitions and deputations as inadequate before the juggernaut of apartheid. The Programme called instead for bolder political action in order to build a mass African movement and pressure the white authorities into a thorough reformation of South African society. It proclaimed a two-pronged, nonviolent strategy in order to help bring about a democratic South Africa free of racial discrimination: economic pressure through strikes and boycotts, and massive noncooperation with white authorities in order to render discriminatory legislation unenforceable. The Youth League underscored this historic change in African political strategy in the Union by helping elect Dr. James Moroka, known to be sympathetic to mass political action, as president of the ANC in place of the more conservative incumbent, Dr. Alfred Xuma, and by putting six of its own members on the national ANC executive council.[97]

American observers in South Africa noted with apprehension the "bitterness" of the ANC delegates toward the government's apartheid policy and the entire traditional system of "Native administration" typified by the pass laws. Bernard Connelly, the acting head of the U.S. Embassy, reported to Acheson a week after the Bloemfontein convention that the Congress emphasized that it did not oppose white people, but only white oppression.[98] Connelly considered it significant that the ANC's rising militancy was rooted in a color-conscious African nationalism that eschewed communism as a solution for the problems of black South Africans. There were some Communist Party members active and respected in the ANC, but what Connelly called the "vanguard organization" of African nationalism in the Union was not threatened by Soviet control. The more important external influence on black South Africans at the end of 1949 came instead from the example of other peoples of color, such as those in Indonesia, taking over the governments of their own countries.[99] For the Afrikaner nationalists in power in the Union, however, the political commitments taken by Africans at Bloemfontein represented merely "ridiculous braggadocio and sheer insolence."[100] The architects of apartheid took little notice of the effects of their policies on the majority of South Africans, and they seemed unaware of the significance of the changing African response to white oppression.

PART THREE

STAYING
TOGETHER

The Korean War and the Cementing of the United States– South African Alliance: 1950

Rising domestic anticommunism in the United States and South Africa and the alliance of the two nations in the Korean War led them to a series of agreements in late 1950 that firmly established American support for the apartheid regime. In the United States the traumatic events of the previous fall, when the Soviet Union had produced its own atomic weapon and China had been "lost" to communism, were followed by a series of fearful developments in the first six weeks of the new year. Former high State Department official Alger Hiss was convicted of perjury on January 21 for denying his alleged connections to a communist spy ring. On January 31, President Truman gave his official approval to the military's proposed program for developing a thermonuclear hydrogen bomb, which would be vastly more destructive than the fission weapons that had incinerated Hiroshima and Nagasaki. Three days later, British atomic scientist Klaus Fuchs, who had worked at Los Alamos on the original Manhattan Project during World War II, was arrested in England on charges of providing classified information about atomic weapon design to Soviet agents. On February 9 a little-known Republican U.S. senator, Joseph McCarthy, stood before a partisan audience in Wheeling, West Virginia, held aloft a sheaf of papers, and claimed that he had a list of 205 Communist Party members working in the State Department with the knowledge and approval of Secretary of State Dean Acheson. The era of McCarthyism, with its search for domestic traitors to explain international setbacks, was now fully under way.[1]

Anxieties about subversion in the United States in early 1950 were matched by American fears that growing Soviet power and confidence, fueled by atomic weaponry and the addition of China to the communist camp, might lead to overt Soviet military aggression against the noncommunist world. In April, the National Security Council, in conjunction with the State and Defense Departments, produced an enormously influential study of American "objectives and programs for national security," known as NSC-68. The document called for a massive military buildup in order to deter what it believed was the fanatical determination of the Soviet Union to gain world domination by whatever means necessary. NSC-68 viewed the world as divided into only two camps, which it called simply "slave" and "free," and warned that the Soviets might use other communist countries as proxy forces with which to capture further territory. When North Korean troops invaded South Korea on June 25, the recommendations of NSC-68 seemed fully confirmed to American policymakers, who assumed the North Koreans were under the control of the Kremlin. American involvement in the Korean War over the next three years led to a thorough militarization of the Cold War, greater fears of a direct Soviet-American clash, and even less tolerance of dissent in the United States against official anticommunism. In September, Congress passed the Internal Security ("McCarran") Act to tighten existing espionage and sabotage laws and require the registration of all members of groups that fell under a very broad definition of "Communist" or "communist action" organizations.[2]

The McCarran Act echoed very similar legislation passed by the South African government just three months earlier. The Suppression of Communism Act in South Africa outlawed the Communist Party and also "communism," an ideology defined broadly enough to include almost any substantive dissent against the official state policy of racial segregation and white supremacy. The Suppression of Communism Act and a handful of other key statutes, most notably the Group Areas Act, laid the legislative basis in 1950 for apartheid, tying anticommunism firmly to white racism in southern Africa. This was also the year in which the Nationalist Party gained enough electoral strength to assert the hegemony over South African politics it would maintain for decades thereafter. Black South Africans found their already tenuous position in the Union further eroded, and impoverished Africans took to the streets for the first time in large numbers to protest directly their increasing oppression at the hands of absolute white authority. The success of Afrikaner nationalists prompted the younger generation of African nationalists in the African National Congress to respond by initiating large-scale African political organizing in opposition to apartheid. The swift and massive use of violence by the police in reaction to African demonstrations against repressive legislation signaled the Nationalists' utter rejection of any compromise on the issue of white dominion in the Union.[3]

Despite the grim and worsening state of race relations in the Union, which was carefully reported by American diplomats there, the entry of the United States into full-scale war against communist forces in Korea in 1950 ensured that Pretoria's international rather than domestic policies would determine its relationship with Washington. South Africa's unwavering anticommunism kept it an unquestioned ally in what seemed an increasingly dangerous and bipolar world. The Union government's dispatch of a squadron of airmen in September to aid the American cause won it considerable credit with American policymakers. By late November, Chinese communist troops had entered the war in large numbers on the side of North Korea and were driving the American-dominated U.N. armies swiftly backwards. With Truman about to declare a national emergency in the United States, South Africa's final agreement on November 23 to produce and sell large quantities of uranium ore to the United States and Britain entrenched the Union firmly in Washington's good graces. Within two months American loans and arms sales to the Union had been arranged, and American weapons were soon being used to guarantee the domestic stability of the apartheid regime. The igniting of the Cold War into actual large-scale fighting welded the common interests of South Africa and the United States into a solid alliance.[4]

I

By 1950, the Truman administration was focusing more attention on the African continent than it had in any previous year. This resulted largely from the postwar decolonization of Asia, which had left Africa as the last great bastion of white rule in the nonwhite Third World. "Africa" and "the colonial world" were becoming increasingly synonymous. In the context of communist insurgencies and successes in Asia, the Truman administration took comfort in the reassuring situation in Africa. In the summer of 1950, Assistant Secretary of State George McGhee found it "gratifying to be able to single out a region of 10 million square miles in which no significant inroads have been made by communism, and to be able to characterize the area as relatively stable and secure."[5] American policymakers recognized the growing power of nationalist movements in every colonial area and realized that this "dynamic tide" could not be stopped.[6] Instead, the United States needed to use this period of "relative quiet in Africa," before nationalism there became as powerful as it was in Asia and the Middle East, to help guarantee the long-term loyalty of African peoples to the Western cause in the Cold War.[7] This difficult task would be best accomplished, in the view of the State Department, by working to build new cooperative relations between Africans and European colonial administrators to replace older exploitative ones. The Truman administration therefore continued to seek a middle position between the colonial powers and the anticolonial peoples and nations in order to keep both groups aligned with its anticommunist cause.[8]

American policymakers realized that the independence of most Asian colonies by 1950 had sharply increased the importance of Africa for the economic and strategic strength of the Western European nations. One of Washington's chief concerns about its European allies was their dollar shortage stemming from their imbalance of trade with the United States. The production and export of direct dollar-earning commodities from the African colonies helped significantly in reducing the persistent trade deficits of Britain, France, Belgium, and Portugal with the United States.

The economic stability of the NATO countries in 1950 depended to no small degree on steady agricultural and mineral production in Africa.[9]

Direct American interests in the colonies of southern Africa included some trade and investment but centered mostly on the production and transportation of strategic raw materials. Uranium ore from the Belgian Congo remained by far the most important concern, but other minerals from the Congo and the Rhodesias, including copper, chromite, and manganese, also figured prominently in the American stockpiling effort. Consequently, the Truman administration was determined that such enormously valuable military materials not fall into the hands of the Soviet Union or its allies. Throughout 1950, especially after the outbreak of war in Korea, the Defense Department indicated considerable interest in improving the limited transportation facilities of southern Africa in order to increase the flow of strategic minerals to the West.[10]

The ability of the Truman administration to achieve its goals in regard to colonial Africa depended primarily on its relationship with the metropolitan countries still in authority there. The creation of the Western alliance through NATO and the Marshall Plan had linked the United States closely with the Western European powers, but the allies had some real differences of opinion regarding Africa. The Truman administration was troubled by continuing European discrimination against American trade and investment in colonial areas, while Europeans tended to resent American insistence on further expanding the already dominant economic position of the United States in the world. Truman's advisers worried about the security of mining operations in southern Africa, believing that colonial administrators did not appreciate the serious potential for communist sabotage of key resources there. The intensity of conflict at the United Nations over colonial issues resulted in considerable metropolitan defensiveness about the administration of "dependent" areas, and the Western European powers did not appreciate the efforts of the United States to take a middle position and avoid siding completely with them against the anti-colonial nations.[11] The pressure applied to the U.S. by European diplomats was no doubt due, in part, to their awareness that Americans could conceivably go beyond an intermediary position to provide more than merely rhetorical support to colonies bent on declaring their independence from the powers of Europe, as the United States itself had once done.

The Truman administration was convinced that the "severe strains" over colonial issues that had emerged between the United States and its Western European allies at the 1949 U.N. sessions played directly into the hands of international communism.[12] The State Department sought to avoid any repetition of such problems in 1950 by arranging extensive discussions beforehand with the British, French, and Belgian governments. These talks in July laid the foundation for a more unified Western front at the U.N., with the United States placing greater emphasis on convincing the anticolonial delegations of the reasonableness of the Europeans in their colonial administration.[13] The North Korean invasion of South Korea and the U.N. resolution approving military support for South Korea further strengthened the American effort at shifting priorities away from anticolonialism and towards unity against aggression by communist forces. It also made the United States, now actively involved in a war with the communist world, more susceptible to pressures applied by the surviving imperial powers of Western Europe, countries that were surrendering control of enormous resources in Asia and that were in no hurry to concede their colonial dominion in Africa. By the end of the year, the Truman administration had repeatedly assured its European allies of its opposition to what it called "indiscriminate self-government" and "a premature according of political independence to the peoples of Africa."[14]

American support for the European imperial powers and Washington's "keen appreciation" of the need for "time and patience" in the "orderly, guided development" of colonial independence dismayed people who sought basic political and economic freedoms in Africa.[15] Internally, the State Department acknowledged the aspirations of educated Africans, paraphrasing their suspicion that the Marshall Plan and NATO might be merely the latest in a long tradition of plans for "manacling the African peoples with the chains of Western imperialism."[16] The metropolitan countries rather than the generally impoverished colonial areas were clearly the beneficiaries of Marshall Plan aid, while NATO's strategic interests received much higher priority in Washington than did African economic or political development.[17] African nationalists knew by intimate experience the human costs of decades of what the State Department was now acknowledging were the distorted economies of the African colonies, resulting from European overinvestment in the production of strategic minerals for export and underinvestment in agriculture for local consumption.[18]

American support for white dominion in Africa seemed to dovetail with continuing racial discrimination and segregation in the United States. The State Department admitted in April 1950 that "no American problem receives more wide-spread attention, especially in dependent areas, than our treatment of racial minorities, particularly the Negro."[19] The Department began to consider recruiting more African Americans as Foreign Service officers in order to assign them to areas like British West Africa, where they might help "offset the widespread and growing African criticism of racial practices in the United States."[20] In its September 1950 issue, *The Christian Century* framed its applause for voluntary school desegregation in some areas of the American South in terms of the importance of race relations in the United States for the country's effectiveness as a world leader. "In the draining of the reservoirs of good will toward America," wrote the magazine's editors, "no single factor has proved quite so disastrous as our unchristian, undemocratic pattern of race relationships."[21] The Truman administration recognized that the further removal of racial barriers in the United States would significantly increase "the faith of other countries in this country's capacity for leadership."[22]

The problems that American racial practices and ties with imperial powers created for the relationship of the United States to the Third World were highlighted anew at the fall 1950 sessions of the United Nations, especially on the issue of South Africa's treatment of its nationals of Indian descent. The implementation of apartheid legislation by the Malan government had exacerbated this old conflict between the Union and India. Preliminary U.N.-sponsored talks between the two countries in February had seemed to indicate hope for a resolution to the problem, but the Malan government's passage of the Group Areas Act in June, with its provisions for total racial segregation in the Union, destroyed Indian hopes of a compromise.[23] With the outbreak of war in Korea and the need to gain as much participation as possible from member nations in the U.N. "police action" there, the Truman administration sought to moderate what it called "this case of discord among two non-Communist governments which opens promising avenues to Soviet propagandists."[24] Determined to avoid further alienating the Union and perhaps causing it to withdraw from the United Nations, Washington urged renewed talks between the two countries as a substitute for India's resolution in the General Assembly asking South Africa to move away from apartheid and bring its treatment of people of Indian origin into line with the principles of the U.N. Charter.[25] Internally, the State Department acknowledged the importance of this issue for American relations with the world's nonwhite majority, concluding in September that "we do not wish to be in the position of either voting against or abstaining on a resolution which may have the support of two-thirds of the General Assembly."[26]

As the Indian resolution neared a vote in November, discussions within the U.S. delegation revealed the depth of American anxieties about racial issues and their influence on the course of international affairs. Some of the American delegates worried that an ambiguous U.S. position on the resolution would place the United States "in disrepute with [the] colored peoples of the world and display exactly the kind of weakness on [the] racial issue of which [the] Soviets already [have] made unceasing propaganda capital."[27] Calling race relations "our Achilles' heel before the world," Henry Cabot Lodge noted that "all over the United States there were violations of our basic civil rights policies." Lodge emphasized to his colleagues in the U.S. delegation the symbolic importance of this vote and argued that "we should say South Africa was wrong in this matter just as we are, and we could admit we were wrong." Other delegates warned about the danger of using a double standard for human rights violations, condemning them vigorously in Eastern Europe while claiming that they were strictly a domestic matter in South Africa. John Hickerson of the State Department admitted that Americans had "a beam or two in our own eyes," such as the segregation laws of his native state of Texas, and agreed that the South African government was wrong to treat

Indians as it did, although he reminded his colleagues that in other respects—such as helping in Korea—the South Africans "were pretty good people." [28]

After trying unsuccessfully to amend the Indian resolution so as to remove the flat declaration that segregation constituted discrimination, the Truman administration finally decided to vote in favor of it in early December. The dramatic Chinese entry into the Korean War just a week earlier influenced this choice, as the United States sought renewed support for the war effort from other Asian countries. Acheson explained the vote to a disappointed South African representative in terms of "the critical situation in Asia at the moment and the effect of our vote on the peoples of Asia." [29]

One of the greatest fears of American policymakers in the crisis atmosphere of 1950 was that Third World resentment of American and European racial discrimination might encourage nonwhite peoples to seek closer relations with the Soviet Union. Aware that nationalism and anti-colonialism were fast becoming permanent features of African public life, the State Department emphasized the need to "differentiate between Communist infiltration and the justifiable political ambitions of the native population." [30] The Department was pleased that, in contrast to much of Asia, communist ideals and loyalties seemed not yet to have penetrated Africa in any substantial way. [31] In order to keep Africans oriented toward the West in the long run, Assistant Secretary of State George McGhee considered it imperative for the United States to use "this period of grace," while communist pressure was absent, to help build better living conditions for the African peoples so that poverty and discrimination at the hands of the West would not make communism attractive in contrast. [32] The State Department worried that the white supremacist attitudes of colonial officials and white settlers in southern Africa and the apartheid policies of the South African government would "play into the hands of Communist agitators" and help turn Africans in the region away from the West. [33]

The best way to avoid this danger, according to Washington, was for the administering authorities in Africa to develop progressive colonial policies that would bring greater benefits to the African population and thereby engender the more harmonious race relations "essential to the welfare of the entire free world." [34] Acknowledging that "there has been a tendency to place the emphasis on Europe's need for Africa rather than on the mutual need of Africa and Europe for each other," the State Department declared in April 1950 that "it is now our view that the mutuality of this need should be emphasized." [35] McGhee urged Acheson to work with the European colonial powers for "a reasonable acceleration" of the political and economic development of Africa. [36]

The outbreak of war in Korea increased the enormous American concern for preserving "stability" in the non-communist world. Whether stability was best achieved by honoring the immediate needs and inherited attitudes of the European imperial nations or by supporting and even championing the independent economic and political aspirations of the nonwhite majority in the United Nations remained an open question, at least in theory. In practice, U.S. officials concluded that stability required staying close to the metropolitan powers in the short run, while also trying to gain the favor of the colonial peoples of Africa in the longer term.[37] The difficulty of accomplishing both of these tasks simultaneously haunted the Truman administration. At best they were straddling a difficult fence; at worst they were caught on the horns of a painful dilemma—some might even say a glaring contradiction. When forced to choose between the two opposing options in the atmosphere of international crisis arising from the war in Korea, American policymakers assigned first priority to the immediate need for preserving the Western alliance.[38]

II

The difficulties the Truman administration faced in maintaining an anti-communist alliance that included both the white rulers of Africa and the nonwhite peoples under their authority were clearest in South Africa. African resentment of the apartheid policies of the Malan government spilled into the streets during 1950, manifesting itself in organized demonstrations and prompting a ferocious and deadly response from the white authorities. The Nationalist regime made it clear that it would have no truck with previous South African governments' talk of blacks gaining rights and privileges in the Union when they became more "civilized"; under apartheid, they would *never* be granted the same political and economic rights as whites. African nationalists within the ANC found themselves hurtled forward by escalating racial tensions into taking more radically democratic positions. Whether with reluctance or exhilaration, they felt obliged to sever the strands of hope for gradualist reform that tied them to white South African liberals.[39]

While unwavering in its emphasis on racial pride and on African leadership for Africans, the now ascendant Youth League of the ANC specifically rejected what it called an "extreme and ultra revolutionary" policy of "hurl[ing] the Whiteman [in]to the sea."[40] The ANC insisted on an end to white domination under any guise—"segregation, apartheid, trusteeship, or White leadership"—but offered an explicitly Christian vision of a nonracial future for the Union in which whites would also have an important place.[41] Despite the Programme of Action's focus on African racial unity, the political and material aspirations of most of the highly Westernized leaders of the ANC tended to be very similar to those espoused by Western societies. Ideologically diverse in its own leadership, the Congress from 1950 onwards reacted to the tightening administration of apartheid laws in part by developing alliances with democrats of other colors, including Indians, Coloreds, and white radicals. The Youth League's Robert Sobukwe noted that "we are prepared to work with any man who is fighting for the liberation of Africa [from white domination] *within our life-time.*"[42] In South Africa in 1950, the small but dedicated Communist Party remained the group other than African nationalists that most prominently opposed apartheid or any other form of white supremacy. Initially suspicious that communists were merely another version of manipulative whites, African nationalists by early 1950 were appreciating the financial resources, organizational abilities, and often remarkable courage of white communists in an apartheid country and were beginning to build an important alliance with them.[43]

The possibility of substantial political ties between white radicals and blacks fanned the flames of Pretoria's fears of subversion and was hardly welcome news in Washington. The South African police closely monitored the activities of the Youth League, which the American Embassy believed was "violently anti-European and threatens to eventually oust [the] white man from power in South Africa."[44] As the ANC moved away from its traditional strategy of petitioning the authorities for desired changes and began to use militantly democratic language and to organize anti-apartheid demonstrations, the white authorities targeted the organization's leaders in their increasing harassment of Africans. Crushing poverty remained the greatest single obstacle to African political organizing, as most Africans in the Union had to focus all of their energies on sheer economic survival. The illegality and risk of political involvement for people with no political rights also hindered the work of the ANC and other black organizations. But the increasing humiliation and degradation of Africans at the hands of the South African authorities more than offset these hindrances, evoking unprecedented resistance to white domination in the early months of 1950.[45]

Simmering tensions between residents of the sprawling African locations around Johannesburg and white police patrolling the areas flared into large-scale violence in January and February. Africans bitterly resented the increasingly frequent and arbitrary enforcement of the pass laws, which required them to carry an identification card at all times and show it upon demand by the police. Similarly, they took offense at the random police raids of their homes in the middle of the night to enforce laws banning African possession of liquor. The arrest of a man in Newclare for alcohol possession on the night of January 29 sparked an armed clash between police and some fifteen hundred Africans in the location, during which six hundred more Africans were arrested. The U.S. Embassy reported to Washington that this was "a further indication of the current deterioration of race relations" in the Union, which the Communist Party of South Africa would seek to exploit for its own subversive ends.[46]

Two weeks later, the arrest of another Newclare resident for not carrying his pass escalated into three days of violent conflict between police and hundreds of Africans there and in the neighboring location of

Sophiatown. The shocked American consul in Johannesburg, Sydney Redecker, reported that "it was necessary" for the police to use "pistols, rifles and even machine guns to disperse the rioters," who were largely unarmed. He detailed injuries to police officers and even the damage police cars had sustained, but made no mention of casualties among those on the receiving end of machine-gun fire. Redecker hinted at "grievances of the natives against the white authorities" but registered astonishment at the level of anger expressed by Africans against the police; he warned that if the residents of the location had had more than just a few pistols, the results would have been "infinitely worse and incalculable." As it was, the extent of violence between whites and Africans made the February clashes "the most serious to occur thus far against the established European authority of South Africa."[47]

An even more ominous feature of the street fighting in Newclare and Sophiatown was the involvement of armed white vigilantes. Unimpressed by the use of machine guns against unarmed people, and determined to prevent the violence from spreading into Johannesburg proper, residents of the nearest white neighborhoods believed that the police were not mobilizing adequate force to restore order. Many defied police orders by driving into the locations and beating Africans at random in order to "teach them a lesson."[48] White citizens throughout Johannesburg were now enormously anxious about the possibility of further unrest as they feared that Africans might be losing all respect for white laws and authority.[49] A government commission established to investigate "acts of violence committed by Natives" in the locations during the previous four months concluded in March that the police had shown "remarkable restraint" in employing no greater force than was absolutely necessary to end the disorder. The commission did note that Africans genuinely detested the "brutal" nighttime police raids on their homes, and it admitted that there "seems to be some justification for the complaints against some of the younger members of the South African police" who, the commission conceded, apparently treated Africans with "undue harshness." But the commission concluded that Communist agitators, irresponsible youth gangs, and even African women egging on their husbands and lovers contributed at least as much to the outbreaks of violence in the African locations.[50]

American governmental observers in the Union believed the causes of the clashes to be more deeply rooted in the discriminatory character of South African society, especially as exacerbated by the Nationalist government. Consul Redecker pointed to the "natives' increasing restlessness and dissatisfaction with their entire status, economic and living conditions, and more immediately, the increasingly stringent police control measures to which they have been subjected during the last two years." He described the overcrowded "slums unsuitable for human habitation" in which urban Africans were forced to live, and the extraordinary amounts of time they had to spend commuting by inadequate public transportation to any jobs they were fortunate enough to find in the white sectors of the city. Redecker cited the absence of street lighting, sanitation, and recreational facilities in the African locations as contributing to Johannesburg's ranking as one of the world's cities with the highest crime rates. From an official American perspective, the ultimate danger posed by these conditions and the South African government's lack of interest in changing them could be traced to Moscow. The U.S. Embassy in Capetown emphasized that the recent disturbances in the African locations had not been caused by communist organizers, but it agreed with Redecker that "communist elements are very active among the natives and take every opportunity to intensify their feelings of injustice and frustration, and to foment trouble between the native and ruling European population[s]." Apartheid, it seemed, might be weakening the allegiance of the majority of South Africans to the West.[51]

Organized black resistance to apartheid reached a new level of seriousness in the events of "Freedom Day," 1 May 1950. Joseph Sweeney, a former Los Angeles social worker and former OSS agent with a doctorate in political science who was now the political officer of the U.S. Embassy in South Africa, believed that these incidents offered "the first authentic glimpse of the Nationalist Government in action in a racial crisis."[52] Since the adoption of the Programme of Action five months earlier, the ANC had been moving to implement its new policy of complete noncooperation with the Union government.[53] Five thousand people turned out to welcome ANC president-general Dr. James Moroka when he arrived in Johannesburg on March 26 to chair a "Defend Free Speech Convention" protesting the government's barring of the most prominent South African communists, including Sam Kahn, Yusuf Dadoo, and labor organizer J. B. Marks, from public speaking of any kind. African, Colored, Indian, and Communist Party leaders in the Transvaal issued a joint call for a boycott of work by all nonwhites on May Day as a protest against the entire array of discriminatory restrictions on nonwhites.[54]

Some of the younger African nationalists in the ANC still distrusted the Communist Party and hesitated to work closely with it and with other non-African organizations, but the Congress as a whole agreed to the call for a general "Freedom Day" strike on the traditional labor holiday used for demonstrations of worker solidarity in the communist world.[55] The U.S. Embassy was impressed by "the unusually high degree of organization that has characterized the planning for 'Freedom Day' [and that] reflects the new militancy of the African National Congress." The Embassy recognized that this would not be "a preponderant Communist show" but rather "a protest by the Natives against the many restrictions that are imposed on them."[56] Concerned that a successful work stoppage of even a day might encourage further African resistance, the South African government inundated the African locations with announcements of the banning of all public meetings of more than a dozen people for the entire May Day weekend and the illegality of staying away from work as a protest. Joseph Sweeney recalled later that

> no one who did not live in South Africa at this time can fully appreciate what a stoppage of African labor would have meant. Not only would most of white South Africa not have received its early morning tea, breakfast, or any other meal, but little housework would have been done, no children minded, no artisan would have had his tools handed to him, all heavy lifting would have stopped, and industry would have virtually ceased. It would have been comparable to New York City without electrical current.[57]

The Malan regime was determined to prevent blacks in the Union from gaining the confidence and empowerment which might result from a dramatic demonstration of the country's utter dependence on their labor.[58]

The leaders of all the major black organizations publicly urged their followers not to disobey the government ban on demonstrations, which the protest organizers had cancelled. With the Union Defense Forces on full alert and ready to back them up, heavily armed police units patrolled the entire Rand area, especially the African locations, on Monday, May 1. A tense calm prevailed until late afternoon in the Benoni location, where a crowd of several hundred Africans had gathered on a sports field to listen to two Indians speaking on the need for racial equality in South Africa. A police detachment arrived, ordered the crowd to disperse, and began cursing and beating the people nearest them. When the civilians failed to leave at once, the police charged them once with batons and a second time with bayonets. After their enthusiastic use of bayonets carried them into the middle of the large crowd, they panicked at the fear of being surrounded and opened fire with rifles and at least one machine gun. A dozen Africans were killed and several dozen wounded, while a handful of police were injured by rocks thrown from the crowd. News of the violence spread quickly into nearby African locations, resulting in further clashes with the police. Official summaries put the total number of African casualties at thirty wounded and eighteen dead, including several children, but Africans present at the incidents reported that the real numbers were considerably higher.[59]

From the U.S Embassy, Sweeney cabled Secretary of State Acheson that the May Day clashes were "the most serious in recent South African history" and "uglier in mood" than any previous conflicts between police and Africans. He warned that the outbreaks of violence formed "part of a pattern of racial tension which threatens the internal stability of the Union."[60] The increasing brutality of police raids into the African locations around Johannesburg, clearly intended since the year before to punish and intimidate whole populations rather than to catch specific criminals, was encouraging greater African resentment of the white authorities. American observers and the South African government were greatly surprised by the success of the stay-at-home strike on the Rand, as at least half of all African workers did not report for work on May 1.[61] This indicated increasing cohesion and organization in the black communities in the face of greater white restrictions on the daily lives of black South Africans.[62] Sweeney also recognized that a major reason the clashes had not been even worse was the restraint shown by black leaders in urging their followers to avoid violence regardless of police provocation. What Sweeney called "signs of a new spirit of nationalism among the Natives" loomed behind the immediate demands for decent wages and the elimination of the pass system.[63]

The eagerness of the police to use overwhelming and deadly force to silence even nonviolent dissent indicated the ominous direction in which white South African society was moving. The police had been given orders to shoot to kill whenever the authority of the government was disputed, and they had shown what the U.S. Embassy called "an aggressive overwillingness to forestall even the hint of violence with bullets."[64] Margaret Ballinger and the handful of other liberals in the South African Parliament sought a public investigation of the clashes and their underlying causes in hopes of preventing such incidents in the future, but Malan rejected any discussion of what he saw as strictly a matter of internal security. Most tellingly, Smuts and the other United Party leaders did not support Ballinger's proposal as they were determined to appear supportive of the police and to avoid being portrayed as "*kaffir-boeties*" (roughly, "nigger-lovers") by the Nationalists. As Smuts put it in agreeing with his old nemesis Malan, "force must be met with force."[65]

Joseph Sweeney reported home to the State Department that future riots in South Africa could only be prevented by significant improvements in African living conditions, but that the Union government had no interest in implementing reforms.[66] The racial violence on the Rand seemed instead to have confirmed Nationalist leaders in their conviction that only rigid control of Africans could "keep the Native in his place." This meant increased police and military strength, more effective counter-intelligence, a continued low standard of living for Africans, and more thorough apartheid legislation and administration.[67] A prominent Transvaal attorney captured the deepest feeling of most Afrikaners, and of many whites of English descent, when he commented privately in the wake of the "Freedom Day" clashes: "This is a white country and we are going to keep it white if we have to kill all of the others."[68] Faced with an historic movement among black South Africans towards greater political unity and boldness, the Union government remained determined neither to compromise on its racial policies nor to allow any further public demonstrations of dissent. At this critical juncture, the Nationalist regime moved vigorously to preserve what Sweeney summarized as "white supremacy in an Afrikaner republic—the beginnings of modern Africa's first police state."[69]

In late May the National Executive Committee of the ANC decided to call for a national day of protest against the government's proposed Suppression of Communism Bill (originally titled the Unlawful Organizations Bill) and Group Areas Bill, and a day of mourning for those killed by the police on "Freedom Day." With the support of the other major black organizations and the Communist Party, the ANC called on all "Africans, Indians, Coloureds and European democrats" to "stay quietly in their homes" on Monday, June 26, as a display of strength and unity against the Nationalist government's "policy of apartheid, tyranny and oppression."[70] Some conservative African nationalists, in a manner remarkably similar to that of the government, had blamed the "Freedom Day" deaths of Africans on the manipulative determination of communist organizers to "stamped[e] our people into the May Day demonstrations" in order to gain a propaganda victory for communism rather than a real victory for the African people.[71] But the leading edge of African nationalism in the Union, the Congress Youth League, rallied strongly behind the plans for June 26, issuing a dramatic plea for democratic unity and concluding, "Up You Mighty Race!"[72]

Mixed results from the "Day of Protest and Mourning" suggested both the organizational difficulties confronting black South Africans and their growing sense of political unity and determination in 1950. The effort proved largely ineffective in the Transvaal and in Capetown, but it resulted in an almost complete shutdown of Port Elizabeth and a serious dislocation of daily life in Durban.[73] The U.S. consul in Port Elizabeth, Harold Robison, reported to the State Department that the protest there was thoroughly peaceful and "highly successful."[74] In order to avoid conflicts with the large and heavily armed police forces patrolling the nation's cities that day, protest organizers worked hard to keep people at home and off the streets.[75] In contrast to the "Freedom Day" protests, which had been limited to Johannesburg and the surrounding Transvaal area, the "Day of Protest and Mourning" marked, in the ANC's words, "the first attempt at a political strike on a national scale by the Non-European people of this country."[76] The U.S. Embassy also sensed the significance of the June 26 stay-at-home, reporting to Washington that "it was one of the many warm-ups that will occur in South Africa before the Natives feel strong enough to launch a full-scale offensive against 'White-supremacy.' "[77]

ANC president-general Moroka offered a glimpse of some of the larger meaning of the "Day of Protest and Mourning" in a public statement a few days later. He acknowledged the limited participation in the protest and credited the effectiveness of the South African government and many white employers in threatening to fire black workers who failed to show up for work. But he lauded the large number of disciplined protestors who refused to be intimidated or provoked into violence by police harassment, despite being "treated as though we were the private property of White South Africa." Moroka warned the government that this protest signified that "we are in dead earnest about our intention to live in this land untrammelled, to live under human and humane conditions, to live in peace and harmony with those other human beings whom it has pleased providence to place in this part of the globe." The ANC president-general pointed out that these events in South Africa could not be separated from the larger global struggle for the self-determination of all peoples, including the conflagration in Korea, which had begun just one day before the "Day of Protest and Mourning": "The good wishes of the democratic outside world have been with us . . . [in our] struggle for [our] very existence and to keep the campfires of democracy flickering." It was not at all clear, however, that the most powerful nation of that democratic world outside the Union, the United States, while eager to stoke those campfires in Korea, would be part of "the wide democratic and Christian world" which Moroka believed was "with us in our tribulation" in southern Africa.[78]

For the rest of 1950, the reports of American diplomats in South Africa remained grim about the prospects for a peaceful resolution of the problems that were widening the gulf between blacks and whites in the Union. In response to escalating police harassment and intimidation of blacks and the enactment of severe new apartheid laws, the ANC issued an unprecedented public statement in early August calling for "unqualified fundamental rights" for all Africans and warning of a "racial explosion" if the current trend of racial animosity continued.[79] New U.S. Ambassador John Erhardt told Acheson in October in his first report from South Africa that "racial relations have deteriorated so badly in South Africa since the advent of the Nationalist Government that there are few white people in the country who have anything like an adequate understanding of what is going on among Native leaders and Native organizations." Erhardt noted that among whites in the Union "it is popular to say that Native opinion does not exist, but this is wishful thinking on the part of advocates of 'white supremacy.' " The U.S. Embassy, he concluded, "believes the cohesiveness of Native opinion is generally underestimated."[80] Joseph Sweeney added that information about black political organizing was "extremely scanty," but that "all the present evidence is that cooperation among non-European groups is unusually high."[81] White South Africans seemed to have little knowledge of, and even less interest in, the dramatic changes under way among the majority of their countrymen.[82]

American governmental observers feared that as South Africa continued "on its way to becoming a police state," the country's black majority might either convert to communism or at least ally itself closely with communists as the best available means of resisting oppression.[83] The problem confronting American diplomats in South Africa was that communists seemed to be more on the side of racial justice and elemental decency than any other whites in the country. While claiming that communists were perhaps "not sincere," Ambassador Erhardt admitted to Acheson in a cable in October that "the legitimate grievances of Natives are legion and among the few persons who espouse these grievances the majority of vocal ones are Communists." Until it dissolved itself on June

20 in anticipation of being banned by the government six days later, the Communist Party of South Africa had remained the only political party Africans could join. Erhardt noted the utter lack of communication between even the most liberal whites and their fellow residents of darker hues, and contrasted this with the lack of racial elitism among white communists in the Union "who *know* the Natives . . . and often know them very well."[84]

Even if black South Africans did not seek to create a Soviet-style communist state, Erhardt shared the concern of the country's few white liberals that increasing governmental oppression could lead blacks to conclude that "whether Communism is a good or bad thing, it is the only outside force they can call upon for assistance." The courage and long-standing commitment of many black Communist Party members, including Yusuf Dadoo, J. B. Marks, and Moses Kotane, to the cause of racial justice in South Africa helped give the Party real credibility among the country's nonwhite population. Erhardt reported to Washington that the more difficult the Nationalist government made the achievement of racial equality in South Africa, the more black leaders would have to seek help from all potential allies, among whom communists would rank very high.[85]

Even more disturbing for the Truman administration in the second half of 1950 was the possibility that apartheid's radicalization of South Africa's black majority at home might spill over into the international arena. The reinforcement of the color line in the Union inclined black South Africans to be suspicious of other countries practicing racial discrimination, including the segregated United States and the colonialist Western European nations. The tendency of those same states to defend South Africa at the United Nations and to keep close relations with the Nationalist regime increased black uncertainty about the anticommunist West. With the United States at war in Korea, African doubts about the values and practices of the West were not a welcome development from the perspective of Washington. Bernard Connelly reported in mid-August that Africans in the Union were "growing increasingly sympathetic toward the North Koreans, because they interpret events in Korea as a racial struggle and without being fully aware of all aspects of the Korean situation they favor any side that bears the epithet 'Gooks.' "[86] In his January 1951 review of the previous year in South Africa, Erhardt noted that African opinion in the Union was generally opposed to participation on the side of the United Nations in the Korean War, "which it looked upon as a color clash in which its sympathies were with the colored side, i.e. the North Koreans."[87] The official attitude of the ANC "that the Korean people are competent to solve their own problems" suggested considerable distrust of the American view of the war.[88]

The highest priority in Washington by the end of 1950 was what American officials saw as the international struggle between the democratic nations of the West and the communist countries allied with the

Soviet Union. In southern Africa, however, the experience of apartheid and continued white settler dominion were casting doubt on that formulation in the minds of the region's nonwhite majority, for whom anticommunism seemed to be closely linked with white supremacy. The ruthlessness of the white authorities in South Africa in dealing with Africans showed no signs of abating: on November 27 in the Witzieshoek Native Reserve, police opened fire with machine guns on an unarmed crowd of Africans who failed to disperse immediately when ordered to. More than a dozen people were killed and almost a hundred wounded.[89] American observers in the Union believed there was little chance of an effective black challenge to white rule in the immediate future, but they foresaw only more trouble on the horizon in South Africa. Joseph Sweeney, whose role as the political officer of the U.S. Embassy and whose relatively liberal racial attitudes enabled him to get a better sense of African opinion than other American officials at the time, warned his superiors in Washington that "no one could spend much time in South Africa without recognizing that the white population is sitting on a volcano which could explode at any time."[90]

III

In addition to dividing white from black more clearly than ever before in South Africa, the Nationalist Party in 1950 also established beyond question its hegemony within the small but crucial realm of white politics in the Union. Having accepted a devaluation of the South African pound and brought the country successfully through the financial crisis of the previous year, the Nationalists used the racial crisis they had fostered to move white politics sharply to the right. In their quest to establish perpetual white supremacy in an Afrikaner republic, Malan and the other Nationalist leaders put the foundational legislation for apartheid into effect in 1950 with the enthusiastic support of the majority of white South Africans. Implementing apartheid meant, above all else, channeling the historic processes of industrialization and urbanization in a manner that would severely limit social mixing and economic interdependence across race lines. In this endeavor the Nationalists mobilized increasing physical force against black opposition, while assuming extraordinary legal powers under the guise of defending the traditional Afrikaner way of life from the threat of international communism. The Malan government played masterfully on white racial fears to gain support for its equation of any movement toward greater racial equality with communism and subversion.[91]

By further widening the racial chasm in South African society and establishing itself as the premier defender of white supremacy, the Nationalist Party eliminated the tenuous middle ground in Union politics and forced the United Party opposition to move either right or left. The party of Smuts, thoroughly grounded in its own version of white dominance and especially sensitive to the need for an inexpensive, tractable African labor force for South African industry and mining, chose a defensive posture of acquiescing in the establishment of apartheid by refusing to offer a clear alternative to it.[92] The Nationalists' determination and fervor in pursuing racial segregation and the annexation of South West Africa and the British High Commission territories impressed almost all white South Africans, whose sensitivity to international criticism of their country had heightened their feelings of patriotism. By contrast, the United Party's efforts to sound more "reasonable" in the inflamed racial atmosphere of 1950 made it seem indecisive and even dangerous to fearful white South Africans. The United Party also suffered from its traditional association with England, as the British government was linking itself very cautiously, but publicly, to a policy of eventual racial equality in Africa by its political reforms in West Africa and by such symbolic gestures as including Africans in social gatherings for visiting British officials in Kenya.[93]

Such events pushed most English-speaking white South Africans to identify themselves fully as South Africans and no longer as even partially British. Very few white South Africans desired guidance from a country with an undercurrent of racially egalitarian ideas; many more understood Malan when he warned of the "bitter fruit" of African political participation in British West Africa.[94] Nationalist Party calls for a mass expatriation of South Africans of Indian descent also won it considerable support among English-speaking whites in Natal, who had traditionally backed the United Party but who loathed Indians. By exacerbating racial tensions and by defining white politics in South Africa as primarily the protection of white interests and privileges, the Nationalists succeeded in establishing themselves as the preferred representatives of a growing majority of white South Africans.[95]

In the late spring and early summer of 1950, the Nationalist Party pushed through the South African Parliament four important pieces of legislation. These laid much of the statutory groundwork for apartheid and what one American diplomat called at the time "the South African police-state-in-the-making."[96] Just as the long-standing ban on marriages between whites and Africans had been amended a year earlier to include marriages between whites and any nonwhites, the Immorality Amendment Act of 1950 extended the decades-old prohibition of extramarital sexual intercourse between whites and Africans to include any sex between whites and all nonwhites. This bill targeted the Colored community in particular, as the Nationalists sought to prevent any further slippages in what they saw as white South African racial purity. Second, the Population Registration Act of 1950 classified each South African by identifiable racial categories, a sometimes difficult task but a prerequisite for making any system of more rigorous segregation enforceable. Finally, the Group Areas Act and the Suppression of Communism Act proved the most significant determinants of the direction of South African social and political development.

The Group Areas Act empowered the government to proclaim residential and business areas as being for the exclusive ownership or occupation of one of the particular "racial groups" defined by the Population Registration Act. This meant a wholesale unscrambling of South Africa's many urban neighborhoods that were not fully segregated in order to prevent all social relationships, especially of a peer nature, across racial lines.[97] The Indian community in the Union would suffer particularly grievous losses from the implementation of this racial zoning, as many middle-class Indians owned land in largely white neighborhoods and made their livings through commerce with non-Indians.[98]

As the vehicle for absolute residential segregation, the Group Areas Act demonstrated more clearly than any other piece of apartheid legislation that South African racial practices were moving in a direction opposite from that of the rest of the world. *The New Republic* commented that the United States was "losing its grim distinction as the country where racial discrimination is worst"; with this law South Africa "now seems to be in the number-one place."[99] Henry S. Villard, the former head of the State Department's first Division of African Affairs and now the U.S. Ambassador in Norway, reported to Washington from Oslo that Norwegians were appalled by the Group Areas Act. He summarized their feeling that "with this reactionary step which is nothing but sheer Hitlerism, the [South African] Government has deprived itself of any understanding and sympathy from democratic world opinion. People may to a certain extent understand racial problems, but they cannot sympathize with a government which consciously works for an increase of racial discrimination."[100] Whether this "democratic world opinion" would include the government Villard worked for remained to be seen.

The Suppression of Communism Act outlawed the Communist Party of South Africa and, even more significantly, created the offense of statutory communism to include all extralegal efforts at social change. The bill defined "Communism" as "any doctrine or scheme which aims at bringing about any political, industrial, social or economic change within the Union by the promotion of disturbance or disorder" or "which aims at the encouragement of feelings of hostility between the European and non-European races of the Union."[101] The law gave the government the right to deprive those it named "Communists" of their property and freedom without redress to any court.[102] This sweeping exception to the idea of civil liberty for whites, in which the public law of South Africa was at least theoretically grounded, formed the most important of what Joseph Sweeney called "the traditional trappings of the police state" that the Malan government was taking on.[103] By defining all but the mildest critics of apartheid as "Communists," the Nationalists were able to eliminate all meaningful public political dialogue in the Union. Most white South

Africans found reassurance in the idea of a communist conspiracy, which offered an easy explanation for dissatisfaction with the status quo and relieved them of responsibility for the worsening racial crisis in their land.[104]

There were, of course, a small number of real communists in the Union, even after the Communist Party of South Africa had dissolved itself just a few days prior to being outlawed. They included some of the foremost political organizers of all races who believed in and worked for racial equality, and they opposed apartheid and all other forms of white supremacy. But the Suppression of Communism Act, with a definition of communism so broad that actual Communist Party ideologues must have found at least some amusement in it, had much more ambitious intentions than simply silencing Member of Parliament Sam Kahn or South African Indian Congress leader Yusuf Dadoo. Through this ultimate measure of "red-baiting," the Malan government sought to create a Manichaean world in which all serious dissent against apartheid would be discredited as subversion emanating from Moscow. While talking about "Communism," the Nationalists intended to remove all liberal influences from South African public life.[105] American observers recognized that the final purpose of this Nationalist strategy was "to perpetuate White supremacy in an Afrikaans republic."[106] In achieving their goal of absolute political control of the Union, the Nationalists had no scruples about using force against even nonviolent dissent, as one shocked U.S. Embassy officer learned by chancing upon the police's brutal dispersion of a mostly black crowd gathered peacefully outside the Parliament building in Capetown on June 14 to protest the Suppression of Communism Bill.[107]

The political strength of Afrikaner nationalism among white voters reached a critical mass with the 30 August 1950 elections in South West Africa. While not annexing the territory and thereby avoiding provocation of the international community, the Malan government in 1949 had created six new seats in the South African House of Assembly and four in the Senate for South West Africa. In the August 1950 elections to fill those positions, white South West Africans chose all Nationalist candidates.[108] This gave the Nationalist Party for the first time an absolute majority in Parliament even without its small coalition partner, the Afrikaner Party. The Nationalists claimed that their thorough sweep of the South West African elections, coming so soon after the enactment of their major legislative initiatives, constituted a resounding white mandate for apartheid. Americans in the Union recognized that the Nationalists were in the process of building themselves an almost unassailable position of dominance in South African white minority politics.[109]

Certain British policies toward South Africa also strengthened the Nationalists' political position in the Union and in the southern African region in 1950. Facing the threat of preemptive action by South Africa against Bechuanaland, the London government issued its decision in March to ban Seretse Khama and his English wife from the territory.[110] Britain sought to bolster its security links with Commonwealth nations, arranging with American approval for the exchange of classified military information with South Africa and the other member states.[111] Allied in their support of the United States in Korea and fearful of communist aggression elsewhere, England and South Africa reached an agreement along with Australia and New Zealand for the use of Commonwealth forces in any prospective conflict in the Middle East.[112] By the end of the summer, the South African Navy was cooperating in frequent joint exercises with the South Atlantic Squadron of the British Royal Navy.[113] While not happy with Pretoria's domestic policies, the British government chose not to emphasize its differences with South Africa but rather to focus on certain interests the two governments shared in the international realm.[114]

Following hard on the United Party's devastating defeat in the South West African elections, the death of Jan Smuts on September 11 further assured the ascendancy of the Nationalist Party in the Union. Smuts had managed almost singlehandedly to keep together the diverse factions of the United Party, ranging from the few white liberals in the country to a much larger bloc of conservatives who differed little from the Nationalists. American observers noted that this combination made the United Party parallel in many ways to the Democratic Party in the United States.[115] Many United Party supporters had been more loyal to Smuts than to the party itself, and after his death large numbers of them were likely to switch to supporting the Nationalists.[116] Americans stationed in the Union worried that the United Party might be disintegrating, especially since the two most dynamic candidates for replacing Smuts as party leader were both political liabilities among white voters in the inflamed racial atmosphere of 1950: Harry Oppenheimer, who was of Jewish descent; and Sir de Villiers Graff, who had an English title and was believed to have some "Coloured blood" in his family line.[117] J. G. N. Strauss was chosen instead, leading Ambassador Erhardt to report to Washington his "reputation for mediocrity."[118]

The death of Smuts from a stroke at the age of eighty did not immediately affect South African politics, for, as the U.S. Embassy noted, "his dissent was more one of degree than principle, and the road this country has taken has been evident for some time."[119] Joseph Sweeney admired Smuts' "vision" and "reckless courage" but regretted that "he had never once used this courage on behalf of the Africans" due to his fundamental agreement with Malan on racial issues.[120] Nevertheless, his removal from the political scene did mean the loss of the Union's most prominent promoter of South African ties with the outside world, particularly Great Britain and its more liberal traditions. Smuts' death therefore appropriately symbolized the thorough victory of Afrikaner nationalism in South Africa.[121]

Malan's elevation of Dr. Hendrik F. Verwoerd to Minister of Native Affairs in a reshuffling of the Cabinet in October provided one other momentous sign of the direction in which South African society was moving in 1950. Verwoerd was one of the younger generation of fervent

Afrikaner nationalists, mostly from the Transvaal, who wanted the elderly Malan, a product of the Cape province and its relatively more restrained racial customs, to move faster with the apartheid program. While frankly labeling Verwoerd "a rabid racialist" and disagreeing completely with his approach to solving South Africa's racial problems, Joseph Sweeney admitted he was "far and away the ablest and most energetic man" ever put in charge of the Department of Native Affairs.[122]

Verwoerd quickly became the leading ideologue of apartheid and provided much of the drive behind the government's extensive efforts at implementing complete racial segregation over the next several years. After eight years of reordering South African society through his control of "Native Affairs," he would be elected Prime Minister in 1958, reminding the world that "our motto is to maintain white supremacy for all time to come over our own people and our own country."[123] With Hofmeyr and now Smuts dead, the United Party in decline, and Verwoerd rising quickly in influence, the U.S. Embassy warned Acheson that the South African government would utterly disregard the welfare of the vast majority of South Africans who were black and would draw "ever closer to its ideal of an Afrikaner Republic in which civil liberties as they are known in the western world will be curtailed." Because it saw "no evidence of any spirit of moderation on the horizon," the Embassy believed "these plain, and admittedly alarming, forecasts are justified."[124]

IV

While tensions in Europe and the outbreak of war in Korea kept the Truman administration focused largely on other parts of the globe in 1950, American strategic interests in South Africa and the escalating racial conflict in that country did encourage Washington to pay more attention to the Union than ever before. Truman asked NAACP president Walter White for a report on South Africa if White went on his planned tour of Africa in the spring, and Republican leader Harold Stassen visited the Union in December.[125] Assistant Secretary of State George McGhee, whose area of responsibility included Africa, spent a week in South Africa in March and talked at length with Malan and other government officials. McGhee sought to encourage Malan in his allegiance to the West, reminding him that "we viewed with tolerance the steps which the [South African] Government was taking to handle its [domestic] problems."[126] In later reflections on that trip, the Texan Assistant Secretary demonstrated the continuing tendency of affluent white Americans to identify with affluent white South Africans more than with anyone else on the African continent. He described feeling amazed at the "progressive spirit and dynamism of the Johannesburg businessmen" whose new skyscrapers and industrial plants created "an atmosphere more like Chicago than Africa. Indeed, there was nothing else in Africa like it."

Nowhere else in Africa, it seemed, could a well-to-do white American feel more at home.[127]

Traditional white American attitudes toward Africans had changed little in the years since World War II. Americans still had minimal contact with Africans in the Union and no effective intelligence about African political organizations and their plans.[128] The intensification of the Cold War and anticommunism in the United States had rendered more ominous the long-standing American assumption that Africans lacked substantial cultures of their own: their supposed cultural void now seemed a ready invitation to communist influence. Sydney Redecker, the U.S. consul in Johannesburg, expressed this concern to the State Department in a revealing manner on 15 September 1950: "The African natives . . . offer an unusual [opportunity] for the propagation of communism, especially since, unlike the populations of China, India, Indonesia, [the] Near East, etc., which have ancient and deep-rooted cultures and religions of their own for serving as a barrier or deterrent to their absorption of the communist philosophy, the African natives are virtually completely lacking in any cultural or religious background or any intellectual or spiritual resources of their own." Redecker believed that Africans were materially better off in the Union than anywhere else in Africa, and that life in an industrialized society, even under apartheid, was therefore preferable to life in more pastoral areas of the continent. Even the gold mines, he added, were a "civilizing force" for Africans "from remote parts of Africa," who thereby came into direct contact for the first time with the "advanced modern European civilization" represented by "the great office buildings of Johannesburg" and "the beautiful European homes." Arguing that it would require "not years, but decades and generations to prepare the natives for democratic self-rule," Redecker warned that only the maintenance of white authority in southern Africa could prevent the "disorders, anarchy and retrogression"—and eventual communist victory—inevitable in any swift transition to majority rule.[129]

The U.S. Embassy's political officer, Joseph Sweeney, recalled later his frustration in 1950 that "no one in the Department of State paid any serious attention to South Africa except as a source of strategic minerals." Sweeney found that he "could not interest our people" in Washington in the "Freedom Day" riots of May 1 and their significance as an indicator of the Nationalist government's refusal to seek any mutual accommodation with the country's black majority.[130] The degree to which the Truman administration quietly supported white authority in the Union was suggested by the small but symbolic role of the United States in the events of May Day on the Rand. Two American B-50 bombers arrived at Palmeitfontein Airport outside Johannesburg on April 26, the twenty-ninth anniversary of the founding of the South African Air Force, for a scheduled four-day visit from England. The South African Air Force and the white public showed extraordinary interest in the American "super-fortresses," with a crowd of seventy-five thousand people, the largest ever at the airfield, gathering to admire the most recent addition to the military arsenal of the United States.[131]

Apparently at the request of the South African government, the planes did not leave as planned on April 30 but instead extended their stay for three more days. On May 1, they flew up and down the Rand on an unannounced flight, convincing "large numbers" of Africans that the planes were in the Union in order to intimidate and perhaps even bomb them if trouble were to break out in the townships and locations.[132] The American pilots of the B-50s may have been unaware of the political significance of their aerial work that day, but their South African hosts could hardly have been so naïve. American diplomats in the Union, who knew that British authorities had used a comparable display of air power over African communities in Kenya ten months earlier in order to intimidate protestors against white rule there, understood the significance of the presence of the American bombers on the Rand.[133]

The passage of the major apartheid laws in May and June troubled the Truman administration, but not nearly enough to cause any reorientation of American policy toward the Union. The U.S. Embassy in Capetown noted that the Afrikaner nationalists' "tactics of raising the cry of 'Communism' at all and sundry who oppose apartheid" rendered the Suppression of Communism Act "a distinctly unhealthy sign of the times . . . [that] supports the contention of the Anti-Government groups that the Nationalist Government is aiming at the creation of a 'police state.' "[134] The American press registered dismay at the direction of official South African racial policies, which the editors of *The Crisis* called "a full-fledged totalitarian philosophy with a master-race policy as brutal and reactionary as anything ever cooked up by the Nazis."[135] But the rising tide of anticommunism in the segregated United States, typified by the Internal Security Act about to be approved overwhelmingly by Congress, made it almost impossible for American officials to criticize an even more anticommunist country, even had they been inclined to. Malan announced on June 2 that South Africa would not recognize the new communist government of China but would maintain relations with the Chinese Nationalist regime in Taiwan instead.[136] Under heavy attack from Senator McCarthy and other conservative Republicans for "losing" China and being "soft" on communism, the State Department had no interest in rebuking a government with such compatible views of the international situation.[137]

The most important events tying South Africa to the United States were the outbreak of war in Korea on June 25 and South Africa's support for the American forces that moved swiftly to the defense of South Korea. The Union's Suppression of Communism Act, enacted the very next day, could hardly have upset an American administration now certain that it was at war with the allied forces of international communism. The white South African press, public, and armed forces wholeheartedly approved of the U.N.-sanctioned American actions in Korea.[138] Temporarily putting aside its resentment of the United Nations, the Malan regime also declared its support for the U.N. "police action" against North Korea.[139] After some initial hesitation, the South African government decided on August 4 to contribute a fighter squadron to the U.N. forces; the South African Air Force group left Durban three weeks later and arrived in Korea in September.[140] The commitment of actual South African personnel to the war in Korea confirmed for the Truman administration the trustworthiness of South Africa as an ally in the now militarized Cold War.[141]

The entry of the United States into a full-scale military conflict in Korea determined Washington's priorities for the rest of Truman's term in office. The administration feared that the North Korean invasion might be merely the first move of a general communist assault against the "free world." Concern for domestic reforms in the United States and in other countries it was allied with disappeared as the American government focused almost entirely on the crisis abroad. The Truman administration paid little further attention to its civil rights programs and sought unity among the noncommunist nations; criticism of the racial policies of allied countries seemed to have no place in the perilous situation facing the West.[142] Secretary of State Acheson later recalled his disdain in 1950 for "purists who would have no dealings with any but the fairest of democratic states, going from state to state with litmus paper testing them for true-blue democracy." He resented what he saw as their irresponsibility and "escapism in [not] dealing with the world as it was."[143] George Kennan explained in September that "what we require in the public personality of other states is less 'democracy' than stability and correctness of attitude with respect to international life."[144] By these criteria, the South African government was proving itself thoroughly acceptable to the United States.

With South Africa on board as a full-fledged ally in the Korean War, the Truman administration continued its policy of mediating between the Union and the rest of the members of the United Nations in order to keep South Africa from leaving the organization. The International Court of Justice had handed down its advisory opinion on South West Africa on July 11, concluding that South Africa was not legally obligated to place the territory under the U.N. trusteeship system but that it was required to continue making annual reports to the United Nations and to transmit any petitions from the inhabitants of the area to the U.N.[145] The United States worked with Britain to urge Pretoria to abide by the Court's compromise decision, and got U.N. approval for establishing a smaller, more sympathetic committee to work with South Africa toward implementing the decision.[146] Under considerable pressure from other member nations, the Truman administration agreed in September to sidestep the antiradical immigration restrictions of the new Internal Security Act and allow the Rev. Michael Scott into New York to address the U.N. Trusteeship Council on behalf of the Africans of South West

Africa.[147] But Washington made it clear to Pretoria that it shared white South Africa's view of Scott as a dangerous radical with long-standing connections to the Communist Party in both Britain and South Africa.[148] Joseph Sweeney recalled that Scott's opposition to Malan on the issue of South West Africa was too isolated to be effective "with the Western democracies looking the other way, or at any rate checking their strategic stockpiles."[149]

The entry of tens of thousands of Chinese troops into the Korean War on the side of North Korea in late November ended months of American military successes. The swift American retreat from the Yalu River renewed the feeling of crisis in Washington, where Truman told a national television and radio audience on December 15 that "our homes, our Nation, [and] all the things we believe in, are in great danger."[150] The next day the President declared the existence of a national emergency due to "the increasing menace of the forces of communist aggression" organized by Moscow.[151] The National Security Council concluded that "the United States and its allies of the free world are fighting a war of survival against the aggression of Soviet Russia."[152] Senator Arthur Vandenberg captured the widespread American fear of a general war in a letter to Acheson: "I hope the Good Lord will make us worthy of His benediction. In times like these all that counts is our country."[153] Military strategists in the Truman administration believed that a great window of American vulnerability had opened up because of increasing Soviet military strength, and they feared that the Chinese support for the North Koreans might be the start of a global war masterminded by the Soviets. The U.S. government determined that only a massive American military buildup around the globe could save the world from communist aggression, and it proceeded to accomplish that task by a threefold increase in U.S. military spending during the course of the Korean War.[154]

Any expansion of the critical nuclear portion of the American military arsenal required, of course, more uranium ore. The Soviet achievement of atomic weaponry less than a year earlier had already provoked the Truman administration to seek increased production of fissionable materials, and events in Korea further accelerated that search. U.S. Air Force planners contributed urgency to the task by using improved American intelligence capacities to raise their estimates of crucial Soviet targets to be eliminated in a general war between the two nations.[155] The Defense Department acknowledged in September that its program "to increase the production of fissionable material calls for an expansion of production at a rate as rapid as the limiting factor of ore permits."[156] The war in Korea also sharpened American concerns for nuclear security and preventing any Soviet procurement of fissionable materials from the West.[157] "If the free countries of Asia and Africa should fall to Soviet Russia," President Truman announced in his State of the Union address on 8 January 1951, "we would lose the sources of many of our most vital raw materials, including uranium, which is the basis of our atomic power."[158]

In 1950, the Belgian Congo remained by far the greatest single source of uranium ore for the United States. The State Department considered Belgium a dependable ally with whom the United States had relations "as untroubled as those with any other country"; Belgium solidly supported NATO and the Marshall Plan and was a "fundamentally conservative country" that feared and distrusted the Soviet Union.[159] While the Belgian government continued to press the Truman administration to fulfill the 1944 Tripartite Agreement by bringing Belgium into research and development work on atomic energy for nonmilitary uses, the Belgians guaranteed the flow of ore from the Shinkolobwe mine to the United States and did not hinder a growing American trade in other goods with the Congo.[160] Union Minière, which managed the mine, expanded its uranium production after the start of the Korean War at the request of the Americans and the British, and received a price increase from the Combined Development Agency in October to offset the costs of doing so.[161] In early November the Belgian government allowed the U.S. Ambassador in Belgium, Robert Murphy, to visit the Congo in order to evaluate the security of the area against outside attacks.[162]

American nuclear planners were acutely conscious in 1950 that the Congolese supply of uranium ore might run out in the near future, and they looked to South Africa to become the next major supplier.[163] Problems that had slowed the negotiations between the Combined Development Agency and the South African Atomic Energy Board for a final contract for the production and sale of South African ore were being solved. Processes for efficiently separating uranium ore from gold ore were approaching completion. Secretary of Defense Louis Johnson, distrusting British security measures after the arrest of Klaus Fuchs for atomic espionage, wanted an exclusive contract between the United States and South Africa, but Acheson and the U.S. Atomic Energy Commission persuaded him not to interfere with the ongoing negotiations by the CDA.[164] Acheson and other strategists in the administration anticipated that South Africa would seek involvement in atomic energy research and development as part of any agreement on selling ore; the Americans, along with the British, preferred a purely commercial contract, but were willing to include the South Africans in the nuclear "club" if they insisted on it.[165] With the United States at war in Korea and urgently seeking to expand its nuclear stockpile, Acheson pressed Malan to complete the negotiations and expedite uranium production in the Union.[166] On November 23, representatives of the United States and Britain signed a contract with the South African government for the production of uranium ore and its sale to the Combined Development Agency over a period of ten years.

Both sides indicated considerable satisfaction with the uranium arrangement. The white South African press and public received the announcement of the new contract with great pride. They ranked it alongside the discoveries of diamonds and gold in the nineteenth century as the third great mineral to be produced in the Union and one that demonstrated South Africa's unusual strategic importance. One Nationalist newspaper declared that South African uranium might prove to be "the chief weapon in preserving Western civilization" against Soviet aggression.[167] The American and British governments agreed to provide in the form of loans all of the capital necessary for financing the establishment of the six projected uranium extraction plants on the Rand. The Truman administration was particularly pleased with the helpful attitude of the Malan government, which successfully pressured the hesitant South African gold mining companies to take on the uranium production project and thereby enter into unprecedentedly close financial relations with the United States.[168] Despite its troubling racial policies and problems, the Pretoria regime had again proven itself a reliable ally of the United States in matters of the highest priority to the Truman administration. "Perhaps most encouraging of all about the present [South African] Government's attitude," concluded Ambassador Erhardt, "is that internationally it has come of age."[169]

South Africa's agreement to produce and sell uranium ore to the United States was followed by swift satisfaction of the Union's longstanding but previously unsuccessful efforts to get substantial military equipment and loans from the United States. Partly in anticipation of closer relations with Pretoria, the Truman administration pushed through Congress an amendment to the Mutual Defense Assistance Act that gave the President wider latitude in extending assistance for the procurement of military supplies to "free countries whose security is important to us."[170] In talks with South African Minister of Defense F. C. Erasmus in New York on 4 October 1950, Acheson was acutely aware that the uranium negotiations were nearing completion and indicated his appreciation for South Africa's contribution of a fighter squadron to the American-directed U.N. military effort in Korea.[171] Erasmus then went on to Washington to discuss details of military equipment desired by his government with George Marshall, recently brought out of retirement to replace Louis Johnson as Secretary of Defense.[172] The Central Intelligence Agency warned that "South African military planning, to a degree unknown in North Atlantic Treaty states, focuses on the basic requirement of internal security," but the Truman administration was encouraged by South Africa's recent commitment to helping the NATO powers in the defense of the rest of the African continent and the Middle East.[173] On 5 February 1951, with South African uranium newly under contract to the United States, Acheson notified South African Ambassador Jooste that the United States government would now give "the most sympathetic consideration" to requests by the Union for military equipment.[174]

The continuing modernization of South Africa's economic infrastructure required a steady inflow of capital from abroad, and the Malan government had been seeking substantial loans from the U.S.-dominated World Bank, the United States' Export-Import Bank, and private banks in New York since its early days in office. Pretoria had been disappointed in 1949 to arrange only a $10 million credit from a group of New York banks. With the conclusion of the uranium contract, however, U.S. governmental funds began to flow swiftly to the Union, and Truman administration officials acknowledged privately that strategic minerals were the key to this new American attitude.[175] On 23 January 1951, the World Bank announced that it had granted two loans totalling $50 million to South Africa: one of $30 million for developing electric power facilities, and one of $20 million for overhauling and expanding the entire national transportation system. Eight leading American commercial banks announced on the same day that they were granting a $30 million loan to the South African government for purposes complementary to those of the World Bank loans. Five months later the Export-Import Bank, at the request of the U.S. Atomic Energy Commission, completed its arrangements for a $35 million loan to various mining companies in South Africa for the uranium production project.[176]

By the end of 1950, the relationship of the United States and the Union of South Africa had entered a new stage of unprecedented closeness. As the Cold War flared into full-scale hot war on the Korean peninsula and the United States declared a national emergency, the Malan government proved itself a dependable ally of the West and as vociferous an opponent of the Soviet Union and communism as any American Cold Warrior could want. By sending troops to fight alongside the Americans in Korea and by promising to provide a new source of uranium ore to fuel the American nuclear arsenal, the Nationalist regime demonstrated its profound importance to the Truman administration. In return, the United States government agreed to provide large loans and weapons, which would be used principally for internal security against opponents of apartheid. American corporations and investors noted this signal from Washington of the Union's significance, and increased their involvement in South African economic ventures.[177] Considerations of national security had proven vastly more important for American policymakers than concern for democracy or racial equality, for the tighter bonds between Washington and Pretoria came in the same year that the Union government consolidated its apartheid policies and demonstrated the brutality with which it would treat any sign of dissent by the vast majority of South Africans who were not white. The Truman administration did not favor the direction South African racial politics were heading, but it was more than willing to accept an apartheid ally for reasons of national security.[178]

CHAPTER 8

Apartheid and the Cold War: Confirming the Ties, 1951–1952

he last two years of the Truman administration coincided with a period of enormous unrest in South Africa. In its efforts to implement a more rigorous version of racial segregation and to stamp out domestic dissent, the government of Daniel Malan provoked an intense but ephemeral organizing effort by white opposition groups and a full-scale constitutional crisis over the powers of the Nationalist-controlled Parliament. More significantly for the future of the Union, traditionally divided black opposition organizations united in 1952 for a sustained, nonviolent Defiance Campaign against what they called the "unjust laws" of apartheid. While not immediately successful in changing the country's racial legislation, the unprecedented degree of discipline and black participation in the Defiance Campaign marked the historic beginning of a unified movement for a nonracial, democratic South Africa. In the short run, however, the Nationalist Party extended its control of the country by ultimately crushing the Defiance Campaign, defusing the constitutional crisis, which threatened white unity, and increasing its hegemony in white politics with a resounding victory in the national elections of April 1953.

The war in Korea had established priorities for the United States government that remained in effect for the rest of the Truman administration's tenure in office. Western unity against the forces of international communism took precedence over all other considerations. The NATO allies, including the British, Belgian, and Portuguese rulers of colonial southern Africa, provided the backbone of military and political support for the American defense of South Korea. The anticommunist government of South Africa also contributed military forces to that effort and, in the fall of 1952, began fulfilling its promise to supply uranium ore for the American nuclear arsenal. Amidst the decisive events of 1950, apartheid had settled in among the "free" nations of the West, where it would remain for decades to come. The last years of the Truman administration saw the consolidation of this relationship.

I

The constitutional crisis that created unusual animosity and instability within white South Africa in 1951 and 1952 arose over the Malan government's effort to remove Colored voters in the Cape province from the common voters' roll. Unlike Africans, who—if they met the property and income requirements—could only vote on a separate roll for three Members of Parliament to represent all Africans in the entire Union, Coloreds of sufficient means in the Cape voted in the same manner as whites. The Separate Representation of Voters Act ("Colored Voters Act") aimed to strengthen the Nationalist Party by eliminating a bloc of nonwhite voters who provided the necessary electoral margin for several United Party representatives in Parliament. But the legislation touched on more fundamental issues in the governance of the Union.

The South African Act of Union of 1909 formed the constitution of modern South Africa. It allowed for amendments to itself by a simple parliamentary majority, with the exception of two "entrenched clauses," which could be altered only by a two-thirds vote of Parliament. These clauses guaranteed the voting rights of Cape Coloreds and the legal equality of English and Afrikaans as national languages. The Nationalist government believed, however, that since the Statute of Westminster in 1931, in which the British government had affirmed the complete sovereignty of the Union Parliament over South African affairs, Parliament could do whatever it wished by a simple majority vote, including amending the "entrenched clauses." Since the Nationalists held a majority but not two-thirds of the seats in Parliament, this difference was critical.

The authoritarian tendencies of the Nationalist government had already aroused concerns among moderate white opponents who differed little with Malan on issues of racial segregation. The United Party naturally opposed the disenfranchisement of voters who consistently supported their candidates. But more fundamentally, the Nationalists' willingness to alter one of the two "entrenched clauses" of the constitution did not bode well for their respect for the other one, and English-speaking South Africans were alarmed. War veterans had always resented the Nationalists' support for Nazi Germany, and they reacted to this new threat to the balance of white power by organizing the Torch Commando as an extra-parliamentary citizens' movement and lobbying group in April 1951. The formation of the short-lived Torch Commando represented a last stand by white moderates against the rising tide of Nationalist Party power. Their specific goal was the defeat of the Colored Voters Bill, although their refusal to allow Colored war veterans into their organization illuminated the profound degree of white agreement about racial issues in the Union.[1]

Colored voters in the Cape province registered unhappiness about their threatened disenfranchisement with a peaceful protest march in Capetown by eight thousand people on 8 March 1951, the day the Colored Voters Bill was introduced in Parliament. They followed this with a general strike on May 7, which received some support from black South Africans and encouraged the trend towards greater nonwhite unity. The Torch Commando then flexed its political muscle by organizing a huge parade by torchlight through the streets of Capetown; tens of thousands of South Africans of all races turned out to demonstrate their displeasure with the authoritarian direction of the Malan government's policies. When the authorities barred a deputation of marchers from entering the Parliament building, violence broke out as police charged the restive crowd with fixed bayonets and the protestors fought back with flaming torches and pieces of iron fence. Over a hundred people were injured. The government then wielded the incident as supposed proof of the revolutionary danger posed by opponents of apartheid and the need to prevent further demonstrations as threats to the national security of the Union. Malan reiterated that South Africa was more threatened by communism than any other country due to the Union's large nonwhite population, and that any agitation of South Africa's blacks played directly into the hands of the Soviet Union.[2]

The South African Parliament passed the Separate Representation of Voters Act in June. In the same month, it drastically strengthened the already severe Suppression of Communism Act by amending it to become indefinitely retroactive; now anyone who at any point in the past had spoken or acted in ways the government wished to define as "communistic" could be banned from public life. Minister of the Interior T. E. Donges explained that it was difficult to fight communism in a nation where "agitators" of any race "did not always preach out-and-out Communism" but instead cleverly seized every opportunity to "foment" civil disobedience, dissent, and dissatisfaction.[3] The ruling Nationalists were succeeding in defining South African politics as a choice between apartheid and communism, with no middle ground.[4]

American diplomatic representatives in the Union, while accustomed to a broad definition of communism by their own government, did worry about the talk of "civil war" that circulated among some unhappy English-speaking South Africans in the summer of 1951. Chargé d'affaires Bernard Connelly kept Washington apprised of their resentment of the "authoritarian trend" of the Nationalist government and their determination "to maintain parliamentary democracy for white people."[5] Despite apartheid's progress and the tensions it had created, however, Connelly reported the U.S. Embassy's opinion that "it will take a great many years before a fully authoritarian regime would be possible in South Africa."[6]

The main white opposition group, the United Party, found itself pulled along toward apartheid by the Nationalists' polarizing tactics. Saddled with weak leadership and a position fraught with contradictions, the United Party proved unable to articulate policies of any substantial difference with the Nationalists on such major issues as racial segregation, South West Africa, and the British High Commission territories.[7]

In October the United Party, admitting it had no contact with African organizations or leaders, commissioned a private study of African political attitudes. Joseph Sweeney of the U.S. Embassy noted how "it is a reflection on the white South African approach to the Native problem that the simple task of finding out what the Native thinks politically should be such a mystery and require such a secretive approach."[8] By early 1952, United Party leader J. G. N. Strauss announced that if returned to power, his party would preserve the Group Areas Act and only amend it in minor ways. Both of the major parties in the Union now stood on an apartheid platform.[9]

Growing numbers of Africans in South Africa recognized the false dichotomy of apartheid and communism and understood that the perceived threat masked by the Nationalists' red-baiting was the idea of nonracial democracy. Urban Africans particularly resented the government's repression of all efforts to improve their impoverished condition, as they sought to enter into the Western economic life enjoyed by their white countrymen through better access to education and jobs.[10] The new U.S. Ambassador in South Africa, Waldemar J. Gallman, a career diplomat who would prove a sympathetic friend to the Malan regime during his three years in the Union, reported to Washington in November 1951 that the continuing implementation of apartheid was inevitably provoking African unrest and that "relations between the Natives and Whites have deteriorated to the lowest level in the Union's history." Gallman discounted rumors of an imminent widespread African uprising and believed that the South African government had enough forces at hand to quell almost any rebellion that might happen. He warned, however, that the Malan regime's insistence on keeping sizable military forces in the Union in the event of any war indicated its unspoken respect for Africans' organizing abilities. More troubling to the American ambassador was the fact that there was "no non-Communist white person who is on the 'inside' of thinking and planning among the non-European leaders." The only whites fully trusted by black South Africans appeared to be those of radical political commitments.[11]

When Americans in the Union made efforts to discover how educated Africans felt about conditions in their country and about the United States, they were disappointed to receive some sharp criticisms. Bitter African resentment of white supremacy in the Union translated into disappointment with the United States for not opposing apartheid. A U.S. Embassy officer reported a conversation with a group of Africans who said they could understand support for the Malan government by the British government, given its long record of colonialism, "but America was now the great western exponent of freedom and they expected her to use her influence in their favor." While very few Africans in the Union were communists, they said that they could not help but notice that the Soviet Union and local communists sided with them in their struggle against white oppression, while the United States supported the apartheid government at the United Nations. These Westernized Africans feared that their own "advocacy of racial equality might lead to their arrests as Communists under the Suppression of Communism Act"; they had heard in the news of people being arrested as communists in the United States, and they wondered if there were a similar motive of white supremacy involved in those detentions. Their association of anticommunism with white supremacy made black South Africans reluctant recruits for the Cold War that dominated Washington's view of the world.[12]

The increasing legal and administrative debilitation of black South Africans under apartheid encouraged the developing sense of unity among black political organizations in the Union. With the government's attack on Colored voting rights and other privileges in 1951, the Colored community in the Cape Province, which had long kept itself apart from less privileged Africans, began to seek to form a common front with other blacks. The ANC and the South African Indian Congress (SAIC) had already worked together, along with the Communist Party, on the Freedom Day and Day of Mourning protests of the previous year. At a meeting on 29 July 1951 in Johannesburg, representatives of the ANC, SAIC, and the (Colored) Franchise Action Committee (FRAC) agreed to plan a massive "Defiance Campaign" of peaceful civil disobedience as a demonstration of resistance to apartheid. A joint planning council of the three organizations recommended in November that an ultimatum be given to the government to repeal the "unjust laws" of apartheid by February 1952. This report was endorsed by the ANC in December, and a national action council was set up to direct the campaigning. In January, Prime Minister Malan received an ultimatum signed by James Moroka and Walter Sisulu of the ANC, calling for the repeal of six areas of legislation created or exacerbated by the Nationalist government since 1948: pass laws, stock limitation laws for rural areas, the Bantu Authorities Act (which sought to restructure political and economic relations in the native reserves), the Group Areas Act, the Colored Voters Act, and the Suppression of Communism Act. The ultimatum was summarily rejected by Malan. The State Department observed these events carefully, noting in September 1951 that "the most significant political trend in the Union today is the growing cooperation among Indian, Native and Colored groups" fostered by the Nationalists' "blatant deprivation of non-European rights."[13]

Political uncertainty in the Union increased anew when the South African Appeals Court, the nation's highest judiciary body, declared on 20 March 1952 that the government's Colored Voters Act was unconstitutional and therefore invalid. While United Party and Torch Commando leaders called for the Malan government to resign, the Nationalists responded by introducing a "High Court of Parliament Act" to make the legislature itself the highest court in the land and thereby overrule the Appeals Court. The measure passed both houses by a simple majority and became law on June 3. By this blatant attempt to remove constitutional restraints on its power to rule the country by party fiat, the Nationalists provoked renewed tensions within the white political community, even as the threat of organized black resistance to apartheid loomed larger than ever.[14]

In the spring of 1952, the government began to use the authority of the amended Suppression of Communism Act to silence its opponents, forbidding their membership in certain organizations, restricting their freedom of movement, and barring them from public speaking.[15] When Solly Sachs, the general secretary of the interracial Garment Workers' Union, refused to abide by the government's decree, the Nationalist regime arrested him in the middle of a speech he was giving to ten thousand union members, most of them Afrikaner women, outside the Johannesburg City Hall on May 24. The enraged crowd, who revered Sachs for his decades of work on their behalf, responded by booing lustily and hurling small missiles at the police. Large numbers of police then stormed out of City Hall and charged the crowd with batons. The American consul general in Johannesburg, Marselis Parsons, described the resulting action: "These policemen then moved among the crowd, hitting women and non-Europeans seemingly without provocation." Parsons reported to Washington that the timing of Sachs' arrest and the "gratuitous brutality of the police" indicated that the government had apparently desired to provoke serious riots and bloodshed.[16]

The Malan government's heavyhanded manner of dealing with its more radical opponents did not bode well for its traditional rivals in the United Party. The English-language press began to compare the Union to a police state, and an all-white "Democratic Front," made up of the United Party, the Torch Commando, and the small Labour Party, demonstrated that it could bring out tens of thousands of white opponents of the government to open-air protest rallies.[17] The United Party remained, however, just as committed to white dominion in South Africa as the Nationalists, and in its disagreements with the government it never threatened to join forces with the majority of South Africans who were not white. As apartheid polarized the country more completely into black and white camps, the United Party refused to provide an alternative vision of the Union's racial future to that offered by the architects of apartheid.[18] On the eve of the Defiance Campaign, Assistant Secretary of State George Perkins warned Dean Acheson that in recent months in South Africa, "racial tension has increased at such a rate, primarily because of the Government's heavy-handed apartheid policies, as to raise the possibility of serious disorders within the next few years."[19] John Foster Dulles, a special adviser to Truman on foreign affairs, articulated Washington's concern that apartheid might destabilize the entire region by igniting "an explosion that will spread the fire of revolution throughout Africa and shake the colonial rule of England, France and Belgium."[20]

By 1952, blacks in South Africa had little reason to hope for liberation through the established political system. The few white liberals in the country failed to stand clearly for color-blind democracy and an end to racial discrimination.[21] Distrusting the supposed liberalness of English-speaking white South Africans, many blacks preferred to deal with the Afrikaner nationalists, for at least "you know where you are with the Dutchman," as one African proverb put it. An African in Sophiatown, outside Johannesburg, explained this phenomenon to journalist Anthony Sampson:

> Yes, man, with Danny Malan you know where you are. "I'm going to keep the Kaffirs in their place," he says to the Dutchmen, and he does. He means it. Police, guns, passes, prison. We know who we're fighting. But if things got bad with Slim Jannie Smuts, he'd get Congress [the ANC] along and shake hands and say, "Good morning, Mister Xuma," and everyone said, "Old Smuts is a good guy really!" And we'd forget all about apartheid and all the bad laws; I'm telling you![22]

The debased conditions under which all Africans lived and worked, whether in the mines, on farms, in prisons, in the cities, or in the African locations on the edges of the urban areas, contrasted dramatically with the growing affluence and comfort of most white South Africans. As resentment of their economic oppression built among the nation's impoverished majority and no hope for political change and eventual enfranchisement issued from the existing system, black South Africans indicated a new readiness to challenge white authority.[23]

Afrikaners and other white South Africans held large celebrations in Capetown on 6 April 1952 to mark the tercentenary of Jan Van Riebeeck's landing at the Cape of Good Hope with the first white settlers in southern Africa in 1652. Black South Africans greeted the day with massive, peaceful protest rallies in the major cities of the Union, at which resolutions were passed approving further stages of protest against the government's racial laws.[24] In his address to a rally in Johannesburg that day, Dr. Moroka, the president-general of the ANC, explained that while whites indeed had much to celebrate in terms of their good health and the wealth they had extracted from the land over three centuries, they had also created "a record of sadness," of slavery and continuing exploitation, by seeing nonwhites solely "as servants and enemies." Moroka responded to the steady Nationalist drumbeat of proclaiming the red and black menaces while escalating oppressive measures against blacks:

> We are said to be influenced by communism. That accusation is loudest when we are most insistent on a just recognition of our rights. Anyone who asserts the rights of the downtrodden is labelled a communist. . . . Any and everyone who raises his voice for justice and fair-play is said to be a communist. I wish to state here most emphatically that we, the African National Congress, are not communists.

It was the conditions blacks lived under, not communism, concluded Moroka, that made them cry out in protest.[25]

Encouraged by the success of the April 6 rallies, the Joint Planning

Council of the ANC, the SAIC, and the FRAC decided to begin the Defiance Campaign on June 26. Nelson Mandela, as "Volunteer-in-Chief," and Walter Sisulu, the only paid ANC official, as secretary-general of the organization, played key roles in organizing the campaign and were among the first resisters arrested. Volunteers, mostly African but also Indian and Colored, who had been trained in nonviolent civil disobedience broke minor regulations regarding racial segregation throughout the Union. When arrested and fined, they almost all refused to pay and spent time in jail instead. Their acts of defiance were watched by a much larger crowd of supporters, and the Campaign helped build a spirit of resistance in the black communities while also filling the jails to overflowing in many areas. The Campaign was infused in much of the country with a religious fervor, including daily prayer meetings. The resistance effort had its greatest participation in the eastern Cape Province, around Port Elizabeth and New London, where it merged with black trade union sentiment and strikes in support of the Campaign. Rather than petering out as expected by whites, the Defiance Campaign continued steadily through the summer, reaching its peak in September with twenty-five hundred arrests that month. An astonished Ambassador Gallman cabled Acheson on September 11 that the resistance seemed now to "pose a very serious problem" for the South African government. The white ambassador admitted he was "surprised to find at this stage of development in So[uth] Afr[ica] so impressive a measure of responsible leadership and discipline" among blacks.[26]

Despite a boost at the beginning of October from India's successful effort to get the United Nations to debate South Africa's entire apartheid policy, the Defiance Campaign ground almost to a halt with the outbreak of violence in Port Elizabeth on October 18 and in East London on November 9. In the first incident, a riot flared after a policeman apparently assaulted two Africans he was questioning at a railroad station. When they resisted, he fired into the crowd that was gathering, killing one and injuring several others. Police reinforcements arrived and fired again into the stone-throwing crowd, killing at least six more Africans, although American observers believed the actual African death toll to be as high as 160. Four whites were then killed by the enraged crowd in a series of attacks on white-owned property.[27]

In the second incident, heavily armed police employed a bayonet charge to break up a peaceful Sunday "prayer meeting" in East London for which local ANC officials had previously received approval from the white authorities, but which the police said had become instead a political gathering. As the police drove them into the nearby African "location," or ghetto, those attending the meeting brutally killed two whites, including a Dominican nun. The police then cordoned off the location and continued firing into it for hours, killing seven Africans and wounding twenty-seven, according to police reports. The American consul in Port Elizabeth noted that hospital sources put the actual death toll closer to one hundred. The police also killed a number of other Africans in smaller riots in early November in Kimberley and Johannesburg.[28]

Dismayed ANC leaders immediately denounced the violence. Major General J. A. Brink, the South African Commissioner of Police, claimed that communist influences had caused the riots, and that the police should be allowed a completely free hand to deal with those elements accordingly.[29] American observers in the Union recognized, however, that the riots were spontaneous in origin and had no direct connection to the peaceful Defiance Campaign, although months of active resistance to the white authorities had inevitably increased tensions between blacks and police and had thus helped lay the groundwork for the outbreaks.[30] Henri La Tendresse, the attaché to the U.S. Embassy, emphasized to Washington that many of the South African police were "inexperienced and not noticeably endowed with a sense of responsibility"; instead, they seemed "anxious to impress the Natives with a show of force."[31]

Writing in *The Nation* a few months later, Harry Warner suggested that the eager provocation of violence by the police indicated their desire for opportunities to clash with Africans. Since the government had not been able to derail the disciplined campaign of peaceful passive resistance by ordinary means, Warner argued, it apparently sought to convert the protests to violence in order to crush them by the use of greater force.[32] Albert Lutuli, soon to be elected president-general of the ANC, agreed, claiming that the government had sent in *agents provocateurs* to help spark the riots and thus enable the government to reclaim the initiative from the passive resisters.[33] The editors of *The Nation* observed that the Malan government's handling of the disturbances demonstrated that it welcomed them, at least in part as a campaign strategy for the upcoming election to distract white voters from the South African courts' rulings in August and November that the High Court of Parliament Act was unconstitutional.[34]

The number of volunteers for the Defiance Campaign tapered off sharply in the late autumn of 1952, although the discipline and commitment of the protestors did win some symbolically important converts to their cause late in the year. The first whites joined the Campaign and were arrested in early December. They included Patrick Duncan, a former British colonial administrator and the son of a respected former governor-general of South Africa. He was joined by Manilal Gandhi, son of the late revered leader of India, who had earlier argued against the Defiance Campaign on the grounds that Africans in the Union were not yet sufficiently committed to the nonviolence at the heart of his father's principle of *satyagraha*.[35] The English monastic Father Trevor Huddleston, whose work among the poorest Africans in Johannesburg over the previous decade had made him a rare trusted white among South African blacks, publicly gave his support to the Campaign early in 1953. "It has been the teaching of the Church through the centuries," he declared at an ANC meeting, "that when government degenerates into tyranny . . . laws cease to be binding upon its subjects."[36]

Moroka, Mandela, Sisulu, and seventeen other leaders of the Defiance Campaign were put on trial by the government in December 1952 and convicted of "statutory communism" for their role as organizers. They were given suspended sentences. Moroka's efforts at the trial to distance himself from the other defendants in order to receive milder treatment hurt his standing in the ANC, and Albert Lutuli defeated him that same month in the election for president-general of the Congress, while Mandela won the post of deputy president.[37] Two harsh new laws passed by the Union government in February 1953 brought the Campaign to a final halt. The Public Safety Law allowed the government to declare a state of emergency at any time and enact whatever regulations it deemed necessary to deal with any situation. The Criminal Law Amendment Act created severe penalties for anyone guilty of protesting or encouraging protest against any law, including long jail sentences, astronomical fines, and even public floggings. This latter legislation made it nearly impossible to recruit volunteers for arrest. With the United Party almost unanimously supporting these laws, the idea of protected civil liberties seemed more distant than ever for most South Africans.[38]

The significance of the Defiance Campaign for South Africa's future lay in its demonstration of growing black unity in opposition to apartheid and its ability to win support from private citizens in the United States and England. Eight thousand "defiers" had been voluntarily arrested with what even whites acknowledged as remarkable self-discipline. The ANC had gained considerable visibility and prominence in South Africa, and its membership jumped from less than ten thousand to more than 100,000 in the course of a few months. Under Lutuli's guidance in early 1953, the ANC emphasized its ideological diversity and inclusiveness. Lutuli indicated his own preference for the variant of socialism represented by the British Labour Party, but he insisted that the Congress's only criterion for membership was a commitment to nonracial democracy in South Africa.[39] The Defiance Campaign showed with finality that black South Africans were now determined to control their own future and would no longer be interested in working under the tutelage of liberal whites, as even the South African Liberal Association admitted.[40]

Early in 1952, a handful of Americans with progressive political beliefs and an interest in Africa founded a group called Americans for South African Resistance (AFSAR) in New York. AFSAR provided publicity in the United States for the Defiance Campaign and raised five thousand dollars for the ANC, just as liberals in England undertook similar efforts. Songs by the famous African American performer and proponent of racial equality, Paul Robeson, were played over loudspeakers at rallies in South Africa in support of the Campaign. The struggle of black South Africans against apartheid was beginning to seep into the consciousness of educated people in the United States and England, laying the groundwork for the important support that would come from those sources in later decades.[41]

The ANC still meant little to the top policymakers in the Truman administration, but the Defiance Campaign did impress American observers in the Union. In response to Acheson's query in January 1953 about a report in the *New York Times* that the Malan government was considering moderating some of the restrictions on African land ownership in urban areas, the U.S. Embassy noted that the Campaign had been "a significant influence" in increasing Pretoria's interest in proclaiming the "positive" aspects of apartheid.[42] A month later, Ambassador Gallman reported to Washington that the successful execution of the sustained resistance effort indicated both the deteriorating state of race relations in South Africa and the growing political awareness and organization of the black majority there. Gallman argued that the Nationalist government needed to rescind its most egregiously oppressive laws, allow better economic and educational opportunities for blacks, and set up some kind of mechanism for at least consulting with nonwhites. The Ambassador believed that political rights were at the heart of the struggle in South Africa and that the Union government could best avoid revolutionary change in the future by granting the franchise now to a limited number of educated blacks. He warned against the dangers of too much democracy, however, emphasizing that "there can be no question of a general franchise for Natives" as the vast majority were "at this stage totally incompetent" to use the vote "properly." The result of universal suffrage, Gallman concluded, would be "a breakdown of the political structure of the Union, and at the extreme, chaos. It could open the gates to seizure of power by irresponsible elements or by Communists."[43]

The condescending attitude of white American officials about the capacities of black South Africans, combined with Washington's continuing support of the South African government at the United Nations, did not endear the Truman administration or its successors to those working for nonracial justice and freedom in the Union. ANC leaders identified their own struggle against white supremacy with the efforts of people of color throughout the colonial world to free themselves from imperial control by white Europeans. The ANC understood that the United States government, despite its democratic rhetoric, provided the strongest support to the purveyors of white dominion in the Third World. In his presidential address to the Transvaal chapter of the ANC in September 1953, Nelson Mandela condemned the brutal repression of the Mau Mau uprising in Kenya by the British and "the criminal attacks by the imperialists against the people of Malaya, Vietnam, Indonesia, Tunisia, and Tanganyika," and he opposed what he called "the efforts of imperialist America and her satellites to drag the world into the rule of violence and brutal force."[44] The Cold War assumptions that preoccupied the

United States were clearly proving less convincing to black South Africans.

As the Truman administration came to the end of its term in early 1953, racial polarization continued throughout southern Africa. In response to red- and black-baiting by the Nationalists, the United Party were determined not to be outdone as champions of white supremacy in the campaign leading up to the South African national elections of April 15. In the resulting atmosphere of exacerbated white racial fears, the relentless Nationalists won another large victory, doubling the size of their parliamentary majority and bolstering their plans for extending apartheid.[45] In the British colonies in central Africa, the return to power in London of a Conservative government paved the way for the creation of the white settler–dominated Central African Federation in August 1953, despite strenuous African objections. Intended by the British to create a more economically viable unit out of the Rhodesias and Nyasaland and to preserve British influence while minimizing that of South Africa, the short-lived Central African Federation functioned instead as a spur to the African nationalist struggle for independence from white rule.[46] And in the Belgian Congo, white settlers, fearful of the United Nations, the trend toward decolonization in much of the colonial world, and the example of self-government in the Gold Coast, sought to create a "White International" of European settlers in the region to lobby against the granting of any further power to Africans. They openly admired South Africa's racial policies, and they looked to the Malan government to rescue them and their wealth and status if Belgium ever pulled out of the Congo.[47]

II

In its policy toward the colonial world in general, and southern Africa in particular, the Truman administration in its last two years continued to seek what it called the "difficult middle course" between the European imperial powers and the people of color they ruled.[48] This effort was profoundly affected by the United States' being at war in Korea with what it believed were the united forces of international communism headed by the Soviet Union. The Truman administration considered its colonialist NATO allies crucial for the defense of the "free world" against further Soviet aggression, while the "dependent" peoples of the Third World could as yet offer little military strength to help with this foremost American priority. In the current "power struggle with the strongest and most dangerous dictatorship in history," the State Department believed that "there would be little value in a policy designed to create strong and democratic friends [in the Third World] 50 years hence at the cost of sacrificing the strength and stability of the nations upon which our security depends at this moment."[49]

American policymakers continued to recognize that certain problems accompanied the close alignment of the United States with other countries symbolizing white dominion over people of color, such as the Western European powers and South Africa. Waging counter-revolutionary warfare against people seeking political liberty could threaten the very identity of democratic states, as "nations of the Western world cannot at the same time maintain their own democratic political institutions and take the measures which would be required to stifle the demands of the dependent peoples" for self-government.[50] The State Department also believed that the United States "should avoid the danger of such a close identification with reactionary colonial policies that liberal opinion in the world will no longer be influenced by our leadership," since "liberals are today anti-Communist and it is to our interest that they should remain so."[51] With most African Americans still unable to vote in their own country, it could be seen as consistent that the United States would not support swift African independence from white rule. The National Security Council admitted that race relations in the United States were "psychologically damaging" to American interests in the colonial world. The NSC realized, too, that Cold War concerns were not paramount in the minds of unfree colonial peoples: "In underdeveloped countries, past or present white domination is a far greater psychological reality than the Soviet menace."[52]

In a world endangered by the pervasive threat of communist expansion, however, the United States government feared "premature independence" much more than any potential consequences of delaying national liberation in the Third World. "It is a hard, inescapable fact," explained Assistant Secretary of State Henry A. Byroade, "that premature independence can be dangerous, retrogressive, and destructive." According to this imagery, the Third World infant, "born" before it had reached full term (a point to be determined by the Western powers), would lack the vitality necessary to fend off the Soviet wolf, which would seek to devour it. The resulting damage to the "legitimate economic interests" of the Europeans in those areas "might seriously injure the European economies upon which our Atlantic defense system depends."[53] Secretary of State Acheson emphasized that the United States therefore needed to be very careful about how it expressed any sympathy toward those seeking self-government in the colonial world.[54] The men of the Truman administration distrusted the "extremist elements in the dependent territories" who, even if not communist in orientation, seemed similar to the anti-colonial representatives of the new nonwhite nations who had created what American policymakers considered "the relatively psychopathic atmosphere" of the U.N. Trusteeship Council.[55] From Washington's perspective, such emotional, irresponsible people could hardly compare in value to a dependable NATO ally like Great Britain or Belgium.

The Truman administration demonstrated its tendency to heavily favor European rather than Third World interests in its apportionment of economic assistance abroad. The President himself spoke in glowing terms of the Point Four program and its supposedly central place in American diplomacy: "There is nothing of greater importance in all our foreign policy. There is nothing that shows more clearly what we stand for and what we want to achieve."[56] In reality, however, as administration officials acknowledged privately, the program received minimal funding from the U.S. Congress and little support from the colonial powers in Africa. It represented more of a shift in propaganda tactics than a substantial change in the European priorities of American foreign policy.[57]

These facts were not lost on African nationalists. "If Point Four is going to capture the imagination of Africa," one ANC leader pointed out to a visiting journalist, "it will have to mean more than partnership between white and white, which is what it means now. It will have to mean partnership between white and black, and that we don't see a sign of."[58] With the war in Korea and the American rearmament effort in full swing, American economic aid under the new Mutual Security Administration, established in November 1951, became increasingly tied to activities contributing to American defense industries. Marshall Plan assistance reaching African colonial territories by late 1951 was being channeled to increase local food supplies for workers engaged in the production of strategic minerals.[59]

The relative absence of crises in Africa in the last two years of the Truman administration allowed Americans to continue focusing their attention elsewhere in the volatile international arena. Budgetary constraints and other priorities prompted the State Department in 1951 to reduce its already limited personnel and facilities on the African continent, as Assistant Secretary of State for Near Eastern and African Affairs George McGhee admitted that "the volume of 'hot news' from Africa south of the Sahara is somewhat limited."[60] Only during Truman's final months in office did the Defiance Campaign in South Africa and the Mau Mau rebellion in Kenya reveal the seriousness of African discontent with white rule and suggest the swiftness with which colonial rule would soon be driven out of most of the continent. The editors of *The Crisis* predicted in November 1952 that the now-evident determination of Africans to rule themselves would "eventually blast Europe out of Africa."[61] In an article entitled "All Africa Is Moved by a Wave of Unrest," which appeared a month later in the *New York Times,* C. L. Sulzberger warned that the quiescent days of white authority in Africa were gone. He worried about the Soviet Union's benefitting from anticolonial efforts there, but acknowledged that the struggle for self-government in Africa "cannot conveniently be labeled 'made in Moscow.'"[62]

Political turmoil south of the Sahara in 1952 could only spell trouble for an American government at war in the Far East and dependent on southern Africa for several key minerals for the manufacture of military hardware. Critical quantities of copper, chromite, cobalt, industrial diamonds, tantalum, manganese, tin, asbestos, and, most important, uranium, were produced with minimal labor costs and exported to the United States and its Western European allies.[63] American policymakers thought of Africa as "a relatively secure repository of raw materials highly useful to the military strength of the West," which would also provide important geographical positions in the event of any future war.[64] The Truman administration's relative disregard for the well-being of African peoples in its pursuit of strategic minerals left it, as the State Department acknowledged privately, "vulnerable to the charge that we were interested only in what we could get out of Africa in the way of strategic materials."[65] Unrest in colonial Africa also threatened significant economic interests of the Western European nations and a small but growing number of private American investments in the region, both of which profited considerably from cheap labor and the abundance of valuable raw materials.[66]

Late in 1953, the Central Intelligence Agency outlined the foremost American interests in sub-Saharan Africa and the nature of the most serious threats to them. "The chief problem in Tropical Africa," explained the Agency, "is that increasing discontent and demands for self-government, although varying widely in different colonial dependencies, will gradually weaken European control and pose a threat to Western access to Tropical Africa's strategic resources." The CIA registered optimism about the increasing quantity of strategic minerals and foodstuffs being exported from the region to the West, but warned that the days of exploiting low-cost African labor might be numbered: "Production costs of strategically significant raw materials will be increased by African pressures for more social benefits and higher wages." The gathering drive by Africans for political independence would mean, eventually, their control of "a greater share in the management of their own economic resources," a situation certain to reduce the privileged access of the United States and Western Europe to the wealth of the African continent. Communism "so far has had little impact on Tropical Africa," the Agency reported, despite "the growing anti-Western sentiment of Africans." The real danger to American interests south of the Sahara was the determination of Africans to be free of white rule.[67]

By its last year in office, the Truman administration, despite its own preoccupation with the Soviet Union, recognized that Africans found colonialism a much more real and present impediment to their lives than communism. The U.S. Ambassador in Liberia, Edward R. Dudley, reported that "the literate African studies the use of the term 'free world' with . . . [great] interest, but if this means support of colonial rule in Africa he is against it." Educated Africans viewed the supposed American neutrality toward British plans for the Central African Federation as supportive of white-settler power. Dudley reminded his superiors in Washington that West Africans were aware of American arms shipments to South Africa, for they saw South African gold being flown in payment to the United States on Pan American planes that stopped in Nigeria, the Gold Coast, and Liberia. "Africa[ns] know," he pointed out, "that more arms can prolong white rule of Africa." Dudley concluded that the bottom line for Africans would be "whether a partially color-conscious U.S. favors black men or white men as ultimate masters of a black continent."[68]

Developments in British West and East Africa in 1951 and 1952 suggested that the United States could not much longer assume the ready availability of the material riches of the southern end of the continent. The British grant of limited self-government to the Gold Coast and the victory of Kwame Nkrumah and his Convention Peoples' Party in the first colony-wide elections in February 1951 marked a critical step towards decolonization in sub-Saharan Africa, leading to the establishment of the independent country of Ghana six years later. Ripples from these momentous events washed over the rest of the continent. Surprised by how "developments in one area rapidly become known in other parts of Africa despite the scarcity of modern communications," the CIA observed that "the progress toward self-government in the Gold Coast is widely known in the [other] Tropical African territories."[69] Nkrumah's success inspired African nationalists in the British central African colonies, who saw in the Gold Coast a model for their own future altogether different from that offered by the Central African Federation or the Malan government to the south.[70]

The beginning of the Mau Mau rebellion in Kenya in the autumn of 1952 provided a compelling example of the escalating cost of maintaining white rule in colonial Africa. In contrast to West Africa, Kenya was home to a considerable number of white settlers who utterly opposed African self-government in the colony. Long-standing frustration and impoverishment at the hands of wealthy whites brought African resentment to a boil in an armed uprising of the Kikuyu people, which the local white community proved unable to suppress without massive and often brutal intervention by British forces. The violence and determination employed by the Kikuyu demonstrated dramatically that African quiescence under white rule could no longer be assumed. Observers around the world drew differing lessons from Mau Mau: in the Third World it was seen as further evidence that colonialism must end very soon, while in South Africa, whites believed that its potential influence on the local Defiance Campaign must be countered by stronger measures of "law and order."[71] The United States government tacitly supported the British in their campaign to suppress the rebellion, but recognized that tensions along the color line south of the Sahara would only get worse as long as whites remained in authority.[72]

While the 1950 contract with South Africa and increasing domestic production on the Colorado Plateau promised much future ore for the United States, the Truman administration remained acutely aware for the rest of its tenure in office that uranium from the Belgian Congo provided over three quarters of the fuel for the American nuclear arsenal.[73] The cheap price of Congolese uranium, stemming from the low wages paid to African miners, enabled Acheson and the administration's nuclear planners to agree to pay a substantial increase in the export tax on the ore in 1951. This helped alleviate the Belgian government's concern about not yet being included in the research and development aspects of the American nuclear energy program. In September 1951, the World Bank extended $70 million in loans to Belgium and the Belgian Congo for the improvement of the Congolese transportation infrastructure in order to facilitate exports of strategic materials.[74]

After the outbreak of war in Korea, Washington's concern for the security of the Shinkolobwe mine escalated sharply. A joint U.S.-Belgian military mission visited the region in late 1950 to make a systematic evaluation of its security needs. The Defense Department believed that a direct air attack by the Soviets on the mine was unlikely, but the Joint Chiefs of Staff began making contingency plans for "the seizure of critical areas in the Congo by force" in case of a Soviet occupation of Western Europe, including Belgium. Secretary of Defense George Marshall emphasized that "the primary source of danger" to American access to Congolese uranium was "a large-scale uprising of the natives in the area or considerable disaffection of the natives employed at the mines."[75] American sources in the Congo reported that relations between Africans and Europeans were deteriorating in the colony late in 1952, including African efforts at passive resistance to colonial rule that mirrored the contemporaneous Defiance Campaign in South Africa. Doubting that "the natives are suddenly developing 'iron in the spine,' " the U.S. vice-consul in Leopoldville suspected that communists were instead trying to start "an organized campaign of induced disaffection."[76] The Truman administration considered African discontent in the Congo subversive and sought to bolster Belgian authority there. The Joint Chiefs of Staff approved the shipment of $7 million worth of American military equipment for additional Belgian troops being sent to the Katanga Province, and the CIA planted a "controlled source" in the area to provide early warning of any problems and initiated "plans and preparations for covert counter-sabotage."[77]

The absence of organized political unrest in Portuguese Africa in the last years of the Truman administration allowed Washington to pay relatively little attention to Angola and Mozambique. Three factors inclined American policymakers to hope for continued quiet there. First, the agreement between Portugal and the United States granting American military use of the Azores continued in effect. Second, Portugal was a member of NATO. Third, Lobito in Angola and Lourenco Marques and Beira in Mozambique served as important ports for the transshipment of strategic minerals from the Rhodesias and the Congo to the West. The United States government recognized that the vast majority of people in the two Portuguese colonies lived under authoritarian rule that helped keep them impoverished, illiterate, and disenfranchised. The State Department admitted that "the forced recruitment of native labor for work on Portuguese plantations and public projects may generate a substantial measure of native resentment." By 1952, the colonial government of Mozambique itself indicated concern that such unabashed exploitation of African workers might lead to serious trouble, especially with the influence of rising resistance to apartheid across the border in South Africa. But in the early 1950s, the revolutions that would eventually drive the Portuguese out of Africa remained still in the future, and the Truman administration could afford to support tacitly Lisbon's colonial authority.[78]

The United States had even less interest in seeing any serious African resistance to British colonial rule in southern Africa. Expanding American needs for military hardware because of the Korean War led the administration's defense planners to pay close attention to the production and export of Northern Rhodesian copper and Southern Rhodesian chrome. Unrest among African miners and railroad workers in the region distressed American policymakers, as did the inadequate Rhodesian railway system.[79] During its last two years in office, the Truman administration arranged for more than $70 million in grants and loans from the United States government and the World Bank for the expansion of mining industries and transportation systems in British central Africa. Further U.S. assistance reached the region through Marshall Plan funds for Britain. The U.S. Export-Import Bank also loaned $18 million to Portugal in 1952 to finance the construction of the Mozambican portion of a new railroad link from Southern Rhodesia to Lourenco Marques and to improve the Benguela Railroad in Angola so that it could help with copper exports from Northern Rhodesia.[80]

The State Department monitored the investment climate in the Rhodesias on behalf of American business interests and lobbied British colonial officials to adopt policies attractive to foreign private capital. By the end of the Truman years, private American interests had invested $250 million in the region. Most of this was in mineral production, but American entrepreneurs also sought to expand into industries serving the local population.[81] One such attempt involved an American brewery's seeking to establish a plant in Northern Rhodesia, which colonial officials opposed, to the dismay of the State Department. Secretary of State Acheson explained his particular interest in the case:

> Although it is possible that the fostering of American breweries abroad might not be considered the most desirable type of capital development, it should be remembered that the success or failure of one American investor in an area plays an important role in the decisions of other would-be investors. If an American brewery proves successful in Northern Rhodesia, it would tend to attract other investments in other fields of manufacturing.

Opportunities for investment capital, especially in politically stable areas, remained an important concern of American policymakers.[82]

As British plans for establishing the Central African Federation took clearer shape in 1952, the Truman administration sought to appear neutral about the controversial idea, but in fact favored it.[83] While generally pleased to have a Conservative Party government back in power in England, the State Department knew of African unhappiness with the idea of white-settler rule in the area and therefore doubted London's insistence that there was "no way to determine the wishes of the [African] inhabitants" about federation.[84] Washington, however, shared Britain's hopes that federation would spur central African economic development and tie the region more closely to the West. This would encourage political stability and thereby assure continued American access to the strategic minerals of the area.[85] White American diplomats in the area also tended to identify with white settlers and colonial officials more than with Africans, and sympathized with their situation as a ruling racial minority. For example, Southern Rhodesia's fiercely segregationist racial policies, which were at the heart of African opposition to federation, received praise from the American consul general in Salisbury in December 1952.[86] By the summer of 1953, American policymakers spoke of the imminent creation of the Central African Federation as "one of the most favorable political developments yet to take place in Africa."[87]

III

A variety of American interests in the Union of South Africa during the final two years of the Truman administration helped confirm the close alliance established between the two nations at the end of 1950. Economic links continued to increase, with the United States solidly entrenched in second place behind Great Britain as a leading supplier of imports to South Africa. Private American capital, encouraged by the example of large United States government and World Bank loans to the Union, flowed into the booming South African economy in increasing amounts, especially in the areas of mining and manufacturing. American capital and the U.S.-funded uranium extraction project helped reinvigorate the South African gold-mining industry. Favorable South African policies regarding taxes and the repatriation of investment profits encouraged several large American corporations to establish manufacturing plants in the Union by 1952, including General Motors, IBM, Ford, Chrysler, Firestone, Goodyear, Bethlehem Steel, and Frigidaire. By 1953, direct American investments in South Africa had quadrupled in the eight years since the end of World War II, and the Union's continued economic growth had come to depend heavily on foreign capital from the United States as well as Great Britain.[88]

The constitutional crisis and the Defiance Campaign in South Africa did evoke some concern in American corporations and their allies in the State Department. There was even anxiety in Peoria, Illinois, whence the Caterpillar Tractor Company wrote to Acheson in May 1952 asking for his assessment of the Union's political and economic future. The State Department responded to such queries by emphasizing the "stable, buoyant economy" of South Africa and the Union government's ability to "maintain internal order in the event of any domestic disturbances."[89] The Truman administration openly encouraged private American investment in the apartheid state, citing its significance for the economy of an important ally and the moderating influence that the supposedly more liberal racial attitudes of American businesses could have on white South African opinion and policies.[90] American companies doing business in the Union remained somewhat apprehensive at the end of 1952, but took solace from what the U.S. Embassy referred to as their "normal optimism and [the] clear promise of profitable future activities."[91] David Ladin, the general manager of the General Motors plant in Port Elizabeth, assured his company's top management back in the United States that the ministers of the Nationalist government, despite their stern reaction to domestic political dissent, had proven "extremely cooperative on any worthwhile problem the business man or manufacturer takes to them for help." In estimating the future prospects of General Motors in South Africa, Ladin concluded that "we can afford to be somewhat more optimistic when we consider the stock which forms the basis of most of the white population—Dutch, British, [and] French Huguenots."[92]

The ongoing war in Korea confirmed the military ties between the United States and South Africa. The British Commonwealth as a whole constituted the strongest and most dependable ally of the United States.[93] Malan's commitment in principle in the fall of 1952 to an anticommunist defense pact for Africa along the lines of NATO provided another sign of the Nationalists' willingness to subordinate their isolationist tendencies to the broader Western interest of containing communist expansion.[94] Preliminary American and British plans before 1953 for a Middle East Defense Organization were to include South African participation.[95] Some tensions surfaced between Pretoria and Washington early in 1952 over South Africa's unhappiness that its air squadron in Korea had not yet been equipped with jets by the United States. When the Union government threatened to ground its airmen until this was done, Acheson worried that such an action might lead to a "chain reaction" of force reductions by other U.S. allies in Korea looking to demobilize their troops in anticipation of an armistice. The Secretary of State was relieved when he was able to persuade the South Africans to keep their squadron flying by accelerating plans to modernize its equipment.[96] Arrangements for the sale of American military equipment to the South African government for internal use, approved in principle in February 1951 under the Mutual Defense Assistance Program, were finalized on 9 November 1951, followed by an additional sale in October 1952.[97]

South Africa's mineral resources remained the primary interest of the United States in its relations with the Union in the last years of the Truman administration. Manganese, chromite, and amosite asbestos were among the most important of these, as American defense industries depended heavily on South African sources of all three for the production

of military hardware.[98] Since the outbreak of the Korean War, an unusual American sensitivity to the quantity and security of the Union's
manganese exports indicated how critical Washington considered the resources of its South African ally for American national security.[99]

The Truman administration believed the key South African resource
for the United States in the long run would be uranium. The South
African Atomic Energy Board agreed in November 1951 to undertake
uranium ore production at several other mines in addition to those originally contracted for a year earlier, and the Atomic Energy Commission
began to consider expanding American facilities for processing uranium.[100] The first uranium extraction plant in the Union opened at
Krugersdorp outside Johannesburg on 8 October 1952, and AEC chairman Gordon Dean predicted that "within two or three years South Africa will be our most important uranium supplier."[101] Dean reminded
the State Department that the AEC "naturally has an important interest
in the political and economic stability" of the Union, given "the substantial contribution that this country will be making to the strength of the
United States." He was therefore relieved to hear the Department's reassurance that "it is unlikely that the political disturbances in the Union
of South Africa will affect our uranium ore program in that area" in the
foreseeable future.[102]

Arrayed against the economic, military, and strategic interests of the
United States in the Union were the political problems caused by what
the State Department called "the reactionary racial policies" of the South
African government.[103] The Malan regime rejected any supervisory role
of the United Nations in South West Africa, and timed its implementation in 1951 of the Group Areas Act to undermine its proposed talks
with the Indian government about the Union's treatment of South Africans of Indian descent.[104] Warren Austin, the head of the U.S. delegation to the United Nations, reminded Acheson that the Malan government had always openly proclaimed its intention "to turn the clock back
and institute in the territories under the control of the South African
Gov[ernmen]t a political and social system which the great majority of
UN members find contrary to the purposes and aspirations of the UN."[105]
Even Waldemar Gallman, who became the U.S. Ambassador to South
Africa in 1951 and manifested considerable sympathy with the Union
government during his tenure there, registered surprise at the "callous-
ness" of South African officials regarding the treatment of Indians and
other blacks and their lack of concern for the "moral issues involved."[106]

The Truman administration's foremost concern about South Africa's
apartheid program was that it not become a major liability for the West
in the Cold War.[107] Acheson considered this especially important in the
context of the war in Korea, as he wanted to avoid alienating Asian
nations that did not appreciate white South African racial attitudes.[108]
Debates within the U.S. delegation at the United Nations reflected
awareness that American condemnation of Eastern bloc countries as "un-

free" was not matched by comparable concern about liberty in southern Africa. The more liberal members of the delegation agreed with Dr. Channing Tobias that "we should take the same attitude with the South Africans as with the Soviets in cases of such extreme violations of human rights." The administration's position, however, adhered more closely to the view of others in the delegation who emphasized South Africa's wholehearted support of American positions on all non-racial issues, and contrasted that with the resistance of Third World nations to American Cold War priorities.[109] Acheson regarded South African uranium as critical for determining American attitudes at the United Nations on discussion items regarding the Union, and the United States continued throughout 1951 and 1952 to seek to moderate criticisms of its apartheid ally and keep South Africa from withdrawing from the international organization.[110]

In September 1952, at the height of the Defiance Campaign, Arab and Asian members increased international pressure on South Africa by going beyond the specific problems of South West Africa and the treatment of South Africans of Indian descent to raise the entire issue of apartheid for discussion in the United Nations. This move intensified the American dilemma of how to support the Union without appearing to identify with its racial policies. Officials in the Truman administration with responsibilities for Third World areas argued that the American delegation needed to support the resolution condemning apartheid as a violation of fundamental human rights if the United States wished to maintain credibility among peoples of color.[111] Acheson shared this concern but worried even more about alienating South Africa and perhaps pushing it to the point of leaving the U.N. and isolating itself from international affairs. The Secretary of State believed that public rebukes would only harden Pretoria's resistance to change and would thus actually serve to reinforce apartheid. Mindful of continuing racial discrimination in the United States, the administration also wished to avoid setting a precedent of the U.N. investigating the domestic race relations of a member state. In an effort to avoid siding with either the Union or its numerous critics, the United States chose to abstain on the successful December 1952 resolution condemning apartheid.[112]

Dissatisfied with such lukewarm public gestures, the Nationalist government in Pretoria saw itself as an inadequately appreciated ally of the United States. White South Africans bitterly resented the ongoing efforts in the United Nations to force them to change their racial policies, as they considered race relations in the Union a strictly domestic matter. In the fall of 1952, South African Ambassador Jooste told Acheson that his government considered the mere discussion in the U.N. of racial tensions in South Africa an act of overt hostility, because it was providing "a major impetus to the present passive resistance movement."[113] While committed to a close relationship with the Truman administration because of the leading role of the United States in the anticommunist Western alliance and the importance of American capital for the South African economy, the apartheid regime disdained American efforts to accommodate the opinions of the liberal and anticolonial forces in the United Nations. The Nationalists emphasized that South Africa, in contrast to many anti-colonial countries, strongly supported the U.N.-sanctioned American military effort in Korea and therefore deserved praise rather than abuse at the U.N.[114] Malan poked some fun at the American effort to straddle the issue of whether Africans from South West Africa should be invited to appear before the U.N. Trusteeship Council, asking Ambassador Gallman in a "somewhat jocular manner" what the American position would be "if American Negroes were invited to appear before . . . [the U.N.] to testify on how they were treated." This was precisely the sort of comparison Gallman and Acheson wished to avoid.[115]

Intense concern within the State Department about the precedent a U.N. condemnation of South African racial policies might set revealed the vulnerability felt by American policymakers about racial discrimination and segregation in their own country.[116] Proponents of racial equality in the United States, unwilling to subordinate the goal of democracy at home to the task of containing communism abroad, also recognized the opportunity for exposing what they saw as official American hypocrisy about "freedom." They hoped thereby to force the United States to bring its racial practices into closer line with its democratic rhetoric. In the fall of 1951, William Patterson and Paul Robeson of the left-wing Civil Rights Congress presented a petition to the United Nations entitled *We Charge Genocide: The Historical Petition to the United Nations for Relief from a Crime of the United States Government against the Negro People*. Dismissing the charges as mere communist propaganda, the Truman administration sought to minimize the petition's impact on world opinion.[117] In discussions in October 1952 of the South African item on the U.N. agenda, Assistant Secretary of State George Perkins urged Acheson to avoid encouraging any precedent for United Nations involvement in American domestic practices like "our immigration laws, U.S. treatment of Communists, segregation laws in our eleven southern states, etc."[118] Acheson agreed that "because of domestic implications it was very important that the South African case should be regarded as not creating a broad precedent and that therefore it should be described as if it involved a dog with a green tail and pink eyes and blue legs, so that it could be distinguished from other cases not having the same precise characteristics."[119]

Despite signs of gradual improvement in the treatment of African Americans, racial segregation and discrimination remained standard in the United States during Truman's last two years in office.[120] Southern governors like James Byrnes of South Carolina—Truman's former Secretary of State—vowed that their public school systems would never allow the integration of white and black students.[121] The State Department itself, in spite of its concern with the democratic image of the United

States abroad, employed very few blacks above the custodial or clerical levels and provided little encouragement to those interested in becoming Foreign Service officers.[122] White violence against blacks continued, especially in the South, although lynchings mostly disappeared and were replaced by more secretive bombings as the preferred method of racial intimidation and murder.[123] Public executions in the South of black men convicted of raping white women, such as that of Willie McGee in Mississippi in 1951, provided some of the same satisfaction to white crowds as extralegal lynchings had done in the past. Such displays of anti-black hatred received great attention abroad, on both sides of the ideological divide in Europe as well as in the Third World. In a similar vein, the NAACP journal *The Crisis* reported an incident involving a group of fifty-three foreign exchange students who planned to tour the Tennessee Valley Authority as part of their program of orientation to the United States. When the students learned that two dark-skinned Panamanians in the group would be denied entrance to the group's hotel in Knoxville and would have to stay elsewhere, they all refused to go. "What a strange way of teaching democracy to foreigners," observed the journal's editors.[124]

The predominance of anticommunism in the United States in the early 1950s channeled most dissenting opinions about American relations with South Africa into a narrow criticism that failed to challenge fundamental American interests in supporting the apartheid state. Liberal religious, labor, and civil rights organizations registered their dismay at the South African government's racial policies and called on the Truman administration to admonish Pretoria. Leaders in this effort were the handful of social and political activists who formed the committee called Americans for South African Resistance to support the Defiance Campaign in 1952.[125] The U.S. government did acknowledge feeling some pressure as a result of such activities.[126] But these actions were carefully planned to fall within the chauvinistic anticommunist consensus in the United States, and therefore tended to focus on South Africa alone rather than on American support for the status quo there.[127] Critics of apartheid who pointed to the close relationship of Washington and Pretoria and who condemned American support for European colonialism in southern Africa as well were dismissed by the government and the mainstream press as subversives in league with the forces of international communism. Black dissenters like Robeson and W. E. B. Du Bois attracted additional negative attention and harassment from the State Department and the FBI, who revoked their passports and effectively denied them audiences abroad or at home.[128]

IV

Foreign policy had always received the highest priority in the Truman administration, a status reinforced after 1950 by being at war in Korea.

Washington's overriding concern with what it defined as American national security ensured that the alliance between the United States and South Africa would only grow stronger during Truman's final two years in office. The President himself confirmed this, as Secretary of State Acheson recorded after a conversation with Truman in June 1951 about new ambassadorial appointments: "We talked particularly about South Africa. The President is well aware of the delicacy of that situation and the importance of having a proven man there."[129] Acheson thought of the Union as an "important member [of the] free community of nations."[130] Pretoria's consistent support for the anticommunist policies of the United States won it considerable credit in Washington. Benjamin Gerig, the director of the State Department's Office of Dependent Area Affairs, captured the administration's sense of shared goals with the Nationalist government in his recollection of a conversation with South African Ambassador Jooste: "On the big issues, such as Korea, the East-West conflict, etc., we agreed. It was only on certain other minor matters that we had differed. . . ."[131] In its March 1951 policy statement on South Africa, the State Department concluded succinctly that "it is in our interest to maintain friendly relations with South Africa because of strategic considerations and also because South Africa represents a good market for our products."[132]

By 1951, American policymakers were expressing relief that Malan had moderated his earlier emphasis on taking South Africa out of the British Commonwealth and establishing a fully independent republic. This change in Nationalist strategy bolstered the military and economic strength of the Commonwealth and reduced anxiety among English-speaking South Africans about the future of their country. The State Department believed that South Africa's "dependence on the UK for capital, fear of Communism, and concern for the future of white supremacy in Africa have counter-balanced extreme isolationist and nationalist sentiments."[133] Malan's thorough support for American positions on international issues surpassed even Great Britain's, Washington's closest ally, as Pretoria refused to follow London in extending recognition to the new communist government of the Peoples' Republic of China.[134] In an important speech to the South African House of Assembly on 25 January 1951, Malan emphasized that the Union's attitude toward the international situation was "based on the view that Communism was a double danger because it made a special appeal to the non-Europeans. If Communism gained a footing among them it would sound the death knell to white civilization." Joseph Sweeney, the U.S. Embassy's political officer, called this address "a sincere attempt to make a statesman-like speech aligning South Africa on the side of the U.S. . . . His speech indicates that he is through with isolationism and that he has become, at least in part, an internationalist." Sweeney, who represented the most critical perspective on the South African government available within the Truman administration, considered it very important that Malan's "espousal of Western views meet with a friendly response on the international level."[135]

The increased tensions in South Africa that accompanied the constitutional crisis and the Defiance Campaign provoked a ripple of concern within the Truman administration. "Developments in the Union will continue to embarrass the West in its prosecution of the Cold War . . . by furnishing ammunition for Communist and anti-colonial propaganda," the State Department admitted privately. American officials worried that deteriorating race relations in the Union would exacerbate racial unrest in other parts of Africa and promote distrust of the West among the nonwhite nations. The State Department was dismayed that "the white minority consciously is playing with fire by being at loggerheads on constitutional questions and racial policy when relations between them and the great non-white majority are worsening" dramatically.[136] But the Department recognized that white dissent in the Union would not go far enough to threaten the stability of the country seriously, as the conservative leadership of the United Party shared the Nationalists' fundamental commitment to white supremacy.[137]

Black dissent was another matter. The U.S. Embassy in South Africa, the State Department, the Defense Department, and the CIA all agreed with the National Security Council that "over the long run the repressive racial policy of the whites will almost certainly lead to [a] rebellion of the non-white population."[138] The Malan government's "policy of subverting the constitution and the courts" would further diminish African respect for white laws, and black unity seemed to be growing in proportion to white oppression.[139] While South Africa was "heading for serious trouble" that could eventually affect American access to its strategic minerals, American policymakers took solace in 1952 that such a scenario seemed to remain at least several years in the future.[140]

The American press also indicated alarm at the turbulent events of 1952 in South Africa. In a series of articles on the Union in *The Christian Century,* Homer Jack called apartheid second only to the anti-Semitism of Hitler's Third Reich as a system of discrimination and repression. Discussing the pass laws, the restrictions on civil liberties, the migratory labor system for the mines, and the crushing poverty of the African "shantytowns," Jack emphasized black South Africans' awareness of the progress of other nonwhite peoples toward greater freedom and self-government and the growing unwillingness of Africans to remain docile under white control.[141] In a front page article in early April, the *New York Times* worried about the degree of communist influence in the developing Defiance Campaign.[142] *Time* excoriated apartheid as "manifest absurdity" and blamed Malan for having "dragged South Africa far along the road to fascism" in his three years in office.[143]

The editors of *Time* seemed fascinated by Malan's physical unattractiveness. In a cover story in May 1952, they described him as "a bold paunchy Boer with restless little eyes and a pale square face" whose much younger wife served as "nursemaid to her aging, ailing and absent-minded husband": she "holds his hand at public functions, [and] mops his brow when he sweats over meals." They compared him unfavorably to Jan Smuts, calling Malan a hypocritical coward and, in reference to his college days, "an obscure little swot."[144] *Business Week* took a broader view of the problems in the Union, noting the uncertainty of American investors about the future of the country: "As things look now, a backward-looking racial policy is taking South Africa straight for a police state, a civil war, or both. Even if the trend doesn't go that far, the situation will inevitably hurt the prestige of the West in the United Nations and give comfort to Communists everywhere."[145]

While receiving some attention in Washington, the uncertain future of South Africa's race relations did not begin to offset crucial American interests in the region. The State Department acknowledged privately in April 1952 that "because of the United States interest in the planned uranium production in South Africa, it is unlikely that the US Government would be willing to consider any measures which might have repercussions on this program. . . . In sum, we need more from South Africa than she needs from us."[146] The Truman administration chose to cast its policy of remaining close to the apartheid regime in a more idealistic light as well. The administration argued that by remaining a friend of Pretoria, it could exercise a liberalizing influence on white South Africans that it would never have as a critic of the country.[147] Acheson believed that private American businessmen in South Africa, "by their influence and example, can make a real contribution" to increasing mutual respect between the different races in South Africa.[148] The U.S. Embassy in South Africa hoped that the United States would be able to capitalize, "through careful nurturing and endless patience, on existing potential latent forces for moderation" in the Union.[149]

Ambassador Gallman thought this a particularly reasonable course due to the mutual affinity and understanding he felt with the members of the apartheid government. He noted that in his thirty years in the Foreign Service he had never worked in a country—including wartime England—"where close, informal relations with officials were more quickly established." Gallman appreciated the "most encouraging reservoir of good will . . . on all levels and in all sections of society for the United States" and applauded Pretoria's ready cooperation with the United States on manganese exports, the Korean War, and defending the "free world" against the threat of communism.[150] Regarding racial tensions, the American Ambassador concluded that

> about all that can be done here on this issue is for me to be on so friendly and informal [a] basis with Malan and [the] members of his Cabinet that whenever [the] atmosphere sh[ou]ld appear propitious, when I am with them, I can inject a word of caution and make some suggestions. In my contacts with these officials, I am finding them daily more approachable, open and friendly.[151]

Three decades later, in the early 1980s, this same approach by the administration of Ronald Reagan would be known as "constructive engagement."

The sweeping victory of Malan and the Nationalist Party in the South African elections of 15 April 1953 and the accelerating implementation of apartheid legislation that followed suggested that white South Africa was not particularly susceptible to liberal influence from outsiders, no matter how friendly they were.[152] Americans of liberal and even moderate political persuasions, sensitive to continuing racial discrimination in their own country, recoiled at the news of another success for evangelical racism. Noting "the sense of shame that all civilized persons must feel at this victory," the *New York Times* predicted that "there will be a day of reckoning for these men, since human beings will not endure injustice and the loss of freedom interminably."[153] At the direction of Secretary of State John Foster Dulles of the new Eisenhower administration, Ambassador Gallman made a discreet mention to Malan of American concerns that any further exacerbation of racial tensions in South Africa might threaten the stability of the Union, especially in "connection [with] uranium operations." The Prime Minister, confident of his government's control of the country, dismissed the idea out of hand.[154] The situation in South Africa at the end of the Truman years was not developing according to American preferences for a gradual liberalization of race relations, but the State Department emphasized that "at the present delicate stage in the political and economic development of South Africa, it is important that American influence be furthered. No United States Government action should be taken which would lower our prestige or cast doubt on our interest in a strong South Africa."[155] Faced with the juggernaut of apartheid in a country of profound strategic importance to the United States, the Truman administration had chosen to ally itself closely with the world's leading apostles of racial discrimination.

Conclusion

The escalating tensions between the United States and the Soviet Union have so dominated Western views of the international politics of the decade after World War II that it has become difficult to avoid describing these years as "the early Cold War." For the majority of the world's population, however, this period was marked by a different pattern. The dominant international issue for the people of most of Asia, Africa, and the Middle East was colonialism: the control of their lives, land, and resources by Western Europeans. Movements for national independence in these areas, which had been under way for decades, received a powerful impetus from World War II and its grave weakening of the imperial powers of Britain, France, Belgium, and the Netherlands. The Jewish Holocaust at the hands of Hitler's Third Reich exposed the almost incredible evil that could flow from ideas of racial superiority, and the international community by the end of the war was reaching an unusually broad agreement about the moral rightness of the ideal of racial equality. The newly established United Nations became a forum for promoting both the principle of human equality and the reality of decolonization, which were closely associated in the minds of Third World nationalists. For most of these people, the Cold War and the supposed dangers of communism were merely distractions from the historic opportunity provided by World War II for ending the European colonialism that had long dominated the lives of most of the world's people.

The overlaying of a new East–West conflict on an older geography of North–South colonial issues after 1945 created a dilemma for the United States government in its relationship with what would soon be called the Third World. The threat of Soviet expansion dominated Washington's perspective. The Western European nations, the historic allies of the United States, occupied the front lines in any likely confrontation with the Soviet Union, and the Truman administration gave its highest priority to strengthening them. Their power, in turn, depended to no small extent on access to the raw materials of their colonies. But the strongest anticommunist alliance would be one that would also include the genuine, uncoerced allegiance of the nonwhite peoples of those colonial areas, whose independence now seemed imminent, at least in Asia and the Middle East. Not surprisingly, the colonized looked with some skepticism on the idea of a close relationship with those whose bondage they had been struggling for years to free themselves from. It was the ambitious goal of the Truman administration to keep both colonizers and colonized together as part of the "free world," which would contain the expansion of Soviet and left-wing influence.

Washington's preferred solution to tensions in the Western alliance between the Europeans and their colonies was gradual but steady movement toward decolonization. Ideally, noncommunist indigenous governments would slowly replace colonial regimes. Americans considered their own grant of independence to the Philippines in 1946 a model of progressive colonial administration, and they were pleased with Britain's withdrawal from India and most of its other Asian colonies by 1948. The end of the European mandates in the Middle East also seemed an encouraging sign of an evolving independent, pro-Western Third World. The attempted reassertion of colonial control through bloody wars in Indochina, Indonesia, Malaya, Algeria, and Madagascar indicated, however, that the American strategy was not fully accepted in the imperial capitals of Europe. The ultimate test of the American plan of creating a multiracial alliance with the Third World and Western Europe against the Soviet bloc came in southern Africa, for it would prove to be the last great stronghold of white supremacy and European colonialism.

Harry Truman's tenure as President coincided with a period of extraordinary racial polarization in southern Africa. Tensions along the color line increased in the British, Portuguese, and Belgian colonies of the region, as African workers and nationalists manifested increasing discontent with their impoverished colonial status. In the Union of South Africa, the heart of the region, white oppression of blacks redoubled in the face of mounting international criticism. Seeking to fend off the rising tide of Afrikaner nationalism, the government of Jan Smuts showed the limits of its "moderateness" in its anti-Indian policies and its brutal repression of the African mine workers' strike of 1946. With its seizure of power in the white elections of 1948, the Nationalist Party government of Daniel Malan ended all talk of moderation on racial issues as it set about establishing an apartheid state. The resulting increase in oppression of black South Africans led to new levels of street violence between white police and Africans in 1949 and 1950. The Nationalists' determination to create a much more authoritarian national government, to be ruled essentially by Nationalist Party fiat, led to a brief constitutional crisis with English-speaking white South Africans in 1951 and 1952. Malan and his colleagues then reconfirmed their control of South Africa with harsh new legislation to prevent anti-government protests, followed by an overwhelming victory in the white elections of 1953.

The vast majority of South Africans did not passively receive the triumph of resurgent Afrikaner nationalism and unbridled white racism in these years. African resistance to increasing brutality by white authorities led to frequent confrontations in the black locations and townships on the outskirts of the country's urban areas. In response to the deteriorating situation of South Africans of color, the Youth League of the African National Congress helped rekindle the fires of the black liberation movement with the policy of noncooperation declared in its 1949 Programme of Action. In combination with other democrats of all colors, including Indians, Coloreds, and white radicals, the ANC organized large-scale protests on 1 May 1950 ("Freedom Day") and 26 June 1950 ("Day of Protest and Mourning"). The six-month Defiance Campaign of 1952 represented a new level of black cohesiveness and national organization. Apartheid in its first few years helped drive previously divided black communities together, thereby unintentionally pointing the way toward a more unified movement for nonracial democracy in South Africa.

The increased polarization of southern Africa along color lines in these years presented the Truman administration with the acutest version of its dilemma about how to deal with the Third World. Though the region received less attention in Washington than areas like Europe, Asia, and the Middle East where Cold War crises abounded, this reflected, not a lack of significant American interests, but rather an assumption that colonial and white settler authority was firmly in control. The United States government monitored developments in the region carefully and was fully aware of the sharp escalation in racial tensions that accompanied the establishment of apartheid. The Truman administration hoped to distance itself from this virulent strain of white racism, especially in view of ongoing racial discrimination and segregation in the United States. But its Cold War concerns and its European priorities, embodied in the Marshall Plan and NATO, led the administration into a close embrace of the imperial authorities in southern Africa, and the outbreak of war in Korea resulted in a series of agreements with Pretoria that bound the United States government to the apartheid regime. In its pursuit of the preoccupying goals of containing communism and preserving the "free world," the Truman administration provided critical assistance to the reassertion of white authority in southern Africa after World War II. The United States acted, in sum, as a reluctant uncle—or godparent—at the baptism of apartheid.

There were many reasons for this. Historic, geostrategic, and economic considerations provided some of the logic for American support of the status quo. In the previous thirty years, the United States had fought in two world wars that it defined as struggles to protect liberty against the expansion of tyranny; in both of those wars South Africa had been an ally, along with the British and the Belgians. The location of South Africa alongside major East–West shipping lanes, especially in the event of a closure of the Suez Canal, and the Union's industrial and economic dominance of the region gave it a geostrategic significance worthy of consideration. Similarly, tacit American support of Portuguese authority in Angola and Mozambique seemed to Washington a small price to pay for continuing access to the valuable air bases of the Azores. While American relations with southern Africa in these years were not ultimately a tale of the Open Door, American trade with and investment in the area were substantial and growing rapidly. The booming market of South Africa matched up well with the expanding need of American manufacturers to export their products. During the Truman years, the United States became the second leading provider of South Africa's imports and a critical source of capital for the Union's industrial expansion, while the buying power of its small white population made South Africa an American export market of unusual importance for its size.

In addition to this first layer of common interests connecting the Truman administration to the white authorities of the region, a more important second layer consisted of political considerations and strategic minerals. The emergence of the Cold War and the tendency of Americans to view it as a struggle of transcendent good and evil guaranteed all opponents of the Soviet Union a warm welcome in Washington. The most important American allies were the British Commonwealth nations, which included South Africa, and the Western European nations, which controlled the rest of southern Africa. South Africa's particularly close relationship to England was personified until 1948 by Prime Minister Jan Smuts, whose status as the senior statesman of the Commonwealth gave him great credibility with the Truman administration. The ascendancy of anticommunism as the cardinal political virtue for the United States after World War II meant that even the frankly undemocratic and racist government of Daniel Malan would be kept well within the fold of the "free world." Loathing the Soviet Union and all left-wing ideas and resentful of the long-standing British influence in their country, the Afrikaner nationalists turned logically to the United States as a more compatible ally.

The most important single interest of the United States in southern Africa during the Truman administration was the uranium of the southern Belgian Congo and the South African Rand. The Belgian ores fueled the American nuclear arsenal, which undergirded all American actions in the early Cold War, and South African uranium was expected to replace the Belgian supply when it ran out. A variety of other strategic minerals from the region, including copper, cobalt, manganese, chrome, and industrial diamonds, also figured prominently in the sustenance of American military power. "In the case of those minerals where we lack self-sufficiency," explained Paul Nitze of the State Department in 1947, "continuing access to the minerals of the rest of the world is an absolute requirement of the very life of our nation."[1] Official Washington looked upon the white authorities of southern Africa, oppressive as they may have been, as the guarantors of that availability. Conversely, the United States government viewed even the most disciplined and peaceful event of the black liberation struggle in this period, the Defiance Campaign, above all as a threat to American mineral access in South Africa. The discovery of rich uranium deposits on the Colorado Plateau by itinerant prospector Charlie Sheen just months before the close of Truman's tenure in office promised an eventual end to the heavy dependence of the United States on overseas sources of the critical material.[2] But until 1952, their large supplies of the invaluable ore gave the Belgian Congo and South Africa—and the preservation of their political stability—a unique significance in the eyes of the Truman administration.

If supporting the status quo in southern Africa offered substantial tangible benefits to the United States government, the policy contained certain political disadvantages as well. The defeat of the Nazis in World War II, the subsequent decolonization of most of Asia and the Middle East, and the rhetorical emphasis of the Cold War on freedom from tyranny had helped create an international environment inhospitable to the racial beliefs of Afrikaner nationalists. Sensitive to growing criticism of South Africa and of Washington's close relationship with the Afrikaner regime, the Truman administration hoped in vain that the Malan government would restrain its implementation of repressive apartheid measures.

Administration members, like many other Americans, recognized their own country's vulnerability on the issue of racial discrimination and worried that South Africa's present course reflected the darker side of their own society.[3] It was with some relief that the prominent American historian C. Vann Woodward wrote a few years later: "In its present plight the [American] South might cast a glance back over its shoulder to South Africa, with which it once identified itself and seemed to see eye to eye. The South no longer identifies herself with South Africa and no longer has reason to fear the madness of self destruction."[4] Racial prejudice at home and among its allies could only hinder the United States in its Cold War struggle for the loyalty of the new nations of the Third World. In a brief filed with the Supreme Court in December 1952 regarding school desegregation cases, Truman's Attorney General argued that "it is in the context of the present world struggle between freedom and tyranny that the problem of racial discrimination must be viewed. . . . Racial discrimination furnishes grist for the Communist propaganda mills, and it raises doubts even among friendly nations as to the intensity of our devotion to the democratic faith."[5]

While the racial attitudes and practices of the Malan government concerned American policymakers, the men of the Truman administration nonetheless found themselves sharing a deep sense of cultural and racial identity with their counterparts in Pretoria. Ambassador Waldemar Gallman cited the "common heritage and experience that have left an identical imprint on the character and outlook of both peoples," such as their common effort to "force the frontier back." "Let us remember," he urged in his final report from South Africa before leaving his post there, "that Western civilization was brought to the tip of Africa by the forebears of these friendly people" who now ruled the Union.[6] The Nation-

alists' explicit rejection of such supposed features of "Western civilization" as a belief in civil liberties and the principle of equality for all people
failed—perhaps understandably—to overcome the feeling of white American officials that these were still people much like themselves.

The State Department occasionally acknowledged in private the explicitly racial character of this feeling of common identity, pointing out
what it considered the importance for American policy of South Africa's
"having the largest white population on the African continent."[7] American diplomats realized that "our people in the Union have very little
contact with the Native leaders and are completely dependent on white
sources for their information on what is really happening among the
Native elements."[8] By its own admission, the Truman administration took
its understanding of South Africa almost exclusively from the perspective
of the white minority there, as symbolized by the frequent American use
of the dubious phrase "the Native problem" to describe the results of
apartheid. Trevor Huddleston, an Anglican priest working and living
among the poorest blacks of Johannesburg in these years, offered a different construction of the issue: "There is no such thing as a Native
problem in South Africa, only a European problem."[9]

The ease that white Americans felt with white South Africans in the
Truman years reflected their experiences at home in a segregated United
States. American policymakers and diplomats could almost never have
known black people as peers. A country in which white people held the
preponderance of power and people of color were widely disenfranchised, impoverished, and physically intimidated could not have seemed
strange to representatives of the United States in the 1940s and early
1950s. The explicitness of white South African racism may have been
surprising on occasion, especially under the Malan government, but the
structure of South African society could hardly have shocked an American. A nation that genuinely eschewed racial discrimination would have
been much more of a novelty to American diplomats and businessmen
abroad. The dim view that most white Americans took of the capacity of
Africans for self-government mirrored their generally pessimistic and
prejudiced notions about the social, economic, and political position of
blacks in the United States. Any changes in their perspective on Africans
would necessarily have affected how white Americans thought about and
treated their black countrymen at home, as the parallel development of
African decolonization and the American civil rights movement was to
demonstrate in the late 1950s and 1960s.[10]

American support for the white supremacist authorities of southern
Africa in the early Cold War raises troubling questions about the relationship between racism and anticommunism, two of the most prominent features of recent American history. Do racism and anticommunism
go hand in hand? Is there any inherent tension between them? Does
anticommunism function as a cover for the repression of other perceived
threats to the social order, such as demands for racial equality? The sa-

lience of these questions derives from the fact that the nations that formed the core of the Western alliance against the Soviet Union were the very countries with the strongest traditions of white dominion over people of color, through colonialism, slavery, and segregation.

Its blatant racism belied the self-proclaimed title of "free world" much touted by Americans in these years. Despite their respective claims of lusotropicalism, superior colonial administration, and constitutional liberalism, the Portuguese, Belgian, and British authorities of southern Africa held tightly to their control over the lives of Africans in their territories. The Afrikaner nationalists in South Africa lumped all serious opponents of apartheid together as "communists," as they turned back the clock of race relations in their country. And the United States government focused the greatest part of its attention on supposed communists at home and abroad—including southern Africa—even as American society remained profoundly divided by pervasive racial discrimination and inequality.

In some ways, apartheid and Jim Crow made natural allies during the brief period between the rise of the former and the decline of the latter. Racial politics in South Africa and the United States had certain parallels. White Southerners, who wielded a disproportionate influence in the Congress, shared a similar spirit with Afrikaner nationalists. Parallels between the Dixiecrat revolt of 1948 in the United States and the rise of the Nationalist Party in South Africa were not lost on participants and observers. For the United Party and the Democratic Party each represented unwieldy coalitions of liberals and conservatives, whose ideological diversity left them vulnerable in the Cold War to assaults from the right. Jan Smuts and Harry Truman were both firm anticommunists who defined themselves as political moderates in the racial and political storms of the late 1940s. The vigilante riots at the Paul Robeson concerts in Peekskill in 1949 demonstrated the explosive potential in the United States for racial violence in the guise of suppressing communism, just as the institutionalized violence of apartheid, in suppressing the "Freedom Day" protest of 1950 and the Defiance Campaign of 1952, battered the causes of racial equality and political radicalism in South Africa.

But in other ways, the confluence of racism and anticommunism in the ascendancy of the Nationalist Party made the close American relationship with South Africa an uncomfortable one for the Truman administration. In contrast to Daniel Malan and the Afrikaner nationalists, for whom white supremacy and anticommunism were inseparable, Harry Truman and other moderate and liberal Americans did not believe, in principle, in racial exceptions to the idea of a "free world." While the Nationalist Party concerned itself almost entirely with affairs inside South Africa, the United States government was taking a much more global perspective. A considerable part of American competition with the Soviet Union was for the loyalty of the nonwhite majority of the world's population. Truman's support for greater civil rights for African Americans stemmed not only from his evolving belief in the rightness of racial equality, but also from his administration's awareness of American vulnerability in a world increasingly in accord in its condemnation of racial discrimination. Thus the logic of a global crusade for liberty from communism, while allying Washington with an array of undemocratic regimes abroad, also helped push the United States toward greater compliance at home with its own avowed principles.

Though the dilemma the United States faced in dealing with southern Africa was tangible and troubling, in retrospect there can be little surprise at how it was resolved, given the strongly held priorities of American policymakers. Almost to a man, they believed without question that Soviet and communist expansion constituted a much greater and more imminent threat to American interests than did the entrenched racial tyranny of the Western nations, among whom they included South Africa. The hopes of the liberal and moderate Cold Warriors of the Truman administration to create a more racially egalitarian and inclusive Western alliance were therefore sacrificed to the newer but deeper American conviction of the importance of embracing all anticommunists. These priorities stemmed from their experiences as powerful white Americans, screened off from any transforming firsthand experience of the injustice within their own society. All had grown up as willing beneficiaries of a long heritage of racial discrimination, and all were much quicker to perceive a beam in the eye of distant communist regimes than to feel a mote in their own eye at home.

Were other policy options seriously considered within the Truman administration? Debates among American officials about southern Africa in these years lacked the breadth of perspective available on regions like the Middle East and East Asia. There was no equivalent, for example, to the "China hands" and their cogent, if unsuccessful, argument for ending support for an unpopular authoritarian regime. Dissenting opinions from outside the government, such as those of the Council on African Affairs, were drowned in the rising tide of anticommunist repression. Even American diplomats in South Africa who seemed the most troubled by Afrikaner nationalism, like Thomas Holcomb, and the most sympathetic to black South Africans, like Joseph Sweeney, did not question the necessity and wisdom of working closely with the Union government.

This lack of alternatives stemmed in part from the rudimentary state of black organization in southern Africa in the late 1940s and early 1950s. The ANC and other black associations not only lacked a successful army in the field, comparable to those of Mao Zedong or the Indonesian nationalists, but remained at that point still committed to nonviolent protest. From Washington's perspective, the legitimacy of the South African government was not yet in question. The absence of real options in its policy on southern Africa also derived in part from the obvious benefits—most especially uranium—that the status quo in the region provided an American government obsessed with the threat of Soviet expansion.

But the circumscribed debate resulted ultimately from the limited efforts of elite white policymakers in a Jim Crow society to transcend their own racial consciousness. Had the oppressed proponents of greater democracy and liberty in southern Africa been white, for example, they would almost certainly have gained considerable attention and sympathy in Washington. The Truman administration's increasing racial liberalism at home did not, in this case, extend beyond the water's edge.

The policy of the United States toward southern Africa in the years of the early Cold War inevitably had some effect on American relations with other parts of the Third World. Explaining the dubious character of certain governments allied to the United States during World War II, Franklin Roosevelt occasionally cited a traditional Balkan proverb: "My children, it is permitted you in time of grave danger to walk with the devil until you have crossed the bridge."[11] The choice by 1950 to side with white authority south of the Sahara surely made subsequent decisions in support of anticommunism in the Third World easier. Having accepted the flagrant contradiction of apartheid and "the free world," the United States government would soon orchestrate the overthrow of elected governments in Iran and Guatemala and provide critical assistance to a whole host of authoritarian forces on the periphery of the Cold War. In swallowing apartheid, the Truman administration helped lay the groundwork for decades of American policy toward the Third World and also for the anti-American sentiment so evident in many of those regions today.

The attitudes and policies of the United States government were not lost on Africans in southern Africa. People who lived under foreign control or under the authority of a brutal minority regime found the Cold War priorities of the United States considerably less urgent than did the Truman administration. Their experience of anticommunism, especially in South Africa, made them suspicious of its relationship to freedom and democracy. One African opponent of apartheid in the Union explained in 1950 that "one day we shall all be called Communists. It does not matter whether a man is minister of a church, if he belongs to a movement struggling for freedom, the [Suppression of Communism] Act will be used against him."[12] *The West African Pilot* in Nigeria elaborated on this perspective in an editorial in June 1953:

> Judging from what we see and experience from day to day, we feel that all this talk of the so-called "free world" and "iron curtain" is a camouflage to fool and bamboozle colonial peoples. . . . We shall judge every nation strictly on the merits of the attitude of that nation towards our national aspirations. We have every cause to be grateful to the Communists for their active interest in the fate of colonial peoples and for their constant denunciation of the evils of imperialism [and apartheid]. It is then left to the so-called "free" nations to convince us that they are more concerned about our welfare than the Communists, and in this regard we believe more in action than in mere words.[13]

The overwhelming majority of the fifty million people of southern Africa could only have experienced the early Cold War as a tragic development, one that slowed their quest for greater self-government and human dignity by eliciting critical American support for apartheid and colonialism. In his presidential address to the Transvaal branch of the ANC on 21 September 1953, Nelson Mandela encouraged his colleagues to stand firm in their struggle for democracy, while reminding them that "there is no easy walk to freedom anywhere."[14] On that journey for most people of southern Africa, the Truman administration had proven itself willing only to increase, not lighten, the load to be carried.

Appendix

Table 1—Heads of U.S. Mission/Embassy in South Africa, 1942–1954

Name	Title	Tenure
Lincoln MacVeagh	Minister	21 May 1942–21 Nov. 1943
Thomas Holcomb	Minister	21 Mar. 1944–30 May 1948
North Winship	Minister Ambassador	24 Mar. 1948–promotion 2 Mar. 1949–20 Dec. 1949
John G. Erhardt	Ambassador	23 May 1950–18 Feb. 1951
Waldemar J. Gallman	Ambassador	22 Aug. 1951–15 Aug. 1954

Source: U.S. Department of State, *United States Chiefs of Mission, 1778–1982* (Washington: U.S. Government Printing Office, 1982), 207.

Table 2—Sources of U.S. uranium concentrates, 1947–1952 (in tons)

Fiscal year	Domestic	Canada	Belgian Congo	Total
1947 (6 mos.)	0	137	1440	1577
1948	116	206	1689	2011
1949	115	217	1909	2241
1950	323	235	2505	3063
1951	639	255	2792	3686
1952	824	210	2623†	3657

Source: Adapted from Richard G. Hewlett and Francis Duncan, *A History of the United States Atomic Energy Commission*, vol. 2, *Atomic Shield, 1947/1952* (University Park: Pennsylvania State University Press, 1969), p. 647.

†Includes a small amount from the Union of South Africa.

Table 3—South African imports from the United States, 1945–1952

Year	U.S. goods as a percentage of all S.A. imports	Rank of U.S. among exporters to S.A.	Value of S.A. imports from U.S. ($)
1945	29	2	131 mil
1946	26	2	227 mil
1947	35	1	414 mil
1948	35	1	492 mil
1949	26	2	266 mil
1950	16	2	125 mil
1951	19	2	247 mil
1952	21	2	204 mil

Source: "Basic Data on the Economy of the Union of South Africa," *Economic Reports* (May 1955), 11; U.S. Department of Commerce, *1949 Statistical Supplement to the Survey of Current Business* (Washington: U.S. Government Printing Office, 1949), 107; idem, *Business Statistics 1955: A Supplement to the Survey of Current Business* (Washington: U.S. Government Printing Office, 1955), 104; idem, *Investment in Union of South Africa,* 118, 123–24; Alphaeus Hunton, "Postscript," in *Resistance Against Fascist Enslavement,* 53.

Table 4—U.S. private capital investment abroad and in South Africa for selected years, 1943–1952 (in millions of dollars)

Year	U.S. private capital investment in South Africa	Total U.S. private capital investment abroad
1943	51	7,862
1949	105	10,700
1950	140	11,788
1951	157	13,089
1952	194	14,820
1953	213	16,000

Source: "Basic Data on the Economy of the Union of South Africa," *Economic Reports* (May 1955), 4; U.S. Department of Commerce, *Historical Statistics of the United States: Colonial Times to the 1970* (Washington: U.S. Government Printing Office, 1975), 869; idem, *U.S. Business Investments in Foreign Countries* (Washington: U.S. Government Printing Office, 1960), 1; Samuel Pizer and Frederick Cutler, "Growth in Private Foreign Investments," *Survey of Current Business* (January 1954), 7; U.S. Department of Commerce, Office of Business Economics, *Foreign Investments of the United States* (Washington: U.S. Government Printing Office, 1953), 7–8.

Notes

Preface

1. In his otherwise delightful book about Wyoming geologist David Love, *Rising from the Plains* (New York: Farrar, Straus & Giroux, 1986), for example, John McPhee claims that "the rock that destroyed Hiroshima had come out of the Colorado Plateau" (p. 206), when in fact it was mined in the southern Belgian Congo.

For other examples, see Steven Metz, "Congress, the Antiapartheid Movement, and Nixon," *Diplomatic History* 12 (Spring 1988): 181, which claims that in 1973 "for the first time southern Africa's deposits of strategic minerals became a critical factor in [U.S.] discussions of policy toward the region"; Stephen E. Ambrose, *Rise to Globalism: American Foreign Policy Since 1938,* 3rd rev. ed. (Harmondsworth, England: Penguin, 1983), 376, which posits that "events in the Congo, meanwhile [in 1960], brought the Cold War to central Africa for the first time"; Anthony Lake, "Caution and Concern: The Making of American Policy toward South Africa, 1946–1971" (Ph.D. diss., Princeton University, 1974), 44, which argues that "the situation in South Africa has not been closely or immediately related to the Cold War, except very occasionally"; and Martin Bauml Duberman, *Paul Robeson: A Biography* (New York: Ballantine Books, 1989), 340, which mentions in passing "the South African government [in 1949]—about to become a loyal U.S. ally in the Cold War, in return for Washington's working to postpone any direct UN action on South-West Africa."

In the same vein, a National Public Radio interview of political scientist and South African specialist Thomas Karis on 19 June 1990, the eve of Nelson Mandela's first visit to the United States, discussed the U.S. government's collusion with the South African government in the 1950s in terms of shared anticommunism and did not mention uranium at all.

2. The archival basis of this study is not multinational. American policymakers generally occupy center stage in this story, and the research is therefore grounded in American documents. While the footnotes have not been "internationalized," my analysis has been deeply informed by the secondary literature on southern Africa in these years. This study is thus intended as a small contribution to the broad effort to make the history of American foreign relations less parochial, specifically by examining race relations as an international issue in the early Cold War period. For one of the most insightful discussions of the question of "internationalizing" American diplomatic history, see Robert J. McMahon, "The

Study of American Foreign Relations: National History or International History?" *Diplomatic History* 14 (Fall 1990): 554–64.

Introduction

1. There has not yet been a comprehensive study of United States–South African relations in the Truman years. The most important work to date can be found in the appropriate chapters in William Minter, *King Solomon's Mines Revisited: Western Interests and the Burdened History of Southern Africa* (New York: Basic Books, 1986); and Thomas J. Noer, *Cold War and Black Liberation: The United States and White Rule in Africa, 1948–1968* (Columbia: University of Missouri Press, 1985). On the economic relationship between the two countries, see, in addition to Minter's book, Richard W. Hull, *American Enterprise in South Africa: Historical Dimensions of Engagement and Disengagement* (New York: New York University Press, 1990). See also Thomas J. Noer, "Truman, Eisenhower, and South Africa: The 'Middle Road' and Apartheid," *Journal of Ethnic Studies* 11 (Spring 1983): 75–104; Anthony Lake, "Caution and Concern: The Making of American Policy Toward South Africa, 1946–1971" (Ph.D. diss., Princeton University, 1974); Stanford D. Greenberg, "U.S. Policy toward the Republic of South Africa, 1945–1964" (Ph.D. diss., Harvard University, 1965).

2. Leonard Thompson, "The Parting of the Ways in South Africa," in *The Transfer of Power in Africa: Decolonization, 1940–1960,* ed. Prosser Gifford and William Roger Louis (New Haven: Yale University Press, 1982), 417–44; Allister Sparks, *The Mind of South Africa* (New York: Alfred A. Knopf, 1990), 184–85. On American awareness of the Soviet Union's public opposition to the practice of racial discrimination, see, for example, E. Talbot Smith (U.S. Consul in Durban), "Memorandum on the Natal Indian Situation," 26 March 1945, enclosed in U.S. Legation in Capetown to the Department of State, 3 April 1945, 848A.00/4-345, Department of State Records, Record Group 59, National Archives, Washington, D.C., in *Confidential U.S. State Department Central Files, South Africa: Internal Affairs and Foreign Affairs, 1945–1949* (Frederick, Md.: University Publications of America, 1985 [microfilm, 14 reels with printed guide]), 1 (hereafter *CSDCF, 1945–49,* followed by reel number).

3. For a useful definition and discussion of racism, see Pierre L. van den Berghe, *Race and Racism: A Comparative Perspective* (New York: John Wiley & Sons, 1967), 11.

Chapter 1

1. Michael McCarthy, *Dark Continent: Africa as Seen by Americans* (Westport, Conn.: Greenwood Press, 1983), 148–49.

2. On the matter of African Americans being essentially invisible to white Americans in the Truman period, see the revealing novel by Ralph Ellison, *Invisible Man* (New York: Random House, 1952).

3. Martin Flavin, *Black and White: From the Cape to the Congo* (New York: Harper, 1950), 1, 140; Edward H. McKinley, *The Lure of Africa: American Interests in Tropical Africa, 1919–1939* (Indianapolis: Bobbs-Merrill, 1974), 203; McCarthy, *Dark Continent,* xvi, 145–53; Edward Baum, "The United States, Self-Government, and Africa: An Examination of the Nature of the American Policy on Self-Determination with Reference to Africa in the Postwar Era" (Ph.D.

diss., University of California, Los Angeles, 1964), 118–23; Chester Bowles, *Africa's Challenge to America* (Berkeley: University of California Press, 1956), 1. Americans' relative lack of interest in Africa continues today, as suggested by the contrast between the bare trickle of United States aid going to desperately poor sub-Saharan nations and the considerable sums approved almost overnight for countries in Eastern Europe after their political liberalization in late 1989. See Neil Henry, "Will Foreign Donors to Eastern Europe Remember Africa?" *Seattle Times*, 26 January 1990, sec. A, p. 3.

4. McCarthy, *Dark Continent*, xvi-xvii, 77–84, 126–41.

5. Richard Wright, *Native Son* (New York: Harper & Brothers, 1940; repr., New York: Harper & Row, 1966), 32, 35–36; James R. Nesteby, *Black Images in American Films, 1896–1954: The Interplay Between Civil Rights and Film Culture* (Washington: University Press of America, 1982), 115–35; Jean-Donald Miller, "The United States and Colonial Sub-Saharan Africa, 1939–1945" (Ph.D. diss., University of Connecticut, 1981), 224–26; McKinley, *Lure of Africa*, 165–67, 201–3.

6. McKinley, *Lure of Africa*, 195–96; McCarthy, *Dark Continent*, 77–92.

7. Michael H. Hunt, *Ideology and U.S. Foreign Policy* (New Haven: Yale University Press, 1987), 46–91; McCarthy, *Dark Continent*, 27–29, 77–84; McKinley, *Lure of Africa*, 156; Frederickson, *White Supremacy*, 187–89. On American science and racial categorization, see Stephen Jay Gould, *The Mismeasure of Man* (New York: W.W. Norton, 1981). On race in American foreign policy, see, in addition to Hunt, George W. Shepherd, Jr., ed., *Racial Influences on American Foreign Policy* (New York: Basic Books, 1970); Rubin F. Weston, *Racism in U.S. Imperialism: The Influence of Racial Assumptions on American Foreign Policy, 1893–1946* (Columbia: University of South Carolina Press, 1972); Paul Gordon Lauren, *Power and Prejudice: The Politics and Diplomacy of Racial Discrimination* (Boulder: Westview Press, 1988). Assumptions about differences between racial groups, even among respected authorities, have not disappeared easily. State Department historians writing in 1972, for example, apparently agreed that "the degree of civilization" that "dependent peoples" had attained—civilization being supposedly a unitary concept—could determine the amount of independence they would be allowed. See *Foreign Relations of the United States* (Washington: United States Government Printing Office [volumes to be cited in this work were published between 1967 and 1986]), *1946*, 1:600, n. 58, (hereafter *FRUS*).

8. McKinley, *Lure of Africa*, 173, 194; McCarthy, *Dark Continent*, 104–5, 112–13. Melville J. Herskovits provided a penetrating analysis of white American assumptions about the African history of African Americans in his 1941 book entitled *The Myth of the Negro Past* (New York: Harper & Brothers, 1941).

9. McKinley, *Lure of Africa*, 154–55. Quotation is on p. 148.

10. Melville J. Herskovits, *Dahomey: An Ancient West African Kingdom* (New York: J. J. Augustin, 1938); McKinley, *Lure of Africa*, 150, 158–62 (Bowman quotation is on p. 170). The prevalence in the United States of portrayals of Africa focusing on wildlife and denigrating people moved Eslanda Robeson to end her 1945 book describing her own visit to southern Africa with a simple declaration: "Africans are *people*." Robeson, *African Journey* (New York: John Day, 1945), 154 (emphasis in original). Another manifestation of the assumption that creativity and disciplined accomplishment among black people could happen only with white influence was the belief of many, if not most, Southern

whites that "outside agitators" were creating the civil rights movement in the black communities of the American South in the 1950s and 1960s. Africans were not the only people of color who white Americans tended to assume had merely imitative rather than creative abilities, as suggested by the common attitude in the United States in those same decades that Japanese manufacturers could only copy what innovative Americans and Europeans thought up.

11. H. V. Morton, *In Search of South Africa* (New York: Dodd, Mead, 1948), 17; McCarthy, *Dark Continent*, 56–60, 66–73, 92–95.

12. This commonly used term misleadingly suggests that colonial areas could somehow not survive without (i.e., were dependent on) imperial administration and outside authority. The economic reality of colonialism was, in fact, quite different: the economic power of the small metropolitan powers depended precisely on their ability to exploit the vast resources of their colonial holdings.

13. Geoffrey Barraclough, *An Introduction to Contemporary History* (Harmondsworth, England: Penguin, 1967), 153. See also Lauren, *Power and Prejudice*, 197.

14. *The Public Papers and Addresses of Franklin D. Roosevelt*, comp. Samuel I. Rosenman (New York: Macmillan, 1938–50), 9:672.

15. The text of the joint declaration can be found in Ruth B. Russell, *A History of the U.N. Charter: The Role of the United States, 1940–1945* (Washington: Brookings Institution, 1958), Appendix B, 975.

16. A term to be used advisedly, given its potential for suggesting inferiority to the industrialized nations of the Northern Hemisphere.

17. Thomas Karis and Gwendolen M. Carter, eds., *From Protest to Challenge: A Documentary History of African Politics in South Africa, 1882–1964* (Stanford: Hoover Institution Press, 1972–77), vol. 2, *Hope and Challenge, 1935–1952,* by Thomas Karis, 87–90; and "Africans' Claims in South Africa," in ibid., 209–23; E. Talbot Smith, "Natal's Indian Problem," 13 November 1944, enclosed in Smith to Secretary of State, 5 April 1945, 848A.00/4-545, *CSDCF, 1945–49,* 1.

18. The Committee on Africa, the War, and Peace Aims, *The Atlantic Charter and Africa from an American Standpoint* (New York: n.p., 1942), 12, 17, 30–31; M. S. Venkataramani, "The United States, the Colonial Issue, and the Atlantic Charter Hoax," *International Studies* (New Delhi) 13 (January-March 1974): 23–27.

19. See, for example, Walter LaFeber, *The New Empire: An Interpretation of American Expansion, 1860–1898* (Ithaca: Cornell University Press, 1963).

20. "An Open Letter from the Editors of *Life* to the People of England," *Life,* 12 October 1942, p. 34 (emphasis in original). The magazine continued, "We don't like to put the matter so bluntly, but we don't want you to have any illusions." See also Gary R. Hess, *America Encounters India, 1941–1947* (Baltimore: Johns Hopkins Press, 1971), 184–85; William Roger Louis and Ronald Robinson, "The United States and the Liquidation of the British Empire in Tropical Africa, 1941–1951," in Gifford and Louis, *Transfer of Power in Africa,* 34; Hollis R. Lynch, "Pan-African Responses in the United States to British Colonial Rule in Africa in the 1940s," in ibid., 79; William Roger Louis, "American Anti-Colonialism and the Dissolution of the British Empire," in *The 'Special Relationship': Anglo-American Relations Since 1945,* ed. Wm. Roger Louis and Hedley Bull (Oxford: Clarendon Press, 1986), 263.

21. See Miller, "United States and Colonial Sub-Saharan Africa," 187–93,

for an interesting discussion of the significance of Roosevelt's experiences in Gambia for his attitude towards European, and especially British, colonial rule.

22. Louis and Robinson, "United States and the Liquidation of the British Empire," 34–37. Quotation is from memorandum of conversation by the Advisor on Caribbean Affairs, Charles Taussig, 15 March 1945, *FRUS, 1945*, 1:124.

23. David Killingray and Richard Rathbone, *Africa and the Second World War* (Basingstoke, England: Macmillan, 1986), 3–4; Michael Crowder, "The Second World War: Prelude to Decolonisation in Africa," in *The Cambridge History of Africa*, ed. J. D. Fage and Roland Oliver, vol. 8, *From c. 1940 to c. 1975*, ed. Michael Crowder (Cambridge: Cambridge University Press, 1984), 24; Peter Duignan and Lewis H. Gann, *The United States and Africa: A History* (Cambridge: Cambridge University Press, 1984), 284.

24. William Roger Louis, *Imperialism at Bay: The United States and the Decolonization of the British Empire, 1941–1945* (New York: Oxford University Press, 1978), 9; Louis and Robinson, "United States and the Liquidation of the British Empire," 34; John J. Sbrega, "Determination versus Drift: The Anglo-American Debate over the Trusteeship Issue, 1941–1945," *Pacific Historical Review* 55 (May 1986): 257–58, 279–80; Miller, "United States and Colonial Sub-Saharan Africa," 193–94; Hess, *America Encounters India*, 130–56, 185.

25. Taussig memo, *FRUS, 1945*, 1:124; Louis and Robinson, "United States and the Liquidation of the British Empire," 41–42; Lynch, "Pan-African Responses in the United States," 63.

26. Noer, " 'Non-Benign Neglect,' " 271. Most studies of U.S.-African relations in the twentieth century focus on the post-1956 period and have often been the domain of journalists and political scientists. The best of these include Waldemar Nielsen, *The Great Powers and Africa* (New York: Praeger, 1969); Vernon McKay, *Africa in World Politics* (New York: Harper and Row, 1963); Rupert Emerson, *Africa and United States Policy* (Englewood Cliffs, N.J.: Prentice Hall, 1967); Edward W. Chester, *Clash of Titans: Africa and U.S. Foreign Policy* (Maryknoll, N.Y.: Orbis Books, 1974); Walter R. Goldschmidt, ed., *The United States and Africa* (New York: Praeger, 1963); Harin Shah, *The Great Abdication: American Foreign Policy in Asia and Africa* (Delhi: Atma Ram & Sons, 1957); Miller, "United States and Colonial Sub-Saharan Africa"; G. Macharia Munene, "The Truman Administration and the Decolonization of Sub-Saharan Africa, 1945–1952" (Ph.D. diss., Ohio University, 1985). For southern Africa in particular, see the sources listed in Chapter 1, note 1, as well as William Hance, ed., *Southern Africa and the United States* (New York: Columbia University Press, 1968) and René Lemarchand, ed., *American Policy in Southern Africa: The Stakes and the Stance* (Washington: University Press of America, 1978). For earlier U.S.-African relations, see Duignan and Gann, *United States and Africa: A History;* and Russell Warren Howe, *Along the Afric Shore: A Historical Review of Two Centuries of U.S.-African Relations* (New York: Barnes & Noble, 1975).

27. Henry S. Villard, *Affairs at State* (New York: Thomas Y. Crowell, 1965), 65; Miller, "United States and Colonial Sub-Saharan Africa," 14, 30, 39; Noer, " 'Non Benign Neglect,' " 272; Duignan and Gann, *United States and Africa*, 288; Bowles, *Africa's Challenge to America*, 57. Not surprisingly, the Library of Congress assigned its staff in a manner similar to that of the State Department, with the European Affairs Division responsible for African affairs as well. Bowles, *Africa's Challenge to America*, 2.

Responsibility in the State Department for southern Africa was divided between the Division of British Commonwealth Affairs within the Office of European Affairs (reorganized in 1949 as the Office of British Commonwealth and Northern European Affairs within the Bureau of European Affairs), which dealt with South Africa, and the Division of African Affairs within the Office of Near Eastern and African Affairs (reorganized in 1949 as the Office of African Affairs within the Bureau of Near Eastern, South Asian, and African Affairs), which managed the colonial areas constituting the rest of the region.

28. Policy manual, "The Foreign Policy of the United States," 1 April 1945, enclosed in Stettinius to Truman, 16 April 1945, Box 159, President's Secretary's File, Harry S Truman Papers, Harry S Truman Library, Independence, Missouri; Miller, "United States and Colonial Sub-Saharan Africa," 178; Baum, "United States, Self-Government, and Africa," 119.

29. Miller, "United States and Colonial Sub-Saharan Africa," 48; Harold R. Isaacs, *The New World of Negro Americans* (New York: John Day, 1963), 150; John Hope Franklin, *From Slavery to Freedom: A History of Negro Americans,* 3rd ed. (New York: Alfred A. Knopf, 1967), 574, 600. See also William R. Scott, *The Sons of Sheba's Race: African-Americans and the Italo-Ethiopian War, 1935–1941* (Bloomington: Indiana University Press, 1991).

30. Ralph J. Bunche to Conyers Read, 6 February 1942, *OSS/State Department Intelligence and Research Reports* (Washington: University Publications of America, 1980), part 13, *Africa, 1941–1961* (microfilm, 11 reels with printed guide), 1 (hereafter *OSS/SD, Africa,* followed by reel number); OSS, "Survey of Mozambique (Portuguese East Africa)," 30 July 1942, *OSS/SD, Africa,* 9; Miller, "United States and Colonial Sub-Saharan Africa," 1–4, 8–9, 50–52, 94, 112–16, 131–32, 250; Dumett, "Africa's Strategic Minerals," 393–400.

31. "West and Equatorial Africa," vol. 1, 31 January 1942, *OSS/SD, Africa,* 1; Miller, "United States and Colonial Sub-Saharan Africa," 5–7, 30–34, 229–31; Louis, *Imperialism at Bay,* 170–72. Welles is quoted in Hunt, *Ideology and U.S. Foreign Policy,* 162.

32. Miller, "United States and Colonial Sub-Saharan Africa," 6, 37, 228–29.

33. The novel *Invisible Man* was published in 1952 but had been copyrighted in 1947.

34. Joseph Boskin, "Sambo: The National Jester in the Popular Culture," in *The Great Fear: Race in the Mind of America,* ed. Gary B. Nash and Richard Weiss (New York: Holt, Rinehart and Winston, 1970), 166–67, 177, 182. See also Nesteby, *Black Images in American Films*; Thomas Cripps, *Slow Fade to Black: The Negro in American Film, 1900–1942* (New York: Oxford University Press, 1977); Donald Bogle, *Toms, Coons, Mulattoes, Mammies, and Bucks: An Interpretive History of Blacks in American Films* (New York: Viking Press, 1973).

35. An impressive exception is Neil R. McMillen, *Dark Journey: Black Mississippians in the Age of Jim Crow* (Urbana: University of Illinois Press, 1989).

36. Herbert Shapiro, *White Violence and Black Response: From Reconstruction to Montgomery* (Amherst: University of Massachusetts Press, 1988), 310–41; Franklin, *From Slavery to Freedom,* 597–98. See also Robert L. Zangrando, *The NAACP Crusade Against Lynching, 1909–1950* (Philadelphia: Temple University Press, 1980); and Robert Shogan, *The Detroit Race Riot: A Study in Violence* (Philadelphia: Chilton Books, 1964).

37. Harvard Sitkoff, "Racial Militancy and Interracial Violence in the Second World War," *Journal of American History* 58 (December 1971): 667–81;

Shapiro, *White Violence and Black Response,* 305–10, 333, 335; Walter F. White, *A Man Called White: Autobiography of Walter White* (New York: Viking, 1948), 277–93; Miller, "United States and Colonial Sub-Saharan Africa," 227. On the struggle for racial equality in the armed services, see Richard M. Dalfiume, *Desegregation of the U.S. Armed Forces: Fighting on Two Fronts, 1939–1953* (Columbia: University of Missouri Press, 1969). See also Morris J. MacGregor, *Integration of the Armed Forces, 1940–1965* (Washington: Center of Military History, United States Army, 1981).

38. Franklin, *From Slavery to Freedom,* 589–90.

39. J. Edgar Hoover (Director of the FBI) to James Byrnes, 7 July 1945, Folder 627, James F. Byrnes Papers, Special Collections, Robert Muldrow Cooper Library, Clemson University, Clemson, South Carolina; War Department, "Questionable Statements," 21 April 1945, Box 55, Confidential File, White House Central Files, Truman Papers.

40. Gunnar Myrdal, *An American Dilemma: The Negro Problem and Modern Democracy* (New York: Harper & Brothers, 1944), xix; Horace R. Cayton, "The Negro's Challenge," *Nation,* 3 July 1943, pp. 11–12; Walter J. Brown, Notes of 11 July 1944, Folder 74(2), Byrnes Papers; Doris E. Saunders, "1944 Pre-Convention Maneuverings: The Day Dawson Saved America from a Racist President," *Ebony* 27 (July 1972): 45–50; White, *Man Called White,* 266–68; Franklin, *From Slavery to Freedom,* 598–99. See also Richard M. Dalfiume, "The 'Forgotten Years' of the Negro Revolution," *Journal of American History* 55 (June 1968): 90–106; Rayford Logan, ed., *What the Negro Wants* (Chapel Hill: University of North Carolina Press, 1944); Doug McAdam, *Political Process and the Development of Black Insurgency, 1930–1970* (Chicago: University of Chicago Press, 1982); Aldon D. Morris, *The Origins of the Civil Rights Movement: Black Communities Organizing for Change* (New York: Free Press, 1984); John Modell, Marc Goulden, and Sigurdur Magnusson, "World War II in the Lives of Black Americans: Some Findings and an Interpretation," *Journal of American History* 76 (December 1989): 838–48; Harvard Sitkoff, "The Preconditions for Racial Change," in *A History of Our Time: Readings on Postwar America,* ed. William H. Chafe and Harvard Sitkoff, 2nd ed. (New York: Oxford University Press, 1987), 151–60.

Chapter 2

1. Non-European Unity Committee, Capetown, "A Declaration to the Nations of the World," 8 August 1945, enclosed in H. Earle Russell to Secretary of State, 15 August 1945, 848A.00/8–1545, *CSDCF, 1945–49,* 1. On *Herrenvolk* ideology, see George Frederickson, *White Supremacy: A Comparative Study in American and South African History* (New York: Oxford University Press, 1981); and Kenneth P. Vickery, "'Herrenvolk' Democracy and Egalitarianism in South Africa and the U.S. South," *Comparative Studies in Society and History* 16 (1974): 309–28.

The assumption that the failure of an individual to accept the norms of racial domination indicated mental imbalance would find one poignant echo in the United States thirteen years later. When Clennon King, a black minister and part-time college professor from Albany, Georgia, applied for admission to the all-white University of Mississippi in 1958, Mississippi authorities responded by seizing him during a visit to the campus admissions office and committing him to the state mental institution explicitly on the grounds that "only an insane Negro would seek admission to Ole Miss." Taylor Branch, *Parting the Waters: America in the King Years, 1954–63* (New York: Simon & Schuster, 1988), 233.

2. Tom Lodge, *Black Politics in South Africa Since 1945* (New York: Longman, 1983), 23–24; Leo Kuper, "African Nationalism in South Africa," in *The Oxford History of South Africa,* ed. Monica Wilson and Leonard Thompson (London: Oxford University Press, 1969–1971), vol. 2, *South Africa, 1870–1966,* 444–45; Albert Luthuli, *Let My People Go* (New York: McGraw-Hill, 1962), 101–2; Dr. Alfred B. Xuma, Presidential Address to the ANC Annual Conference of 14–16 December 1941, in Karis and Carter, *From Protest to Challenge,* 2:181–83. Black South Africans serving in the armed forces were bitterly aware that they were paid almost the exact same wages for actively supporting the South African government and the Allied cause as were allotted as stipends to families of white opponents of the war who had been incarcerated as threats to the security of the country. See Xuma, Presidential Address.

3. Crowder, "Second World War," 8–9.

4. Noer, " 'Non-Benign Neglect,' " 278; Killingray and Rathbone, *Africa and the Second World War,* 2–3; Crowder, "Second World War," 20–22.

5. Raymond Dumett, "Africa's Strategic Minerals During the Second World War," *Journal of African History* 26 (1985): 381–82, 404–5.

6. Killingray and Rathbone, *Africa and the Second World War,* 14–17; Crowder, "Second World War," 30–33; United States Office of Strategic Services, R & A No. 2279, "Nationalist Trends in British West Africa," 30 August 1944, *OSS/SD, Africa,* 3; George Padmore, "Anglo-American Plan for Control of Colonies," *Crisis* 51 (November 1944): 357; Basil Davidson, *Africa in Modern History: The Search for a New Society* (London: Allen Lane, 1978), 202–3; Office of Strategic Services, R & A No. 2852, "Regulations and Practices Concerning Native Troops in British, French, Spanish, Belgian, Portuguese, and Ex-Italian Africa," 27 February 1945, *OSS/SD, Africa,* 3.

7. Davidson, *Africa in Modern History,* 199; Richard D. Ralston, "American Episodes in the Making of an African Leader: A Case Study of Alfred B. Xuma," *International Journal of African Historical Studies* 6 (1973): 72–73; OSS, "Regulations and Practices Concerning Native Troops"; Lynch, "Pan-African Responses in the United States," 85.

8. Quoted in Davidson, *Africa in the Modern World,* 203.

9. Basil Davidson, *Report on Southern Africa* (London: Jonathan Cape, 1952), 258.

10. René De Villiers, "Afrikaner Nationalism," in Wilson and Thompson, *Oxford History of South Africa* 2:365–423. Other sources on Afrikaner history include T. Dunbar Moodie, *The Rise of Afrikanerdom: Power, Apartheid and the Afrikaner Civil Religion* (Berkeley: University of California Press, 1975); Willem A. DeKlerk, *The Puritans in Africa: A Story of Afrikanerdom* (London: R. Collings, 1975); David Harrison, *The White Tribe of Africa: South Africa in Perspective* (Berkeley: University of California Press, 1982); Dan O'Meara, *Volkskapitalisme: Class, Capital and Ideology in the Development of Afrikaner Nationalism, 1934–1948* (Cambridge: Cambridge University Press, 1983); Newell M. Stultz, *Afrikaner Politics in South Africa, 1934–1948* (Berkeley: University of California Press, 1974). For general histories of South Africa since the beginning of white settlement, see T. R. H. Davenport, *South Africa: A Modern History,* 3rd ed. (Toronto: University of Toronto Press, 1987); and Leonard Thompson, *A History of South Africa*

(New Haven: Yale University Press, 1990); consult also Sparks, *Mind of South Africa.*

11. Simon Schama, *The Embarrassment of Riches: An Interpretation of Dutch Culture in the Golden Age* (New York: Alfred A. Knopf [distributed by Random House], 1987), 22–50.

12. De Villiers, "Afrikaner Nationalism," 365–66.

13. Frederickson, *White Supremacy,* 171; Schama, *Embarrassment of Riches,* 25–28, 40–42.

14. Thompson, "Parting of the Ways," 419–21; Sam C. Nolutshungu, *South Africa in Africa: A Study in Ideology and Foreign Policy* (Manchester, England: Manchester University Press, 1975), 9–17.

15. James G. Leyburn, "Urban Natives in South Africa," *American Sociological Review* 9 (October 1944): 495; John W. Cell, *The Highest Stage of White Supremacy: The Origins of Segregation in South Africa and the American South* (Cambridge: Cambridge University Press, 1982), 216; Davenport, *South Africa,* 258–60; Gail M. Gerhart, *Black Power in South Africa: The Evolution of an Ideology* (Berkeley: University of California Press, 1978), 22–24; Thompson, "Parting of the Ways," 421–22.

16. Thomas Holcomb (U.S. Minister in South Africa) to Secretary of State, "Second Session of the Ninth Parliament of the Union of South Africa: IV," 31 March 1945, 848A.00/3-3145, *CSDCF, 1945–49,* 1; "Seven Golden Houses," *Fortune* 34 (December 1946): 162; D. Hobart Houghton, *The South African Economy,* 4th ed. (New York: Oxford University Press, 1976), 108, 112.

17. Davidson, *Report on Southern Africa,* 77–79, 114–15, 174–75, 270; Davenport, *South Africa,* 330; Houghton, *South African Economy,* Table 16, p. 286; Eslanda G. Robeson, *African Journey,* 50; Lodge, *Black Politics in South Africa,* 11–12; D. Hobart Houghton, "Economic Development, 1865–1965," in Wilson and Thompson, *Oxford History of South Africa* 2:32–38.

18. Davidson, *Report on Southern Africa,* 48–50; McGregor to Secretary of State, 14 June 1949, 848A.00/6-1449, *CSDCF, 1945–49,* 8.

19. United States Department of Commerce, Bureau of Foreign Commerce, *Investment in Union of South Africa: Conditions and Outlook for United States Investors* (Washington: United States Government Printing Office, 1954), 43.

20. Coordinator of Information, Interview with Frederick Spencer, 17 February 1942, *OSS/SD, Africa,* 10.

21. Hereafter reservedly referred to on occasion (for the purpose of literary felicity) by the somewhat misleading term "Indians."

22. E. Talbot Smith, "Natal's Indian Problem," 13 November 1944, enclosed in Smith to Secretary of State, 5 April 1945, 848A.00/4-545, *CSDCF, 1945–49,* 1. For a representative white Natalian perspective on Indian fellow residents of the province, see "Durban Joint Wards Committee," 9 August 1945, enclosed in Holcomb to Department of State, 25 September 1945, 848A.00/9-2545, *CSDCF, 1945–49,* 1.

23. On the maintenance of residential segregation in the United States, see Kenneth T. Jackson, *Crabgrass Frontier: The Suburbanization of the United States* (New York: Oxford University Press, 1985), especially 190–218; and Arnold R. Hirsch, *Making the Second Ghetto: Race and Housing in Chicago, 1940–1960* (Cambridge: Cambridge University Press, 1983).

24. Smith, "Natal's Indian Problem."

25. State Department Office of European Affairs, "Indian Situation in Natal," 11 January 1945, 848A.00/1-1145, *CSDCF, 1945–49,* 1; Smith, "Memorandum on the Indian Situation," 12 January 1945, enclosed in Holcomb to Secretary of State, 19 January 1945, 848A.00/1-1945, *CSDCF, 1945–49,* 1.

26. Holcomb to Secretary of State, 19 January 1945, 848A.00/1–1945, *CSDCF, 1945–49,* 1; Smith, "Memorandum on the Indian Situation," 23 December 1944, enclosed in Holcomb to Secretary of State, 5 January 1945, 848A.00/1-545, *CSDCF, 1945–49,* 1; Smith, "Memorandum on the Indian Situation," 26 January 1945, enclosed in U.S. Legation (Capetown) to Department of State, 6 February 1945, 848A.00/2-645, *CSDCF, 1945–49,* 1; Smith, "Memorandum on the Indian Situation," 27 February 1945, enclosed in U.S. Legation (Capetown) to Department of State, 6 March 1945, 848A.00/3-645, *CSDCF, 1945–49,* 1; Smith, "Memorandum on the Natal Indian Situation," 26 March 1945, enclosed in U.S. Legation (Capetown) to Department of State, 3 April 1945, 848A.00/4-345, *CSDCF, 1945–49,* 1; "Durban Joint Wards Committee," 9 August 1945, enclosed in Holcomb to Department of State, 25 September 1945, 848A.00/9-2545, *CSDCF, 1945–49,* 1.

27. On African nationalism in South Africa, see Lodge, *Black Politics in South Africa*; Gerhart, *Black Power in South Africa*; Leo Kuper, "African Nationalism in South Africa, 1910–1964," in Wilson and Thompson, *Oxford History of South Africa* 2:426–76; Peter Walshe, *The Rise of African Nationalism in South Africa: The African National Congress, 1912–1952* (Berkeley: University of California Press, 1971); Edward Roux, *Time Longer Than Rope: A History of the Black Man's Struggle for Freedom in South Africa,* 2nd ed. (Madison: University of Wisconsin Press, 1964); Mary Benson, *South Africa: The Struggle for a Birthright* (Harmondsworth, England: Penguin, 1966); Francis Meli, *South Africa Belongs to Us: A History of the ANC* (Bloomington: Indiana University Press, 1988).

28. Department of State, Office of Intelligence Research, "Race Relations in South Africa," 21 October 1952, *OSS/SD, Africa,* 10; Ralston, "American Episodes," 72–73; Kuper, "African Nationalism," 434–36, 445–46; Lodge, *Black Politics in South Africa,* 2–3; Thompson, "Parting of the Ways," 417, 423–24; Thomas J. Noer, *Briton, Boer, and Yankee: The United States and South Africa, 1870–1914* (Kent, Ohio: Kent State University Press, 1978), 120–21.

29. Robeson, *African Journey,* 43.

30. Lodge, *Black Politics in South Africa,* viii-ix, 1, 11–20; Kuper, "African Nationalism," 451; Luthuli, *Let My People Go,* 101.

31. Lodge, *Black Politics in South Africa,* 20–28; Gerhart, *Black Power in South Africa,* 54; Kuper, "African Nationalism," 436.

32. Hereafter referred to by the more commonly used "Nationalist Party."

33. Davenport, *South Africa,* 309–28; Amry Vandenbosch, *South Africa and the World: The Foreign Policy of Apartheid* (Lexington: University of Kentucky Press, 1970), 110–14; De Villiers, "Afrikaner Nationalism," 372; Davidson, *Report on Southern Africa,* 147–49.

34. Quoted in Davidson, *Report on Southern Africa,* 147–49.

35. Harrison, *The White Tribe of Africa: South Africa in Perspective,* 125–31.

36. Holcomb to Secretary of State, 29 May 1945, 848A.00/5-2945, *CSDCF, 1945–49,* 1. Almost thirty thousand Afrikaners, most under the age of sixteen, died in British concentration camps during the Boer War of 1899–1902. See Davenport, *South Africa,* 216–17.

37. "Pan-Netherlandism, South Africa and the War," 1 April 1942, *OSS/SD, Africa,* 10.

38. Earle Russell (Consul General in Cape Town), "Political Report," 28 April 1945, 848A.00/4-2845, *CSDCF, 1945–49,* 1. For an example of such reports on Germany, see "Dachau Captured by Americans Who Kill Guards, Liberate 32,000," *New York Times,* 1 May 1945, p. 1.

39. Bowman (Consul General in Johannesburg), "Political Notes," enclosed in Holcomb to Secretary of State, 2 October 1945, 848A.00/10-245, *CSDCF, 1945–49,* 1; Vandenbosch, *South Africa and the World,* 110. On Malan's view of Germany as a "bulwark" against communism, see Holcomb to Secretary of State, 10 April 1947, 848A.032/4-1047, *CSDCF, 1945–49,* 5.

40. Luthuli, *Let My People Go,* 101. Despite its spelling in his autobiography published abroad, Lutuli apparently preferred his surname written without the "h." For an authoritative if sympathetic biography of Smuts, see W. K. Hancock, *Smuts,* 2 vols. (Cambridge: Cambridge University Press, 1962–1968).

41. Holcomb to Secretary of State, 20 July 1945, 848A.00/7-2045, *CSDCF, 1945–49,* 1.

42. Vandenbosch, *South Africa and the World,* 108; Cell, *Highest Stage of White Supremacy,* 269–70.

43. Holcomb to Secretary of State, "Second Session of the Ninth Parliament of the Union of South Africa: IV," 31 March 1945, 848A.00/3-3145, *CSDCF, 1945–49,* 1 (emphasis added).

44. Ibid.

45. It followed from white South African assumptions about the limited abilities of black South Africans that blacks would not be likely to organize themselves effectively without some white (in this case, white radical) direction and assistance.

46. Holcomb to Secretary of State, 20 July 1945, 848A.00/7-2045, *CSDCF, 1945–49,* 1; Holcomb to Secretary of State, 30 July 1945, 848A.00/7-3045, *CSDCF, 1945–49,* 1.

47. "Excerpts from Address Delivered by Field-Marshal Smuts At Lourenco Marques On July 23, 1945," enclosed in Holcomb to Secretary of State, 27 July 1945, 848A.00/7-2745, *CSDCF, 1945–49,* 1; State Department Office of European Affairs, Division of British Commonwealth Affairs, "Pan-Africanism," 18 January 1945, 848A.00/1-1845, *CSDCF, 1945–49,* 1; George Padmore, "Anglo-American Plan for Control of Colonies," *Crisis* 51 (November 1944): 355; Vandenbosch, *South Africa and the World,* 155–56.

48. Holcomb to Secretary of State, 20 July 1945, 848A.00/7-2045, *CSDCF, 1945–49,* 1.

49. Holcomb to Secretary of State, 16 April 1945, enclosing newspaper clipping of Auspex [pseud.], "Behind the Smokescreen," *Forum* (Capetown[?]), 31 March 1945, 848A.00/4-1645, *CSDCF, 1945–49,* 1; Department of State, Division of British Commonwealth Affairs, "Jan Hofmeyr—South Africa's Next Leader," 17 October 1944, Folder: "South Africa: General," Box 14, Records of the Office of Assistant Secretary of State and Under-Secretary of State Dean Acheson, 1941–1948, 1950, Record Group 59, National Archives.

Chapter 3

1. Alonzo L. Hamby, "The Mind and Character of Harry S Truman," in *The Truman Presidency,* ed. Michael J. Lacey (Cambridge: Cambridge University Press, 1989), 30.

2. Hunt, *Ideology and U.S. Foreign Policy,* 163.

3. Hamby, "Mind and Character of Truman," 30–31; William H. Chafe, "Postwar American Society: Dissent and Social Reform," in Lacey, *Truman Presidency,* 165–67; "President Truman," editorial, *Crisis* 52 (May 1945): 129; Walter J. Brown, Notes of 11 July 1944 and 18 July 1944, Folder 74(2), Byrnes Papers. The best general sources on the Truman administration and civil rights include Barton J. Bernstein, "The Ambiguous Legacy: The Truman Administration and Civil Rights," in *Politics and Policies of the Truman Administration,* ed. Barton J. Bernstein (Chicago: Quadrangle, 1970), 269–314; William Berman, *The Politics of Civil Rights in the Truman Administration* (Columbus: Ohio State University Press, 1970); Donald R. McCoy and Richard Ruetten, *Quest and Response: Minority Rights and the Truman Administration* (Lawrence: University Press of Kansas, 1973); William H. Chafe, "The Civil Rights Revolution, 1945–1960: The Gods Bring Threads to Webs Begun," in *Reshaping America: Society and Institutions, 1945–1960,* ed. Robert H. Bremner and Gary W. Reichard (Columbus: Ohio State University Press, 1982), 67–100.

4. One interesting study of the elite world out of which most of these men came is Walter Isaacson and Evan Thomas, *The Wise Men: Six Friends and the World They Made: Acheson, Bohlen, Harriman, Kennan, Lovett, McCloy* (New York: Simon & Schuster, 1986). See also Richard J. Barnet, "The National Security Managers and the National Interest," *Politics and Society* 1 (February 1971): 257–68.

5. Jonathan Daniels, *The Man of Independence* (Philadelphia: J. B. Lippincott, 1950), 34, 37, 40.

6. Clark M. Clifford oral history interview, 19 April 1971, transcript, pp. 253–55, Truman Library; Hunt, *Ideology and U.S. Foreign Policy,* 162.

7. Editorial, "Byrnes and the Balkans," *Crisis* 52 (December 1945): 345. Byrnes' note to the Bulgarian government in the summer of 1945 demanding free elections inspired some bitter humor among black South Carolinians, such as this poem sent to the Secretary by black educator Horace Mann Bond:

> Dear Mr. Byrnes, we doff our hats, in humblest admiration;
> Your latest note has thrown the Reds in utmost consternation.
> The echo sounds throughout the World—"Free Ballots for the Bulgar!"
> And none would raise a sour note—except, of course, the vulgar. . . .
>
> When you have time, dear Mr. Byrnes, from your high tasks dramatic,
> Please raise your voice in your own State, in accents as emphatic.
> There's Barnwell, and there's Bluffton, and there's Ballentine and Bowman,
> We love to see the Bulgars vote; now how about the Black man?

Horace Mann Bond, "Free Ballots for the Bulgars," enclosed in Bond to Byrnes, 22 August 1945, Folder 532, Byrnes Papers.

8. Hoover to Byrnes, 7 July 1945, Folder 627, Byrnes Papers.

9. Isaacson and Thomas, *Wise Men,* 50–57, 80–90, 125–29. For further information on Acheson, see Gaddis Smith, *Dean Acheson* (New York: Cooper Square, 1972); and David S. McLellan, *Dean Acheson: The State Department Years* (New York: Dodd, Mead, 1976).

10. David Mayers, *George Kennan and the Dilemmas of U.S. Foreign Policy* (New York: Oxford University Press, 1988), 266–67. For an enlightening discussion of Kennan's perspective on the Third World, see Anders Stephanson,

Kennan and the Art of Foreign Policy (Cambridge: Harvard University Press, 1989), 157–75.

11. Hunt, *Ideology and U.S. Foreign Policy,* 162–63; Mayers, *George Kennan and Dilemmas of U.S. Policy,* 271–72.

12. Kennan, "Tasks Ahead in U.S. Foreign Policy," lecture at the National War College, Washington, D.C., 18 December 1952, Box 18, George F. Kennan Papers, Seeley Mudd Library, Princeton University, Princeton, New Jersey.

13. Kennan diary, 1933–1938, "Fair Day, Adieu!" Box 25, Kennan Papers. See also Mayers, *George Kennan and Dilemmas of U.S. Policy,* 49–53; Isaacson and Evans, *Wise Men,* 171–72.

14. "The Acheson-Goldberg Correspondence on Rhodesia," *Africa Report* 12 (January 1967): 56; Dean Acheson, *Among Friends: Personal Letters of Dean Acheson,* ed. David S. McLellan and David C. Acheson (New York: Dodd, Mead, 1980), 306, 312.

15. Mayers, *George Kennan and Dilemmas of U.S. Policy,* 58, 267–71.

16. American diplomats in the field generally followed the lead of their superiors in Washington in assessing blacks in southern Africa as not yet capable of self-government. See, for example, E. Talbot Smith, "Natal's Indian Problem," 13 November 1944, enclosed in Smith to Secretary of State, 5 April 1945, 848A.00/4–545, *CSDCF, 1945–49,* 1.

17. W. E. Burghardt Du Bois, *The Souls of Black Folk: Essays and Sketches* (Chicago: A. C. McClung, 1903; repr., New York: Blue Heron Press, 1953), vii.

18. John Dower portrays the mutual wartime racial animosities of Japanese and Americans in *War Without Mercy: Race and Power in the Pacific War* (New York: Pantheon, 1986). For the significance of race in the Anglo-American alliance in the Pacific theater, see Christopher Thorne, *Allies of a Kind: The United States, Britain and the War Against Japan, 1941–1945* (London: Hamish Hamilton, 1978).

19. Horace R. Cayton, "The Negro's Challenge," *Nation,* 3 July 1943, p. 10.

20. Robert E. Cushman, "Our Civil Rights Become a World Issue," *New York Times Magazine,* 11 January 1948, p. 12.

21. White, *Man Called White,* 260; Shapiro, *White Violence and Black Response,* 318.

22. Alan Barth, "The 'Discovery' of Buchenwald," *Nation,* 5 May 1945, pp. 509–10.

23. "Charter of the United Nations," in Russell, *History of the U.N. Charter,* Appendix M, 1,035.

24. I. F. Stone, "Pie in the 'Frisco Sky," *Nation,* 19 May 1945, pp. 561–63; Louis, *Imperialism at Bay,* 533.

25. Louis, *Imperialism at Bay,* 532, 534–41; Sbrega, "Determination versus Drift," 278–79; Margaret Padelford Karns, "The United States, the United Nations and Decolonization" (Ph.D. diss., University of Michigan, 1975), 30–40. In characteristically blunt fashion, Truman explained a few months later that "those [Pacific] islands we do not need will be placed under U.N.O. trusteeship, and those we need we will keep, as long as we need them." Quoted in Nielsen, *Great Powers and Africa,* 250.

26. Louis, *Imperialism at Bay,* 542; editorial, *Christian Century,* 8 August 1945, p. 899.

27. I. F. Stone, "Truman and the State Department," *Nation*, 9 June 1945, p. 638; "San Francisco," editorial, *Crisis* 52 (June 1945): 161; Hollis Ralph Lynch, *Black American Radicals and the Liberation of Africa: The Council on African Affairs, 1937–1955* (Ithaca: Africana Studies and Research Center, Cornell University, 1978), 29–30; Franklin, *From Freedom to Slavery*, 601–3. One of the most careful students of the subject and a scholar not given to hasty judgements, William Roger Louis, noted the high-toned arguments of the American delegation and concluded, "If self-righteousness is a hallmark of American policy, then in the trusteeship question it found its finest hour." Louis, *Imperialism at Bay*, 115.

28. Minutes of meeting of U.S. delegation to U.N., 26 May 1945, *FRUS, 1945*, 1:894. See also Munene, "The Truman Administration and the Decolonization of Sub-Saharan Africa," 34.

29. Isaacs, *New World of Negro Americans*, 6–9, 16–17.

30. Russell, *History of the U.N. Charter*, 910–18; Hancock, *Smuts*, 2:433.

31. Virginia C. Gildersleeve, *Many a Good Crusade: Memoirs* (New York: Macmillan, 1954), 344–45.

32. Hancock, *Smuts*, 2:445; Barber, *South Africa's Foreign Policy*, 7–10; Jack Spence, "South Africa and the Modern World," in Wilson and Thompson, *Oxford History of South Africa* 2:478–79.

33. Davidson, *Report on Southern Africa*, 241. The quoted phrase is from Martin Flavin, an American journalist who visited the region in the late 1940s. Flavin, *Black and White*, 141.

34. Dumett, "Africa's Strategic Minerals," 389–91; Miller, "United States and Colonial Sub-Saharan Africa," 116–23.

35. "The Economic Resources of West and Southwest Africa," 10 January 1942, *OSS/SD, Africa*, 1; Dumett, "Africa's Strategic Minerals," 385–86, 392–93.

36. "Survey of Post-War Needs: Belgium," Box 1, Office Files of the Assistant Secretary of State for Economic Affairs, 1944–50, and the Under Secretary of State for Economic Affairs, 1946–47 ("Clayton-Thorp" Files), Truman Library.

37. Crawford Young, *Politics in the Congo: Decolonization and Independence* (Princeton: Princeton University Press, 1965), 20–23, 31–32; Jean Stengers, "Precipitous Decolonization: The Case of the Belgian Congo," in Gifford and Louis, *Transfer of Power in Africa*, 315–21.

38. Young, *Politics in the Congo*, 40, 66–67.

39. OSS, "Survey of the Belgian Congo," 28 September 1942, *OSS/SD, Africa*, 7; Dumett, "Africa's Strategic Minerals," 391–92; Davidson, *Africa in Modern History*, 201. One contribution to maintaining a stable work force that the Belgian colonial authorities hoped the United States would make was to export to the Congo "incentive goods to keep Congo natives willing to work by providing them with attractive articles their wages could buy," such as bicycles, mirrors, sewing machines, and gramophones. Max Horn, counselor of government of Belgian Congo, quoted in Nancy MacLennan, "Congo Role Hailed in Post-War Trade," *New York Times*, 6 May 1945, p. 16.

40. The weapon that destroyed Hiroshima was made from uranium-235. Plutonium actually fueled the bomb that incinerated Nagasaki three days later, but plutonium was created by being separated from uranium. David Alan Rosenberg, "U.S. Nuclear Stockpile, 1945 to 1950," *Bulletin of the Atomic Scientists* 38

(May 1982): 25; Richard G. Hewlett and Oscar E. Anderson, Jr., *A History of the United States Atomic Energy Commission*, vol. 1, *The New World, 1939/46* (University Park, Pa.: Pennsylvania State University Press, 1962), 209–12, 222–23.

41. Hewlett and Anderson, *New World*, 16–17, 26, 65; Jonathan E. Helmreich, *Gathering Rare Ores: The Diplomacy of Uranium Acquisition, 1943–1954* (Princeton: Princeton University Press, 1986), 3–7.

42. "The Economic Resources of West and Southwest Africa," 10 January 1942, *OSS/SD, Africa*, 1.

43. Leslie R. Groves, *Now It Can Be Told: The Story of the Manhattan Project* (New York: Harper & Brothers, 1962), 35–37, 179; Hewlett and Anderson, *New World*, 85–86; Helmreich, *Gathering Rare Ores*, 7–9.

44. Gregg Herken, *The Winning Weapon: The Atomic Bomb in the Cold War, 1945–1950* (New York: Alfred A. Knopf, 1980), 102.

45. Helmreich, *Gathering Rare Ores*, 15–41.

46. Robert H. Ferrell, "Truman's Place in History," *Reviews in American History* 18 (March 1990): 7. Clark Clifford, one of Truman's closest advisers, maintains, however, that Truman did not learn of the existence of the Manhattan Project until twenty minutes after being sworn in as President. Clifford with Richard Holbrooke, "Annals of Government (The Truman Years—Part I)," *New Yorker*, 25 March 1991, p. 45.

47. J. Samuel Walker, "The Decision to Use the Bomb: A Historiographical Update," *Diplomatic History* 14 (Winter 1990): 112.

48. OSS, "Survey of Mozambique (Portuguese East Africa)," 30 July 1942, *OSS/SD, Africa*, 9; Kenneth Maxwell, "Portugal and Africa: The Last Empire," in Gifford and Louis, *Transfer of Power in Africa*, 337–44.

49. Angus Ward (U.S. Consul General at Nairobi) to Department of State, 25 August 1951, *FRUS, 1951*, 5:1,228; Maxwell, "Portugal and Africa," 338.

50. Gerald Bender and Allen Isaacman, "The Changing Historiography of Angola and Mozambique," in *African Studies Since 1945: A Tribute to Basil Davidson*, ed. Christopher Fyfe (London: Longman, 1976), 228–33; Allen Isaacman and Jennifer Davis, "U.S. Policy Towards Mozambique, 1946–1976: 'The Defense of Colonialism and Regional Stability,' " in Lemarchand, *American Policy in Southern Africa*, 22; Davidson, *Report on Southern Africa*, 277. For further discussion of "luso-tropicalism," see Charles R. Boxer, *Race Relations in the Portuguese Colonial Empire, 1415–1825* (Oxford: Clarendon Press, 1963); and Gerald J. Bender, *Angola Under the Portuguese: The Myth and the Reality* (Berkeley: University of California Press, 1978).

51. Noer, *Cold War and Black Liberation*, 6; OSS, "Survey of Mozambique"; Bender and Isaacman, "Changing Historiography of Angola and Mozambique," 228; Miller, "United States and Colonial Sub-Saharan Africa," 234–36.

52. Noer, *Cold War and Black Liberation*, 6; Maxwell, "Portugal and Africa," 349. The OSS, watching for Axis subversion in southern Africa during the war, knew that such ideological leanings could have serious consequences; it was dismayed that the Mozambican colonial government paid little attention to the several hundred "well organized and very active" Nazi supporters in the colony. See OSS, "Survey of Mozambique."

53. George F. Kennan, "Problems of Diplomatic-Military Collaboration," lecture at the National War College, Washington, D.C., 7 March 1947, Box 16, Kennan Papers; Byrnes to Crocker (U.S. chargé d'affaires in Portugal), 30 Jan-

uary 1946, *FRUS, 1946,* 5:962; Maxwell, "Portugal and Africa," 349–50. See also John A. Marcum, *Portugal and Africa: The Politics of Indifference (A Case Study in American Foreign Policy)* (Syracuse: Program of Eastern African Studies, Syracuse University, 1972).

54. McCarthy, *Dark Continent,* 56–60, 92–95. Quotation is on p. 56.

55. Noer, *Briton, Boer, and Yankee,* 126–30.

56. Frederickson, *White Supremacy,* 98, 197–98; Noer, *Briton, Boer and Yankee,* 132–33. See also Cell, *Highest Stage of White Supremacy.*

57. For example, U.S. Minister in South Africa Lincoln MacVeagh, an old New York acquaintance of Roosevelt's who had worked for his first presidential campaign in 1932, wrote to the President in 1942 that the future of South Africa "will always be stormy and uncertain." Lincoln MacVeagh, *"Dear Franklin . . ."* *Letters to President Roosevelt from Lincoln MacVeagh, U.S. Minister to South Africa, 1942–1943* (Pasadena: California Institute of Technology, Munger Africana Library Notes, Issue #12, March 1972), 25.

58. MacVeagh warned Roosevelt that Smuts was one of the last representatives of an "amazing crop of unusual men" produced by the Boer War. These were "the best of the real Boers, trained to the saddle, the gun, and the frontier, with clear eyes still, and clear heads. Unfortunately their children do not reproduce the mold." With the passing of Smuts' generation, MacVeagh concluded, "the days of King Arthur and his Round Table, 'when every chance called forth a noble knight,' are no more in South Africa." Ibid., 42–43. Truman spoke admiringly of Smuts, claiming once with some exaggeration that "Jannie Smuts and I started the United Nations together." Quoted in E. S. M., "Preface," in ibid., 3.

59. Dumett, "Africa's Strategic Minerals," 384; Spence, "South Africa and the Modern World," 477–78; Vandenbosch, *South Africa and the World,* 109–10; Barber, *South Africa's Foreign Policy,* 7–10.

60. Board of Economic Warfare memorandum, "Urgent Necessity of Shipping American Materials to the Union of South Africa and Southern Rhodesia," 2 April 1942, enclosed in Thomas McCabe to Harry Hopkins, 2 April 1942, Box 713, Geographic File, 1942–1945, Record Group 218 (Records of the United States Joint Chiefs of Staff), National Archives. For the long-standing policy of the United States government to encourage close South African ties with England, see Noer, *Briton, Boer, and Yankee,* especially pp. 26–28, 36–40, 135.

61. The best sources for tracing this development in detail are Ward A. Spooner, "United States Policy Toward South Africa, 1919–1941: Political and Economic Aspects" (Ph.D. diss., St. John's University, New York, 1979); Minter, *King Solomon's Mines Revisited;* Hull, *American Enterprise in South Africa.*

62. Quoted in Hull, *American Enterprise in South Africa,* 180. See also ibid., 182–89; and Spooner, "United States Policy Toward South Africa," 3, 313–17, 347–48, 353–54.

63. Spooner, "United States Policy Toward South Africa," 1–3, 352; Hull, *American Enterprise in South Africa,* 201.

64. Patrick H. Martin, "American Views on South Africa, 1948–1972" (Ph.D. diss., Louisiana State University and Agricultural and Mechanical College, 1974), 257–58; W. Alphaeus Hunton, *Decision in Africa: Sources of Current Conflict,* rev. ed. (New York: International Publishers, 1960), 52–53.

65. Memorandum of conversation in Department of State, 29 June 1945,

848A.24/6-2945, *CSDCF, 1945–49*, 6; Commerce Department, *Investment in Union of South Africa*, 23. General Foods, for example, was delighted by "the sizable quantity of Post Toasties" it was allowed to import. M. E. Brown (Export Manager, General Foods Sales Company) to James A. Ross (Assistant Chief of Division of Commercial Policy, State Department), 19 April 1945, 848A.24/2-245, *CSDCF, 1945–49*, 6.

66. Policy Manual, "The Foreign Policy of the United States"; Commerce Department, *Investment in Union of South Africa*, 13.

67. Spooner, "United States Policy Toward South Africa," 3–4, 333–334, 341, 347–48; Commerce Department, *Investment in Union of South Africa*, 26; Hull, *American Enterprise in South Africa*, 201.

68. Office of European Affairs, Division of British Commonwealth Affairs, "South African Politics and American Commercial Policy," 1 January 1945, 848A.00/1-145, *CSDCF, 1945–49*, 1; Spooner, "United States Policy Toward South Africa," 2; Roderick Peattie, *Struggle on the Veld* (New York: Vanguard Press, 1947), 243–44.

69. Vandenbosch, *South Africa and the World*, 115.

70. Robert A. Pollard, *Economic Security and the Origins of the Cold War, 1945–1950* (New York: Columbia University Press, 1985), 197. See also Stephen D. Krasner, *Defending the National Interest: Raw Materials Investments and U.S. Foreign Policy* (Princeton: Princeton University Press, 1978).

71. Dumett, "Africa's Strategic Minerals," 400–401; Hull, *American Enterprise in South Africa*, 202.

72. Groves (Chairman of Combined Development Trust) to Patterson (Secretary of War and Chairman of Combined Policy Committee), 3 December 1945, *FRUS, 1945*, 2:84; Miller, "United States and Colonial Sub-Saharan Africa," 128–29; Helmreich, *Gathering Rare Ores*, 42–49, 69–70; Dumett, "Africa's Strategic Minerals," 388–89.

73. MacVeagh, *"Dear Franklin . . . ,"* 11, 18–19, 23–24, 31–32, 34, 41; John Seiler, "Introduction," in ibid., 6.

74. "Text of President's Navy Day Speech in Central Park on the Aims of U.S. Foreign Policy," *New York Times*, 28 October 1945, p. 33.

75. Recent white historians in the United States have not been immune to the apparent difficulty of imagining democratic rule in South Africa as a positive phenomenon. Arguing that earlier stages of South African politics had been dominated by Afrikaner-English conflict and by debates among whites about what to do with blacks, Amry Vandenbosch concluded in 1970 that "some pessimists foresee a third phase when South African politics will be a debate among the blacks about what to do with the whites." Vandenbosch, *South Africa and the World*, 20.

76. MacVeagh, *"Dear Franklin . . . ,"* 11, 18.

77. MacGregor, *Integration of the Armed Forces*, 99–103; quotation is on p. 100. A small number of blacks served as enlisted men in the Navy before 1942, but they were assigned almost exclusively as "steward's mates"—or, as the black press sometimes called them, "seagoing bellhops." Ibid., 5.

78. Policy manual, "Foreign Policy of the United States."

79. On the famine, see Holcomb to Secretary of State, 25 September 1945, 848A.5018/9-2545, *CSDCF, 1945–49*, 8; Byrnes to Holcomb, 12 February 1946, 848A.5018/2-1246, *CSDCF, 1945–49*, 8; "Resolution Addressed to General Jan

Christian Smuts, Prime Minister of South Africa," 7 January 1946, enclosed in Paul Robeson and Max Yergan to Henry S. Villard (Chief of African Affairs, State Department), 10 January 1946, 848A.48/1-1046, *CSDCF, 1945–49*, 8.

80. Believing that "the communistic menace in our own country is too grave to ignore," one wealthy Texan wrote to Senator Robert Taft in 1945 that she was "seriously considering emigrating with my small family to the Union of South Africa," a country sure to be safer even than the United States from the dangers of Soviet influence. Emily L. Mueller to Taft, 9 January 1945, enclosed in Taft to Chief Clerk of Department of State, 10 January 1945, 848A.51/1-1045, *CSDCF, 1945–49*, 10. Certain cultural similarities between Afrikaners and white Texans were noted by other observers at the time. See, for example, Flavin, *Black and White*, 5–6.

Chapter 4

1. H. Stuart Hughes, "The Second Year of the Cold War," in *The Origins of the Cold War*, 2nd ed., ed. Thomas G. Paterson (Lexington, Mass.: D. C. Heath and Company, 1974), 102. See also Melvyn P. Leffler, "Was 1947 a Turning Point in American Foreign Policy?" in *Centerstage: American Diplomacy Since World War II*, ed. L. Carl Brown (New York: Holmes & Meier, 1990), 19–42.

2. Munene, "Truman Administration and the Decolonization of Sub-Saharan Africa," 59; Robert C. Good, "The United States and the Colonial Debate," in *Alliance Policy in the Cold War*, ed. Arnold Wolfers (Baltimore: Johns Hopkins Press, 1959), 234–36; Bruce R. Kuniholm, "U.S. Policy in the Near East: The Triumphs and Tribulations of the Truman Administration," in Lacey, *Truman Presidency*, 337.

3. For discussions of McCarthyism before McCarthy, see Richard M. Freeland, *The Truman Doctrine and the Origins of McCarthyism: Foreign Policy, Domestic Politics, and Internal Security, 1946–1948* (New York: Alfred A. Knopf, 1972); and Athan Theoharis, *Seeds of Repression: Harry S Truman and the Origins of McCarthyism* (Chicago: Quadrangle, 1971). A useful survey and bibliography of the history of anticommunism in the United States is Peter H. Buckingham, *America Sees Red: Anticommunism in America, 1870s to 1980s: A Guide to Issues and References* (Claremont, Calif.: Regina Books, 1988).

4. James L. Roark, "American Black Leaders: The Response to Colonialism and the Cold War, 1943–1953," *African Historical Studies* 4 (1971): 253–70.

5. Vernon McKay, "Africa Plays New Role in Western Strategy," *Foreign Policy Bulletin*, 27 February 1948, pp. 2–3.

6. Karns, "United States, the United Nations and Decolonization," 13; Louis and Robinson, "United States and the Liquidation of the British Empire," 54.

7. Quoted in Davidson, *Africa in Modern History*, 203.

8. Karns, "United States, the United Nations and Decolonization," 16; Shah, *Great Abdication*, 20, 29.

9. D. A. Low, "The Asian Mirror to Tropical Africa's Independence," in Gifford and Louis, *Transfer of Power*, 3; I. F. Stone, "Pie in the 'Frisco Sky," *Nation*, 19 May 1945, p. 562; James Mayall, "Africa in Anglo-American Relations," in Louis and Bull, *'Special Relationship,'* 322; Robert J. McMahon, "Toward

a Post-Colonial Order: Truman Administration Policies toward South and Southeast Asia," in Lacey, *Truman Presidency*, 347.

10. Harry S Truman, text of speech before joint session of Congress, 12 March 1947, quoted in full in *Major Problems in American Foreign Policy: Documents and Essays*, vol. 2, *Since 1914*, ed. Thomas G. Paterson (Lexington, Mass.: D. C. Heath and Company, 1978), 289–92. For the text of Kennan's influential "long telegram" of 22 February 1946, see ibid., 276–80. See also Kennan, "Psychological Background of Soviet Foreign Policy," 31 January 1947, Folder "1947," Box 1, Kennan Papers.

11. R. F. Millon, "Fascism, Philippine Style," *Nation*, 21 September 1946, pp. 320–22; Low, "Asian Mirror," 9, 15; "Report on Argentina," *Nation*, 9 June 1945, pp. 649–50; J. Alvarez del Vayo, "Argentina, Nazi Paradise," *Nation*, 7 January 1950, pp. 6–7; "Braden Denounces Self-Proclaimed 'Savior' in Implied Attack on Tactics of Peron," *New York Times*, 28 October 1945, p. 10; Shah, *Great Abdication*, 75.

12. Paul Hutchinson, "America in the Postwar World," *Christian Century*, 12 March 1947, p. 327.

13. George Marshall, memorandum of conversation with M. S. Raymond-Laurent and T. C. Achilles, 15 July 1948, *FRUS, 1948*, 3:469.

14. Joint Strategic Survey Committee, "United States Assistance to Other Countries from the Standpoint of National Security," 29 April 1947 (appendix to SWNCC 360/1, Enclosure B, "Memorandum by the Joint Chiefs of Staff to the State-War-Navy Coordinating Committee," 12 May 1947), *FRUS, 1947*, 1:740–42.

15. Timothy P. Ireland, *Creating the Entangling Alliance: The Origins of the North Atlantic Treaty Organization* (Westport, Conn.: Greenwood Press, 1981), 222.

16. Jefferson Caffery (U.S. Ambassador in France) to Marshall, 12 May 1947, *FRUS, 1947*, 3:709–13; Department of State, Office of the Secretary, "Summary of Telegrams," 29 October 1947, Box 21, Naval Aide Files, Truman Papers; Bradford Perkins, "Unequal Partners: The Truman Administration and Great Britain," in Louis and Bull, '*Special Relationship*,' 53; Crowder, "Second World War," 28.

17. The most comprehensive study of the Marshall Plan is Michael J. Hogan, *The Marshall Plan: America, Britain, and the Reconstruction of Western Europe, 1947–1952* (Cambridge: Cambridge University Press, 1987). See also Melvyn P. Leffler, "The United States and the Strategic Dimensions of the Marshall Plan," *Diplomatic History* 12 (Summer 1988): 277–306.

18. Caffery to Marshall, 18 April 1947, *FRUS, 1947*, 3:699–701; Caffery to Marshall, 24 October 1947, *FRUS, 1947*, 3:786–90; George Shepperson and Thomas Price, *Independent Africa: John Chilembwe and the Origins, Setting, and Significance of the Nyasaland Native Rising of 1915* (Edinburgh: The University Press, 1958), 400–401; McMahon, "Toward a Post-Colonial Order," 353; Pollard, *Economic Security and the Origins of the Cold War*, 202; Good, "United States and the Colonial Debate," 233; Louis and Robinson, "United States and the Liquidation of the British Empire," 46.

Rumors during the unsuccessful revolt in Madagascar that black American troops were coming to bring arms to the insurgents proved wildly optimistic, although they suggested the extent to which Third World nationalists at the outset of the Cold War still hoped the United States would be supportive of the principle of self-government in the colonial world. George Shepperson, "Notes on Negro American Influences on the Emergence of African Nationalism," *Journal of African History* 1 (1960): 312; John D. Hargreaves, *Decolonization in Africa* (London: Longman, 1988), 92–93. See also Douglas Little, "Cold War and Colonialism in Africa: The United States, France, and the Madagascar Revolt of 1947," *Pacific Historical Review* 59 (November 1990): 527–52.

19. McMahon, "Toward a Post-Colonial Order," 350. For further detail, see Robert J. McMahon, *Colonialism and Cold War: The United States and the Struggle for Indonesian Independence, 1945–1949* (Ithaca: Cornell University Press, 1981).

20. Louis and Robinson, "United States and the Liquidation of the British Empire," 48–49; Good, "United States and the Colonial Debate," 237–38; Nielsen, *Great Powers and Africa*, 253–54.

21. W. E. B. Du Bois called 15 August 1947—the date of Indian independence—"the greatest historical date of the nineteenth and twentieth centuries" because it marked the freeing of four hundred million people of color from white domination. Du Bois, "The Freeing of India," *Crisis* 54 (October 1947): 301.

22. Louis, "American Anti-Colonialism and the Dissolution of the British Empire," 267–68; Tony Smith, "Patterns in the Transfer of Power," in Gifford and Louis, *Transfer of Power in Africa*, 87–89; Perkins, "Unequal Partners," 46–47, 51. William Roger Louis and Ronald Robinson concluded that "like most empires, the British Empire improved its morality as its power declined." Louis and Robinson, "United States and the Liquidation of the British Empire," 38.

23. Vernon McKay, "New African Opportunities Attract Western Capital," *Foreign Policy Bulletin*, 5 March 1948, p. 2; Lloyd C. Gardner, "Economic Foreign Policy and the Quest for Security," in *The National Security: Its Theory and Practice, 1945–1960*, ed. Norman A. Graebner (New York: Oxford University Press, 1986), 91; Baum, "United States, Self-Government, and Africa," 111, 130; Duignan and Gann, *United States and Africa*, 285.

24. George Padmore, "British Labour and the Colonies," *Crisis* 52 (October 1945): 291–94; Louis and Robinson, "United States and the Liquidation of the British Empire," 37–38; Lynch, "Pan-African Responses in the United States," 85; George W. Shepherd, "Comment" on Immanuel Wallerstein's "Africa, the United States, and the World Economy: The Historical Bases of American Policy," in *U.S. Policy Towards Africa*, ed. Frederick S. Arkhurst (New York: Praeger, 1975), 42–44.

25. U.S. delegation working paper, 15 September 1947, *FRUS, 1947*, 1:290; Baum, "United States, Self-Government, and Africa," xi, 156, 167–71.

26. Dean Acheson, *Present at the Creation: My Years in the State Department* (New York: W. W. Norton, 1969), 671.

27. Memorandum of conversation between Raja Sir Maharaj Singh (Indian Delegation), H. E. Mr. Liu Chieh (Chinese Delegation), Mr. Awni Khalidy (Iraqi Delegation), and Ambassador Francis B. Sayre (U.S. Representative on the Trusteeship Council), 29 October 1947, *FRUS, 1947*, 1:309; Lynch, "Pan-African Responses in the United States," 67.

28. Memorandum of conversation with General Carlos P. Romulo of the Philippines, by Harley A. Notter of the U.S. Delegation Staff of Advisers to the U.N., 14 November 1947, *FRUS, 1947*, 1:317–21; S. Chandrasekhar, "Imperialism Returns to Asia," *Crisis* 53 (March 1946): 79–81, 91–92.

29. Paul Robeson, "Some Reflections on *Othello* and the Nature of Our Time," *The American Scholar* 14 (Autumn 1945): 392.

30. Andrew Rotter, *The Path to Vietnam: Origins of the American Commitment to Southeast Asia* (Ithaca: Cornell University Press, 1987), 4, 8.

31. "The Diplomat Who Did Not Want to Be Liked" (obituary for Dean Acheson), *Time*, 25 October 1971, p. 20; Good, "United States and the Colonial Debate," 236. For a discussion of long-standing American ambivalence about and distrust of foreign revolutions, see Hunt, *Ideology and U.S. Foreign Policy*, 92–124.

32. Hamby, "Mind and Character of Harry S Truman," 49. Quotation is from Shah, *Great Abdication*, 56.

33. Pollard, *Economic Security and the Origins of the Cold War*, 202.

34. Joint Strategic Plans Committee, J.S.P.C. 814/3, "Estimate of Probable Developments in the World Political Situation Up to 1957," 11 December 1947, *The Declassified Documents Reference System* (Washington: Carrolton Press, 1975), #75B. See also Mayall, "Africa in Anglo-American Relations," 331.

35. Freeland, *Truman Doctrine and the Origins of McCarthyism*, 115–50; Walter LaFeber, *America, Russia, and the Cold War, 1945–1984*, 5th ed. (New York: Alfred A. Knopf, 1985), 53; Robert J. Donovan, *Conflict and Crisis: The Presidency of Harry S Truman, 1945–1948* (New York: W. W. Norton, 1977), 292–97. Donovan observed that by 1951 Washington was "honeycombed with loyalty-security boards and loyalty review boards." Donovan, *Tumultuous Years: The Presidency of Harry S Truman, 1949–1953* (New York: W. W. Norton, 1982), 366.

36. For an illuminating discussion of the relationship between white racism and anticommunism in the American South, see Wayne Addison Clark, "An Analysis of the Relationship Between Anti-Communism and Segregationist Thought in the Deep South, 1948–1964" (Ph.D. diss., University of North Carolina, 1976). An important novel suggestive of similar themes in the North is Richard Wright's *Native Son*.

37. Aldon D. Morris, *The Origins of the Civil Rights Movement: Black Communities Organizing for Change* (New York: Free Press, 1984), 1–4; Chafe, "Postwar American Society," 166.

38. *To Secure These Rights: The Report of the President's Committee on Civil Rights* (New York: Simon & Schuster, 1947), 24; Thomas R. Brooks, *Walls Come Tumbling Down: A History of the Civil Rights Movement, 1940–1970* (Englewood Cliffs, N.J.: Prentice Hall, 1974), 54–55; White, *Man Called White*, 325–26; "Massacre," editorial, *Crisis* 54 (August 1947): 233; Shapiro, *White Violence and Black Response*, 365–70. See also Zangrando, *NAACP Crusade Against Lynching*.

39. Harold Preece, "Klan 'Murder, Inc.,' in Dixie," *Crisis* 53 (October 1946): 299–301; Shapiro, *White Violence and Black Response*, 353–57, 369–70.

40. Quoted in Branch, *Parting the Waters*, 129.

41. "Terror in Tennessee," editorial, *Crisis* 53 (April 1946): 105; White, *Man Called White*, 310; Brooks, *Walls Come Tumbling Down*, 55–56; Shapiro, *White Violence and Black Response*, 362–65.

42. "Brotherhood Week, 1946," editorial, *New York Times*, 17 February 1946, sec. 4, p. 8.

43. Cover, *Time*, 22 September 1947; Jules Tygiel, *Baseball's Great Experi-*

ment: Jackie Robinson and His Legacy (New York: Oxford University Press, 1983), 3–9, 35.

44. Robert A. Garson, *The Democratic Party and the Politics of Sectionalism, 1941–1948* (Baton Rouge: Louisiana State University Press, 1974), 186; Steven Lawson, *Black Ballots: Voting Rights in the South* (New York: Columbia University Press, 1976), 139; Brooks, *Walls Come Tumbling Down*, 54, 61–65; Franklin, *From Slavery to Freedom*, 612.

45. William Attwood, "Outwitted in the War of Ideas," 5 September 1947, Appendix B in Henry Cabot Lodge, "Memorandum on Information Program," enclosed in Arthur Vandenberg to George Marshall, 20 October 1947, Folder 2, Box 3, Papers of Arthur H. Vandenberg, Jr., Bentley Historical Library, University of Michigan, Ann Arbor, Michigan; "Democracy Defined at Moscow," editorial, *Crisis* 54 (April 1947): 105; St. Clair Drake, "The International Implications of Race and Race Relations," *Journal of Negro Education* 20 (Summer 1951): 264; Harold R. Isaacs, "Race and Color in World Affairs," in *Racial Influences on American Foreign Policy*, ed. George W. Shepherd, Jr. (New York: Basic Books, 1970), 33–36; David W. Southern, *Gunnar Myrdal and Black-White Relations: The Use and Abuse of "An American Dilemma," 1944–1969* (Baton Rouge: Louisiana State University Press, 1987), 102.

46. Quoted in *To Secure These Rights*, 146–47; and in "Foreign Policy and FEPC," editorial, *Crisis* 54 (May 1947): 137.

47. Quoted in Southern, *Gunnar Myrdal and Black-White Relations*, 123.

48. Cover, *Time*, 6 January 1947; Southern Conference for Human Welfare, Committee for Charleston, handbill, enclosed in Lawrence M. Pinckney to Byrnes, 5 March 1946, Folder 532, Byrnes Papers. The fame of Byrnes' racial views prompted newscaster Edward R. Murrow to send him a tongue-in-cheek invitation to a fund-raising dinner in New York:

> Dear Mr. Byrnes: I am writing to you because I feel you will be as interested as I in Sydenham Hospital, the first interracial hospital giving Negroes scientific opportunities equal to those of white citizens. During the three years that it has been in existence, Sydenham has demonstrated that an interracial hospital is a workable undertaking. . . . I am certain of the value of your support as a sponsor.

Murrow to Byrnes, 29 October 1947, Folder 668(2), Byrnes Papers. Byrnes apparently did not respond.

49. Lauren, *Power and Prejudice*, 192.

50. *A Petition to the United Nations on Behalf of 13 Million Oppressed Negro Citizens of the United States of America* (New York: National Negro Congress, 1946); *An Appeal to the World: A Statement on the Denial of Human Rights to Minorities in the Case of Citizens of Negro Descent in the United States and an Appeal to the United Nations for Redress* (New York: National Association for the Advancement of Colored People, 1947); Franklin, *From Slavery to Freedom*, 604–5; Lauren, *Power and Prejudice*, 172–74; Bernstein, "Ambiguous Legacy," 279, 307.

51. Martin, "American Views on South Africa," 63; Drake, "International Implications of Race," 265–66; Lauren, *Power and Prejudice*, 187–90, 193.

52. Garson, *Democratic Party and the Politics of Sectionalism*, 186–87. One wealthy French physician of generally sympathetic views toward the United States told an American inquirer in 1947: "Of course, we realize that medical science is

way ahead in America of what it is in France, but then we also know that you have all those colored people over there on whom your doctors constantly experiment." Lodge, "Memorandum on Information Program," enclosed in Vandenberg to Marshall, 20 October 1947, Folder 2, Box 3, Vandenberg Papers.

53. *To Secure These Rights,* 23; Franklin, *From Slavery to Freedom,* 605–6; Shapiro, *White Violence and Black Response,* 357–58; "Democracy Defined at Moscow," editorial, *Crisis* 54 (April 1947): 105.

54. Text of "Truman's Address," *Crisis* 54 (July 1947): 200; "Truman to the NAACP," editorial, *Crisis* 54 (August 1947): 233; Donovan, *Conflict and Crisis,* 333–34.

55. Lauren, *Power and Prejudice,* 191–92.

56. Garson, *Democratic Party and the Politics of Sectionalism,* 186; Chafe, "Postwar American Society," 166–67; Brooks, *Walls Come Tumbling Down,* 59–61; Donovan, *Conflict and Crisis,* 333. See also McCoy and Ruetten, *Quest and Response,* 31–54.

57. *To Secure These Rights,* passim; Donovan, *Conflict and Crisis,* 334–35.

58. Donovan, *Conflict and Crisis,* 336–37; Garson, *Democratic Party and the Politics of Sectionalism,* 230–31. Quotation appears in Chafe, "Postwar American Society," 167. Clifford argued at the time that, unless Truman came out strongly for civil rights, "the Negro bloc, which, certainly in Illinois and probably in New York and Ohio, *does* hold the balance of power, will go Republican." Clifford has written recently that "we did not realize how quickly Southern whites would abandon the President if he supported equal civil rights for all Americans." Clark Clifford with Richard Holbrooke, "Annals of Government (The Truman Years—Part II)," *New Yorker,* 1 April 1991, p. 60.

59. Harold R. Isaacs, "The American Negro and Africa: Some Notes," *The Phylon Quarterly* 20 (Fall 1959): 219–33; Lynch, "Pan-African Responses," 57–60, 64–66, 69, 85–86; Hollis Ralph Lynch, *Black American Radicals and the Liberation of Africa: The Council on African Affairs, 1937–1955* (Ithaca: Africana Studies and Research Center, Cornell University, 1978), 24, 26, 31–33, 54.

60. Lynch, "Pan-African Responses," 67–68; Lynch, *Black American Radicals,* 35–37; Roark, "American Black Leaders," 253–70; R. E. Murphy (Department of State, Office of European Affairs) to Donald Russell, "Attacks on Secretary in the Negro Press," 26 August 1946, enclosed in Russell to Cassie Connor, 30 August 1946, Folder 552, Byrnes Papers; "Keep an Eye on the Communnists [*sic*]," editorial, *Crisis* 55 (April 1948): 105.

61. Holcomb to Secretary of State, 10 September 1946, 848A.5045/9–1046, *CSDCF, 1945–49,* 10.

62. Joint Passive Resistance Council of Natal and Transvaal, "How We Live . . . ," enclosed in U.S. Minister in Pretoria to Department of State, 8 November 1946, 848A.4016/11-846, *CSDCF, 1945–49,* 6; Flavin, *Black and White,* 3; Lodge, *Black Politics in South Africa,* 11–12. Alan Paton powerfully evokes these circumstances in his novel *Cry, the Beloved Country* (New York: Charles Scribner's Sons, 1948).

63. "The African Mine Workers' Strike—A National Struggle," flyer issued by the ANC Youth League, August 1946, in Karis and Carter, *From Protest to Challenge,* 2:318–19; Flavin, *Black and White,* 4, 28–30; Lodge, *Black Politics,* 18–19. Within the comfortable confines of the State Department offices in Washington, however, doubts remained about whether the pay and working conditions of African laborers in the Union constituted actual exploitation. See,

for example, Mulliken to Wailes and Timberlake, 24 October 1946, 848A.504/10-2446, *CSDCF, 1945–49*, 9.

64. Charles E. Dickerson, Jr. (chargé d'affaires in Pretoria) to Secretary of State, 1 July 1947, enclosing Michael Scott, "In Modern Bethal," 848A.504/7-147, *CSDCF, 1945–49*, 9; Dickerson to Secretary of State, 15 July 1947, 848A.504/7-1547, *CSDCF, 1945–49*, 9; Dickerson to Secretary of State, 26 July 1947, 848A.00/7-2647, *CSDCF, 1945–49*, 3; Anthony Sampson, *Drum: A Venture into the New Africa* (London: Collins, 1956), 38–43.

65. Flavin, *Black and White*, 22. The first chapter of Flavin's book appeared originally as an article in the April 1949 issue of *Harper's*.

66. Holcomb to Secretary of State, 9 April 1946, 848A.4016/4-946, *CSDCF, 1945–49*, 6; "Memorandum on the Indian Situation in Natal," 12 September 1945, enclosed in Holcomb to Secretary of State, 14 September 1945, 848A.00/9-1445, *CSDCF, 1945–49*, 1. See also Alan Paton, *Hofmeyr* (London: Oxford University Press, 1964). On the fate of liberalism in the Union after Hofmeyr, see Janet Robertson, *Liberalism in South Africa, 1948–1963* (Oxford: Clarendon Press, 1971).

67. Thompson, "Parting of the Ways," 425–26.

68. E. Talbot Smith, "Memorandum on the Indian Situation in Natal," 26 January 1946, enclosed in Holcomb to Department of State, 1 February 1946, 848A.00/2-146, *CSDCF, 1945–49*, 1; Smith, "Memorandum on Indian Situation," 21 August 1946, enclosed in U.S. Legation in Pretoria to Department of State, 21 August 1946, 848A.00/8-2146, *CSDCF, 1945–49*, 2; Hancock, *Smuts*, 2:461-67; Davenport, *South Africa*, 351–52.

69. Howard Donovan (U.S. Consul General in Bombay) to Secretary of State, 21 June 1946, 848A.4016/6-2146, *CSDCF, 1945–49*, 6; Smith, "Memorandum on the Indian Situation," 7 June 1946, enclosed in Holcomb to Department of State, 18 June 1946, 848A.00/6-1846, *CSDCF, 1945–49*, 2.

70. J. William Henry (U.S. Vice-Consul in Mombasa) to Secretary of State, 25 September 1946, 848A.4016/10-2546, *CSDCF, 1945–49*, 6.

71. "India Struggle in S. Africa," *Kenya Daily Mail*, 28 September 1946, enclosed in Joseph I. Touchette (U.S. Consul in Nairobi) to Secretary of State, 30 September 1946, 848A.4016/9-3046, *CSDCF, 1945–49*, 6.

72. Quoted in *The Passive Resister* (official bulletin of the Passive Resistance Council of the Transvaal Indian Congress), June 1946, enclosed in Holcomb to Secretary of State, 1 July 1946, 848A.00/7-146, *CSDCF, 1945–49*, 2.

73. Holcomb to Secretary of State, 1 July 1946, 848A.00/7-146, *CSDCF, 1945–49*, 2; Smith, "Memorandum on the Indian Situation," 26 July 1946, enclosed in U.S. Embassy in Pretoria to Department of State, 6 August 1946, 848A.4016/8-646, *CSDCF, 1945–49*, 6.

74. Holcomb to Secretary of State, 21 May 1946, 848A.504/5-2146, *CSDCF, 1945–49*, 8; Correll memorandum, 22 March 1946, enclosed in Holcomb to Secretary of State, 15 April 1946, 848A.5045/4-1546, *CSDCF, 1945–49*, 10; Holcomb to Secretary of State, 13 January 1947, 848A.504/1-1347, *CSDCF, 1945–49*, 9; Dan O'Meara, "The 1946 African Mine Workers' Strike and the Political Economy of South Africa," *Journal of Commonwealth and Comparative Politics* 13 (July 1975): 147–58.

75. Holcomb to Secretary of State, 13 August 1946, 848A.5045/8-1346, *CSDCF, 1945–49*, 10; Holcomb to Secretary of State, 15 August 1946, 848A.5045/8-1546, *CSDCF, 1945–49*, 10; Holcomb to Secretary of State, 21

August 1946, 848A.5045/8–2146, *CSDCF, 1945–49,* 10; O'Meara, "1946 African Mine Workers' Strike," 159–61.

76. Holcomb to Secretary of State, 14 August 1946, 848A.5045/8-1446, *CSDCF, 1945–49,* 10; Holcomb to Secretary of State, 21 August 1946, 848A.5045/8-2146, *CSDCF, 1945–49,* 10; Davidson, *Report on Southern Africa,* 106–7.

77. Smith, "Memorandum on the Natal Indian Situation," 26 March 1945, quoting 13 March 1945 editorial in *Die Transvaler,* enclosed in U.S. Legation in Capetown to Department of State, 3 April 1945, 848A.00/4-345, *CSDCF, 1945–49,* 1; Holcomb to Secretary of State, 3 September 1946, 848A.00/9-346, *CSDCF, 1945–49,* 2; Holcomb to Secretary of State, 21 October 1946, 848A.404/10-2146, *CSDCF, 1945–49,* 8.

78. Holcomb to Secretary of State, 26 July 1946, 848A.00/7-2646, *CSDCF, 1945–49,* 2.

79. Holcomb to Secretary of State, 3 September 1946, 848A.00/9-346, *CSDCF, 1945–49,* 2.

80. Holcomb to Secretary of State, 24 October 1946, 848A.918/10-2446, *CSDCF, 1945–49,* 13; Acheson (Acting Secretary of State) to U.S. Legation in Pretoria, 25 October 1946, 848A.918/10-2446, *CSDCF, 1945–49,* 13; "Smuts on the Defensive," editorial, *Crisis* 53 (December 1946): 361. Quotation is from Holcomb to Secretary of State, 8 July 1946, 848A.00/7-846, *CSDCF, 1945–49,* 2.

81. Correll to Mulliken, 30 August 1946, 848A.504/8-3046, *CSDCF, 1945–49,* 9.

82. "Gold!" *Fortune* 34 (October 1946): 105–12, 233–36, 240–45.

83. Smith, "Memorandum on the Indian Situation," 15 April 1946, enclosed in Holcomb to Department of State, 23 April 1946, 848A.00/4-2346, *CSDCF, 1945–49,* 1.

84. Correll, "Memorandum: Biennial Transvaal Indian Congress Election," 2 October 1947, enclosed in Dickerson to Secretary of State, 2 October 1947, 848A.00/10-247, *CSDCF, 1945–49,* 3; "Joint Declaration of Cooperation," 9 March 1947, in Karis and Carter, *From Protest to Challenge* 2:272–73; Lodge, *Black Politics in South Africa,* 20–24; Gerhart, *Black Power in South Africa,* 101–5; O'Meara, "1946 Mine Workers' Strike," 161–70; Kuper, "African Nationalism," 456.

85. Holcomb to Secretary of State, 31 March 1947, 848A.00/3-3147, *CSDCF, 1945–49,* 2; Holcomb to Secretary of State, 22 April 1947, 848A.00/4-2247, *CSDCF, 1945–49,* 2; Holcomb to Secretary of State, 22 May 1947, 848A.00/5-2247, *CSDCF, 1945–49,* 2; Holcomb to Secretary of State, 28 May 1947, 748A.00/5-2847, *CSDCF, 1945–49,* 14; Holcomb to Secretary of State, 11 June 1947, 848A.032/6-1147, *CSDCF, 1945–49,* 5; Holcomb to Secretary of State, 1 December 1947, 848A.00/12-147, *CSDCF, 1945–49,* 3; "South African Political and Economic Developments," 1 January 1948, enclosed in Holcomb to Secretary of State, 31 December 1947, 848A.00/12-3147, *CSDCF, 1945–49,* 3.

86. "Is UNO Intruding?" editorial, *Economist,* 14 December 1946, enclosed in Robert Coe to Secretary of State, 17 December 1946, 848A.4016/12-1746, *CSDCF, 1945–49,* 6.

87. See, for example, Charles E. Dickerson, Jr., to Secretary of State, 2 October 1947, 848A.00/10-247, *CSDCF, 1945–49,* 3.

88. Acheson, "Memorandum for the President," 27 November 1946, Box 170, President's Secretary's File, Truman Papers.

89. Quoted in Hancock, *Smuts* 2:450–51.

90. Quoted in ibid., 2:447.

91. Barber, *South Africa's Foreign Policy*, 10–13, 22–23, 59–60; Spence, "South Africa and the Modern World," 508–9, 525–26; Hancock, *Smuts* 2:448–49.

92. Kuper, "African Nationalism," 454–56; Barber, *South Africa's Foreign Policy*, 33.

93. Paul Robeson (Chairman, Council on African Affairs) and Max Yergan (Executive Director, CAA) to Henri Laugier (Assistant Secretary General for Social Affairs, United Nations), 10 May 1946, 848A.00/5-1046, *CSDCF, 1945–49*, 2; Robeson and Yergan to Herschel V. Johnson (U.S. Delegation to the U.N.), 28 June 1946, enclosed in Johnson to Secretary of State, 2 July 1946, 848A.00/7-246, *CSDCF, 1945–49*, 2.

94. "3 African Leaders Assail Gen. Smuts," *New York Times*, 9 November 1946, 7; Barber, *South Africa's Foreign Policy*, 20–21; Spence, "South Africa and the Modern World," 509–10.

95. "India and the U.N.," editorial, *New York Times*, 25 June 1946, p. 20; Barber, *South Africa's Foreign Policy*, 24–26.

96. Edward T. Wailes (Chief of Division of British Commonwealth Affairs, Department of State) to Smith (U.S. Consul in Durban), 7 May 1946, *FRUS, 1946*, 5:126–27; "Is UNO Intruding?" editorial, *Economist*, 14 December 1946, enclosed in Robert Coe to Secretary of State, 17 December 1946, 848A.4016/12-1746, *CSDCF, 1945–49*, 6; Barber, *South Africa's Foreign Policy*, 30–33. The problem of white citizens' acting to keep people of color from moving into their neighborhoods, as in Natal, was not unfamiliar to the United States government in 1946 and 1947. Crowds of several thousand white people rioted in the Chicago area, for example, in efforts to prevent blacks from taking up residence in what had been exclusively white neighborhoods. See Shapiro, *White Violence and Black Response*, 375–77. An important difference between the two situations, which reflected the different directions of American and South African societies in the late 1940s, however, was that white Americans could not get new segregationist federal legislation passed to bolster their cause. For more on this comparison, see Frederickson, *White Supremacy*.

97. "Memorandum on South West Africa" and "Economic Conditions in South West Africa," both enclosed in Holcomb to Secretary of State, 11 January 1945, 848A.00/1-1145, *CSDCF, 1945–49*, 1; Holcomb to Secretary of State, 9 August 1945, 848A.50/8-945 CS/EG, *CSDCF, 1945–49*, 8; HF to Hickerson, 4 September 1945, attached to 848A.50/8-945 CS/EG, *CSDCF, 1945–49*, 8; Allan D. Cooper, *U.S. Economic Power and Political Influence in Namibia, 1700–1982* (Boulder: Westview Press, 1982), 20–24, 31–32.

98. "African Plebiscite Urged," *New York Times*, 12 November 1946, p. 2; Lynch, "Pan-African Responses in the United States," 67; J. Harold Shullaw (Secretary of U.S. Legation in Pretoria) to Secretary of State, 25 June 1946, 848A.00/6-2546, *CSDCF, 1945–49*, 2; Thomas J. Hamilton, "Soviet Would Bar Africa Annex Plan," *New York Times*, 9 November 1945, p. 1.

99. Minutes of U.S. delegation to U.N., 21 November 1946, *FRUS, 1946*, 1:683; Cooper, *U.S. Economic Power*, 31.

100. Acheson to Holcomb, 18 June 1946, 848A.00/6-1846, *CSDCF, 1945–*

49, 2; Holcomb to Secretary of State, 2 July 1946, 848A.00/7-246, *CSDCF, 1945–49,* 2; Holcomb to Byrnes, 26 July 1946, *FRUS, 1946,* 5:121; Clayton (Acting Secretary of State) to Holcomb, 24 September 1946, *FRUS, 1946,* 5:122–23; minutes of meeting of U.S. delegation to U.N., 21 October 1946, *FRUS, 1946,* 1:657. A generation later Acheson was still inclined to take South Africa's view of the disposition of the territory that had by then become more widely known as Namibia. See Acheson, "On South Africa," *New York Times,* 21 April 1971, p. 47; and Arthur Rovine, letter to the editor, *New York Times,* 5 May 1971, clipping in Box 4, Papers of Joseph Sweeney, Truman Library.

101. Groth to Secretary of State, 21 March 1945, 848A.00/3-2145, *CSDCF, 1945–49,* 1; Barber, *South Africa's Foreign Policy,* 26–29. U.S. Minister Holcomb found Smuts' attitude toward South West Africa revealing:

> The noticeable high-handedness of the Union Government in its capacity as Mandatory Power does not appear to be tempered in the least by the "internationalism" of General Smuts. The interesting conclusion is therefore reached that in matters close to home General Smuts is not nearly so inclined to take the "world view" as he does at great international conferences such as San Francisco. In the South Africa of General Smuts, the "trusteeship" principle is honored more by lip service than by actual practice. . . .

Holcomb to Secretary of State, 22 October 1945, 848A.00/10-2245, *CSDCF, 1945–49,* 1.

102. "South Africa Rebuked," editorial, *Crisis* 54 (January 1947): 9.

103. Holcomb to Secretary of State, 20 January 1947, 848A.00/1-2047, *CSDCF, 1945–49,* 1.

104. Holcomb to Secretary of State, 20 March 1947, 848A.00/3-2047, *CSDCF, 1945–49,* 2; Holcomb to Secretary of State, 12 April 1947, 848A.00/4-1247, *CSDCF, 1945–49,* 2; Holcomb to Secretary of State, 27 May 1947, 848A.014/5-2747, *CSDCF, 1945–49,* 5; Davenport, *South Africa,* 474–75.

105. Duggan, "Memorandum on Indian Situation," 23 December 1946, enclosed in U.S. Minister in Pretoria to Department of State, 3 January 1947, 848A.4016/1-347, *CSDCF, 1945–49,* 6.

106. U.S. Embassy in Moscow to Secretary of State, 19 May 1947, 848A.4016/5-1947, *CSDCF, 1945–49,* 6; Durbrow to Secretary of State, 31 May 1947, 848A.00/5-3147, *CSDCF, 1945–49,* 2.

107. Petition from various chiefs in South West Africa, conveyed to the U.N. by the Rev. Michael Scott, 26 September 1947, Document A/C.4/96, Box 34, Papers of John Foster Dulles, Seeley Mudd Library, Princeton University, Princeton, New Jersey; Council on African Affairs, "South West Africans Speak for Themselves," 30 October 1947, 848A.00/10-3047, *CSDCF, 1945–49,* 3; Michael Scott, *A Time to Speak* (Garden City, N.Y.: Doubleday, 1958), 220–21.

108. U.S. delegation working paper, 15 September 1947, *FRUS, 1947,* 1:291; memorandum by Sandifer (Principal Executive Officer of the U.S. Delegation to the U.N.) to all political officers, 8 October 1947, *FRUS, 1947,* 1:293–94; Vandenbosch, *South Africa and the World,* 194–95.

109. See, for example, R. Austin Acly (chargé d'affaires in Rangoon, Burma) to Secretary of State, 26 November 1947, 848A.4016/11-2647, *CSDCF, 1945–49,* 7.

110. Vinson to Secretary of State, 6 November 1945, 848A.24/11-645, *CSDCF, 1945–49,* 6; Gold to Angell, 22 March 1945, and memorandum of the

Foreign Economic Administration's Executive Policy Committee, both enclosed in Crowley to Secretary of State, 28 May 1945, 848A.24/5-2845, *CSDCF, 1945–49,* 6; memorandum of conversation, 2 July 1946, enclosed in Holcomb to Secretary of State, 3 July 1946, 848A.24/7-346, *CSDCF, 1945–49,* 6.

111. Holcomb to Secretary of State, 23 January 1946, 848A.24/1-2346, *CSDCF, 1945–49,* 6; Holcomb to Secretary of State, 22 April 1947, enclosing "That Dollar Sign," editorial, *Cape Times,* 19 April 1947, 848A.24/4-2247, *CSDCF, 1945–49,* 6.

112. Holcomb to Secretary of State, 23 February 1946, 848A.24/2-2346, *CSDCF, 1945–49,* 14; Holcomb to Secretary of State, 31 January 1946, 848A.032/ 1-3146, *CSDCF, 1945–49,* 5.

113. Harry Andrews (South African Minister in the U.S.) to Secretary of State, 22 April 1946, 848A.24/4-2246, *CSDCF, 1945–49,* 6; Byrnes to Andrews, 27 May 1946, 848A.24/5-2746, *CSDCF, 1945–49,* 6; Chester Lane (Lend-Lease Administrator) to William Clayton (Under Secretary of State for Economic Affairs), 29 August 1946, 848A.24/8-2646, *CSDCF, 1945–49,* 6.

114. Holcomb to Department of State, 2 October 1946, 848A.24/10-246, *CSDCF, 1945–49,* 6.

115. Maher (First Secretary in U.S. Legation in Pretoria) to Secretary of State, 23 September 1946, 848A.24/9-2346, *CSDCF, 1945–49,* 6.

116. Chester Lane, "Memorandum for Mr. Byrnes," 1 November 1946, Box 3, Office Files of the Under Secretary of State for Economic Affairs, Truman Library; Chester Lane, memorandum, 19 November 1946, 848A.24/11-1946, *CSDCF, 1945–49,* 6.

117. Holcomb to Secretary of State, 28 May 1947, 748A.00/5–2847, *CSDCF, 1945–49,* 14; "Royal Family Visits South Africa," *Life,* 10 March 1947, pp. 27–33; Barber, *South Africa's Foreign Policy,* 13–20.

118. "Gold!" *Fortune* 24 (October 1946): 111–12; Gallman (chargé d'affaires in London) to Marshall, 28 January 1948, *FRUS, 1948,* 3:1067; Ritchie Ovendale, *The English-Speaking Alliance: Britain, the United States, the Dominions and the Cold War, 1945–1951* (London: George Allen & Unwin, 1985), 257–58; Mayall, "Africa in Anglo-American Relations," 338–39; Barber, *South Africa's Foreign Policy,* 34–40.

119. Dr. Alphaeus Hunton, "A Postscript for Americans," in *Resistance Against Fascist Enslavement in South Africa,* text of November 1952 memorandum to the U.N. from the ANC and the South African Indian Congress (New York: Council on African Affairs, 1953), 52–53; "New U.S. Stake in South Africa," *Business Week,* 29 November 1947, pp. 81–82; "Nababeep and East O'okiep," *Fortune* 36 (July 1947): 77–80, 159; James F. Byrnes, *All in One Lifetime* (New York: Harper & Brothers, 1958), 171, 187; H. E. Dodge (Secretary of Board of Directors of Newmont Mining Corporation) to the Directors, 12 January 1948, Folder 670, Byrnes Papers. Another small but thriving economic link between the two countries in 1947 was the illegal exportation to the United States of marijuana ("dagga" in the street dialect of Capetown) and opium bought by American sailors in the Union for profitable resale at home. See Carol H. Foster (U.S. Consul General in Capetown) to Secretary of State, 16 January 1947, 848A.114 NARCOTICS/1-1647, *CSDCF, 1945–49,* 5; Foster to Secretary of State, 14 May 1947, 848A.114 NARCOTICS/5-1447, *CSDCF, 1945–49,* 5; Foster to Secretary of State, 10 June 1947, 848A.114 NARCOTICS/6-1047, *CSDCF, 1945–49,* 5.

120. Robert Lovett (Acting Secretary of State), in meeting of U.S. members of Combined Policy Committee with Sen. Hickenlooper (Chairman of Joint Committee on Atomic Energy) and Sen. Vandenberg (Chairman of Senate Foreign Relations Committee), 26 November 1947, *FRUS, 1947,* 1:872–73; notes on Attlee-Smuts conversation, late November 1947 (specific date not given), *FRUS, 1947,* 1:895–96; Ovendale, *English-Speaking Alliance,* 257.

121. Correll, "Communism in South Africa," 25 February 1946, 848A.00B/2-2546, *CSDCF, 1945–49,* 4; Dickerson to Secretary of State, 23 October 1947, 848A.00/10-2347, *CSDCF, 1945–49,* 4.

Chapter 5

1. *New York Times Book Review,* 1 February 1948, p. 6; *New Republic,* 22 March 1948, p. 26; *Yale Review,* n.s., 37 (Spring 1948): 573. The novel received awards from *The Saturday Review,* the Newspaper Guild of New York, and *The Times* of London. South Africans who visited the United States were impressed by how much Americans' views of the Union had been shaped by Paton's book. See, for example, Morris Dembo (Third Secretary of U.S. Embassy in Pretoria), "South African Political and Economic Developments," 23 November 1949, enclosed in North Winship (U.S. Ambassador in South Africa) to Secretary of State, 23 November 1949, 848A.00/11-2349, *CSDCF, 1945–49,* 4.

2. Alan Paton, *Cry, the Beloved Country* (New York: Charles Scribner's Sons, 1948).

3. PPS/20, "Effect Upon the United States If the European Recovery Program Is Not Adopted," 22 January 1948, in [United States Department of State, Policy Planning Staff], *The State Department Policy Planning Staff Papers* (New York: Garland, 1983) 2:77–79; PPS/23, "Review of Current Trends: U.S. Foreign Policy," 24 February 1948, *FRUS, 1948,* 1:510–11.

4. Department of State, Office of the Secretary, "Summary of Telegrams," 2 March 1948, Naval Aide Files, Box 21, Truman Papers.

5. "Report on Soviet Intelligence Prepared by the Joint Intelligence Committee, American Embassy, Moscow," 1 April 1948, *FRUS, 1948,* 1:555. See also Kennan to Marshall, 15 March 1948, *FRUS, 1948,* 3:848–49, quoted in Wilson D. Miscamble, "George F. Kennan, the Policy Planning Staff and American Foreign Policy, 1947–1950" (Ph.D. diss., University of Notre Dame, 1979), 86; Caffery to Marshall, 12 May 1947, *FRUS, 1947,* 3:709–13.

6. Central Intelligence Agency, ORE 25–48, "The Break-Up of the Colonial Empires and Its Implications for U.S. Security," 3 September 1948, President's Secretary's File, Box 255, Truman Papers; Pollard, *Economic Security,* 197–98.

7. Report by Strategic Materials Working Group to Executive Committee on Economic Foreign Policy, 21 June 1948, *FRUS, 1948,* 1:581.

8. PPS/23, "Review of Current Trends: U.S. Foreign Policy," 24 February 1948, *FRUS, 1948,* 1:524. Norman A. Graebner has estimated that the share of the world's capital wealth in American hands in the late 1940s was actually closer to 67 percent than 50 percent. Graebner, "Introduction: The Sources of Postwar Insecurity," in *The National Security: Its Theory and Practice, 1945–1960,* ed. Norman A. Graebner (New York: Oxford University Press, 1986), 11–12.

9. Marshall to diplomatic and consular offices, 20 July 1948, *FRUS, 1948,* 1:595. The State Department noted a few months later that the dissemination of

"information regarding the international economic objectives of the United States" should have "the general purpose of counteracting charges that the United States is bent on 'economic imperialism.'" Department of State, policy statement on South Africa, 1 November 1948, *FRUS, 1948,* 5:529.

10. Memorandum by John Foster Dulles, 24 March 1948, *FRUS, 1948,* 1:544; [James Forrestal], *The Forrestal Diaries,* ed. Walter Millis (New York: Viking, 1951), 387, 394–95; Donovan, *Conflict and Crisis,* 358–61.

11. Perkins, "Unequal Partners," in Louis and Bull, '*Special Relationship,*' 57; Walter LaFeber, *America, Russia, and the Cold War, 1945–1984,* 5th ed. (New York: Knopf, 1985), 74–75; John Ranelagh, *The Agency: The Rise and Decline of the CIA* (New York: Simon & Schuster, 1986), 176–77.

12. Holcomb to Secretary of State, 12 March 1948, 848A.00/3-1248, *CSDCF, 1945–49,* 3; Holcomb to Secretary of State, 12 April 1948, 848A.00/4-1248, *CSDCF, 1945–49,* 3.

13. Nolutshungu, *South Africa in Africa,* 39–41; Davidson, *Report on South Africa,* 151–52; Barber, *South Africa's Foreign Policy,* 40–41; Vandenbosch, *South Africa and the World,* 119.

14. "Statement of the Nationalist Party's 'Apartheid' Policy," 29 March 1948, enclosed in Holcomb to Secretary of State, 31 March 1948, 848A.00/3-3148, *CSDCF, 1945–49,* 3.

15. Holcomb to Secretary of State, 12 April 1948, enclosing "Report of the Native Laws Commission, 1946–1948," March 1948, 848A.4016/4-1248, *CSDCF, 1945–49,* 7.

16. Holcomb to Secretary of State, 12 January 1948, 848A.00/1-1248, *CSDCF, 1945–49,* 3; Holcomb to Secretary of State, 4 June 1946, 848A.032/6-446, *CSDCF, 1945–49,* 5; De Villiers, "Afrikaner Nationalism," in Wilson and Thompson, *Oxford History of South Africa* 2:372; Minter, *King Solomon's Mines Revisited,* 75–78; Barber, *South Africa's Foreign Policy,* 49–52; Davidson, *Report on Southern Africa,* 154–60. One other way to look at the Nationalist Party victory in the 1948 elections is in the context of the anticolonial, sometimes xenophobic, often isolationist independence movements throughout the colonial world in this period. Though obviously quite different in ideology, especially regarding racial issues, the Nationalist stand against British influence can be seen within the limited sphere of white politics in South Africa as anti-imperial and relatively democratic.

17. See, for example, Frederickson, *White Supremacy,* 239–41.

18. Kuper, "African Nationalism in South Africa," in Wilson and Thompson, *Oxford History of South Africa* 2:459–60; Thompson, "Parting of the Ways," in Gifford and Louis, *Transfer of Power,* 426–27; Sparks, *Mind of South Africa,* 190–91. See also Harold Wolpe, "Capitalism and Cheap Labour-Power in South Africa: From Segregation to Apartheid," *Economy and Society* 1 (November 1972): 425–56.

19. Davidson, *Report on Southern Africa,* 153. South African historian Arthur Keppel-Jones offered a similar evaluation of the limitations of white political debate in the Union in this period: "Political discussion in South Africa is distinguished from the polemics of most countries by its unreality." Keppel-Jones, *When Smuts Goes: A History of South Africa from 1952 to 2010, First Published in 2015* (London: Victor Gollancz, 1947), 7.

20. Holcomb to Secretary of State, 16 January 1948, 848A.00/1–1648, *CSDCF, 1945–49,* 3; Holcomb to Secretary of State, 27 January 1948, 848A.032/

1-2748, *CSDCF, 1945–49,* 5; J. Harold Shullaw (Second Secretary of U.S. Legation in Pretoria), "South African Political and Economic Developments," 1 March 1948, enclosed in Holcomb to Secretary of State, 1 March 1948, 848A.00/3-148, *CSDCF, 1945–49,* 3. The idea that proponents of racial equality and supporters of explicit racial oppression formed the two extremes—the Scylla and Charybdis—between which responsible leaders had to navigate was frequently expressed in the United States a few years later by those who viewed the NAACP and the Ku Klux Klan as comparably dangerous organizations.

21. Huston (U.S. Ambassador in Oslo) to Secretary of State, 2 June 1948, 848A.00/6-248, *CSDCF, 1945–49,* 3; Caffery (U.S. Ambassador in Paris) to Secretary of State, 2 June 1948, 848A.00/6-248, *CSDCF, 1945–49,* 3; W. Stratton Anderson, Jr. (Second Secretary of U.S. Embassy in London), to Secretary of State, 2 June 1948, 848A.00/6-248, *CSDCF, 1945–49,* 3; G. H. Archambault, "Smuts Resigns, Leaves Public Life; Nationalist Asked to Form Cabinet," *New York Times,* 29 May 1948, pp. 1, 4.

22. G. H. Archambault, "Smuts Loses Seat In Parliament; Foes, Some Pro-Nazi, Are Swept In," *New York Times,* 28 May 1948, pp. 1, 10; "Foreign News: South Africa," *Time,* 7 June 1948, p. 34; Martin, "American Views on South Africa," 17–25. Smuts reiterated his and the United Party's position on South Africa's racial problems four months later in a speech before the Union Parliament: "We stand and have always stood for European supremacy in this country" and for "the avoidance of all racial mixture." Quoted in Vandenbosch, *South Africa and the World,* 23.

23. "South Africa Turns Backward," *New Republic,* 5 July 1948, p. 9.

24. "The Shape of Things," *Nation,* 5 June 1948, pp. 617–18.

25. Winship to Secretary of State, 16 June 1948, 848A.00/6-1648, *CSDCF, 1945–49,* 3; Winship to Secretary of State, 13 July 1948, 848A.032/7-1348, *CSDCF, 1945–49,* 5.

26. Department of State, Office of Intelligence Research, "South Africa After the General Election," 6 July 1948, *OSS/SD, Africa,* 10.

27. Minutes of meeting of U.S. members of Combined Policy Committee, 28 May 1948, *FRUS, 1948,* 1:707–8; Lilienthal in meeting of U.S. members of Combined Policy Committee, 5 November 1947, *FRUS, 1947,* 1:857; report to President by Special Committee of National Security Council on Atomic Energy Policy with Respect to United Kingdom and Canada, 2 March 1949, *FRUS, 1949,* 1:449; Herken, *Winning Weapon,* 239.

28. NSC 30, "United States Policy on Atomic Warfare," 10 September 1948, Records of the National Security Council, Record Group 273, National Archives; minutes of meeting of Policy Planning Staff on international control of atomic energy, 12 October 1949, *FRUS, 1949,* 1:191–92; minutes of meeting of Policy Planning Staff, 3 November 1949, *FRUS, 1949,* 1:573; Matthew A. Evangelista, "Stalin's Postwar Army Reappraised," *International Security* 7 (Winter 1982/1983): 110.

29. Groves to Acheson, 29 April 1946, *FRUS, 1946,* 1:1,240–41.

30. Acheson to Executive Session of Joint Congressional Committee on Atomic Energy, 12 May 1947, *FRUS, 1947,* 1:809.

31. Shrouded in secrecy even from Truman and most of his top advisers, the actual number of weapons in the American nuclear arsenal in 1948 was approximately fifty. These were not immediately available for military use as they required two days just for assembly. Delivery systems for the weapons were plagued

by serious difficulties, including a dearth of suitable planes and personnel trained for assembling the bombs. These constraints on the American nuclear deterrent were kept highly secret, however, even from most of the administration, and thus did not have any apparent effect on policy decisions. As Truman's hopes for an international agreement on the control of atomic energy finally dissipated in the Cold War crises of 1948, his administration—in addition to seeking more uranium ore—moved to build bombs more quickly, expand delivery systems, and improve weapon designs. By 1950, the American nuclear arsenal included more than six times as many weapons as it had had two years earlier. See David Alan Rosenberg, "The Origins of Overkill: Nuclear Weapons and American Strategy, 1945–1960," *International Security* 7, no. 4 (Spring 1983), 3–71; and Rosenberg, "U.S. Nuclear Stockpile," 25–30.

32. Report to President by Special Committee of NSC on Atomic Energy Policy with Respect to United Kingdom and Canada, 2 March 1949, *FRUS, 1949,* 1:445. See also NSC staff draft report, "Measures Required to Achieve U.S. Objectives with Respect to the U.S.S.R.," 30 March 1949, *FRUS, 1949,* 1:275; and Helmreich, *Gathering Rare Ores,* 247–62.

33. Hewlett and Duncan, *Atomic Shield,* 147–49, 173, 674 (Appendix 5).

34. Statement by Lovett before Joint Congressional Committee on Atomic Energy, 21 January 1948, *FRUS, 1948,* 1:688–91; Vandenberg, *Private Papers of Senator Vandenberg,* 360–61; Hewlett and Duncan, *Atomic Shield,* 274–84; Margaret Gowing, "Nuclear Weapons and the 'Special Relationship,'" in Louis and Bull, *'Special Relationship',* 119–22. Given the Truman administration's willingness to use the threat of not funding the Marshall Plan to force concessions from Britain in December 1947, there was some irony in Secretary of State Marshall's pointed refusal five months earlier to "link uranium supply or atomic energy development with [the] question of European rehabilitation" when doing so would have redounded to the advantage of Belgium or another country besides the United States. Marshall to William L. Clayton (Under Secretary of State for Economic Affairs), 24 July 1947, *FRUS, 1947,* 1:829.

35. Groves to Byrnes, 24 October 1946, *FRUS, 1946,* 1:1,258; NSC staff draft report, "Measures Required to Achieve U.S. Objectives with Respect to the U.S.S.R.," 30 March 1949, *FRUS, 1949,* 1:275; Jean-Luc Vellut, "Mining in the Belgian Congo," in *History of Central Africa,* ed. David Birmingham and Phyllis M. Martin (London: Longman, 1983), 2:143–61; Herken, *Winning Weapon,* 239, 380.

36. [Walter Brown], "W.B.'s book," 24 September 1945, Folder 602, Byrnes Papers.

37. Quoted in Herken, *Winning Weapon,* 50. See also minutes of meeting of Secretaries of State, War, and Navy, 16 October 1945, *FRUS, 1945,* 2:60.

38. Edmund A. Gullion (Special Assistant to Secretary of State) to Lovett, 7 April 1948, *FRUS, 1948,* 1:703–4.

39. Department of State, Office of the Secretary, "Summary of Telegrams," 30 November 1948, Naval Aide Files, Box 21, Truman Papers.

40. Lovett to U.S. Embassy in Belgium, 11 December 1948, *FRUS, 1948,* 3:314.

41. Memorandum of conversation by T. C. Achilles, 10 December 1948, *FRUS, 1948,* 1:791–92.

42. Memorandum of conversation by George W. Perkins (Assistant Secretary of State for European Affairs), 25 July 1952, *FRUS, 1952–1954,* 11:406.

43. Alan Kirk (U.S. Ambassador in Belgium) to Acheson, 14 May 1947, *FRUS, 1947,* 1:812.

44. Kirk to Byrnes, 18 April 1946, *FRUS, 1946,* 1:1233; Kirk to Byrnes, 18 May 1946, *FRUS, 1946,* 1:1247–48; Kirk to Secretary of State, 5 February 1947, *FRUS, 1947,* 1:792–93. One of the strategies Spaak suggested to the Truman administration in this regard was for the United States to invite Belgian scientists to participate in American research and development of atomic energy for industrial applications, an idea the Americans had agreed to in principle in the Tripartite Agreement (Kirk to Secretary of State, 10 January 1947, *FRUS, 1947,* 1:783–84). Marshall demurred, however, citing the 1946 U.S. Atomic Energy Act's ban on the exchange of information with other nations regarding uses of atomic energy for even nonmilitary purposes (Marshall to U.S. Embassy in Belgium, 10 February 1947, *FRUS, 1947,* 1:793–94). A year later Marshall instructed the American Embassy in Belgium to explain to Spaak that the United States did indeed plan to fulfill all of its obligations under the Tripartite Agreement, but that nonmilitary use of atomic energy remained far off in the future; for now, the primary concern of the United States was with the strategic use of uranium ore. Marshall also noted that the presence of some Communist Party members in executive positions in the Belgian atomic research program would have made it very difficult for the United States government to convince the American public that it would be in the national interest of the United States to share nuclear information with Belgium. Marshall to U.S. Embassy in Belgium, 9 March 1948, *FRUS, 1948,* 1:693–94.

45. Marshall to U.S. Embassy in Belgium, 9 March 1948, *FRUS, 1948,* 1:693–94; Millard (chargé d'affaires in U.S. Embassy in Belgium) to Secretary of State, 7 February 1948, *FRUS, 1948,* 1:691–92; memorandum by Gullion (special assistant to Under-Secretary of State), 9 June 1947, *FRUS, 1947,* 1:819–20; Marshall to Clayton, 24 July 1947, *FRUS, 1947,* 1:829.

46. Acheson to Kirk, 27 June 1947, *FRUS, 1947,* 1:822.

47. Franklin A. Lindsay (Executive Officer of U.S. Delegation to U.N. Atomic Energy Commission) to Warren Austin (U.S. Representative at U.N.), 31 January 1947, *FRUS, 1947,* 1:391; Acheson to Executive Session of Joint Congressional Committee on Atomic Energy, 12 May 1947, *FRUS, 1947,* 1:807. A more exotic threat to Shinkolobwe was suggested by a Viennese newspaper in 1952 when it reported the sighting of "two fiery disks" hovering over the uranium mines. The Belgian commander of the nearby Elisabethville airfield, "regarded as a dependable officer and a zealous flyer," set off in a fighter plane to give chase, but gave up after fifteen minutes as the "saucers" disappeared in a straight line toward Lake Tanganyika to the northeast at an estimated speed of fifteen hundred kilometers per hour. "Flying Saucers Over Belgian Congo Uranium Mines," 29 March 1952, *CIA Research Reports: Africa, 1946–1976* (Frederick, Md.: University Publications of America, 1982–1983), microfilm, 3 reels, reel 1. The uniqueness of this resource seemed able to induce considerable anxiety in those responsible for or dependent on it.

48. Minutes of meeting of U.S. members of Combined Policy Committee with Sen. Bourke Hickenlooper (Chairman of Joint Congressional Committee on Atomic Energy) and Sen. Arthur Vandenberg (Chairman of Senate Foreign Relations Committee), 26 November 1947, *FRUS, 1947,* 1:872–73.

49. Minutes of meeting of U.S. Atomic Energy Commission spokesmen with Lovett, Hickenlooper, Vandenburg, and U.S. delegates of Combined Policy

Committee, 26 November 1947, *FRUS, 1947,* 1:874; Helmreich, *Gathering Rare Ores,* 186; Hewlett and Duncan, *Atomic Shield,* 174.

50. Minutes of meeting of U.S. members of Combined Policy Committee, 28 May 1948, *FRUS, 1948,* 1:708; notes on Attlee-Smuts Conversation (late November 1947: specific date not given), *FRUS, 1947,* 1:895–96.

51. Minutes of meeting of U.S. members of Combined Policy Committee, 28 May 1948, *FRUS, 1948,* 1:708; Gordon Arneson to Acheson, 6 August 1949, *FRUS, 1949,* 1:510.

52. Lovett to Hickenlooper, 16 June 1948, *FRUS, 1948,* 1:711–12.

53. Lovett to U.S. Legation in Pretoria, 2 June 1948, 848A.00/6-248, *CSDCF, 1945–49,* 1; Winship to Secretary of State, 11 June 1948, 848A.00/6-1148, *CSDCF, 1945–49,* 1.

54. Auspex (pseud.), "Behind the Smokescreen," *Forum* (Capetown[?]), 31 March 1945, enclosed in Holcomb to Secretary of State, 16 April 1945, 848A.00/4-1645, *CSDCF, 1945–49,* 1.

55. Commerce Department, *Investment in Union of South Africa,* 16, 21, 23; U.S. Department of Commerce, World Trade Information Service, "Basic Data on the Economy of the Union of South Africa," *Economic Reports,* May 1955; L. O. V. Gander, "The Economic Policy of South Africa's New Government," enclosed in McGregor to Secretary of State, 31 August 1948, 848A.50/8-3148, *CSDCF, 1945–49,* 8; policy statement, "Union of South Africa," 1 November 1948, *FRUS, 1948,* 5:527–28, 531; Spooner, "United States Policy Toward South Africa," 352 (Appendix: Table 1); Baum, "United States, Self-Government, and Africa," 118, Table 2; Hunton, "Postscript," in *Resistance Against Fascist Enslavement,* 52–53; Hull, *American Enterprise in South Africa,* 205.

In a less publicized part of the South African–United States trade relationship, complaints continued to come to the attention of American diplomatic personnel in the Union during 1948 about the involvement of American seamen in the narcotics trade in South Africa. Willard Stanton (U.S. Consul in Capetown) to Secretary of State, 848A.114 Narcotics/7-1348, 13 July 1948, *CSDCF, 1945–49,* 6.

56. "South Africa: Complications in the Land of Opportunity Plus," *Newsweek,* 21 June 1948, pp. 74–76.

57. Commerce Department, *Investment in Union of South Africa,* 9–11; Spooner, "United States Policy toward South Africa," chapter 1.

58. William L. Kilcoin (Department of State, Office of British Commonwealth and Northern European Affairs) to Brown (Director of Office of International Materials Policy), 17 April 1952, *FRUS, 1952–1954,* 11:910.

59. Central Intelligence Agency, CIA/RE 27–50, "South African Politics and US Security," 17 November 1950, President's Secretary's File, Box 250, Truman Papers; Commerce Department, "Basic Data on the Economy of the Union of South Africa"; Commerce Department, *Investment in Union of South Africa,* 41, 43.

60. Samuel Pizer and Frederick Cutler, "Growth in Private Foreign Investments," [U.S. Department of Commerce, Office of Business Economics], *Survey of Current Business,* January 1954, pp. 6–7 (Tables 1 and 2); Commerce Department, *Investment in Union of South Africa,* 26; Hunton, "Postscript," in *Resistance Against Fascist Enslavement,* 51; Martin, "American Views on South Africa," 257–58.

61. Commerce Department, *Investment in Union of South Africa,* 13, 24;

CIA, "South African Politics and US Security"; Musedorah Thoreson, "Capital Investment in South Africa," [16 September 1952], *FRUS, 1952–1954,* 11:932–33.

62. Eckes, *United States and the Global Struggle for Minerals,* 121–73; Pollard, *Economic Security,* 197.

63. Report by Strategic Materials Working Group to Executive Committee on Economic Foreign Policy, 21 June 1948, *FRUS, 1948,* 1:581.

64. CIA, "Break-Up of the Colonial Empires."

65. Lovett to U.S. Legation in Pretoria, 7 January 1949, 848A.6359/1-749, Record Group 59, National Archives. See also Lovett to U.S. Embassy in Moscow, 20 October 1948, 848A.6359/10-1248, Record Group 59, National Archives; Dickerson to Secretary of State, 21 October 1948, 848A.50/10–2148, *CSDCF, 1945–49,* 8; Hunton, "Postscript," in *Resistance Against Fascist Enslavement,* 53.

66. Policy statement, "Union of South Africa," 528–29.

67. Report by the SANACC Subcommittee for Rearmament, "Military Aid Priorities," 18 August 1948, *FRUS, 1949,* 1:261–67.

68. Arneson to James Webb (Under-Secretary of State), "Tripartite Atomic Energy Negotiations," 6 July 1949, *FRUS, 1949,* 1:472; Satterthwaite (Deputy Director, Office of British Commonwealth and Northern European Affairs) to Thompson (Deputy Assistant Secretary of State for European Affairs), "Assessment and Appraisal of U.S. Objectives, Commitments, and Risks in Relation to Military Power," 8 February 1950, *FRUS, 1950,* 1:143–44.

69. "General Considerations with Respect to Allies of the United States," 8 February 1951, *FRUS, 1951,* 1:45–46.

70. Department of State, Office of European Affairs, Division of British Commonwealth Affairs, "Pan-Africanism," 18 January 1945, *CSDCF, 1945–49,* 1; policy statement, "Union of South Africa," 527; Ovendale, *English-Speaking Alliance,* 261–62, 265–66.

71. Central Intelligence Agency, ORE 1–49, "The Political Situation in the Union of South Africa," 31 January 1949, President's Secretary's File, Box 256, Truman Papers; Holcomb to Secretary of State, 16 April 1948, 848A.50/4-1648, *CSDCF, 1945–49,* 8; Holcomb to Secretary of State, 19 May 1948, 848A.50/5-1948, *CSDCF, 1945–49,* 8; Winship to Secretary of State, 23 July 1948, 848A.50/7-2348, *CSDCF, 1945–49,* 8.

72. Policy statement, "Union of South Africa," 532; Department of State, Office of the Secretary, "Summary of Telegrams," 18 June 1948, Naval Aide Files, Box 2, Truman Papers; position paper prepared by State-Defense Military Information Control Committee, 10 January 1950, *FRUS, 1950,* 3:1,606; documents relating to exchange of classified military information between United States and United Kingdom, 27 January 1950, Document C, "Policy with Respect to Commonwealth Nations," *FRUS, 1950,* 3:1,621.

73. Memorandum by John Hickerson (Director of Office of European Affairs), 10 May 1948, *FRUS, 1948,* 3:999.

74. SWNCC 38/46, "Memorandum by the Joint Chiefs of Staff to the State-War-Navy Coordinating Committee," 9 September 1947, *FRUS, 1947,* 1:766–68; NSC 2/1, "A Report to the President by the National Security Council on Base Rights in Greenland, Iceland, and the Azores," 25 November 1947, Record Group 273, National Archives; "Views of the Joint Chiefs of Staff on Military Rights in Foreign Territories" (undated; sent by Louis Johnson [Secretary of

Defense] to Acheson on 19 May 1949), *FRUS, 1949,* 1:304; John Wiley (U.S. Ambassador in Portugal) to Marshall, 4 February 1948, *FRUS, 1948,* 3:995.

75. SWNCC 202/2, "Policy Concerning Provision of United States Government Military Supplies for Post-War Armed Forces of Foreign Nations," 21 March 1946, *FRUS, 1946,* 1:1,155.

76. Policy manual, "The Foreign Policy of the United States," 1 April 1945, enclosed in Stettinius to Truman, 16 April 1945, President's Secretary's Files, Box 159, Truman Papers; Baruch to Byrnes, 13 May 1946, *FRUS, 1946,* 5:976; Baruch to Byrnes, 16 May 1946, *FRUS, 1946,* 5:980.

77. Maxwell, "Portugal and Africa," in Gifford and Louis, *The Transfer of Power,* 346–50.

78. George Kennan, "Problems of Diplomatic-Military Collaboration," lecture at National War College, Washington, D.C., 7 March 1947, Box 16, Kennan Papers; Kennan to Perkins, 24 July 1951, Box 29, Kennan Papers.

79. Acheson, *Present at the Creation,* 53, 627–28. Acheson also included Salazar's picture in the photo section of this collection of memoirs. Official American admiration for the authoritarian style of Portuguese governance in this period was not restricted to Salazar. Assistant Secretary of State George McGhee recalled liking and respecting Admiral Gabriel Texeira, Governor-General of Mozambique, when he met him on a tour of southern Africa in 1950. McGhee admired Texeira as a strong figure and "a real aristocrat," even though he admittedly ruled the colony "with an iron hand," prevented any "local participation in government," and was responsible for there being "few amenities for the mass of black inhabitants." George C. McGhee, *Envoy to the Middle World: Adventures in Diplomacy* (New York: Harper and Row, 1983), 118–19.

80. Committee on Colonial Problems to Allan Evans, 21 January 1948, Box 8, Records of Policy Planning Staff, 1947–1953, Record Group 59, National Archives; policy statement prepared in Department of State, "Portugal," 20 October 1950, *FRUS, 1950,* 3:1,543–46; Marcum, *Portugal and Africa,* 3.

81. MacVeagh to Marshall, 30 November 1948, *FRUS, 1948,* 3:1,015. MacVeagh spoke with some authority about undemocratic regimes of the right, having been posted previously in South Africa and Greece. He clearly enjoyed Portugal, choosing to live there after his retirement from the Foreign Service. Seiler, "Introduction," in MacVeagh, *"Dear Franklin,"* 5.

82. Central Intelligence Agency, ORE 68–48, "Opposition to ECA in Participating Countries," 10 February 1949, President's Secretary's File, Box 256, Truman Papers.

83. Jaime da Silva, "Portugal: How to Win Elections," *Nation,* 1 January 1949, pp. 16–17; William Minter, *Portuguese Africa and the West* (Harmondsworth, England: Penguin, 1972), 16–24, 37–49.

84. Minutes of meeting of U.S. Delegation to U.N., 4 October 1948, *FRUS, 1948,* 1:277–79.

85. Policy statement, "Union of South Africa," 530–31.

86. CIA, "Break-Up of the Colonial Empires."

87. Shah, *Great Abdication,* 56, 101–2.

88. Harvard Sitkoff, "Harry Truman and the Election of 1948: The Coming of Age of Civil Rights in American Politics," *Journal of Southern History* 37 (November 1971): 597–616; Chafe, "Civil Rights Revolution," 74–79; Berman, *Politics of Civil Rights,* 79–128; Bernstein, "Ambiguous Legacy," 271–92.

89. Policy statement, "Union of South Africa," 526.

90. On dissent in the United States, see Mark Solomon, "Black Critics of Colonialism and the Cold War," in *Cold War Critics: Alternatives to American Foreign Policy in the Truman Years,* ed. Thomas G. Paterson (Chicago: Quadrangle, 1971), 205–39; Lynch, *Black American Radicals*; idem, "Pan-African Responses in the United States," in Gifford and Louis, *Transfer of Power,* 57–86.

91. Marshall to Diplomatic and Consular Offices, 20 July 1948, *FRUS, 1948,* 1:595.

92. Marshall, address to U.N. General Assembly, 23 September 1948, *FRUS, 1948,* 1:289.

93. Policy statement, "Union of South Africa," 524, 527; Chafe, "Civil Rights Revolution," 72–74, 79.

94. Minutes of meeting of U.S. Delegation to U.N. General Assembly, 28 September 1948, *FRUS, 1948,* 1:275–77; CIA, "Political Situation in the Union of South Africa"; position paper prepared in Department of State for U.S. Delegation to U.N. General Assembly, "Question of South West Africa: Advisory Opinion of International Court of Justice," 4 September 1950, *FRUS 1950,* 2:481–84. For most Americans the really important issues at the United Nations continued to be those concerning the Soviet Union and its allies; problems within the Western group of anticommunist nations were seen largely as a distraction. Thus George Kennan had in mind Eastern Europe rather than southern Africa when he argued at a public forum in New York on 20 October 1948 that "the conflict which exists inside the U.N. is not a conflict between the U.S. and the U.S.S.R. It is a conflict between the majority of the U.N. members, acting in support of the Charter, and a group of governments who refuse to abide by its provisions or to recognize the over-riding international obligation which the Charter constitutes." Kennan, "The United States and the United Nations," address at Herald-Tribune Forum, New York, 20 October 1948, Box 1, Kennan Papers.

95. Robert E. Cushman, "Our Civil Rights Become a World Issue," *New York Times Magazine,* 11 January 1948, p. 12; George Kennan, "Where Do We Stand?" lecture at National War College, 21 December 1949, Box 17, Kennan Papers; paper prepared by Colonial Policy Review Sub-Committee of the Committee on Problems of Dependent Areas, "United States Policy Toward Dependent Territories," 26 April 1950, *FRUS, 1952–1954,* 3:1,097, 1,102; CIA, "Political Situation in the Union of South Africa"; Rupert Emerson and Martin Kilson, "The American Dilemma in a Changing World: The Rise of Africa and the Negro American," *Daedalus* 94 (Fall 1965): 1,058–60, 1,072–74; Harry S. Ashmore, *Hearts and Minds: The Anatomy of Racism from Roosevelt to Reagan* (New York: McGraw-Hill, 1982), 155–56.

96. "Candidate Wallace," editorial, *Crisis* 55 (February 1948): 41; "President Truman's Orders," editorial, *Crisis* 55 (September 1948): 264; Southern, *Gunnar Myrdal and Black-White Relations,* 101–2; Chafe, "Postwar American Society," 167; Alonzo L. Hamby, "The Clash of Perspectives and the Need for New Syntheses," in *The Truman Period as a Research Field: A Reappraisal, 1972,* ed. Richard S. Kirkendall (Columbia: University of Missouri Press, 1974), 136.

97. Harvard Sitkoff, "Harry Truman and the Election of 1948," 613; "The Southern Negro: 1952," *Nation,* 27 September 1952, p. 243. On the significance of Truman's anticommunism in the presidential campaign, see Robert A. Divine, "The Cold War and the Election of 1948," *Journal of American History* 59 (June 1972): 90–110.

98. M. G. de B. Epstein (managing editor of *The South African Financial*

News [Johannesburg]) to Truman, 11 November 1948, and Truman to Epstein, 26 November 1948, White House Central Files, Box 585, Truman Papers; Berman, *Politics of Civil Rights,* 129–33. The United Party in South Africa apparently took some encouragement from Truman's victory, feeling that if the Democrats could defeat the more conservative Republicans in the United States, then perhaps it could come back from its loss to the Nationalists and win in the next election in South Africa. Raymond A. Valliere (Third Secretary of U.S. Legation in Pretoria), "South African Political and Economic Developments," 16 November 1948, enclosed in Winship to Secretary of State, 16 November 1948, 848A.00/ 11-1648, *CSDCF, 1945–49,* 4.

99. Policy statement, "Union of South Africa," 525, 531.

100. Winship to Secretary of State, 13 September 1948, 848A.4016/9-1348, *CSDCF, 1945–49,* 7; Winship to Secretary of State, 5 October 1948, 848A.4016/ 10-548, *CSDCF, 1945–49,* 7; Winship to Secretary of State, 28 October 1948, 848A.032/10-2848, *CSDCF, 1945–49,* 5. Winship unwittingly revealed in the latter telegram how thoroughly their own racial experiences and assumptions from the United States could blind Americans to the demographic and political realities of South Africa: "While [the Union government] has demonstrated that it can be ruthless with the *minority* groups . . . ," he began one sentence, referring to black South Africans (emphasis added).

101. "South Africa's Witches' Brew," *Christian Century,* 10 November 1948, p. 1,198.

102. Whitney H. Shepardson, "Report on a Visit to the Union of South Africa" to Council on Foreign Relations, New York, 25 October 1948, Box 5, Papers of John D. Sumner, Truman Library.

103. Winship to Secretary of State, 13 September 1948, 848A.4016/9-1348, *CSDCF, 1945–49,* 7; Winship to Secretary of State, 5 October 1948, 848A.4016/ 10-548, *CSDCF, 1945–49,* 7; Dickerson to Secretary of State, 21 October 1948, 848A.50/10-2148, *CSDCF, 1945–49,* 8. This concern would be proven valid by the course of all black South African political organizing since 1948, which has been characterized by the need to respond to intensifying oppression from the government. While not well prepared at the time to react effectively to the rise of Afrikaner nationalism to power, the African National Congress and other black organizations have since been forced to question the utility of Western liberalism as an adequate world view for people in their situation. See Molopatene Collins Ramusi and Ruth S. Turner, *Soweto, My Love* (New York: Henry Holt, 1989), 70–75; Gerhart, *Black Power in South Africa,* 16; Thompson, "Parting of the Ways," in Gifford and Louis, *Transfer of Power,* 426; Kuper, "African Nationalism," in Wilson and Thompson, *Oxford History of South Africa,* 461.

104. Winship to Secretary of State, 23 November 1948, 848A.00/11-2348, *CSDCF, 1945–49,* 4.

105. CIA, "Political Situation in the Union of South Africa."

106. "South Africa's Witches' Brew," 1,198–99. See also Winship to Secretary of State, 29 November 1948, 848A.00/11-2948, *CSDCF, 1945–49,* 4.

107. Policy statement, "Union of South Africa," 531.

108. Memorandum by Armistead M. Lee and Musedorah Thoreson (Department of State, Office of British Commonwealth and Northern European Affairs), "Summary of Current United States–South African Problems," 16 September 1952, *FRUS, 1952–1954,* 11:929; Commerce Department, *Investment in Union of South Africa,* 16, 21.

109. Winship to Secretary of State, 11 June 1948, 848A.00/6–1148, *CSDCF, 1945–49,* 1; Dickerson to Secretary of State, 21 October 1948, 848A.50/10-2148, *CSDCF, 1945–49,* 8; Winship to Secretary of State, 17 December 1948, 848A.50/12-1748, *CSDCF, 1945–49,* 8; CIA, "Political Situation in the Union of South Africa."

110. CIA, "South African Politics and U.S. Security."

111. Dickerson to Secretary of State, 20 October 1948, 748A.00/10-2048, *CSDCF, 1945–49,* 14; minutes of meeting of Washington exploratory talks, 22 December 1948, *FRUS, 1948,* 3:328; CIA, "Political Situation in the Union of South Africa"; Ovendale, *English-Speaking Alliance,* 250–55.

112. Winship to Secretary of State, 28 December 1948, 848A.00/12-2848, *CSDCF, 1945–49,* 4; Winship to Secretary of State, 17 September 1948, 848A.00/9-1748, *CSDCF, 1945–49,* 4; Lauren, *Power and Prejudice,* 177–82.

113. Policy statement, "Union of South Africa," 524, 531; Lovett, "Memorandum for the President," 23 November 1948, White House Central Files, Box 451, Truman Papers. The change from legations to embassies also altered the title accorded the heads of the two missions from "Minister" to "Ambassador."

Chapter 6

1. Max Beloff, "No Peace, No War," *Foreign Affairs* 27 (January 1949): 224.

2. U.S. Embassy in Pretoria to Secretary of State, 19 July 1949, 848A.4016/7-1349, *CSDCF, 1945–1949,* 8; Raymond A. Valliere, "South African Political and Economic Developments," 19 April 1949, enclosed in Winship to Secretary of State, 19 April 1949, 848A.00/4-1949, *CSDCF, 1945–49,* 4; John C. Fuess (U.S. Consul in Capetown) to Secretary of State, 3 June 1949, 848A.002/6-349, *CSDCF, 1945–49,* 5.

3. St. Clair Drake, "The International Implications of Race and Race Relations," *Journal of Negro Education* 20 (Summer 1951): 269.

4. "Inaugural Address of Harry S Truman," 20 January 1949, Box 36, Papers of George M. Elsey, Truman Library. See also Thomas G. Paterson, "Foreign Aid Under Wraps: The Point Four Program," *Wisconsin Magazine of History* 56 (1972/73): 119–26.

5. Benjamin Hardy to Francis Russell, 23 November 1948, Box 36, Elsey Papers; Hardy, "Point 4: Dynamic Democracy," unpublished manuscript, 21 September 1950, Box 1, Papers of Benjamin H. Hardy, Truman Library.

6. Acheson, State Department press release no. 58, 26 January 1949, *FRUS, 1949,* 1:759. See also George M. Elsey oral history interview, 9 March 1965 and 10 July 1969, transcript, pp. 100–102, 143–48, Truman Library; Donald Edmund Secrest, "American Policy toward Neutralism during the Truman and Eisenhower Administrations" (Ph.D. diss., University of Michigan, 1967), 29–34.

7. Harry S Truman, *Memoirs,* vol. 2, *Years of Trial and Hope, 1946–1952* (Garden City, N.Y.: Doubleday, 1956), 234, 238. See also Daniels, *Man of Independence,* 368–69.

8. [Harry S Truman], *The Autobiography of Harry S Truman,* ed. Robert H. Ferrell (Boulder: Colorado Associated University Press, 1980), 102; Truman to Vandenberg, 6 July 1950, Box 3, Vandenberg Papers.

9. Acheson, *Present at the Creation,* 265–66; memorandum prepared in

Department of State, "Legislative Background of Point Four Program," 20 June 1950, *FRUS, 1950,* 1:846–51; Truman, *Memoirs,* 2:230–34.

10. Editorial note, *FRUS, 1950,* 1:851–52.

11. Webb to U.S. Embassy in London, 12 September 1950, *FRUS, 1950,* 6:866–68.

12. McGhee to Acheson and Webb, "Summary of Conclusions and Recommendations Reached at Lourenco Marques Conference," 12 April 1950, *FRUS, 1950,* 5:1,520; memorandum of conversation by Hare (Deputy Assistant Secretary of State) with Gabriel Van Laethem (Second Secretary of French Embassy), 20 April 1950, *FRUS, 1950,* 5:1,539–40. George Kennan believed the entire Point Four philosophy was misconceived from the start, especially its assumption that the vulnerability of Third World areas to communist pressures arose from poverty and despair. Kennan took the opposite view, arguing that "restlessness does not stem from poverty and disease but in all probability from [the] effects of western education and example on oriental peoples. . . . Poverty and disease were there long before instability and discontent were noted." Kennan believed that the "real source[s] of bitterness" toward the United States "all the way from Egypt to China" were instead "irrational[ity]" and "neurotic" anti-Western nationalism. Kennan, outline for address to Economic Group, Century Club, 8 November 1951, Box 18, Kennan Papers.

13. CIA, ORE 25–48, "The Break-Up of the Colonial Empires and Its Implications for U.S. Security," 3 September 1948, President's Secretary's File, Box 255, Truman Papers.

14. Acheson to U.S. Embassy in Belgium, 8 September 1949, *FRUS, 1949,* 2:356–57; memorandum of conversation by David H. Popper (principal executive officer of U.S. Delegation to U.N.), 8 December 1949, *FRUS, 1949,* 2:369.

15. Millard (U.S. chargé d'affaires in Belgium) to Acheson, 6 September 1949, *FRUS, 1949,* 2:356; memorandum of conversation by G. Hayden Raynor (adviser to U.S. Delegation to U.N.) with Vincent Broustra (French Delegation to U.N.), 24 November 1949, *FRUS, 1949,* 2:358–59.

16. Bedell Smith (U.S. Ambassador in Moscow) to Marshall, 21 August 1948, *FRUS, 1948,* 1:613; minutes of meeting of U.S. Delegation to U.N., 29 October 1948, *FRUS, 1948,* 1:283; minutes of meeting of U.S. Delegation to U.N., 3 November 1948, *FRUS, 1948,* 1:284; Llewellyn E. Thompson (Deputy Director of Office of European Affairs) to Dean Rusk (Assistant Secretary of State for U.N. Affairs) and Charles Bohlen (Counselor of Department of State), 8 April 1949, *FRUS, 1949,* 2:349. Quotation is from British Embassy to Department of State, 18 January 1949, *FRUS, 1949,* 2:341–43.

17. Department of State to British Embassy, 17 February 1949, *FRUS, 1949,* 2:345–47; McMahon, "Toward a Post-Colonial Order," in Lacey, *Truman Presidency,* 357–58; Kennan to Acheson, "United Nations," 14 November 1949, in *State Department Policy Planning Staff Papers,* 3:189; memorandum of conversation by Ambassador Francis B. Sayre (U.S. Representative on U.N. Trusteeship Committee) with British Ambassador Sir Oliver Shewell Franks, 31 December 1949, *FRUS, 1949,* 2:371.

18. Johnson, "The Defense Establishment," transcript of radio address, 22 August 1949, Box 1, Kennan Papers.

19. Department of State policy statement on Indochina, 27 September 1948, *FRUS, 1948,* 6:43–49. See also Louis and Robinson, "United States and the

Liquidation of the British Empire," in Gifford and Louis, 44; *Transfer of Power,* Lauren, *Power and Prejudice,* 204–5; Rotter, *Path to Vietnam,* 4–8.

20. Vandenberg to W. A. McDonald, 29 June 1949, Box 3, Vandenberg Papers.

21. Foster (Acting Administrator for Economic Cooperation) to Kenney (Chief of ECA Mission in the United Kingdom), 18 November 1949, *FRUS, 1949,* 4:450–51. See also memorandum of conversation by John Foster Dulles (U.S. Delegation to U.N.) with Count Carlo Sforza (Italian Minister of Foreign Affairs), 13 April 1949, *FRUS, 1949,* 4:548–49; and Shepherd, "Comment," in Arkhurst, *U.S. Policy Towards Africa,* 43.

22. James Lay (Executive Secretary of NSC), report to the NSC, "United States' Objectives and Programs for National Security," 8 December 1950, *FRUS, 1950,* 1:447. See also map, "Helping African Development and Adding Africa's Resources to Freedom's Cause with Marshall Plan Aid," 2 February 1951, Box 5, Sumner Papers.

23. Background paper for use at East–West African Consular Conference, 1950, "ECA Operations and Economic Development Plans," Box 5, Sumner Papers. See also "Backward-Area Aid Program Set in Motion; ECA Names Dr. Isaiah Bowman as Director," *New York Times,* 24 March 1949, p. 16. For documentation of the tiny percentage—less than 1 percent—of ERP spending targeted for African economic development, see Harry B. Price, *The Marshall Plan and Its Meaning* (Ithaca: Cornell University Press, 1955), 88, 384–85.

24. Escott Reid, *Time of Fear and Hope: The Making of the North Atlantic Treaty, 1947–1949* (Toronto: McClelland and Stewart, 1977), 194.

25. Acheson, "Memorandum for the President," 5 January 1951, Box 66, Acheson Papers, Truman Library; Nielsen, *Great Powers and Africa,* 253; Munene, "Truman Administration and the Decolonization of Sub-Saharan Africa," 165.

26. Ovendale, *English-Speaking Alliance,* 253.

27. JCS study, "Views of the Joint Chiefs of Staff on Military Rights in Foreign Territories" (undated; sent from Johnson to Acheson, 19 May 1949), *FRUS, 1949,* 1:304; Department of State, Office of the Secretary, "Summary of Telegrams," 22 March 1949, Naval Aide Files, Box 21, Truman Papers; Vandenberg to Ronald Brunger, 16 August 1949, Box 3, Vandenberg Papers; Acheson, *Present at the Creation,* 279; Reid, *Time of Fear and Hope,* 195; Maxwell, "Portugal and Africa," in Gifford and Louis, *Transfer of Power,* 345.

28. Mary Heaton Vorse, "The South Has Changed," *Harper's* 199 (July 1949): 27–33. For more on Vorse's life as a feminist and an independent political radical, see Dee Garrison, *Mary Heaton Vorse: The Life of an American Insurgent* (Philadelphia: Temple University Press, 1989). Paul Robeson, campaigning in the South for Progressive Party presidential candidate Henry A. Wallace in 1948, had also been encouraged by the new spirit of boldness he found among African Americans in the region. Martin Bauml Duberman, *Paul Robeson: A Biography* (New York: Ballantine Books, 1989), 326–27.

29. "And Now the Air Force," editorial, *Crisis* 56 (February 1949): 41; "Armed Service Jim Crow Policy Ends," editorial, *Crisis* 56 (May 1949): 137; "Army Still Out of Step," editorial, *Crisis* 56 (August–September 1949): 233.

30. U.S. Minister in South Africa, State Department dispatch no. 175, 25 October 1948, quoted in E. T. Wooldridge, memorandum for Secretary of the

Navy, 28 October 1948, File CD31-1-11, Box 124, Office of Administrative Secretary, Records of the Secretary of Defense, Record Group 330, National Archives.

31. Morris Dembo, "South African Political and Economic Developments," 9 December 1949, enclosed in Winship to Secretary of State, 9 December 1949, 848A.00/12-949, *CSDCF, 1945–49,* 4.

32. "U.S. Acts Against Violence," editorial, *Crisis* 56 (July 1949): 201; "Florida's Little Scottsboro: Groveland," *Crisis* 56 (October 1949): 266–68, 285.

33. For a striking personal description of the difficulties and successes involved in early attempts at desegregation in the U.S. armed forces, see James Forman, *The Making of Black Revolutionaries* (New York: Macmillan, 1972; repr., Washington: Open Hand Publishing, 1985), 60–76. See also Dalfiume, *Desegregation of the U.S. Armed Forces.*

34. "State Department Revisions," *San Francisco Chronicle,* 29 May 1949, newspaper clipping, Box 32, Kennan Papers.

35. Murrey Marder, "Truman Nominates 7 to Fill High State Department Posts," *Washington Post,* 27 May 1949, newspaper clipping, Box 32, Kennan Papers; McGhee, *Envoy to the Middle World,* 146.

36. Memorandum by Raymond A. Valliere, 3 May 1949, enclosed in Winship to Secretary of State, 3 May 1949, 848A.00/5-349, *CSDCF, 1945–49,* 4; "Robeson Speaks for Robeson," editorial, *Crisis* 56 (May 1949): 137. For the most informative biography of Robeson, see Duberman, *Paul Robeson.*

37. "48 Hurt in Clashes at Robeson Rally; Buses Are Stoned," *New York Times,* 5 September 1949, 1; Leo Egan, "Governor Orders Grand Jury Study of Robeson Rioting," *New York Times,* 15 September 1949, p. 1; Shapiro, *White Violence and Black Response,* 378–91; Duberman, *Paul Robeson,* 363–80.

38. Kennan, "Where Do We Stand," lecture at National War College, 21 December 1949, Box 17, Kennan Papers.

39. Memorandum by Valliere, 3 May 1949, enclosed in Winship to Secretary of State, 3 May 1949, 848A.00/5-349, *CSDCF, 1945–49,* 4; Davidson, *Report on Southern Africa,* 117–18, 131–32. Quotation from clergyman is in Bernard Connelley to Department of State, 2 March 1950, 745A.00/3-250, Department of State Records, Record Group 59, National Archives, in *Confidential State Department Central Files, South Africa: Internal Affairs and Foreign Affairs, 1950–1954* (Frederick, Md.: University Publications of America, 1985 [microfilm, 22 reels with printed guide]), 1 (hereafter *CSDCF, 1950–54,* followed by reel number).

40. Winship to Secretary of State, 31 May 1949, 848A.4016/5-3149, *CSDCF, 1945–49,* 8.

41. Chargé d'affaires in Moscow to Department of State, 26 May 1949, 848A.4016/5-2649, *CSDCF, 1945–49,* 8; M. Afonin, "Slave Labor in South Africa," *Izvestiya,* 11 June 1949, enclosed in Chargé d'Affaires to Department of State, 848A.4016/6-1649, *CSDCF, 1945–49,* 8. For more on prison conditions, see Sampson, *Drum.*

42. Winship to Secretary of State, 31 May 1949, 848A.4016/5-3149, *CSDCF, 1945–49,* 8. In a similar vein, the South African Board of Censors in the summer of 1949 banned the American film *Home of the Brave* as a potential disturber of the peace in the Union because it included an African American as one of a group of American soldiers on an important mission in the Pacific during World War II. "Making Us Look Fools," editorial, *Daily Despatch* (Port Elizabeth), 16

August 1949, enclosed in Winship to Department of State, 6 September 1949, 848A.00/9-649, *CSDCF, 1945–49,* 4.

43. Winship to Secretary of State, 8 October 1948, 848A.00/10-848, *CSDCF, 1945–49,* 4.

44. Winship to Secretary of State, 31 December 1948, 848A.4016/12-3148, *CSDCF, 1945–49,* 7; Winship to Secretary of State, 10 January 1949, 848A.4016/1-1049, *CSDCF, 1945–49,* 7; Winship to Secretary of State, 31 May 1949, 848A.4016/5-3149, *CSDCF, 1945–49,* 8.

45. McGregor to Secretary of State, 14 January 1949, 848A.4016/1-1449, *CSDCF, 1945–49,* 7; McGregor to Secretary of State, 31 January 1949, 848A.4016/1-3149, *CSDCF, 1945–49,* 7; George Padmore, "South African Race Riots," *Crisis* 56 (April 1949): 110; Lodge, *Black Politics in South Africa,* 60; Davenport, *South Africa,* 367.

46. McGregor to Secretary of State, 17 January 1949, 848A.4016/1-1749, *CSDCF, 1945–49,* 7; McGregor to Secretary of State, 24 January 1949, 848A.4016/1-2449, *CSDCF, 1945–49,* 7; Winship to Secretary of State, 28 February 1949, 848A.4016/2-2849, *CSDCF, 1945–49,* 7.

47. "Current Status of the South African Indian," 14 March 1949, *OSS/SD, Africa,* 10; McGregor to Secretary of State, 12 October 1949, 848A.4016/10-1249, *CSDCF, 1945–49,* 8; "The Shape of Things," *Nation,* 29 January 1949, pp. 114–15; George Padmore, "South African Race Riots," *Crisis* 56 (April 1949): 110–11, 124–25; "South African Race Riots a Warning," *Christian Century,* 2 February 1949, p. 132; McGregor to Secretary of State, 14 February 1949, 848A.4016/2-1449, *CSDCF, 1945–49,* 7. White South African incitement of different nonwhite communities to violence against one another, accompanied by assertions of the need for white rule as the sole bulwark against chaos, will not seem strange to those familiar with more recent events in South Africa, such as the conflicts between followers of the ANC and the Inkatha movement that flared into widespread violence in 1990.

48. Winship to Secretary of State, 29 August 1949, 848A.00/8-2949, *CSDCF, 1945–49,* 4. See also Davenport, *South Africa,* 362. As was well known but rarely mentioned among whites in the Union, the genealogies of many Afrikaners included nonwhite ancestors—what was sometimes referred to as "a spot of the tar brush." A common joke at this time in South Africa ran thus: "Question, Why is Dr. Malan jealous of Seretse Khama? Answer, Because he has a white wife!" Joseph Sweeney, "South Africa: 1950–52," undated manuscript, Box 5, Sweeney Papers, Truman Library.

49. General Secretary's report, Natal Indian Congress, enclosed in McGregor to Secretary of State, 18 July 1949, 848A.4016/7-1849, *CSDCF, 1945–49,* 8; Winship to Secretary of State, 31 March 1949, 848A.00B/3-3149, *CSDCF, 1945–49,* 5; Winship to Secretary of State, 17 June 1949, 848A.00B/6-1749, *CSDCF, 1945–49,* 5; Dr. J. H. Otto du Plessis (Director of State Information Office of South Africa), address at annual meeting of Johannesburg branch of South African Institute of International Affairs, 26 September 1949, enclosed in U.S. Embassy in Pretoria to Department of State, 6 October 1949, 848A.20200/10-649, *CSDCF, 1945–49,* 6; Winship to Secretary of State, 20 October 1949, 848A.00/10-2049, *CSDCF, 1945–49,* 4; Winship to Secretary of State, 13 December 1949, 848A.00/12-1349, *CSDCF, 1945–49,* 4.

50. Winship to Secretary of State, 3 November 1949, 848A.00/11-349, *CSDCF, 1945–49,* 4. Basil Davidson observed the character of white–black re-

lations in South Africa in the early years of apartheid in a conversation he took part in on a street in the African location of Moroka outside Johannesburg. Stopping to speak with a resident of the location through his African guide and interpreter, Mr. Nkosi, Davidson asked,

> "What else does he say?"
>
> "He asks," Mr. Nkosi said, "whether or not we have come to beat anyone up. He says he would like to know, because then he will go away before we begin."
>
> It was all very quiet, orderly, matter-of-fact. There was the "urbanized native" and there was the visiting white man with his African guide: they might, it is true, have come on peaceful business, but then again they might not. . . .

Davidson, *Report on Southern Africa,* 137.

51. Department of State, Division of Research for Europe, Office of Intelligence Research, "The Union and South West Africa, 1949," 11 August 1949, *OSS/SD, Africa,* 10; Winship to Secretary of State, 21 November 1949, 848A.00/11–2149, *CSDCF, 1945–49,* 4; Ovendale, *English-Speaking Alliance,* 258. Quotation appears in Cooper, *U.S. Economic Power,* 32.

52. Raymond A. Vallière, "South African Political and Economic Developments," 3 June 1949, enclosed in Winship to Secretary of State, 3 June 1949, 848A.00/6-349, *CSDCF, 1945–49,* 4; Scott to Acheson, 31 August 1949, 848A.014/8-3149, *CSDCF, 1945–49,* 5; Scott to Truman, 1 September 1949, 848A.014/9-149, *CSDCF, 1945–49,* 5; Dean Rusk (Deputy Under-Secretary of State) to Scott, 22 September 1949, 848A.014/9-149, *CSDCF, 1945–49,* 5; Scott, *Time to Speak,* 244–45. Quotations are from "South West Africa: Discussions and Proceedings in the United Nations, December, 1948, to December, 1949," Box 5, Sweeney Papers.

53. Morris Dembo, "South African Political and Economic Developments," 30 December 1949, enclosed in Connelly to Secretary of State, 30 December 1949, 848A.00/12-3049, *CSDCF, 1945–49,* 4. See also U.S. delegation working paper, "Summary of Action Taken by the Fourth Regular Session of the General Assembly, September 20–December 10, 1949," *FRUS, 1949,* 2:367; Hickerson to Raynor, 24 January 1950, 745A.00/1-2450, *CSDCF, 1950–54,* 1.

54. Caffery to Marshall, 31 May 1948, *FRUS, 1948,* 3:706–9; Louis and Robinson, "United States and the Liquidation of the British Empire," in Gifford and Louis, *Transfer of Power,* 46–51; Tony Smith, "Patterns in the Transfer of Power: A Comparative Study of French and British Decolonization," in ibid., 93; Lynch, "Pan-African Responses in the United States," in ibid., 84–85; McMahon, *Colonialism and Cold War,* 292–95; Mayall, "Africa in Anglo-American Relations," in Louis and Bull, *'Special Relationship,'* 321–22.

55. Harold Preece, "Africa Awakes," *Crisis* 52 (December 1945): 348–50, 363–64; Lynch, "Pan-African Responses in the United States," 83; Louis and Robinson, "United States and the Liquidation of the British Empire," 42–43, 50, 52; John D. Hargreaves, "Toward the Transfer of Power in British West Africa," in Gifford and Louis, *Transfer of Power,* 135–36. For a prescient analysis of why West Africa would move more swiftly to political independence than the rest of the continent, see W. E. B. Du Bois, "Black Africa Tomorrow," *Foreign Affairs* 17 (October 1938): 103–6.

56. Robert I. Rotberg, *The Rise of Nationalism in Central Africa: The Mak-*

ing of Malawi and Zambia, 1873–1964 (Cambridge: Harvard University Press, 1965), 214–21; Thomas M. Franck, *Race and Nationalism: The Struggle for Power in Rhodesia-Nyasaland* (London: George Allen and Unwin, 1960), 35–38; Davidson, *Report on Southern Africa,* 244–45; Ovendale, *English-Speaking Alliance,* 265–66; Prosser Gifford, "Misconceived Dominion: Federation in British Central Africa," in Gifford and Louis, *Transfer of Power,* 394–95.

57. Basil Davidson, "Whose Continent? Central African Crisis," *Nation,* 23 May 1953, p. 436; Raymond A. Valliere, "South African Political and Economic Developments," 1 February 1949, enclosed in Winship to Secretary of State, 1 February 1949, 848A.00/2-149, *CSDCF, 1945–49,* 4; J. Harold Shullaw, "South African Political and Economic Developments," 1 May 1948, enclosed in Maher to Secretary of State, 1 May 1948, 848A.00/5-148, *CSDCF, 1945–49,* 3; Rotberg, *Rise of Nationalism,* 189–213; Davidson, *Report on Southern Africa,* 248–68; Gifford, "Misconceived Dominion," 387–97.

58. Winship to Secretary of State, 8 June 1949, 848A.504/6-849, *CSDCF, 1945–49,* 9; Department of State, policy statement on Great Britain, 11 June 1948, *FRUS, 1948,* 3:1,106; report by Strategic Materials Working Group to Executive Committee on Economic Foreign Policy, 21 June 1948, *FRUS, 1948,* 1:582; memorandum of conversation of Harriman with Salazar, 25 November 1949, *FRUS, 1949,* 4:716–17; memorandum of conversation of Acheson with Portuguese Ambassador, 12 July 1949, Box 64, Acheson Papers, Truman Library. Another American idea in this period about what central Africa might be used for—suggested by, among others, the U.S. Ambassador in Italy, James C. Dunn, and George Kennan—was large-scale immigration from the defeated Axis powers, Italy and Germany. Department of State, Office of the Secretary, "Summary of Telegrams," 9 August 1948, Naval Aide Files, Box 21, Truman Papers; Munene, "Truman Administration and the Decolonization of Sub-Saharan Africa," 160.

59. [Great Britain] Commonwealth Relations Office, "Bechuanaland Protectorate," March 1950, Box 3, Sweeney Papers; "Notes Taken From: *Presentation of the Position Arising in the Political Crisis Occasioned by the Marriage of Seretse Khama to Ruth Williams in England,*" [n.d.], Box 2, Sweeney Papers; Ruth Khama, "Secret Courtship—Then Marriage," and idem, "My Baby—And the Future," undated newspaper clippings, Box 3, Sweeney Papers.

60. Willard Stanton (U.S. Consul General in Capetown) to Secretary of State, 5 July 1949, 848A.4016/7-549, *CSDCF, 1945–49,* 8; Stanton to Secretary of State, 12 July 1949, 848A.4016/7-1249, *CSDCF, 1945–49,* 8; "The Marriage of Seretse Khama," *Times Survey of the British Colonies,* [n.d.], newspaper clipping, Box 3, Sweeney Papers; Office of Strategic Services, Research and Analysis Branch, R & A No. 2532, "The Problem of the High Commission Territories in Southern Africa," 14 March 1947, Microform Collection, Record Group 59, National Archives; Spence, "South Africa and the Modern World," in Wilson and Thompson, *Oxford History of South Africa,* 496–97; Barber, *South Africa's Foreign Policy,* 108–15.

61. W. Stratton Anderson (Second Secretary of U.S. Embassy in London) to Secretary of State, 22 March 1949, 848A.4016/3-2249, *CSDCF, 1945–49,* 7; Winship to Secretary of State, 23 August 1949, 848A.4016/8-2349, *CSDCF, 1945–49,* 8; Morris Dembo, "South African Political and Economic Developments," 23 November 1949, enclosed in Winship to Secretary of State, 23 November 1949, 848A.00/11-2349, *CSDCF, 1945–49,* 4; Commonwealth Rela-

tions Office, "Bechuanaland Protectorate," March 1950, Box 3, Sweeney Papers; H. V. Hodson, "Seretse Khama and the Colour Bar," *Listener* (weekly publication of the BBC), 30 March 1950, newspaper clipping, Box 3, Sweeney Papers.

62. U.S. Embassy in Capetown to Department of State, 14 April 1950, 745A.00(W)/4-1450, *CSDCF, 1950–54,* 2; Barber, *South Africa's Foreign Policy,* 113.

63. Raymond A. Valliere, "South African Political and Economic Developments," 19 July 1949, enclosed in Winship to Secretary of State, 19 July 1949, 848A.00/7-1949, *CSDCF, 1945–49,* 4.

64. Holmes to Secretary of State, 9 March 1950, 745A.00/3-950, *CSDCF, 1950–54,* 1; "The Protectorates," editorial, *Times* (London), 15 April 1950, 7; Fritz Alfsen (U.S. Consul in Bristol) to Secretary of State, 12 November 1948, 848A.4016/11-1248, *CSDCF, 1945–49,* 7.

65. "Seretse Khama," editorial, *Crisis* 57 (April 1950): 239; Ovendale, *English-Speaking Alliance,* 261–62; memorandum of conversation of Bernard Connelly and Joseph Sweeney with W. A. W. Clark (Chief Assistant to British High Commissioner in Charge of Protectorate Affairs), 9 March 1950, Box 2, Sweeney Papers.

66. Policy Planning Staff, PPS/50, "Premises and Conclusions Relating to Peace and U.S. Security," 22 March 1949, *FRUS, 1949,* 1:270; Johnson to Acheson, 19 May 1949, *FRUS, 1949,* 1:301; memorandum by Arneson to Acheson, 6 August 1949, *FRUS, 1949,* 1:511; Acheson, *Present at the Creation,* 597.

67. CIA, "The Political Situation in the Union of South Africa," 31 January 1949, President's Secretary's File, Box 256, Truman Papers.

68. Houghton, *South African Economy,* 183–84; Ralph A. Boernstein (U.S. Consul in Port Elizabeth) to Winship, 25 March 1949, enclosed in Winship to Department of State, 29 March 1949, 848A.00/3-2949, *CSDCF, 1945–49,* 4; Winship to Acheson, 11 February 1949, *FRUS, 1949,* 6:1,802–3; Raymond A. Valliere, "South African Political and Economic Developments," 19 April 1949, enclosed in Winship to Secretary of State, 19 April 1949, 848A.00/4-1949, *CSDCF, 1945–49,* 4. Quotation is from James A. Farrell, Jr., memorandum to members of Board of Directors of National Foreign Trade Council, "South African Exchange and Trade Conditions," 21 January 1949, enclosed in Farrell to Thorp, 27 January 1949, 848A.51/1-2749, *CSDCF, 1945–49,* 10.

69. "Basic Policies of the Military Assistance Program," 7 February 1949, *FRUS, 1949,* 1:250–54.

70. Editorial note, *FRUS, 1949,* 1:398.

71. Memorandum for Secretary of Defense, 16 August 1949, File CD6-4-48, Office of the Administrative Secretary, Box 32, Record Group 330, National Archives; memorandum of conversation of Under Secretary of State with F. C. Erasmus, 17 August 1949, *CSDCF, 1945–49,* 14; memorandum of conversation of Webb with Erasmus and other South African officials, 17 August 1949, *FRUS, 1949,* 6:1,805–7; Thompson (Deputy Assistant Secretary of State for European Affairs) to Webb, 14 November 1949, 848A.20/11-1449, *CSDCF, 1945–49,* 6.

72. Policy paper approved by Foreign Assistance Correlation Committee, "Objectives of the Military Assistance Program," 25 May 1949, *FRUS, 1949,* 1:314–20.

73. Winship to Secretary of State, 27 September 1948, 848A.51/9-2748, *CSDCF, 1945–49,* 10; Department of State, memorandum of conversation, "Dollar

Exchange Problems of South Africa," 6 October 1948, Box 15, Office Files of the Assistant Secretary of State for Economic Affairs, Truman Library; John Porter (pseud.), "Will South Africa Go Fascist?" *Nation,* 6 November 1948, p. 517; Winship to Secretary of State, 19 August 1949, 848A.50/8-1949, *CSDCF, 1945–49,* 8.

74. Russell G. Smith (Executive Vice-President of Bank of America) to Acheson, 28 September 1949, 848A.51/9-2849, *CSDCF, 1945–49,* 10; Winship to Secretary of State, 14 October 1949, 848A.51/10-1449, *CSDCF, 1945–49,* 10; Winship to Secretary of State, 4 November 1948, 848A.51/11-449, *CSDCF, 1945–49,* 10.

75. Memorandum of conversation by Thorp (Assistant Secretary of State for Economic Affairs), 5 January 1949, *FRUS, 1949,* 6:1,799-802; Winship to Secretary of State, 31 March 1949, 848A.6359/3-3149, Record Group 59, National Archives; Hickerson to Webb, 16 May 1949, *FRUS, 1949,* 6:1,804.

76. Department of State, policy statement on South Africa, 1 November 1948, *FRUS, 1948,* 5:528–29; Willoughby to Brown, 20 December 1948, 848A.51/12–2048, *CSDCF, 1945–49,* 10.

77. Memorandum of conversation of Acheson and Andrews, 29 March 1949, Box 64, Acheson Papers, Truman Library. See also press statement by Erasmus, enclosed in Satterthwaite to Perkins, 19 August 1949, 848A.20/8-1949, *CSDCF, 1945–49,* 6.

78. U.S. Embassy in Pretoria to Secretary of State, 28 September 1949, 848A.20/9-2849, *CSDCF, 1945–49,* 14.

79. CIA, "Political Situation in the Union of South Africa"; McGregor to Secretary of State, 14 October 1949, 848A.00/10-1449, *CSDCF, 1945–49,* 4; Thomas Sancton, "South Africa's Dixiecrats," *Nation,* 28 May 1949, p. 602.

80. Raymond A. Valliere, "South African Political and Economic Developments," 1 February 1949, enclosed in Winship to Secretary of State, 1 February 1949, 848A.00/2-149, *CSDCF, 1945–49,* 4. See also John G. Erhardt to Department of State, 27 October 1950, 745A.00(W)/10-2750, *CSDCF, 1950–54,* 3.

81. Sydney Redecker (U.S. Consul General in Johannesburg) to Secretary of State, 30 September 1949, 848A.428/9-3049, *CSDCF, 1945–49,* 8; Acheson to Redecker, 13 October 1949, 848A.428/11-1349, *CSDCF, 1945–49,* 8.

82. D. D. Forsyth (South African Department of External Affairs) to Winship, 4 June 1949, enclosed in Winship to Secretary of State, 7 June 1949, 848A.111/6-749, *CSDCF, 1945–49,* 5; Acheson to U.S. Embassy in Pretoria, 8 August 1949, 848A.111/8-849, *CSDCF, 1945–49,* 5; Karis and Carter, *From Protest to Challenge* 4:168. On Yergan's personal political reversal—which seems to have been connected to his disappointment with the American Communist Party's rejection in 1945 of its wartime moderation and return to an emphasis on class conflict, as well as to his marriage that same year to a wealthy white physician who may have had a conservative influence on him—see Lynch, *Black American Radicals,* 35–37.

83. Rosenberg, "Origins of Overkill," 23–25; minutes of meeting of Policy Planning Staff on international control of atomic energy, 12 October 1949, *FRUS, 1949,* 1:191–92; minutes of Policy Planning Staff meeting, 3 November 1949, *FRUS, 1949,* 1:573; memorandum by Acheson, 20 December 1949, *FRUS, 1949,* 1:612. Senator Brien McMahon, the influential chairman of the Joint Congres-

sional Committee on Atomic Energy, reminded Secretary of Defense Johnson that the idea that "we may reach a point when we have 'enough bombs'" was simply "false." McMahon to Johnson, 14 July 1949, *FRUS, 1949*, 1:483–84.

84. Report to President by Special Committee of the NSC on Atomic Energy Policy with Respect to the United Kingdom and Canada, 2 March 1949, *FRUS, 1949*, 1:445–49. See also NSC staff draft report, "Measures Required to Achieve U.S. Objectives with Respect to the USSR," 30 March 1949, *FRUS, 1949*, 1:275.

85. Memorandum by Arneson for Acheson, 6 August 1949, *FRUS, 1949*, 1:509–11; Gustafson to Secretary of State, 30 November 1949, 848A.6359/11-3049, Record Group 59, National Archives; summary log of atomic energy work in Office of Under-Secretary of State, 1 February 1949–31 January 1950, *FRUS, 1949*, 1:626.

86. Arneson memorandum for Acheson, 6 August 1949, *FRUS, 1949*, 1:511. Quotation is from Acheson, memorandum of conversation with Francis Biddle, 3 May 1949, Box 64, Acheson Papers, Truman Library.

87. Winship to Secretary of State, 26 October 1949, 848A.00(W)/10-2649, *CSDCF, 1945–49*, 4.

88. Hickerson to Secretary of State, 11 March 1949, 848A.00/3-1149, *CSDCF, 1945–49*, 4.

89. Acheson to U.S. consular officer in charge, Durban, 13 December 1949, 848A.4016/10-1449, *CSDCF, 1945–49*, 14.

90. CIA, "Political Situation in the Union of South Africa."

91. Satterthwaite to Hickerson, 13 May 1949, 848A.00/5-1349, *CSDCF, 1945–49*, 4; Vandenbosch, *South Africa and the World*, 174–75.

92. Erasmus, press statement, enclosed in Satterthwaite to Perkins, 19 August 1949, 848A.20/8-1949, *CSDCF, 1945–49*, 6.

93. Connelly to Department of State, 16 January 1950, 745A.00(W)/1-1650, *CSDCF, 1950–54*, 2; McGregor to Secretary of State, 21 December 1949, 848A.4016/12-2149, *CSDCF, 1945–49*, 8; M. R. Sobukwe, address to graduating class at Fort Hare College, 21 October 1949, in Karis and Carter, *From Protest to Challenge* 2:331–36.

94. Davenport, *South Africa*, 78.

95. Winship to Secretary of State, 5 December 1949, 848A.413/12-549, *CSDCF, 1945–49*, 8; Winship to Secretary of State, 18 December 1949, 848A.4016/12-1849, *CSDCF, 1945–49*, 8; Connelly to Secretary of State, 29 December 1949, 848A.4016/2-2949, *CSDCF, 1945–49*, 8.

96. Quoted in Winship to Secretary of State, 20 December 1949, 848A.4016/12-2049, *CSDCF, 1945–49*, 8.

97. Winship to Secretary of State, 20 December 1949, 848A.4016/12-2049, *CSDCF, 1945–49*, 8; Lodge, *Black Politics in South Africa*, 26–28; Gerhart, *Black Power in South Africa*, 77; Edward Feit, *South Africa: The Dynamics of the African National Congress* (London: Oxford University Press, 1962), 2–5; JoAnne Cornwell, "The United States and South Africa: History, Civil Rights and the Legal and Cultural Vulnerability of Blacks," *Phylon* 47 (December 1986): 289.

98. Connelly to Secretary of State, 23 December 1949, 848A.00(W)/12-2349, *CSDCF, 1945–49*, 4.

99. Connelly to Department of State, 12 January 1950, 745A.00/1-1250, *CSDCF, 1950–54*, 1; Connelly to Department of State, 16 January 1950, 745A.00(W)/1-1650, *CSDCF, 1950–54*, 2.

100. Quoted in Connelly to Department of State, 12 January 1950, 745A.00/ 1-1250, *CSDCF, 1950–54,* 1.

Chapter 7

1. In this context of rising fears of communism abroad and pro-Soviet treason at home, Americans who worried about a nuclear arms race and promoted U.S.-Soviet discussions of banning further development of atomic weaponry were usually seen as either communists or communist sympathizers. See, for example, George Kennan's comments on the "Will We Have Peace?" handbill issued by the Milwaukee Branch of National Labor Conference for Peace at the entrance to a hall where Kennan was giving a speech, "Current Problems in the Conduct of Foreign Policy," Milwaukee, 5 May 1950, Box 2, Kennan Papers.

2. The text of the first draft of NSC-68 can be found in *FRUS, 1950,* 1:234–92. For an enlightening discussion of the conceptual framework of NSC-68, see John Lewis Gaddis, *Strategies of Containment: A Critical Appraisal of Postwar American National Security Policy* (New York: Oxford University Press, 1982), 89–126. On the origins of the Korean War and the importance of Korean, rather than Soviet, factors, see Bruce Cumings, *The Origins of the Korean War: Liberation and the Emergence of Separate Regimes, 1945–1947* (Princeton: Princeton University Press, 1981); and idem, *The Origins of the Korean War,* vol. 2, *The Roaring of the Cataract, 1947–1950* (Princeton: Princeton University Press, 1990). For a prominent Soviet specialist's dissent from the general American fears of a full-scale war with the Soviet Union, see George Kennan, "Is War with Russia Inevitable?" draft of an article for *Reader's Digest,* 21 February 1950, Box 2, Kennan Papers. On the political origins of the McCarran Act, see William R. Tanner and Robert Griffith, "Legislative Politics and 'McCarthyism': The Internal Security Act of 1950," in *The Specter: Original Essays on the Cold War and the Origins of McCarthyism,* ed. Griffith and Athan Theoharis (New York: New Viewpoints, 1974), 172–89.

3. For the ANC's own evaluation of the political significance of 1950 for Africans in the Union, see "Draft Report of the National Executive Committee of the ANC," submitted to ANC annual conference, 15–17 December 1950, in Karis and Carter, *From Protest to Challenge* 2:452–58.

4. For the American Ambassador in South Africa's summary of these crucial events of 1950 for U.S.-South African relations, see Erhardt to Department of State, 25 January 1951, 745A.00/1-2551, *CSDCF, 1950–54,* 1.

5. George C. McGhee, "United States' Interests in Africa," *Department of State Bulletin,* 19 June 1950, p. 1,000. McGhee's article was adapted from an address he made to a meeting of the Foreign Policy Association in Oklahoma City on 8 May 1950. See also policy paper prepared by Bureau of Near Eastern, South Asian, and African Affairs, "Future of Africa," 18 April 1950, *FRUS, 1950,* 5:1,524–25.

6. Paper prepared by Colonial Policy Review Sub-Committee of Committee on Problems of Dependent Areas, "United States Policy Toward Dependent Territories," 26 April 1950, *FRUS, 1952–54,* 3:1,083; draft of position paper from background book for colonial policy discussions with United Kingdom, France, and Belgium, 23 June 1950, *FRUS, 1950,* 2:443–44; U.S. delegate [Jessup] at tripartite preparatory meetings to Acheson, 4 May 1950, *FRUS, 1950,* 3:953.

7. U.S. delegation at tripartite preparatory meetings to Acheson, 3 May 1950, *FRUS, 1950*, 3:948–49; "Future of Africa," *FRUS, 1950*, 5:1,525.

8. Report prepared in Department of State, "Political and Economic Problems of Africa," [February 1950], *FRUS, 1950*, 5:1,504–5; "Regional Policy Statement," *FRUS, 1950*, 5:1,590; "United States Policy Toward Dependent Territories," *FRUS, 1952–54*, 3:1,089.

9. Background paper for use at East–West African Consular Conference, 1950, "United States Import Trade Opportunities," Box 5, Sumner Papers; McGhee, "United States Interests in Africa," 1,001–2; "Regional Policy Statement," *FRUS, 1950*, 5:1,589; "Future of Africa," *FRUS, 1950*, 5:1,525, 1,531–32; "Political and Economic Problems," *FRUS, 1950*, 5:1,505.

10. "Future of Africa," *FRUS, 1950*, 5:1,531; "Regional Policy Statement," *FRUS, 1950*, 5:1,588–89, 1,598; report of Subcommittee D, annex II, "U.S. Statement on Africa," *FRUS, 1950*, 3:1,098; Johnson to W. A. Harriman (U.S. Special Representative in Europe, ECA), 6 January 1950, Geographic File, 1951–1953, Box 51, Records of the U.S. Joint Chiefs of Staff, Record Group 218, National Archives; Johnson to Webb, 8 September 1950, Geographic File, 1951–1953, Box 51, Record Group 218, National Archives; Erhardt to Acheson, 22 November 1950, *FRUS, 1950*, 5:1,581; Erhardt to Acheson, 22 December 1950, *FRUS, 1950*, 5:1,584–85.

11. "Regional Policy Statement," 29 December 1950, *FRUS, 1950*, 5:1,589–93; report of Subcommittee D, annex II, *FRUS, 1950*, 3:1,097–98; paper prepared in Bureau of Near Eastern, South Asian, and African Affairs, "Regional Policy Statement," 29 December 1950, *FRUS, 1951*, 5:1,203; report of Subcommittee D to Foreign Ministers, "Item 7: The Colonial Question," 9 May 1950, *FRUS, 1950*, 3:1,095–97; "Future of Africa," *FRUS, 1950*, 5:1,525.

12. Department of State, Office of the Secretary, "Summary of Telegrams," 3 January 1950, Naval Aide Files, Box 22, Truman Papers; policy statement prepared in Department of State, "Belgium," 8 May 1950, *FRUS, 1950*, 3:1,348; "United States Policy Toward Dependent Territories," *FRUS, 1952–54*, 3:1,098.

13. Hickerson to certain American diplomatic officers, 9 August 1950, Box 13, Records of Office of Assistant Secretary and Under-Secretary of State Dean Acheson, 1941–48, 1950, Record Group 59, National Archives; agreed U.S./U.K. report, "Continued Consultation on and Co-ordination of Policy," 6 May 1950, *FRUS, 1950*, 3:1,072–74; Acheson (in London) to Acting Secretary of State, 14 May 1950, *FRUS, 1950*, 3:1,065; "Regional Policy Statement," *FRUS, 1950*, 5:1,591. This supposed reasonableness of the Europeans, the State Department believed, contrasted starkly with the impetuousness of the governments without administrative responsibility for colonial areas, who "tend to take extreme views on colonial questions." Department of State, Policy Information Committee, "Weekly Review," 16 August 1950, White House Central Files, Box 55, Truman Papers.

14. "Regional Policy Statement," *FRUS, 1950*, 5:1,592; "Regional Policy Statement," *FRUS, 1951*, 5:1,200.

15. The first quotation is from McGhee, "United States Interests in Africa," 1,000. The second two are from Department of State, Policy Information Committee, "Weekly Review," 21 June 1950, White House Central Files, Box 55, Truman Papers.

16. Memorandum by McGhee to Acheson and Rusk, 17 February 1950, *FRUS, 1950*, 5:1,511.

17. On ERP assistance, see, for example, "Lisbon Is Steadied by Marshall Plan," *New York Times,* 23 July 1950, p. 29. On NATO priorities affecting Africa, see policy statement prepared in Department of State, "Portugal," 20 October 1950, *FRUS, 1950,* 3:1,546; and supplement to policy statement on Portugal, 20 October 1950, *FRUS, 1950,* 3:1,547–48.

18. "Political and Economic Problems," *FRUS, 1950,* 5:1,508–9.

19. "United States Policy Toward Dependent Territories," *FRUS, 1952–54,* 3:1,097.

20. "Regional Policy Statement," *FRUS, 1950,* 5:1,598.

21. "The Walls Are Tumbling," *Christian Century,* 27 September 1950, p. 1,128.

22. "United States Policy Toward Dependent Territories," *FRUS, 1952–54,* 3:1,102.

23. Henderson to Secretary of State, 3 July 1950, 745A.00/7-350, *CSDCF, 1950–54,* 1.

24. Position paper prepared in Department of State for U.S. Delegation to U.N. General Assembly, "The Treatment of Indians in South Africa," 2 September 1950, *FRUS, 1950,* 2:561.

25. Austin to Acheson, 7 November 1950, and Acheson to Austin, 8 November 1950, *FRUS, 1950,* 2:562–64.

26. "The Treatment of Indians in South Africa," *FRUS, 1950,* 2:561.

27. Austin to Acheson, 29 November 1950, *FRUS, 1950,* 2:573–74.

28. Minutes of meeting of U.S. Delegation to U.N., 10 November 1950, *FRUS, 1950,* 2:564–69. On the issue of avoiding the use of a double standard for human rights violations, see also "The Shape of Things," *Nation,* 18 November 1950, pp. 449–50.

29. Perkins to Acheson, 6 December 1950, 745A.00/12-650, *CSDCF, 1950–54,* 1.

30. "Political and Economic Problems," *FRUS, 1950,* 5:1,506–7.

31. "United States' Policy Toward Dependent Territories," *FRUS, 1952–54,* 3:1,079–80; memorandum by McGhee to Acheson and Webb, "Summary of Conclusions and Recommendations Reached at Lourenco Marques Conference," 12 April 1950, *FRUS, 1950,* 5:1,516.

32. McGhee, "United States Interests in Africa," 1,000, 1,002–3.

33. Department of State, Policy Information Committee, "Weekly Review," 19 April 1950, White House Central Files, Box 55, Truman Papers. See also "Regional Policy Statement," *FRUS, 1950,* 5:1,587; and memorandum of conversation between various U.S. and U.K. officials, "Communism in Africa," 19 September 1950, *FRUS, 1950,* 5:1,552–53.

34. Policy statement prepared in Department of State, "Belgium," *FRUS, 1950,* 3:1,348. See also "Regional Policy Statement," *FRUS, 1950,* 5:1,590, 1,598.

35. "Future of Africa," *FRUS, 1950,* 5:1,530.

36. Memorandum by McGhee to Acheson and Rusk, 17 February 1950, *FRUS,* 5:1,510.

37. "Summary Record of Colonial Policy Talks with the United Kingdom," 5 July 1950, Box 13, Records of the Office of Assistant Secretary and Under-Secretary of State Dean Acheson, 1941–48, 1950, Record Group 59, National Archives; report of Subcommittee D, annex II, "U.S. Statement on Africa," *FRUS, 1950,* 3:1,097; "United States' Policy Toward Dependent Territories," *FRUS, 1952–54,* 3:1,078–79, 1,094.

38. For a revealing summary of how American policymakers thought of this choice in 1950 as a contrast between the "logic" of the Western industrial democracies and the "emotion" of the peoples of color in the Third World, see memorandum by James F. Green (Deputy Director of Office of U.N. Economic and Social Affairs) to David H. Popper (Principal Executive Officer of U.S. Delegation to General Assembly), 22 December 1950, *FRUS, 1950*, 2:577–82.

39. Michael Scott, "South Africa and South West Africa," *Crisis* 57 (February 1950): 91–93, 124–26; Kuper, "African Nationalism in South Africa," in Wilson and Thompson, *Oxford History of South Africa* 2:461; Gerhart, *Black Power in South Africa*, 16, 37–38.

40. "Basic Policy of Congress Youth League," manifesto issued by National Executive Committee of ANC Youth League, 1948, in Karis and Carter, *From Protest to Challenge* 2:328.

41. "Programme of Action," statement of policy adopted at ANC annual conference, 17 December 1949, in ibid., 2:337. See also the Rev. I. C. Duma, prayer delivered at annual conference of ANC Youth League, 15 December 1949, in ibid., 2:336–37; and Gerhart, *Black Power in South Africa*, 93–101.

42. M. R. Sobukwe, address to graduating class at Fort Hare College, 21 October 1949, in Karis and Carter, *From Protest to Challenge*, 2:334 (emphasis in original).

43. Gerhart, *Black Power in South Africa*, 60–67, 76, 107–19; Lodge, *Black Politics in South Africa*, 28–30. For a fascinating portrayal of white radicals, their connections with Africans, and their political courage in the face of increasing official harassment, see Nadine Gordimer, *Burger's Daughter* (London: Jonathan Cape, 1979).

44. U.S. Embassy in Capetown to Department of State, 14 April 1950, 745A.00(W)/4–1450, *CSDCF, 1950–54*, 2.

45. Feit, *South Africa*, 6–7, 61–65; Thompson, "Parting of the Ways," in Wilson and Thompson, *Oxford History of South Africa* 2:431–32.

46. Connelly to Department of State, 4 February 1950, 745A.00/2-450, *CSDCF, 1950–54*, 1.

47. Sydney B. Redecker to Department of State, 17 February 1950, 745A.00/2-1750, *CSDCF, 1950–54*, 1. See also "African Rioting Abates," *New York Times*, 17 February 1950, p. 12.

48. Redecker to Department of State, 17 February 1950, 745A.00/2-1750, *CSDCF, 1950–54*, 1.

49. Morris Dembo to Department of State, 7 February 1950, 745A.00/2-750, *CSDCF, 1950–54*, 1.

50. "Report of the Commission Appointed to Enquire into Acts of Violence Committed by Natives at Krugersdorp, Newlands, Randfontein and Newclare," 22 March 1950, Box 3, Sweeney Papers.

51. Redecker to Department of State, 17 February 1950, 745A.00/2-1750, *CSDCF, 1950–54*, 1; U.S. Embassy in Capetown to Department of State, 17 February 1950, 745A.00(W)/2-1750, *CSDCF, 1950–54*, 2. On crime in the black sections of Johannesburg, see Sampson, *Drum*, 96–98.

52. Joseph Sweeney, "Freedom Day Riots on the Rand, 1950," unpublished manuscript, p. 1, Box 3, Sweeney Papers.

53. Connelly to Department of State, 7 March 1950, 745A.00/3-750, *CSDCF, 1950–54*, 1.

54. Connelly to Department of State, 31 March 1950, 745A.00(W)/3-3150, *CSDCF, 1950–54*, 2; Lodge, *Black Politics in South Africa*, 33–34.

55. Connelly to Department of State, 2 May 1950, 745A.00/5-250, *CSDCF, 1950–54,* 1; Lodge, *Black Politics in South Africa,* 33.

56. U.S. Embassy in Capetown to Department of State, 28 April 1950, 745A.00(W)/4-2850, *CSDCF, 1950–54,* 2.

57. Sweeney, "Freedom Day Riots on the Rand, 1950," 4.

58. Connelly to Secretary of State, 28 April 1950, 745A.00 MAY DAY/4-2850, *CSDCF, 1950–54,* 2.

59. Sweeney, "Freedom Day Riots on the Rand, 1950," 4–8; Lodge, *Black Politics in South Africa,* 34.

60. Sweeney (for chargé d'affaires, Connelly) to Acheson, "May Day Riots on the Rand," 8 June 1950, *FRUS, 1950,* 5:1824–25.

61. U.S. Embassy in Capetown to Department of State, 12 May 1950, 745A.00(W)/5-1250, copy in White House Central Files, Box 37, Truman Papers; Sweeney, "Freedom Day Riots on the Rand, 1950," 6.

62. U.S. Embassy in Capetown to Department of State, 5 May 1950, 745A.00(W)/5-550, *CSDCF, 1950–54,* 2.

63. Sweeney to Acheson, "May Day Riots on the Rand," *FRUS, 1950,* 5:1,824–25; Lodge, *African Politics in South Africa,* 34.

64. U.S. Embassy in Capetown to Department of State, 5 May 1950, 745A.00(W)/5-550, *CSDCF, 1950–54,* 2. See also Redecker to Department of State, 8 May 1950, 745A.00 MAY DAY/5-850, *CSDCF, 1950–54,* 2. Four days before the May Day violence, American chargé d'affaires Bernard Connelly used intriguing (and telegraphic) language to describe the South African police preparations for demonstrations: "Seems certain this time government security forces fully alerted and will tolerate no nonsense." The apparent equation, even if unintended, of the struggle against apartheid with "nonsense" suggests the difficulty for comfortable white officials from a segregated society of identifying with a struggle for democracy being waged largely by impoverished Africans. See Connelly to Secretary of State, 28 April 1950, 745A.00 MAY DAY/4-2850, *CSDCF, 1950–54,* 2.

65. Quoted in Sweeney, "Freedom Day Riots on the Rand, 1950," 10–11.

66. Sweeney to Acheson, "May Day Riots on the Rand," *FRUS, 1950,* 5:1,825.

67. Sweeney, "Freedom Day Riots on the Rand, 1950," 14.

68. Quoted in ibid., 12.

69. Ibid., 14.

70. "Monday 26th June, National Day of Protest and Mourning," flyer issued by Natal Coordinating Committee, (n.d.), in Karis and Carter, *From Protest to Challenge* 2:448–49; "National Day of Protest and Mourning, Stay at Home on Monday, 26th June!" flyer issued by [Twelve Persons], 15 June 1950, in ibid., 2:449–50.

71. Jordan K. Ngubane, "Post-Mortem on a Tragedy," editorial, *Inkundla ya Bantu,* 20 May 1950, reprinted in Karis and Carter, *From Protest to Challenge* 2:441–42. See also the Rev. J. J. Skomolo to Prof. Z. K. Matthews, 16 June 1950, in ibid., 2:447–48.

72. Central Executive Committee of ANC Youth League (Transvaal), statement on National Day of Protest, 31 May 1950, in Karis and Carter, *From Protest to Challenge* 2:445–46.

73. Lodge, *Black Politics in South Africa,* 35.

74. Harold D. Robison to Department of State, 6 July 1950, 745A.00/7-650, *CSDCF, 1950–54,* 1.

75. Robison to Department of State, 21 June 1950, 745A.00/6-2150, *CSDCF, 1950–54,* 1; Connelly to Secretary of State, 27 June 1950, 745A.00/6-2750, *CSDCF, 1950–54,* 1.

76. "Draft Report of the National Executive Committee of the ANC," 15–17 December 1950, in Karis and Carter, *From Protest to Challenge* 2:456. See also U.S. Embassy in Capetown to Department of State, 2 June 1950, 745A.00(W)/6-250, *CSDCF, 1950–54,* 2.

77. U.S. Embassy in Capetown to Department of State, 30 June 1950, 745A.00(W)/6-3050, *CSDCF, 1950–54,* 2.

78. "Desire of Non-Europeans to Live in Peace and Harmony," *Friend* [Bloemfontein], 4 July 1950, newspaper clipping, Box 3, Sweeney Papers.

79. Sweeney to Department of State, 14 August 1950, 745A.00/8-1450, *CSDCF, 1950–54,* 1.

80. Erhardt to Acheson, 3 October 1950, *FRUS, 1950,* 5:1,835–36.

81. Sweeney to Department of State, 31 August 1950, 745A.00/8-3150, *CSDCF, 1950–54,* 1; Sweeney to Department of State, 5 September 1950, 745A.00/9-550, *CSDCF, 1950–54,* 1.

82. One indicator of this in late 1950 was the government's apparent interest in resurrecting the defunct Native Representative Council as a way to fend off some of the intense criticism of its racial policies. African opinion, however, had become far too radicalized by the end of 1950 to have any interest in accepting a consultative rather than a participatory role in the governing of the Union. See Sweeney to Department of State, 15 August 1950, 745A.00/8-1550, *CSDCF, 1950–54,* 1; and Erhardt to Department of State, 22 December 1950, 745A.00(W)/12-2250, *CSDCF, 1950–54,* 3.

83. Connelly to Department of State, 23 June 1950, 745A.00(W)/6-2350, *CSDCF, 1950–54,* 2.

84. Erhardt to Acheson, 3 October 1950, *FRUS, 1950,* 5:1,835–36 (emphasis in original).

85. Ibid.

86. Connelly to Department of State, 18 August 1950, 745A.00(W)/8-1150, *CSDCF, 1950–54,* 2. See also Connelly to Department of State, 8 September 1950, 745A.00(W)/9-850, *CSDCF, 1945–50,* 2.

87. Erhardt to Department of State, 25 January 1951, 745A.00/1-2551, *CSDCF, 1950–54,* 1.

88. "Draft Report of the National Executive Committee of the ANC," 15–17 December 1950, in Karis and Carter, *From Protest to Challenge* 2: 453.

89. Connelly to Department of State, 1 December 1950, 745A.00(W)/12-150, *CSDCF, 1950–54,* 3.

90. Sweeney to Department of State, 31 August 1950, 745A.00/8-3150, *CSDCF, 1950–54,* 1.

91. Department of State, Division of Research for Europe, Office of Intelligence Research, "Current Status of the Indian Problem in South Africa," 2 August 1950, *OSS/SD, Africa,* 10; Redecker to Department of State, 15 September 1950, 745A.00/9-1550, *CSDCF, 1950–54,* 1; Erhardt to Department of State, 25 January 1951, 745A.00/1-2551, *CSDCF, 1950–54,* 1; Kuper, "African Nationalism in South Africa," in Wilson and Thompson, *Oxford History of South Africa* 2:459.

92. U.S. Embassy in Capetown, 28 April 1950, 745A.00(W)/4-2850, *CSDCF, 1950–54,* 2; Redecker to Department of State, 15 September 1950,

745A.00/9-1550, *CSDCF, 1950–54,* 1; Noer, *Cold War and Black Liberation,* 30–31.

93. Redecker to Department of State, 15 September 1950, 745A.00/9-1550, *CSDCF, 1950–54,* 1. See also "A 'British Dominion,' " editorial, *Die Volksblad,* in "Summary of the Afrikaans Press," 10 June 1952, Box 2, Sweeney Papers.

94. Quoted in Connelly to Department of State, 21 April 1950, 745A.00(W)/4-2150, *CSDCF, 1950–54,* 2.

95. "Current Status of the Indian Problem in South Africa," *OSS/SD, Africa,* 10.

96. Sweeney to Acheson, "May Day Riots on the Rand," *FRUS, 1950,* 1,825–26.

97. U.S. Embassy in Capetown to Department of State, 28 April 1950, 745A.00(W)/4-2850, *CSDCF, 1950–54,* 2.

98. Spence, "South Africa and the Modern World," in Wilson and Thompson, *Oxford History of South Africa* 2:512; Davenport, *South Africa,* 362–63.

99. "Jim Crow to the Hilt," *New Republic,* 12 June 1950, p. 8.

100. Villard to Department of State, 7 July 1950, 745A.00/7-750, *CSDCF, 1950–54,* 1.

101. "Act to Declare the Communist Party of South Africa to Be an Unlawful Organization," 26 June 1950, Box 4, Sweeney Papers. See also Kuper, "African Nationalism in South Africa," in Wilson and Thompson, *Oxford History of South Africa,* 2:459–60. By the latter half of this definition, one could argue that apartheid itself qualified as "Communism."

102. Connelly to Department of State, 9 June 1950, 745A.00(W)/6-950, *CSDCF, 1950–54,* 2.

103. Sweeney to Acheson, "May Day Riots on the Rand," *FRUS, 1950,* 5:1,825–26. See also Davenport, *South Africa,* 368–69.

104. Barber, *South Africa's Foreign Policy,* 53–54.

105. Connelly to Acheson, 27 June 1950, *FRUS, 1950,* 5:1,827–28; Davidson, *Report on Southern Africa,* 161. Brazilian archbishop Helder Camara expressed the dilemma of people working for social justice in a strongly anticommunist culture: "When I feed the poor, I am called a saint. When I ask why they are poor, I am called a communist." Quoted in Colman McCarthy, "From the Eye of the Storm: Jesuits and the Military," *Other Side* 26, no. 2 (March–April 1990), 55.

106. Sweeney to Acheson, "May Day Riots on the Rand," *FRUS, 1950,* 5:1,826.

107. Connelly to Department of State, 16 June 1950, 745A.00(W)/6-1650, *CSDCF, 1950–54,* 2.

108. The acting head of the U.S. Embassy at the time, Bernard Connelly, reported to Washington before the vote that "a measure of South African contrasts is that slightly over 20,000 white South West Africans will elect twice the number of MP's provided for the eight and a half million Natives in the Union." Connelly to Department of State, 14 July 1950, 745A.00(W)/7-1450, *CSDCF, 1950–54,* 2.

109. Redecker to Department of State, 15 September 1950, 745A.00/9-1550, *CSDCF, 1950–54,* 1.

110. R. K. Cope, "The New Scramble for Africa," *Nation,* 20 May 1950, pp. 472–73; Ovendale, *English-Speaking Alliance,* 266.

111. Position paper prepared by State-Defense Military Information Con-

trol Committee, 10 January 1950, *FRUS, 1950,* 3:1,606; documents relating to exchange of classified military information between United States and United Kingdom, Document C, "Policy with Respect to Commonwealth Nations," 27 January 1950, *FRUS, 1950,* 3:1,621.

112. "U.S./U.K. Discussions on Present World Situation," 25 July 1950, *FRUS, 1950,* 3:1,664.

113. Connelly to Department of State, 1 September 1950, 745A.00(W)/9-150, *CSDCF, 1950–54,* 2.

114. Erhardt to Department of State, 25 January 1951, 745A.00/1-2551, *CSDCF, 1950–54,* 1; K. L. Little, letter to the editor, *Times* (London), 7 August 1950, newspaper clipping, Box 5, Sweeney Papers; Ovendale, *English-Speaking Alliance,* 262.

115. See, for example, Connelly to Department of State, 29 November 1950, 745A.00/11–2950, *CSDCF, 1950–54,* 1.

116. Redecker to Department of State, 15 September 1950, 745A.00/9-1550, *CSDCF, 1950–54,* 1.

117. Sweeney to Department of State, 12 September 1950, 745A.00/9-1250, *CSDCF, 1950–54,* 1.

118. Erhardt to Department of State, 13 December 1950, 745A.00/12-1350, *CSDCF, 1950–54,* 1.

119. U.S. Embassy in Pretoria to Department of State, 15 September 1950, 745A.00(W)/9-1550, *CSDCF, 1950–54,* 2.

120. Sweeney, "South Africa, 1950–52," Box 5, Sweeney Papers.

121. G. H. Archambault, "Smuts Dies at 80 on African Farm," *New York Times,* 12 September 1950, newspaper clipping, Box 5, Sweeney Papers; "Foreign News: South Africa," *Time,* 18 September 1950, p. 35.

122. Sweeney to Department of State, 20 October 1950, 745A.00(W)/10-2050, *CSDCF, 1950–54,* 3; Sweeney, "South Africa, 1950–52," Box 5, Sweeney Papers.

123. Quoted in Barber, *South Africa's Foreign Policy,* 137. See also Davenport, *South Africa,* 371–77.

124. U.S. Embassy in Pretoria, 15 September 1950, 745A.00(W)/9-1550, *CSDCF, 1950–54,* 2.

125. White to Truman, 3 May 1950, President's Personal Files: NAACP, Box 393, Truman Papers.

126. Memorandum of conversation (by Bernard Connelly) between Malan and McGhee, 6 March 1950, *FRUS, 1950,* 5:1,817.

127. McGhee, *Envoy to the Middle World,* 143–44.

128. Sweeney, "South Africa, 1950–52," Box 5, Sweeney Papers.

129. Redecker to Department of State, 15 September 1950, 745A.00/9-1550, *CSDCF, 1950–54,* 1.

130. Sweeney, "South Africa: 1950–52," Box 5, Sweeney Papers.

131. U.S. Embassy in Capetown to Department of State, 28 April 1950, 745A.00(W)/4-2850, *CSDCF, 1950–54,* 2; U.S. Embassy in Capetown to Department of State, 5 May 1950, 745A.00(W)/5-550, *CSDCF, 1950–54,* 2; U.S. Embassy in Capetown to Department of State, 12 May 1950, 745A.00(W)/5-1250, *CSDCF, 1950–54,* 2.

132. Sweeney, "South Africa: 1950–52," Box 5, Sweeney Papers.

133. Winship to Secretary of State, 27 June 1949, 848A.00(W)/6-2749, *CSDCF, 1945–49,* 4.

134. U.S. Embassy in Capetown to Department of State, 12 May 1950, 745A.00(W)/5-1250, *CSDCF, 1950–54,* 2.

135. "South African Nationalism," *Crisis* 58 (January 1951): 35; "Foreign News: South Africa," *Time,* 5 June 1950, p. 28; "Foreign News: South Africa," ibid., 18 September 1950, p. 35.

136. Connelly to Department of State, 9 June 1950, 745A.00(W)/6-950, *CSDCF, 1950–54,* 2.

137. Noer, *Cold War and Black Liberation,* 28–29.

138. Connelly to Department of State, 30 June 1950, 745A.00(W)/6-3050, *CSDCF, 1950–54,* 2; Connelly to Department of State, 7 July 1950, 745A.00(W)/7-750, *CSDCF, 1950–54,* 2.

139. Memorandum of conversation of Acheson and G. P. Jooste (South African Ambassador in United States), 3 July 1950, Box 65, Acheson Papers, Truman Library; memorandum of conversation of Acheson and Jooste, 24 July 1950, Box 65, Acheson Papers, Truman Library.

140. Connelly to Department of State, 11 August 1950, 745A.00(W)/8-1150, *CSDCF, 1950–54,* 2; Minter, *King Solomon's Mines Revisited,* 135.

141. Conversation of Erhardt and Malan, *FRUS, 1950,* 5:1,831; Noer, *Cold War and Black Liberation,* 27–28. The South African airmen may have been fighting against communism and with the West, but it seems unlikely that they were risking their lives for the benefit of South Koreans, who in the Union would have been segregated and disenfranchised.

142. Gerald R. Gill, "Afro-American Opposition to the United States' Wars of the Twentieth Century: Dissent, Discontent, and Disinterest" (Ph.D. diss., Howard University, 1985), 68–88, 570; Alonzo Hamby, *Beyond the New Deal: Harry S Truman and American Liberalism* (New York: Columbia University Press, 1973), 441–46.

143. Acheson, *Present at the Creation,* 379.

144. Kennan, draft of letter to Harry H. Harper, Jr., 27 September 1950, Box 26, Kennan Papers.

145. Position paper prepared in Department of State for U.S. Delegation to U.N. General Assembly, "Question of South West Africa: Advisory Opinion of the International Court of Justice," 4 September 1950, *FRUS, 1950,* 2:481–84.

146. Acheson to U.S. Embassy in United Kingdom, 8 August 1950, *FRUS, 1950,* 2:475–76; Douglas (U.S. Ambassador in United Kingdom) to Acheson, 9 August 1950, *FRUS, 1950,* 2:476; Douglas to Acheson, 14 August 1950, *FRUS, 1950,* 2:480; Austin to Acheson, 12 December 1950, *FRUS, 1950,* 2:507–8.

147. Acheson to Henderson (U.S. Ambassador in India), 8 September 1950, *FRUS, 1950,* 2:63–65; minutes of meeting of U.S. Delegation to U.N. General Assembly, 27 September 1950, *FRUS, 1950,* 2:72–74; Austin to Acheson, 29 September 1950, *FRUS, 1950,* 2:74–75.

148. Memorandum of conversation between McGhee and Forsyth, 7 March 1950, *FRUS, 1950,* 5:1,820.

149. Sweeney, "South Africa: 1950–52," Box 5, Sweeney Papers.

150. *Public Papers of the Presidents of the United States: Harry S Truman, 1950* (Washington, 1965), 741.

151. Ibid., 746–47.

152. NSC 100, "Recommended Policies and Actions in Light of the Grave World Situation," 11 January 1951, *FRUS, 1951,* 1:7.

153. Vandenberg to Acheson, 15 January 1951, Box 3, Vandenberg Papers.

154. Trachtenberg, "A 'Wasting Asset,' " *International Security* 13 (Winter 1988/89): 16, 27–28; Gaddis, *Strategies of Containment,* 112–13.

155. Rosenberg, "Origins of Overkill," 23–25; Hewlett and Duncan, *Atomic Shield,* 674.

156. C. Savage, "Increase in Production of Fissionable Material," 26 September 1950, Box 6, Records of the Policy Planning Staff, Record Group 59, National Archives, quoted in Trachtenberg, "A 'Wasting Asset,' " 29.

157. Acheson to certain diplomatic missions, 23 December 1950, *FRUS, 1950,* 1:597–98.

158. *Public Papers of the Presidents of the United States: Harry S Truman, 1951* (Washington, 1965), 8.

159. Policy statement prepared in Department of State, "Belgium," 8 May 1950, *FRUS, 1950,* 3:1,347–52.

160. Paul Van Zeeland (Belgian Foreign Minister) to Acheson, 17 February 1950, *FRUS, 1950,* 1:528; "Note Verbale" from Belgian Embassy to Department of State, 29 September 1949, *FRUS, 1949,* 1:545–47; "Outline Economic Survey of the Belgian Congo," 5 September 1950, Box 5, Sumner Papers.

161. Arneson to Acheson, 14 December 1950, *FRUS, 1950,* 1:594–96.

162. Editorial footnote, *FRUS, 1950,* 1:590.

163. The Associated Press got wind of this possibility and sent one of its London correspondents to South Africa in April to investigate. Bernard Connelly, the acting head of the U.S. Embassy, pleaded ignorance of any plans for such an arrangement. Connelly to Shullaw, 27 April 1950, 745A.00/4–2750, *CSDCF, 1950–54,* 1.

164. Johnson to Acheson, 13 March 1950, Box 55, Office of Administrative Secretary, Record Group 330, National Archives; Acheson to Johnson, 3 April 1950, *FRUS, 1950,* 1:546–47; Hewlett and Duncan, *Atomic Shield,* 426.

165. Memorandum prepared for U.S. members of Combined Policy Committee, "South African Negotiations," 18 April 1950, *FRUS, 1950,* 1:551–52; F. W. Marten (First Secretary in British Embassy) to Arneson, 18 October 1950, *FRUS, 1950,* 1:589; Arneson to Marten, 4 December 1950, *FRUS, 1950,* 1:591–92; memorandum of conversation of Acheson with Dr. T. E. Donges (South African Minister of the Interior), 8 December 1950, Box 65, Acheson Papers, Truman Library.

166. Robert LeBaron to Marshall (Secretary of Defense), 4 October 1950, Box 182, Office of the Administrative Secretary, Record Group 330, National Archives; Webb to Erhardt, 2 October 1950, *FRUS, 1950,* 1:587–88.

167. Quoted in Erhardt to Department of State, 19 December 1950, 845A.2546/12-1950, Record Group 59, National Archives. See also Connelly to Department of State, 5 January 1951, 745A.00(W)/1-551, *CSDCF, 1950–54,* 3.

168. Redecker to Department of State, "Conclusion of Financial Agreement for Uranium Production in South Africa," 19 April 1951, *FRUS, 1951,* 5:1442–44.

169. Erhardt to Secretary of State, 25 January 1951, 745A.00/1-2551, *CSDCF, 1950–54,* 1.

170. Perkins (Assistant Secretary of State for European Affairs) to Acheson,

2 October 1950, *FRUS, 1950,* 5:1,832–33. See also General L. L. Lemnitzer to Secretary of Defense, 5 October 1950, Box 182, Office of the Administrative Secretary, Record Group 330, National Archives.

171. Memorandum by Acheson of conversation with Erasmus and other South African officials, 5 October 1950, *FRUS, 1950,* 5:1,837–39; Perkins to Acheson, 2 October 1950, *FRUS, 1950,* 5:1,832–34.

172. Memorandum of conversation between Marshall and Erasmus, 5 October 1950, *FRUS, 1950,* 5:1,840–41; Colonel K. R. Kreps (Office of Secretary of Defense) to Joint Chiefs of Staff, 1 November 1950, Box 175, Office of Administrative Secretary, Record Group 330, National Archives; W. G. Labor (for Joint Chiefs of Staff) to Secretary of Defense, 15 November 1950, Box 182, Office of Administrative Secretary, Record Group 330, National Archives.

173. CIA, "South African Politics and U.S. Security," 17 November 1950, President's Secretary's File, Box 250, Truman Papers; Erasmus to Johnson, 15 June 1950, Box 182, Office of Administrative Secretary, Record Group 330, National Archives; Walter S. Gifford (U.S. Ambassador in United Kingdom) to Department of State, 21 March 1951, *FRUS, 1951,* 5:1,431.

174. Acheson to Jooste, 5 February 1951, *FRUS, 1951,* 5:1,429–31.

175. Record of meeting no. 169 of National Advisory Council on International Monetary and Financial Problems, "Proposed International Bank Loans to South Africa," 28 December 1950, *FRUS, 1950,* 5:1,844–45.

176. Department of State, policy statement, "Union of South Africa," 28 March 1951, *FRUS, 1951,* 5:1,439; U.S. Department of Commerce, *Investment in Union of South Africa,* 68; "The Shape of Things," *Nation,* 3 February 1951, p. 98; Hunton, "Postscript," in *Resistance Against Fascist Enslavement,* 61.

177. Redecker to Department of State, 19 April 1951, *FRUS, 1951,* 5:1,445–46.

178. CIA, "South African Politics and U.S. Security."

Chapter 8

1. Department of State, Office of Intelligence Research, "The South African Constitutional Crisis," 2 July 1952, *OSS/SD, Africa,* 10; "United Party Does Not Want Colored People at Its Meetings," *Die Burger* (Capetown), 5 May 1952, in "The Afrikaans Press," 7 May 1952, Box 2, Sweeney Papers; Davenport, *South Africa,* 363–64.

2. Sweeney, "South Africa: 1950–52," Box 5, Sweeney Papers; Connelly to Department of State, 18 May 1951, 745A.00(W)/5-1851, *CSDCF, 1950–54,* 3; David A. Robertson (First Secretary of U.S. Embassy in Pretoria) to Department of State, 2 June 1952, 745A.00/6–252, *CSDCF, 1950–54,* 1; "The Shape of Things," *Nation,* 16 June 1951, p. 551.

3. Erhardt to Department of State, 7 February 1951, 745A.00/2-751, *CSDCF, 1950–54,* 1.

4. The ominous direction of Nationalist Party political development was suggested in the parliamentary debates on amendments to the Suppression of Communism Act. A leading Nationalist anti-Semite declared that clergymen preaching the Christian doctrine of the equality of all people were encouraging communism and should be prevented from doing so. When Harry Lawrence, a United Party representative and the former Minister of Justice in the last Smuts government, objected, a Nationalist back-bencher yelled raucously, "In ten years

you'll be hanged!" R. K. Cope, "South Africa: Racist Cauldron," *Nation*, 14 July 1951, p. 32.

5. Connelly to Department of State, 20 June 1951, 745A.00/6-2051, *CSDCF, 1950–54,* 1; Connelly to Department of State, 8 June 1951, 745A.00/6-851, *CSDCF, 1950–54,* 1.

6. Connelly to Department of State, 10 August 1951, 745A.00/8-1051, *CSDCF, 1950–54,* 1.

7. Connelly to Department of State, 4 September 1951, 745A.00/9-451, *CSDCF, 1950–54,* 1; Sweeney to Department of State, 20 September 1951, 745A.00/9-2051, *CSDCF, 1950–54,* 1; Sweeney to Department of State, 2 November 1951, 745A.00/11-251, *CSDCF, 1950–54,* 1.

8. Sweeney to Department of State, 5 October 1951, 745A.00/10-551, *CSDCF, 1950–54,* 1.

9. John A. Birch (commercial attaché to U.S. Embassy) to Department of State, 29 February 1952, 745A.00(W)/2-2952, *CSDCF, 1950–54,* 3.

10. Basil Davidson, "Africa: Emergent Colossus," *Nation*, 8 September 1951, pp. 187–89; Sampson, *Drum*, 20–22.

11. Gallman to Department of State, 9 November 1951, *FRUS, 1951,* 5:1,460–62.

12. Morris Dembo to Department of State, 2 August 1951, *FRUS, 1951,* 5:1,448–49.

13. Department of State, Division of Research for Western Europe, Office of Intelligence Research, "The South African Indian Problem, 1950–51," 6 September 1951, *OSS/SD, Africa*, 10; Lodge, *Black Politics in South Africa*, 40–43; Sampson, *Drum*, 129–32. On traditional Colored arrogance toward Africans in what he called the "pigmentocracy" of South Africa, see Sampson, *Drum*, 198–212.

14. Gallman to Department of State, 21 March 1952, *FRUS, 1952–54,* 11:905–6; Sweeney to Department of State, 26 March 1952, 745A.00/3-2652, *CSDCF, 1950–54,* 1; Robertson to Department of State, 29 April 1952, 745A.00/4-2952, *CSDCF, 1950–54,* 1.

15. Robertson to Department of State, 15 May 1952, 745A.001/5-1552, *CSDCF, 1950–54,* 1; Gallman to Secretary of State, 26 May 1952, 745A.00/5-2652, *CSDCF, 1950–54,* 1.

16. Parsons to Department of State, 28 May 1952, 745A.00/5-2852, *CSDCF, 1950–54,* 1.

17. Parsons to Secretary of State, 26 May 1952, 745A.00/5-2652, *CSDCF, 1950–54,* 1; Robertson to Department of State, 6 June 1952, 745A.00/6-652, *CSDCF, 1950–54,* 1; Seddicum to Secretary of State, 7 June 1952, 745A.00/6-752, *CSDCF, 1950–54,* 1.

18. "Strauss Attempts Appeasement," *Die Burger* (Capetown), 17 May 1952, in "Summary of Afrikaans Press," 23 May 1952, Box 2, Sweeney Papers; Gallman to Department of State, 23 May 1952, 645A.00/5-2352, *CSDCF, 1950–54,* 23.

19. Perkins to Acheson, 11 June 1952, 745A.00/6-1152, *CSDCF, 1950–54,* 1.

20. Quoted in Henri La Tendresse (attaché to U.S. Embassy in Pretoria) to Department of State, 2 April 1952, 745A.00/4-252, *CSDCF, 1950–54,* 1.

21. Thompson, "Parting of the Ways," in Gifford and Louis, *Transfer of Power*, 430–31.

22. Sampson, *Drum*, 159–60.

23. "Dangers of the Apartheid Policy: African Writers' Exposition of the Apartheid Policy from the Africans' Own Stand Point," undated pamphlet (c. 1950), Box 2, Sweeney Papers; Birch to Department of State, 7 March 1952, 745A.00(W)/3-752, *CSDCF, 1950–54,* 3; John Hatch, "South African Racial Patterns," *Crisis* 59 (January 1952): 11–14; Sampson, *Drum,* 52, 99, 175–97; Davidson, *Report on Southern Africa,* 93–94, 100–101, 105–6, 268.

24. Gallman to Secretary of State, 7 April 1952, 745A.00/4-752, *CSDCF, 1950–54,* 1.

25. Dr. J. S. Moroka, address at Johannesburg, 6 April 1952, Box 2, Sweeney Papers.

26. Gallman to Secretary of State, 11 September 1952, 745A.00/9-1152, *CSDCF, 1950–54,* 1; Robison to Department of State, 4 August 1952, 745A.00/8-452, *CSDCF, 1950–54,* 1; Lodge, *Black Politics in South Africa,* 43–45; Karis and Carter, *From Protest to Challenge,* vol. 4, *Political Profiles, 1882–1964,* by Gail M. Gerhart and Thomas Karis (Stanford: Hoover Institution Press, 1977), 72–73, 143–45.

27. Robison to Department of State, 20 October 1952, 745A.00/10–2052, *CSDCF, 1950–54,* 1; Robison to Department of State, 27 October 1952, 745A.00/10-2752, *CSDCF, 1950–54,* 1; Robertson to Secretary of State, 4 November 1952, 745A.00/11-452, *CSDCF , 1950–54,* 1.

28. Robertson to Secretary of State, 10 November 1952, 745A.00/11-1052, *CSDCF, 1950–54,* 1; Robison to Department of State, 12 November 1952, 745A.00/11-1252, *CSDCF, 1950–54,* 2; Lodge, *Black Politics in South Africa,* 59–60.

29. Robertson to Department of State, 25 November 1952, 745A.00/11-2552, *CSDCF, 1950–54,* 1.

30. La Tendresse to Department of State, 12 November 1952, 745A.00/11-1252, *CSDCF, 1950–54,* 1; Robertson to Secretary of State, 12 November 1952, 745A.00/11-1252, *CSDCF, 1950–54,* 1; La Tendresse to Department of State, 18 November 1952, 745A.00/11-1852, *CSDCF, 1950–54,* 1.

31. La Tendresse to Department of State, 21 November 1952, 745A.00/11-2152, *CSDCF, 1950–54,* 1.

32. Harry S. Warner, "South Africa: Who Provoked the Riots?" *Nation,* 21 February 1953, pp. 167–69.

33. Luthuli, *Let My People Go,* 126–27.

34. "The Shape of Things," *Nation,* 22 November 1952, p. 459.

35. Houser, *No One Can Stop the Rain,* 18; Sampson, *Drum,* 136–38.

36. Quoted in Sampson, *Drum,* 168–69. The response of one of the ministers in Malan's government was telling: "In the middle ages people like Michael Scott and Huddleston would have been burned at the stake." Quoted in ibid., 169.

37. Luthuli, *Let My People Go,* 128–29; Sampson, *Drum,* 135, 138.

38. Basil Davidson, "Eyewitness: South African Racism," *Nation,* 27 June 1953, pp. 538–40; Houser, *No One Can Stop the Rain,* 18–19; Sampson, *Drum,* 140–41.

39. U.S. Embassy in Pretoria to Department of State, 20 May 1953, 745A.00/5-2053, *CSDCF, 1950–54,* 2; Gerhart, *Black Power in South Africa,* 89; Luthuli, *Let My People Go,* 125, 130; Sampson, *Drum,* 133–34.

40. Parsons to Department of State, 25 February 1953, 745A.00/2-2553, *CSDCF, 1950–54,* 2.

41. "Defiance of Malan Over 'Unjust' Laws Set in South Africa," *New York*

Times, 7 April 1952, p. 1; Houser, *No One Can Stop the Rain,* 10–17; Sampson, *Drum,* 138.

42. Acheson to U.S. Embassy in Pretoria, 13 January 1953, 745A.00/1-1353, *CSDCF, 1950–54,* 2; Sappington to Department of State, 27 January 1953, 745A.00/1-2753, *CSDCF, 1950–54,* 2.

43. Gallman to Department of State, 24 February 1953, *FRUS, 1952–54,* 11:983–85.

44. "No Easy Walk to Freedom," presidential address by Nelson Mandela, Transvaal branch of ANC, 21 September 1953, in Karis and Carter, *From Protest to Challenge* 3:114. See also presidential address by Chief Albert J. Lutuli at ANC annual conference of 18–20 December 1953, in ibid., 3:124–25.

45. Pamphlet distributed at United Party rally in Bredasdorp, 21 February 1953, enclosed in Johnson to Department of State, 26 February 1953, 745A.00/2-2653, *CSDCF, 1950–54,* 2; Johnson to Department of State, 25 March 1953, 745A.00/3-2553, *CSDCF, 1950–54,* 2; Gallman to Department of State, 9 April 1953, 745A.00/4-953, *CSDCF, 1950–54,* 2; "The Shape of Things," *Nation,* 25 April 1953, p. 339.

46. Rotberg, *Rise of Nationalism in Central Africa,* 236–52; Gifford, "Misconceived Dominion," in Gifford and Louis, *Transfer of Power,* 387–89, 394–400.

47. Mallon (U.S. Consul General at Leopoldville) to Department of State, 19 January 1953, *FRUS, 1952–54,* 11:30–37; "Countering Dr. Malan," *Economist,* 21 April 1951, p. 932.

48. Draft memorandum prepared in Office of Dependent Area Affairs and in Office of U.N. Political and Security Affairs, 8 May 1952, *FRUS, 1952–54,* 3:1,111–15.

49. Memorandum by Ridgway B. Knight (Acting Deputy Director of Office of Western European Affairs), 21 April 1952, *FRUS, 1952–54,* 3:1,104–5; and memorandum prepared by Knight and William Nunley (Office of European Regional Affairs), 9 April 1952, *FRUS, 1952–54,* 1:501.

50. Knight memorandum, *FRUS, 1952–54,* 3:1,104.

51. Draft memorandum, *FRUS, 1952–54,* 3:1,114.

52. Key Data Book prepared by Reporting Unit of National Security Council for the President, enclosed in Lay to Truman, 5 November 1952, *FRUS, 1952–54,* 178–79. See also Francis B. Sayre, "Problems Facing Underdeveloped Areas in Asia and Africa," *Department of State Bulletin,* 21 April 1952, pp. 623–24.

53. Henry A. Byroade, address to World Affairs Council of Northern California at Asilomar, California, 31 October 1953, *FRUS, 1952–54,* 11:56–59.

54. Memorandum of telephone conversation of Acheson with Senator Green, 25 March 1952, Box 67, Acheson Papers, Truman Library. See also Central Intelligence Agency, NIE-69, "Probable Developments in North Africa," 12 September 1952, President's Secretary's File, Box 254, Truman Papers.

55. Knight memorandum, *FRUS, 1952–54,* 3:1,105; memorandum by William Sanders to Hickerson (Assistant Secretary of State for U.N. Affairs), 7 December 1951, *FRUS, 1951,* 2:653.

56. Truman, *Memoirs,* 2:236.

57. McGhee to Edward R. Dudley (U.S. Ambassador in Liberia), 8 November 1951, *FRUS, 1951,* 5:1,234–35; memorandum prepared in Management Staff, "Reorganization of the Point Four Program," 24 November 1951, *FRUS, 1951,* 1:1,663; Basil Davidson, "Cashing In on Old Imperialisms," *Nation,* 13 September 1952, pp. 209–10.

58. Davidson, "Africa: Emergent Colossus," *Nation*, 8 September 1951, p. 187.

59. National Security Council, NSC 110, "Proposed Transfer of the Point IV Program from the Department of State to the Economic Cooperation Administration," 22 May 1951, Record Group 273, National Archives; memorandum prepared in Department of State, [14 September 1951], *FRUS, 1951*, 5:1,232–33.

60. McGhee to Dudley, 8 November 1951, *FRUS, 1951*, 5:1,234–36; memorandum by Nicholas Feld (Officer in Charge of West, Central, and East African Affairs) to Working Group on Colonial Problems, 26 August 1952, *FRUS, 1952–54*, 3:1,147. By contrast, the private Ford Foundation began to increase its spending on development projects in sub-Saharan Africa in this period out of an interest in neutralizing the anti-Western sentiments that it realized colonial peoples were expressing with growing frequency. Memorandum of conversation by Nicholas Feld, 20 February 1952, *FRUS, 1952–54*, 11:1–3.

61. "Africa Awakes," editorial, *Crisis* 59 (November 1952): 578–79.

62. *New York Times*, 21 December 1952, sec. 4, p. 3.

63. Edward T. Dickinson (Vice-Chairman of National Security Resources Board), "A Report on Strategic Ports of West Africa," March 1952, President's Secretary's File, "HSTL staff 27-4-1," Oversize File, Truman Papers; W. B. Thorp (Director of Office of Foreign Economic and Defense Affairs) to Secretary of Joint Chiefs of Staff, 7 November 1952, File CD-500 1952, Box 388, Office of Administrative Secretary, Record Group 330, National Archives.

64. State Department, Office of Intelligence Research, Intelligence Report, "Prospects for African Political Stability in the Event of an Early East–West War," 19 October 1951, *OSS/SD, Africa*, 4.

65. Memorandum of conversation by John W. McBride (Office of African Affairs), "African Economic Development," 21 August 1952, *FRUS, 1952–54*, 11:25.

66. George C. McGhee, "Africa's Role in the Free World Today," *Department of State Bulletin*, 16 July 1951, pp. 97–101; memorandum of conversation by David E. Longanecker (Office of African Affairs), 3 December 1952, *FRUS, 1952–54*, 11:27–28; Davidson, *Report on Southern Africa*, 271–72; Davidson, "Cashing In on Old Imperialisms," *Nation*, 13 September 1952, p. 209.

67. NIE-38, "Conditions and Trends in Tropical Africa," 22 December 1953, *FRUS, 1952–54*, 11:72, 74, 79, 87.

68. Dudley to Department of State, 3 June 1952, *FRUS, 1952–54*, 11:19–20.

69. NIE-38, "Conditions and Trends in Tropical Africa," *FRUS, 1952–54*, 11:78.

70. "What Natives Think of Federation Proposals," *Johannesburg Star*, 27 July 1951; and "Gold Coast Position May Bar Agreement on Federation, Say Nyasaland Settlers," *Johannesburg Star*, 27 August 1951, newspaper clippings, Box 3, Sweeney Papers.

71. John Foster Dulles (Secretary of State) to President Dwight D. Eisenhower, 22 May 1953, Ann Whitman File, Dulles-Herter Series, Box 1, Papers of Dwight D. Eisenhower, Dwight D. Eisenhower Library, Abilene, Kansas; Robertson to Secretary of State, 12 November 1952, 745A.00/11–1252, *CSDCF, 1950–54*, 1.

72. St. Clair Drake, "The Terror That Walks by Day," *Nation*, 29 November 1952, pp. 490–92; Martin L. Kilson, Jr., "Mugo-Son-of-Gatheru," *Crisis* 60

(March 1953): 140–44; Department of State, Intelligence Report, "The Mau Mau: An Aggressive Reaction to Frustration," 12 June 1953, *OSS/SD, Africa*, 7. For more on the Mau Mau, see Robert B. Edgerton, *Mau Mau: An African Crucible* (New York: Free Press, 1989).

73. Dickinson, "A Report on Strategic Ports of West Africa," March 1952, President's Secretary's Files, Oversize File, Truman Papers; Hewlett and Duncan, *Atomic Shield*, 549–52, 674.

74. Memorandum by Arneson to Acheson, 13 September 1949, *FRUS, 1949*, 1:526–28; Murphy to Acheson, 14 March 1951, *FRUS, 1951*, 1:702–3; Murphy to Acheson, 29 June 1951, *FRUS, 1951*, 1:739; *Resources for Freedom: A Report to the President by the President's Materials Policy Commission, June 1952* (Washington: U.S. Government Printing Office, 1952) 5:117–18.

75. Memorandum by Marshall to Acheson and Dean (Chairman of U.S. Atomic Energy Commission), 27 January 1951, *FRUS, 1951*, 1:687–89.

76. U.S. Government memorandum (from Atomic Energy Files), 26 January 1953, *FRUS, 1952–54*, 11:411–12.

77. Marshall to Acheson and Dean, 27 January 1951, *FRUS, 1951*, 1:689; paper prepared in Office of Special Assistant to Acheson, "Summary re Status of Efforts to Improve Security of the Belgian Congo," 6 July 1951, *FRUS, 1951*, 1:742; memorandum of conversation with Baron Silvercruys (Belgian Ambassador in U.S.), Gordon Arneson, and others by George Perkins, 25 July 1952, *FRUS, 1952–54*, 11:408–9.

78. Department of State, Office of Intelligence Research, "Conditions and Trends in Tropical Africa," 24 August 1953, *OSS/SD, Africa*, 4; Donald Lamm (U.S. Consul in Lourenco Marques) to Department of State, 28 March 1952, 745A.00/3-2852, *CSDCF, 1950–54*, 1; Dickinson, "A Report on Strategic Ports of West Africa," President's Secretary's File, Oversize File, Truman Papers.

79. Department of State, Steering Group on Preparations for Talks between the President and Prime Minister Churchill, "Steel and Raw Materials," 3 January 1952, President's Secretary's File, Box 116, Truman Papers; Stott to Fitzgerald, 31 January 1952, *FRUS, 1952–54*, 11:298–300; memorandum of conversation by Samuel J. Gorlitz, 20 February 1952, *FRUS, 1952–54*, 11:301–2; Harold Sims (Consul General in Salisbury) to Department of State, 3 July 1952, *FRUS, 1952–54*, 11:307.

80. W. B. Thorp (Director of Office of Foreign Economic Defense Affairs) to Secretary of Joint Chiefs of Staff, "Rail Transportation in Central and South Africa," 17 October 1952, File CD 531, Office of the Administrative Secretary, Record Group 330, National Archives; Randolph Roberts (U.S. Consul in Salisbury) to Department of State, 10 September 1951, *FRUS, 1951*, 5:1,230–32; Harold Sims, statement to American Consular Conference in Capetown, 11 March 1952, *FRUS, 1952–54*, 11:9; Lamm to Feld (Officer in Charge of West, Central, and East African Affairs), 11 April 1952, *FRUS, 1952–54*, 11:304–5; John P. Hoover (U.S. Consul General in Salisbury) to Department of State, 8 May 1953, *FRUS, 1952–54*, 11:319.

81. Hoover to Department of State, 8 May 1953, *FRUS, 1952–54*, 11:319.

82. Acheson to Consulate General in Salisbury, 7 January 1953, *FRUS, 1952–54*, 11:317; Dulles to Consulate General in Salisbury, 27 July 1953, *FRUS, 1952–54*, 11:326–27.

83. Bruce (Acting Secretary of State) to Consulate General in Salisbury, 4 November 1952, *FRUS, 1952–54*, 11:313–14.

84. Department of State, Steering Group on Preparations for Talks between the President and Prime Minister Churchill, "Summary of Public Attitudes," 28 December 1951, President's Secretary's File, Box 116, Truman Papers; extract from minutes of U.S.-U.K. colonial policy discussions, "Central African Federation," 25 September 1952, *FRUS, 1952–54,* 11:311–12; memorandum by Bourgerie (Director of Office of African Affairs) to Berry (Acting Assistant Secretary of State for Near Eastern, South Asian, and African Affairs), 5 January 1952, *FRUS, 1952–54,* 11:296–97; "African Federation," *Crisis* 60 (February 1953): 107.

85. Hoover to Department of State, 30 October 1952, *FRUS, 1952–54,* 11:313; Davidson, "Cashing In on Old Imperialisms," *Nation,* 13 September 1952, p. 210.

86. Hoover to Department of State, 4 December 1952, *FRUS, 1952–54,* 11:315–17.

87. Memorandum by John D. Jernegan (Deputy Assistant Secretary of State for Near Eastern, South Asian and African Affairs) to Donold *[sic]* B. Lourie (Under Secretary of State for Administration), 19 June 1953, *FRUS, 1952–54,* 11:325.

88. U.S. Department of Commerce, "Basic Data on the Economy of the Union of South Africa," *Economic Reports,* May 1955; memorandum by William L. Kilcoin (Office of British Commonwealth and Northern European Affairs) to Brown (Director of Office of International Materials Policy), "African Manganese and Chrome," 17 April 1952, *FRUS, 1952–54,* 11:910; Musedorah Thoreson, "Capital Investment in South Africa," [16 September 1952], *FRUS, 1952–54,* 11:932–33; U.S. Department of Commerce, *Investment in Union of South Africa,* 25, 86.

89. Avery F. Peterson (Officer in Charge of Dominion Affairs) to F. L. Hull (Export Credit Manager of Caterpillar Tractor Co.), 13 June 1952, enclosed with Hull to Secretary of State, 28 May 1952, 745A.00/5-2852, *CSDCF, 1950–54,* 1; Gallman to Secretary of State, 15 September 1952, 745A.00/9-1552, *CSDCF, 1950–54,* 1; Robertson to Department of State, 4 November 1952, 745A.00/11-452, *CSDCF, 1950–54,* 1; Thoreson, "Capital Investment in South Africa," *FRUS, 1952–54,* 11:933.

90. Acheson to certain diplomatic and consular officers, 10 July 1951, 811.05145A/7–1051, Record Group 59, National Archives; Thoreson, "Capital Investment in South Africa," *FRUS, 1952–54,* 11:933–34; Robertson to Department of State, 2 December 1952, 745A.00/12-252, *CSDCF, 1950–54,* 2.

91. Robertson to Department of State, 2 December 1952, 745A.00/12-252, *CSDCF, 1950–54,* 2.

92. David Ladin to Ivan Dresser (General Motors Overseas Operations, New York), 25 September 1952, enclosed in Robertson to Department of State, 4 November 1952, 745A.00/11–452, *CSDCF, 1950–54,* 1.

93. Paper prepared by Ferguson (Deputy Director of Policy Planning Staff), "General Considerations with Respect to Allies of the United States," 8 February 1951, *FRUS, 1951,* 1:45–46.

94. Dembo to Department of State, 27 August 1952, 745A.00/8-2752, *CSDCF, 1950–54,* 1.

95. Robertson to Department of State, 28 October 1952, *FRUS, 1952–54,* 11:964.

96. Acheson to U.S. Embassy in Capetown, 13 February 1952, 745A.5622/

2-1352, Record Group 59, National Archives; Acheson to U.S. Embassy in Capetown, 1 April 1952, 745A.5622/3-2652, Record Group 59, National Archives; Department of State memorandum, 20 June 1952, 745A.5622/6-2052, Record Group 59, National Archives; Acheson to U.S. Embassy in Capetown, 12 September 1952, *FRUS, 1952–54,* 11:927.

97. Editorial note, *FRUS, 1951,* 5:1,459–60; Hunton, "Postscript," in *Resistance Against Fascist Enslavement,* 62. The Indian government indicated its dismay at these arrangements, citing the suppression of dissent that the equipment would almost certainly be used for. Chester Bowles (U.S. Ambassador in India) to Department of State, 13 December 1952, *FRUS, 1952–54,* 11:980; and Bowles to Department of State, 31 December 1952, *FRUS, 1952–54,* 11:982.

98. Minutes of general staff meeting of Psychological Strategy Board, 13 June 1952, *Declassified Documents Reference System,* 1988, Fiche 114, #1771; National Security Council, "Current Policies of the Government of the United States of America Relating to the National Security, Vol. I: Geographical Area Policies, Part V: Africa," 1 November 1952, *Declassified Documents Reference System,* 1989, Fiche 55, #1013; Central Intelligence Agency, NIE-72, "Probable Developments in the Union of South Africa," 20 October 1952, President's Secretary's File, Box 254, Truman Papers.

99. Acheson to Connelly, 17 April 1950, *FRUS, 1950,* 5:1,823; Connelly to Acheson, 16 September 1950, *FRUS, 1950,* 5:1,829; Acheson to U.S. Embassy in South Africa, 29 December 1951, *FRUS, 1951,* 5:1,462–64; memorandum by Lee and Thoreson, *FRUS, 1952–54,* 11:930–31; Hunton, "Postscript," in *Resistance Against Fascist Enslavement,* 53.

100. Lovett to Chairman of Combined Policy Committee, 15 February 1952, File CD-334 (Combined Development Agency)-1952, Box 348, Office of Administrative Secretary, Record Group 330, National Archives; memorandum for files by J. Bruce Hamilton (Office of Special Assistant to the Secretary) to Acheson, 8 August 1951, *FRUS, 1951,* 1:751; report by Johnson (Director of Raw Materials, AEC), 4 January 1952, *FRUS, 1952–54,* 11:904.

101. Parsons to Department of State, 9 October 1952, 845A.2546/10-952, Record Group 59, National Archives; Dean to Dulles, 16 February 1953, *FRUS, 1952–54,* 2:1,099–1,100.

102. Dean to Dulles, *FRUS, 1952–54,* 2:1,100; Raynor to Arneson, 18 July 1952, 745A.00/7-1152, *CSDCF, 1950–54,* 1.

103. Department of State, policy statement, "Union of South Africa," 28 March 1951, 745A.00/3-2851, *CSDCF, 1950–54,* 1.

104. Discussion brief for bilateral talks on colonial policy at London and Paris, 8 October 1951, *FRUS, 1951,* 2:633; Sweeney, "South Africa: 1950–52," Box 5, Sweeney Papers.

105. Austin to Acheson, 13 December 1951, *FRUS, 1951,* 2:710.

106. Gallman to Department of State, 6 November 1951, *FRUS, 1951,* 5:1,459.

107. Department of State, instruction to U.S. Delegation to U.N. General Assembly, "Treatment of Indians in the Union of South Africa," 20 September 1951, *FRUS, 1951,* 2:843.

108. Acheson to U.S. Embassy in Pretoria, 12 September 1952, *FRUS, 1952–54,* 11:927.

109. Minutes of meeting of U.S. delegation to U.N. General Assembly, 12

December 1951, *FRUS, 1951,* 2:851; minutes of meeting of U.S. delegation to U.N. General Assembly, 16 January 1952, *FRUS, 1951,* 2:730–31.

110. Acheson to Austin, 13 December 1951, *FRUS, 1951,* 2:853; Acheson to U.S. Embassy in South Africa, 18 December 1951, *FRUS, 1951,* 2:714; minutes of meeting of U.S. delegation to U.N. General Assembly, 13 October 1952, *FRUS, 1952–54,* 11:946.

111. Bowles to Department of State, 12 September 1952, *FRUS, 1952–54,* 11:935; Jessup to Acheson, 23 September 1952, *FRUS, 1952–54,* 3:55; U.S. Embassy in New Delhi to Department of State, 7 October 1952, *FRUS, 1952–54,* 11:937; memorandum by Jernegan to Hickerson, 9 October 1952, *FRUS, 1952–54,* 11:943.

112. Acheson to Truman, 25 October 1952, Box 67a, Acheson Papers, Truman Library; memorandum of conversation of Acheson and Casey (Australian Foreign Minister), 7 November 1952, Box 67a, Acheson Papers, Truman Library; Acheson to U.S. Embassy in India, 29 September 1952, *FRUS, 1952–54,* 11:936.

113. Memorandum of conversation of Acheson and Jooste, 14 October 1952, Box 67a, Acheson Papers, Truman Library.

114. Gallman to Acheson, 20 November 1951, *FRUS, 1951,* 2:696; "Summary from the Afrikaans Press," 30 November 1951, Box 5, Sweeney Papers; Gallman to Secretary of State, 23 September 1952, 745A.00/9–2352, *CSDCF, 1950–54,* 1.

115. Gallman to Secretary of State, 14 January 1952, 745A.00/1–1452, *CSDCF, 1950–54,* 1; memorandum by Bancroft to Fisher, "South African Question in the General Assembly," 24 October 1952, *FRUS, 1952–54,* 11:963.

116. One reaction to this perceived weakness was to consider improving the sophistication of American propaganda—for example, emphasizing African American achievements and white American appreciation of those—which reached Africans through the U.S. Information Service and the Voice of America. Dudley to Department of State, "A Revised Information Program for Africa, West Africa in Particular," 3 June 1952, *FRUS, 1952–54,* 11:16.

117. Minutes of meeting of U.S. delegation to U.N. General Assembly, 21 December 1951, *FRUS, 1951,* 2:857; Shapiro, *White Violence and Black Response,* 417–18.

118. Perkins to Acheson, 9 October 1952, *FRUS, 1952–54,* 11:970–71.

119. Memorandum by Bancroft to Fisher, 24 October 1952, *FRUS, 1952–54,* 11:963.

120. For a revealing official acknowledgement of this, see Federal Bureau of Investigation, "The Communist Party and the Negro," February 1953, Office of the Special Assistant for National Security Affairs, Box 16, White House Office Files, Eisenhower Library. For a more optimistic assessment at the time of changes in race relations, see "White Supremacy," editorial, *Life,* 4 August 1952, p. 30.

121. "Along the Color Line," editorial, *Crisis* 59 (February 1952): 103; Lawson, *Black Ballots,* 134.

122. "Meeting of Negro Leaders with Secretary Acheson on April 13, 1951," 16 April 1951, Box 66, Acheson Papers, Truman Library. One African American served as a U.S. ambassador under Truman: Edward R. Dudley, who was posted to Liberia in 1949. Michael L. Krenn, " 'Outstanding Negroes' and 'Appropriate

Countries': Some Facts, Figures, and Thoughts on Black U.S. Ambassadors, 1949–1988," *Diplomatic History* 14 (Winter 1990): 134–35.

123. "Two Bombings," editorial, *Crisis* 59 (April 1952): 238; "The Southern Negro: 1952," *Nation,* 27 September 1952, pp. 243–44.

124. "Racial Incidents," editorial, *Crisis* 58 (October 1951): 530–31; William A. Rutherford, "Jim Crow: A Problem in Diplomacy," *Nation,* 8 November 1952, pp. 428–29; Robert F. Corrigan (U.S. Consul in Dakar) to Department of State, "Some Observations Concerning Racism and Politics in F[rench] W[est] A[frica]," 16 September 1953, *FRUS, 1952–54,* 11:238. Racial incidents in the United States during the Eisenhower years would do little to improve the country's image abroad in this regard. See, for example, United States Information Agency, Office of Research and Intelligence, "Post–Little Rock Opinion on the Treatment of Negroes in the U.S.," January 1958, Box 99, White House Central Files, Eisenhower Papers.

125. John Parker (President of Philadelphia Youth Council of NAACP) to Truman, 4 June 1952, 745A.00/6-452, *CSDCF, 1950–54,* 1; George M. Houser, letter to the editor, *Nation,* 29 November 1952, pp. 503–4; Martin, "American Views on South Africa," 30–31. These efforts were supplemented by an article entitled "The African Response to Racial Laws" by Prof. Z. K. Matthews, a moderate black South African opponent of apartheid, published in the October 1951 issue of *Foreign Affairs* (pp. 91–102). See also Francis A. Kornegay, Jr., "Black America and U.S.–Southern African Relations: An Essay Bibliographical Survey of Developments During the 1950's, 1960's and Early 1970's," in *American–Southern African Relations: Bibliographical Essays,* ed. Mohamed A. El-Khawas and Francis A. Kornegay, Jr. (Westport, Conn.: Greenwood Press, 1975), 138–78.

126. Acheson to U.S. Embassy in Pretoria, 12 September 1952, *FRUS, 1952–54,* 11:927; A. Philip Randolph (International President of Brotherhood of Sleeping Car Porters) to Eisenhower, 17 June 1953, *FRUS, 1952–54,* 11:43–46; memorandum by John E. Utter (Director of Office of African Affairs) to Simmons (Chief of Protocol), "Recommendations for White House Reply to Mr. A. Philip Randolph," 4 September 1953, *FRUS, 1952–54,* 11:51.

127. A particularly clear example of this was the manner in which AFSAR decided to support the Defiance Campaign. See Houser, *No One Can Stop the Rain,* 13–15.

128. FBI, "The Communist Party and the Negro," Box 16, White House Office Files, Eisenhower Library; John Foster Dulles, telephone conversation with Leonard Hall, 6 May 1953, Box 1, Dulles Papers, Eisenhower Library; Gill, "Afro-American Opposition to the United States' Wars," 574–81.

129. Quoted in editorial note, *FRUS, 1951,* 5:1,452–53.

130. Acheson to U.S. Embassy in South Africa, 17 July 1951, *FRUS, 1951,* 2:687.

131. Memorandum of conversation by Gerig, 15 March 1951, *FRUS, 1951,* 2:679.

132. Policy statement, "Union of South Africa," 28 March 1951, 745A.00/3-2851, *CSDCF, 1950–54,* 1.

133. Ibid.

134. Joseph L. Dougherty (Secretary of U.S. Embassy in South Africa) to Department of State, 26 January 1951, 745A.00(W)/1-2651, *CSDCF, 1950–54,* 3.

135. Sweeney to Department of State, 9 March 1951, 645A.00/3-951, *CSDCF, 1950–54,* 23.

136. Department of State, Office of Intelligence Research, "Race Relations in South Africa," 21 October 1952, *OSS/SD, Africa,* 10.

137. Department of State, Office of Intelligence Research, "The South African Constitutional Crisis," 2 July 1952, *OSS/SD, Africa,* 10.

138. NSC, "Current Policies of the Government of the United States," 1 November 1952, *Declassified Documents Reference System,* 1989, Fiche 55, #1013; Gallman to Department of State, 2 March 1953, *FRUS, 1952–54,* 11:988–91; memorandum by Perkins to Acheson, 11 June 1952, 745A.00/6-1152, *CSDCF, 1950–54,* 1; minutes of meeting of U.S. members of Combined Policy Committee, 16 April 1952, *FRUS, 1952–54,* 2:888; CIA, NIE-72, "Probable Developments in the Union of South Africa," 20 October 1952, President's Secretary's File, Box 254, Truman Papers.

139. Department of State, "The South African Constitutional Crisis," *OSS/SD, Africa,* 10.

140. Memorandum by Perkins to Acheson, 11 June 1952, 745A.00/6-1152, *CSDCF, 1950–54,* 1.

141. Homer A. Jack, "South Africa Today," *Christian Century,* 17 September 1952, pp. 1,057–59; idem, "What Is This 'Apartheid'?" *Christian Century,* 24 September 1952, pp. 1,092–93; idem, "Signs of Deterioration in South Africa," *Christian Century,* 1 October 1952, pp. 1,122–25; idem, "Under the Southern Cross," *Christian Century,* 8 October 1952, pp. 1,158–60; idem, "Hope for South Africa," *Christian Century,* 15 October 1952, pp. 1,189–91.

142. "Defiance of Malan Over 'Unjust' Laws Set in South Africa," *New York Times,* 7 April 1952, pp. 1, 3.

143. "South Africa: Reaping the Whirlwind," *Time,* 31 March 1952, pp. 37–38.

144. "South Africa: Of God & Hate," *Time,* 5 May 1952, pp. 32–34.

145. "South Africa Heads for Civil Violence," *Business Week,* 6 September 1952, pp. 172–73.

146. Memorandum by Kilcoin to Brown, 17 April 1952, *FRUS, 1952–54,* 11:909–10.

147. Memorandum by Perkins to Berry, 10 April 1952, *FRUS, 1952–54,* 11:907; Acheson to U.S. Embassy in India, 2 May 1952, *FRUS, 1952–54,* 11:910; Robertson to Department of State, 19 November 1952, 745A.00/11–1952, *CSDCF, 1950–54,* 1; "U.S. Bids U.N. Shun Action on Malan," *New York Times,* 16 November 1952, p. 19.

148. Acheson to U.S. Embassy in Pretoria, 29 December 1952, 745A.00/12-252, *CSDCF, 1950–54,* 2.

149. Robertson to Department of State, 28 October 1952, *FRUS, 1952–54,* 11:964.

150. Gallman to Department of State, 2 March 1953, *FRUS, 1952–54,* 11:986–94.

151. Gallman to Secretary of State, 10 April 1952, 745A.00/4-1052, *CSDCF, 1950–54,* 1.

152. The U.S. Embassy in South Africa reported in June, in reference to the authorities' crackdown on African leadership, that the South African government was no longer making "any pretence of intending to hamstring Communists alone. Several cabinet ministers have publicly stated that a change in the

established order is on a par with a Communist revolution in the United States, and that in this matter there can be little quibbling over ideological orientations." U.S. Embassy in Pretoria to Department of State, 5 June 1953, 745A.00/6-553, *CSDCF, 1950–54*, 2. See also Raynor, "Impressions from a Visit to South Africa," 19 June 1953, *FRUS, 1952–54*, 11:1,000.

153. "A Victory for Evil," editorial, *New York Times*, 17 April 1953, p. 24.

154. Dulles to U.S. Ambassador in Pretoria, 21 April 1953, 745A.00/4-2153, *CSDCF, 1950–54*, 2; U.S. Embassy to Secretary of State, 27 April 1953, 745A.00/4-2753, *CSDCF, 1950–54*, 2.

155. Barringer to Fitzgerald, 20 November 1953, *FRUS, 1952–54*, 11:66–67.

Conclusion

1. Paul H. Nitze, "Minerals as a Factor in U.S. Foreign Economic Policy," *Department of State Bulletin*, 16 February 1947, p. 300. The President's Materials Policy Commission (known as the Paley Commission for its chairman, William S. Paley) explained the American situation in its June 1952 report to Truman:

> The decade of the 1940's marked a crucial turning point in the long-range materials position of the United States. . . . By the midpoint of the twentieth century we had entered an era of new relationships between our needs and resources; our national economy had not merely grown up to its resource base, but in many important respects had outgrown it. We had completed our slow transition from a raw materials surplus Nation to a raw materials deficit Nation.

Noting that there were now only two minerals—magnesium and molybdenum—for which the United States was not at least partially dependent on foreign supplies, the Paley Commission concluded: "If the United States were forced to live within the rigid structure of its present materials position, its future outlook would be bleak indeed." *Resources for Freedom* 1:6–8.

2. See Raye C. Ringholz, *Uranium Frenzy: Boom and Bust on the Colorado Plateau* (New York: W. W. Norton, 1989), especially pp. 57–58.

3. To Afrikaner nationalists in South Africa, such concerns in the United States indicated a hypocritical unwillingness of a fellow white-supremacist society to proclaim traditional American racial discrimination as a positive good that should be preserved rather than a fault that necessitated apology. See, for example, "Color and Conscience in the U.S.A.," editorial, *Die Transvaler*, 12 May 1952, in "Summary of the Afrikaans Press," 15 May 1952, Box 2, Sweeney Papers.

4. C. Vann Woodward, *The Strange Career of Jim Crow* (New York: Oxford University Press, 1955), 151–52. See also Peattie, *Struggle on the Veld*, 150–54.

5. Quoted in Woodward, *Strange Career*, 3rd rev. ed., 132. The Truman administration's concern about the turbulent events in South Africa and their potential international implications was sufficient for the State Department to brief President-elect Eisenhower on them in the transition period at the end of Truman's presidency. Office of the Secretary of State, memorandum for Mr. William Hopkins, "Briefing Materials for Conversations with President-designate," 18 November 1952, *Declassified Documents Reference System*, 1979, #88B.

6. Gallman to Department of State, 6 August 1954, *FRUS, 1952–54,* 11:1,037–38.

7. Department of State, Office of Intelligence Research, "The South African Constitutional Crisis," 2 July 1952, *OSS/SD, Africa,* 10.

8. Sims to Feld, 16 June 1952, *FRUS, 1952–54,* 11:21.

9. Quoted in Sweeney, "South Africa: 1950–52," Box 5, Sweeney Papers.

10. Baum, "United States, Self-Government, and Africa," 278–79.

11. Quoted in Gaddis, *Strategies of Containment,* 3.

12. "Revival of Tribalism Opposed," *Friend* (Bloemfontein), 18 December 1950, 4, newspaper clipping, Box 2, Sweeney Papers.

13. Quoted in Paul Robeson, *Here I Stand* (New York: Othello Associates, 1958), 45–46. A much older Nelson Mandela offered a very similar explanation of the ANC's attitude toward the outside world on his visit to the United States in June 1990, to the consternation of many Americans who assumed that the recently re-legalized ANC would share the same "enemies" with the United States, such as Cuba, Libya, and the Palestine Liberation Organization.

14. Mandela, "No Easy Walk to Freedom," 21 September 1953, in Karis and Carter, *From Protest to Challenge* 3:115.

Selected Bibliography

Archives and Manuscript Collections

Acheson, Dean. Papers. Harry S Truman Library, Independence, Missouri.

Byrnes, James F. Papers. Robert Muldrow Cooper Library, Clemson University, Clemson, South Carolina.

Clifford, Clark M. Oral History. Harry S Truman Library.

Dulles, John Foster. Papers. Dwight D. Eisenhower Library, Abilene, Kansas.

———. Papers. Seeley G. Mudd Library, Princeton University, Princeton, New Jersey.

Eisenhower, Dwight D. Ann Whitman File. Dwight D. Eisenhower Library.

———. White House Office Files: Office of the Special Assistant for National Security Affairs. Dwight D. Eisenhower Library.

Elsey, George M. Oral History. Harry S Truman Library.

———. Papers. Harry S Truman Library.

Hardy, Benjamin H. Papers. Harry S Truman Library.

Henderson, Loy W. Oral History. Harry S Truman Library.

Kennan, George F. Papers. Seeley G. Mudd Library, Princeton University.

Sumner, John D. Papers. Harry S Truman Library.

Sweeney, Joseph. Papers. Harry S Truman Library.

Truman, Harry S. President's Secretary's Files. Harry S Truman Library.

———. White House Central Files. Harry S Truman Library.

U.S. Department of Defense. Joint Chiefs of Staff Records. Record Group 218. Modern Military Records Branch, National Archives, Washington, D.C.

———. Office of the Secretary of Defense Records. Record Group 330. Modern Military Records Branch, National Archives.

U.S. Department of State. Main Decimal File. Record Group 59. Civil Branch, National Archives.

———. Office Files of the Assistant Secretary of State for Economic Affairs. Harry S Truman Library.

———. Office of the Assistant Secretary and Under-Secretary of State (Dean Acheson) Records, 1941–1950. Record Group 59. Civil Branch, National Archives.

————. Policy Planning Staff Records, 1947–1953. Record Group 59. Civil Branch, National Archives.

U.S. National Security Council. Records. Record Group 273. Civil Branch, National Archives.

U.S. Office of Strategic Services. R & A Reports. Microform Collection. Record Group 59. Civil Branch, National Archives.

Vandenberg, Arthur H., Jr. Papers. Bentley Historical Library, University of Michigan, Ann Arbor, Michigan.

Other Unpublished Material

Baum, Edward. "The United States, Self-Government, and Africa: An Examination of the Nature of the American Policy on Self-Determination with Reference to Africa in the Postwar Era." Ph.D. diss., University of California, Los Angeles, 1964.

Bills, Scott L. "Cold War Rimlands: The United States, NATO, and the Politics of Colonialism, 1945–1949." Ph.D. diss., Kent State University, 1981.

Clark, Wayne Addison. "An Analysis of the Relationship between Anti-Communism and Segregationist Thought in the Deep South, 1948–1964." Ph.D. diss., University of North Carolina, 1976.

Gill, Gerald R. "Afro-American Opposition to the United States' Wars of the Twentieth Century: Dissent, Discontent, and Disinterest." Ph.D. diss., Howard University, 1985.

Karns, Margaret Padelford. "The United States, the United Nations and Decolonization." Ph.D. diss., University of Michigan, 1975.

Lake, Anthony. "Caution and Concern: The Making of American Policy toward South Africa, 1946–71." Ph.D. diss., Princeton University, 1974.

Martin, Patrick H. "American Views on South Africa, 1948–1972." Ph.D. diss., Louisiana State University and Agricultural and Mechanical College, 1974.

Miller, Jean-Donald. "The United States and Colonial Sub-Saharan Africa, 1939–1945." Ph.D. diss., University of Connecticut, 1981.

Munene, G. Macharia. "The Truman Administration and the Decolonization of Sub-Saharan Africa, 1945–1952." Ph.D. diss., Ohio University, 1985.

Secrest, Donald Edmund. "American Policy toward Neutralism during the Truman and Eisenhower Administrations." Ph.D. diss., University of Michigan, 1967.

Spooner, Ward A. "United States Policy Toward South Africa, 1919–1941: Political and Economic Aspects." Ph.D. diss., St. John's University, New York, 1979.

Published Documents

[African National Congress and South African Indian Congress.] *Resistance against Fascist Enslavement in South Africa.* With a Postscript for Americans by Dr. Alphaeus Hunton. New York: Council on African Affairs, 1953.

Declassified Documents Reference System. Washington: Carrollton Press, 1975–1982; Woodbridge, Conn.: Research Publications, 1983–1989.

MacVeagh, Lincoln. *"Dear Franklin..." Letters to President Roosevelt from Lincoln MacVeagh, U.S. Minister to South Africa, 1942–1943.* Pasadena, Calif.: California Institute of Technology, Munger Africana Library Notes, Issue #12, March 1972.

[President's Committee on Civil Rights.] *To Secure These Rights: The Report of the President's Committee on Civil Rights.* New York: Simon and Schuster, 1947.

[President's Materials Policy Commission.] *Resources for Freedom: A Report to the President by the President's Materials Policy Commission, June 1952.* 5 vols. Washington, 1952.

Public Papers of the Presidents: Harry S Truman, 1945–1953. Washington, D.C., 1961–1966.

[U.S. Central Intelligence Agency.] *CIA Research Reports: Africa, 1946–1976.* Edited by Paul Kesaris. Frederick, Md.: University Publications of America, 1982–1983. Microfilm, 3 reels and printed guide.

U.S. Department of Commerce. "Basic Data on the Economy of the Union of South Africa." *Economic Reports* (May 1955).

———. Bureau of Foreign Commerce. *Investment in Union of South Africa: Conditions and Outlook for United States Investors,* by Herbert J. Cummings and Bernard Blankenheimer. Washington, 1954.

———. Office of Business Economics. *Foreign Investments of the United States.* Washington, 1953.

———."Growth in Private Foreign Investments," by Samuel Pizer and Frederick Cutler. *Survey of Current Business* (January 1954): 5–10.

[U.S. Department of State.] *Confidential U.S. State Department Central Files. South Africa: Internal Affairs and Foreign Affairs, 1945–1954.* Frederick, Md.: University Publications of America, 1985. Microfilm, 36 reels with printed guides.

———. *Department of State Bulletin.* 1945–1953.

———. *Foreign Relations of the United States, 1945–1952/54.* Washington, D.C., 1967–1983.

[———. Policy Planning Staff.] *The State Department Policy Planning Staff Papers.* [1947–1949.] 3 vols. New York: Garland Publishing, 1983.

U.S. Office of Strategic Services. *OSS/State Department Intelligence and Research Reports.* Part 13. *Africa, 1941–1961.* Washington, D.C.: University Publications of America, 1980.

Bibliographic Aids

Danaher, Kevin. *South Africa and the United States: An Annotated Bibliography.* Washington: Institute for Policy Studies, 1979.

DeLancey, Mark W. *African International Relations: An Annotated Bibliography.* Boulder: Westview Press, 1981.

El-Khawas, Mohamed A., and Francis A. Kornegay, Jr., eds. *American-Southern African Relations: Bibliographic Essays.* Westport, Conn.: Greenwood Press, 1975.

Keto, C. Tsehloane. *American–South African Relations, 1784–1980: Review and*

Select Bibliography. Athens, Ohio: Ohio University Center for International Studies, Africa Studies Program, 1985.

Noer, Thomas J. "'Non-Benign Neglect': The United States and Black Africa in the Twentieth Century." In *American Foreign Relations: A Historiographical Review,* ed. Gerald K. Haines and J. Samuel Walker, 271–92. Westport, Conn.: Greenwood Press, 1981.

Books

Acheson, Dean. *Present at the Creation: My Years in the State Department.* New York: Norton, 1969.

Arkhurst, Frederick S., ed. *U.S. Policy Towards Africa.* New York: Praeger, 1975.

Barber, James P. *South Africa's Foreign Policy, 1945–1970.* London: Oxford University Press, 1973.

Bender, Gerald J. *Angola Under the Portuguese: The Myth and the Reality.* Berkeley: University of California Press, 1978.

Berman, William. *The Politics of Civil Rights in the Truman Administration.* Columbus: Ohio State University Press, 1970.

Bernstein, Barton J., ed. *Politics and Policies of the Truman Administration.* Chicago: Quadrangle, 1970.

Bogle, Donald. *Toms, Coons, Mulattoes, Mammies, and Bucks: An Interpretive History of Blacks in American Films.* New York: Viking Press, 1973.

Bowles, Chester. *Africa's Challenge to America.* Berkeley: University of California Press, 1956.

Brooks, Thomas R. *Walls Come Tumbling Down: A History of the Civil Rights Movement, 1940–1970.* Englewood Cliffs, N.J.: Prentice-Hall, 1974.

Cell, John W. *The Highest Stage of White Supremacy: The Origins of Segregation in South Africa and the American South.* Cambridge: Cambridge University Press, 1982.

Chester, Edward W. *Clash of Titans: Africa and U.S. Foreign Policy.* Maryknoll, N.Y.: Orbis Books, 1974.

Committee on Africa, the War, and Peace Aims. *The Atlantic Charter and Africa from an American Standpoint.* New York: n.p., 1942.

Cooper, Allan D. *U.S. Economic Power and Political Influence in Namibia, 1700–1982.* Boulder: Westview Press, 1982.

Dalfiume, Richard M. *Desegregation of the U.S. Armed Forces: Fighting on Two Fronts, 1939–1953.* Columbia: University of Missouri Press, 1969.

Danaher, Kevin. *The Political Economy of U.S. Policy toward South Africa.* Boulder: Westview Press, 1985.

Davenport, T. R. H. *South Africa: A Modern History.* 3d ed. Toronto: University of Toronto Press, 1987.

Davidson, Basil. *Africa in Modern History: The Search for a New Society.* London: Allen Lane, 1978.

———. *Report on Southern Africa.* London: Jonathan Cape, 1952.

Donovan, Robert J. *Conflict and Crisis: The Presidency of Harry S Truman, 1945–1948.* New York: Norton, 1977.

————. *Tumultuous Years: The Presidency of Harry S Truman, 1949–1953*. New York: Norton, 1982.

Duberman, Martin Bauml. *Paul Robeson: A Biography*. New York: Ballantine Books, 1989.

Du Bois, W. E. B. *The World and Africa*. New York: Viking Press, 1947.

Duignan, Peter, and L. H. Gann. *The United States and Africa: A History*. Cambridge: Cambridge University Press, 1984.

Eckes, Alfred E., Jr. *The United States and the Global Struggle for Minerals*. Austin: University of Texas Press, 1979.

Edgerton, Robert B. *Mau Mau: An African Crucible*. New York: Free Press, 1989.

Emerson, Rupert. *Africa and United States Policy*. Englewood Cliffs, N.J.: Prentice-Hall, 1967.

Feit, Edward. *South Africa: The Dynamics of the African National Congress*. London: Oxford University Press, 1962.

Fieldhouse, D. K. *Black Africa, 1945–1980: Economic Decolonization and Arrested Development*. London: Allen and Unwin, 1986.

Flavin, Martin. *Black and White: From the Cape to the Congo*. New York: Harper, [1950].

Franck, Thomas M. *Race and Nationalism: The Struggle for Power in Rhodesia-Nyasaland*. London: George Allen and Unwin, 1960.

Frederickson, George M. *White Supremacy: A Comparative Study in American and South African History*. New York: Oxford University Press, 1981.

Gaddis, John Lewis. *Strategies of Containment: A Critical Appraisal of Postwar American National Security Policy*. New York: Oxford University Press, 1982.

Garson, Robert A. *The Democratic Party and the Politics of Sectionalism, 1941–1948*. Baton Rouge: Louisiana State University Press, 1974.

Gerhart, Gail M. *Black Power in South Africa: The Evolution of an Ideology*. Berkeley: University of California Press, 1978.

Gifford, Prosser, and William Roger Louis, eds. *The Transfer of Power in Africa: Decolonization, 1940–1960*. New Haven: Yale University Press, 1982.

Goldschmidt, Walter Rochs. *The United States and Africa*. New York: Praeger, 1963.

Hamby, Alonzo. *Beyond the New Deal: Harry S Truman and American Liberalism*. New York: Columbia University Press, 1973.

Hance, William, ed. *Southern Africa and the United States*. New York: Columbia University Press, 1968.

Hancock, W. K. *Smuts: The Fields of Force, 1919–1950*. Cambridge: Cambridge University Press, 1968.

Hargreaves, John D. *Decolonization in Africa*. London: Longman, 1988.

Helmreich, Jonathan E. *Gathering Rare Ores: The Diplomacy of Uranium Acquisition, 1943–1954*. Princeton: Princeton University Press, 1986.

Herken, Gregg. *The Winning Weapon: The Atomic Bomb in the Cold War, 1945–1950*. New York: Knopf, 1980.

Hewlett, Richard G., and Oscar E. Anderson, Jr. *A History of the United States*

Atomic Energy Commission. Vol. 1, *The New World, 1939/1946.* University Park, Pa.: Pennsylvania State University Press, 1962.

Hewlett, Richard G., and Francis Duncan. *A History of the United States Atomic Energy Commission.* Vol. 2, *Atomic Shield, 1947/1952.* University Park, Pa.: Pennsylvania State University Press, 1969.

Hogan, Michael J. *The Marshall Plan: America, Britain, and the Reconstruction of Western Europe, 1947–1952.* Cambridge: Cambridge University Press, 1987.

Horne, Gerald. *Black and Red: W. E. B. Du Bois and the Afro-American Response to the Cold War, 1944–1963.* Albany: State University of New York Press, 1986.

———. *Communist Front? The Civil Rights Congress, 1946–1956.* Rutherford, N.J.: Fairleigh Dickinson University Press, 1988.

Houghton, D. Hobart. *The South African Economy.* 4th ed. Capetown: Oxford University Press, 1964.

Houser, George M. *No One Can Stop the Rain: Glimpses of Africa's Liberation Struggle.* New York: Pilgrim Press, 1989.

Hull, Richard W. *American Enterprise in South Africa: Historical Dimensions of Engagement and Disengagement.* New York: New York University Press, 1990.

Hunt, Michael H. *Ideology and U.S. Foreign Policy.* New Haven: Yale University Press, 1987.

Hunton, W. Alphaeus. *Decision in Africa: Sources of Current Conflict.* Rev. ed. New York: International Publishers, 1960.

Ireland, Timothy P. *Creating the Entangling Alliance: The Origins of the North Atlantic Treaty Organization.* Westport, Conn.: Greenwood Press, 1981.

Isaacman, Allen, and Barbara Isaacman. *Mozambique: From Colonialism to Revolution, 1900–1982.* Boulder: Westview Press, 1983.

Isaacs, Harold R. *The New World of Negro Americans.* New York: John Day, 1963.

Isaacson, Walter, and Evan Thomas. *The Wise Men: Six Friends and the World They Made: Acheson, Bohlen, Harriman, Kennan, Lovett, McCloy.* New York: Simon and Schuster, 1986.

Johnstone, Frederick. *Class, Race and Gold: A Study of Class Relations and Racial Discrimination in South Africa.* London: Routledge and Kegan Paul, 1976.

Kaplan, Lawrence S. *The United States and NATO: The Formative Years.* Lexington: University Press of Kentucky, 1984.

Karis, Thomas, and Gwendolen M. Carter, eds. *From Protest to Challenge: A Documentary History of African Politics in South Africa, 1882–1964.* 4 vols. Stanford: Hoover Institution Press, 1972–1977.

Killingray, David, and Richard Rathbone, eds. *Africa and the Second World War.* Basingstoke, England: Macmillan, 1986.

Kuper, Leo. *Passive Resistance in South Africa.* London: Jonathan Cape, 1956.

Lacey, Michael J., ed. *The Truman Presidency.* Cambridge: Cambridge University Press, 1989.

Lauren, Paul Gordon. *Power and Prejudice: The Politics and Diplomacy of Racial Discrimination.* Boulder: Westview Press, 1988.

Lawson, Steven. *Black Ballots: Voting Rights in the South*. New York: Columbia University Press, 1976.

Lemarchand, René, ed. *American Policy in Southern Africa: The Stakes and the Stance*. Washington, D.C.: University Press of America, 1978.

Lodge, Tom. *Black Politics in South Africa since 1945*. London: Longman, 1983.

Louis, William Roger. *Imperialism at Bay: The United States and the Decolonization of the British Empire, 1941–1945*. New York: Oxford University Press, 1978.

Louis, William Roger, and Hedley Bull, eds. *The 'Special Relationship': Anglo-American Relations Since 1945*. Oxford: Clarendon Press, 1986.

Luthuli, Albert. *Let My People Go*. New York: McGraw-Hill, 1962.

Lynch, Hollis Ralph. *Black American Radicals and the Liberation of Africa: The Council on African Affairs, 1937–1955*. Ithaca: Africana Studies and Research Center, Cornell University, 1978.

Magubane, Bernard M. *The Ties That Bind: African-American Consciousness of Africa*. Trenton: Africa World Press, 1987.

Marcum, John A. *Portugal and Africa: The Politics of Indifference (A Case Study in American Foreign Policy)*. Syracuse: Program of Eastern African Studies, Syracuse University, 1972.

———. *The Angolan Revolution*. Vol. 1, *The Anatomy of an Explosion (1950–1962)*. Cambridge: M.I.T. Press, 1969.

McAdam, Doug. *Political Process and the Development of Black Insurgency, 1930–1970*. Chicago: University of Chicago Press, 1982.

McCarthy, Michael. *Dark Continent: Africa as Seen by Americans*. Westport, Conn.: Greenwood Press, 1983.

McCoy, Donald R., and Richard Ruetten. *Quest and Response: Minority Rights and the Truman Administration*. Lawrence: University Press of Kansas, 1973.

McGhee, George C. *Envoy to the Middle World: Adventures in Diplomacy*. New York: Harper and Row, 1983.

McKinley, Edward H. *The Lure of Africa: American Interests in Tropical Africa, 1919–1939*. Indianapolis: Bobbs-Merrill, 1974.

McMahon, Robert J. *Colonialism and Cold War: The United States and the Struggle for Indonesian Independence, 1945–1949*. Ithaca: Cornell University Press, 1981.

Meli, Francis. *South Africa Belongs to Us: A History of the ANC*. Bloomington: Indiana University Press, 1988.

Minter, William. *King Solomon's Mines Revisited: Western Interests and the Burdened History of Southern Africa*. New York: Basic Books, 1986.

———. *Portuguese Africa and the West*. Harmondsworth, England: Penguin, 1972.

Nesteby, James R. *Black Images in American Films, 1896–1954: The Interplay between Civil Rights and Film Culture*. Washington: University Press of America, 1982.

Nielsen, Waldemar. *The Great Powers and Africa*. New York: Praeger, 1969.

Noer, Thomas J. *Briton, Boer, and Yankee: The United States and South Africa, 1870–1914*. Kent, Ohio: Kent State University Press, 1978.

———. *Cold War and Black Liberation: The United States and White Rule in Africa, 1948–1968.* Columbia: University of Missouri Press, 1985.

Nolutshungu, Sam C. *South Africa in Africa: A Study in Ideology and Foreign Policy.* Manchester, England: Manchester University Press, 1975.

Ovendale, Ritchie. *The English-Speaking Alliance: Britain, the United States, the Dominions and the Cold War, 1945–1951.* London: George Allen and Unwin, 1985.

Peattie, Roderick. *Struggle on the Veld.* New York: Vanguard Press, 1947.

Reid, Escott. *Time of Fear and Hope: The Making of the North Atlantic Treaty, 1947–1949.* Toronto: McClelland and Stuart, 1977.

Ringholz, Raye C. *Uranium Frenzy: Boom and Bust on the Colorado Plateau.* New York: Norton, 1989.

Robeson, Eslanda G. *African Journey.* New York: John Day, 1945.

Robeson, Paul. *Here I Stand.* New York: Othello Associates, 1958.

Rotberg, Robert I. *The Rise of Nationalism in Central Africa: The Making of Malawi and Zambia, 1873–1964.* Cambridge: Harvard University Press, 1965.

Roux, Edward. *Time Longer Than Rope: A History of the Black Man's Struggle for Freedom in South Africa.* Madison: University of Wisconsin Press, 1964.

Russell, Ruth B. *A History of the United Nations Charter: The Role of the United States, 1940–1945.* Washington: Brookings Institution, 1958.

Sampson, Anthony. *Drum: A Venture into the New Africa.* London: Collins, 1956.

Shah, Harin. *The Great Abdication: American Foreign Policy in Asia and Africa.* Delhi: Atma Ram and Sons, 1957.

Shapiro, Herbert. *White Violence and Black Response: From Reconstruction to Montgomery.* Amherst: University of Massachusetts Press, 1988.

Shepherd, George W., Jr., ed. *Racial Influences on American Foreign Policy.* New York: Basic Books, 1970.

Sparks, Allister. *The Mind of South Africa.* New York: Alfred A. Knopf, 1990.

Spence, J. E. *Republic Under Pressure: A Study of South African Foreign Policy.* London: Oxford University Press, 1965.

Tygiel, Jules. *Baseball's Great Experiment: Jackie Robinson and His Legacy.* New York: Oxford University Press, 1983.

Vandenbosch, Amry. *South Africa and the World: The Foreign Policy of Apartheid.* Lexington: University of Kentucky Press, 1970.

Walshe, Peter. *The Rise of African Nationalism in South Africa: The African National Congress, 1912–1952.* Berkeley: University of California Press, 1971.

Weisbord, Robert G. *Ebony Kinship: Africa, Africans, and the Afro-American.* Westport, Conn.: Greenwood Press, 1973.

Westin, Rubin F. *Racism in U.S. Imperialism: The Influence of Racial Assumptions on American Foreign Policy, 1893–1946.* Columbia: University of South Carolina Press, 1972.

Wexler, Immanuel. *The Marshall Plan Revisited: The European Recovery Program in Economic Perspective.* Westport, Conn.: Greenwood Press, 1983.

White, Walter F. *A Man Called White: Autobiography of Walter White.* New York: Viking Press, 1948.

Wilson, Monica, and Leonard Thompson, eds. *The Oxford History of South Africa.* Vol. 2, *South Africa, 1870–1966.* London: Oxford University Press, 1971.

Zangrando, Robert L. *The NAACP Crusade Against Lynching, 1909–1950.* Philadelphia: Temple University Press, 1980.

Articles

Bender, Gerald, and Allen Isaacman. "The Changing Historiography of Angola and Mozambique." In *African Studies since 1945: A Tribute to Basil Davidson,* ed. Christopher Fyfe, 220–48. London: Longman, 1976.

Chafe, William H. "The Civil Rights Revolution, 1945–1960: The Gods Bring Threads to Webs Begun." In *Reshaping America: Society and Institutions, 1945–1960,* ed. Robert H. Bremner and Gary W. Reichard, 67–100. Columbus: Ohio State University Press, 1982.

Crowder, Michael. "The Second World War: Prelude to Decolonisation in Africa." In *The Cambridge History of Africa,* vol. 8, ed. Michael Crowder, 8–51. Cambridge: Cambridge University Press, 1984.

Dalfiume, Richard M. "The Forgotten Years of the Negro Revolution." *Journal of American History* 55 (June 1968): 90–106.

Divine, Robert A. "The Cold War and the Election of 1948." *Journal of American History* 59 (June 1972): 90–110.

Dumett, Raymond. "Africa's Strategic Minerals During the Second World War." *Journal of African History* 26 (1985): 381–408.

Emerson, Rupert, and Martin Kilson. "The American Dilemma in a Changing World: The Rise of Africa and the Negro American." *Daedalus* 94 (Fall 1965): 1,055–84.

Fierce, Milfred C. "Selected Black American Leaders and Organizations and South Africa, 1900–1977: Some Notes." *Journal of Black Studies* 17 (March 1987): 305–26.

Good, Robert C. "The United States and the Colonial Debate." In *Alliance Policy in the Cold War,* ed. Arnold Wolfers, 224–70. Baltimore: Johns Hopkins Press, 1959.

Hero, Alfred O. "American Negroes and U.S. Foreign Policy: 1937–1967." *Journal of Conflict Resolution* 8 (June 1969): 220–51.

Isaacman, Allen, and Jennifer Davis. "United States' Policy toward Mozambique since 1945: The Defense of Colonialism and Regional Stability." *Africa Today* 25 (January-March 1978): 29–55.

Karis, Thomas G. "Revolution in the Making: Black Politics in South Africa." *Foreign Affairs* 62 (Winter 1983): 378–406.

Leffler, Melvyn P. "The United States and the Strategic Dimensions of the Marshall Plan." *Diplomatic History* 12 (Summer 1988): 277–306.

Morris, Milton D. "Black Americans and the Foreign Policy Process: The Case of Africa." *Western Political Quarterly* 25 (September 1972): 451–63.

Noer, Thomas J. "Truman, Eisenhower, and South Africa: The 'Middle Road' and Apartheid." *Journal of Ethnic Studies* 11 (Spring 1983): 75–104.

O'Meara, Dan. "The 1946 African Mine Workers' Strike and the Political Economy of South Africa." *Journal of Commonwealth and Comparative Politics* 13 (July 1975): 146–73.

Ovendale, Ritchie. "The South African Policy of the British Labour Government, 1947–1951." *International Affairs* 59 (1982–1983): 41–58.

Paterson, Thomas G. "Foreign Aid under Wraps: The Point Four Program." *Wisconsin Magazine of History* 56 (1972/73): 119–26.

Roark, James L. "American Black Leaders: The Response to Colonialism and the Cold War, 1943–1953." *African Historical Studies* 4 (1971): 253–70.

Rosenberg, David Alan. "The Origins of Overkill: Nuclear Weapons and American Strategy, 1945–1960." *International Security* 7, no. 4 (Spring 1983), 3–71.

———. "U.S. Nuclear Stockpile, 1945 to 1950." *Bulletin of Atomic Scientists* 38 (May 1982): 25–30.

Sbrega, John J. "Determination versus Drift: The Anglo-American Debate over the Trusteeship Issue, 1941–1945." *Pacific Historical Review* 55 (May 1986): 256–80.

Shepperson, George. "Notes on Negro American Influences on the Emergence of African Nationalism." *Journal of African History* 1 (1960): 299–312.

Sitkoff, Harvard. "Harry Truman and the Election of 1948: The Coming of Age of Civil Rights in American Politics." *Journal of Southern History* 37 (November 1971): 597–616.

Solomon, Mark. "Black Critics of Colonialism and the Cold War." In *Cold War Critics: Alternatives to American Foreign Policy in the Truman Years,* ed. Thomas G. Paterson, 205–39. Chicago: Quadrangle, 1971.

Trachtenberg, Marc. "A 'Wasting Asset': American Strategy and the Shifting Nuclear Balance, 1949–1954." *International Security* 13, no. 3 (Winter 1988/89), 5–49.

Venkataramani, M. S. "The United States, the Colonial Issue, and the Atlantic Charter Hoax." *International Studies* (New Delhi) 13 (January–March 1974): 1–28.

Vickery, Kenneth P. "'Herrenvolk' Democracy and Egalitarianism in South Africa and the U.S. South." *Comparative Studies in Society and History* 16 (1974): 309–28.

Wolpe, Harold. "Capitalism and Cheap Labour-Power in South Africa: From Segregation to Apartheid." *Economy and Society* 1 (1972): 425–56.

Index